THE
SOUTH CAROLINA
ARCHITECTS
1885 - 1935

THE
SOUTH CAROLINA
ARCHITECTS
1885 - 1935

A Biographical
Dictionary

John E. Wells
Robert E. Dalton

New South Architectural Press

Richmond, Virginia
1992

To

Matthew Field Fornaro (b. 1992)

and

Lynette Hamilton Dalton

Contents

ACKNOWLEDGEMENTS

Work on this project began in 1981, and a great many individuals have assisted in various ways. The following persons and institutions, sources of valuable information and assistance, are gratefully acknowledged.

In South Carolina, Martha Walker Fullington, Deborah Allen, Suzanne Pickens, Mary Watson Edmonds, Thomas Shaw, Andrew Chandler, Julie Turner, Norman McCorkle, Charles Lowe, Rebecca Starr, John Blythe, and Dorothy C. Johnson; in North Carolina, Catherine Bishir, Thomas Hanchett, Charlotte Brown, and Drucilla Haley York; in Georgia, Kenneth H. Thomas, Jr.; in Virginia, Richard C. Cote, Wyatt Hibbs, and S. Allen Chambers; in Washington, D.C., Tony P. Wrenn and Antoinette J. Lee; in Philadelphia, Sandra Tatman; and in New York, Zach Watson Rice.

Most of the documentary research for this project was conducted with the assistance of the following libraries and repositories:

In South Carolina, the South Caroliniana Library, University of South Carolina, Columbia; the Cooper Library, University of South Carolina, Columbia; the South Carolina Department of Archives and History, Columbia; the Richland County Public Library, Columbia; the Cooper Library, Clemson University, Clemson; and the Charleston Public Library, Charleston. In North Carolina, the D.H. Hill Library, North Carolina State University, Raleigh; and the Perkins Library, Duke University, Durham.

In other states, the Robert W. Woodruff Library, Emory University, Decatur, Georgia; the Virginia State Library, Richmond, Virginia; the Fiske Kimball Fine Arts Library, University of Virginia, Charlottesville, Virginia; the American Institute of Architects Archives, Washington, D.C.; the Library of Congress, Washington, D.C.; and the Enoch Pratt Free Library, Baltimore, Maryland.

Also, the public libraries of Anderson, Chester, Florence, Greenville, Greenwood, Rock Hill, Spartanburg, and Union, South Carolina; Charlotte, Greensboro, and Wilmington, North Carolina; Augusta and Macon, Georgia; Chattanooga, Memphis, and Nashville, Tennessee; Jacksonville, Florida; Charlottesville, Norfolk, Richmond, and Roanoke, Virginia; Akron and Summit County, Ohio; St. Louis, Missouri; and Tulsa, Oklahoma. The enthusiastic assistance of the librarians in Tulsa and in Wilmington is especially appreciated.

We acknowledge the contributions of Dale Cheek, who assisted in editing and proofing the manuscript; of Jean Dalton, for her help in researching Jacksonville architects; of Tom D. Foster, Jr., for the design of the cover and title page; and Lynette Hamilton Dalton, for her research assistance and encouragement.

INTRODUCTION

Justification: South Carolina's colonial and antebellum architecture has long fascinated antiquarians, scholars, and tourists. Much has been written of the lowcountry plantations, of Robert Mills, and of the city of Charleston. Very little is written, however, on the state's architectural history after 1865. Of published works, only Beatrice Ravenel's *Architects of Charleston* gives serious consideration to the architecture of the post-bellum years.[1] Architecture in all states of the former Confederacy is similarly slighted; histories of American architecture of the years 1865-1935 regularly ignore the South, implying a cultural vacuum.[2] Whether this disregard is an acknowledgement of absent data or a simple ignorance of fact, it is a serious failing that hinders appreciation of architecture in the region and era.[3] It is, at the same time, an indictment of the region's architectural historians.

The necessary data base is evolving, though, indicating an expanding appreciation of southern regional architecture, in proportion to the increased documentation of that architecture. Within the past ten years numerous regional architectural surveys have been published, monographs on regionally important architects, and thematic analyses, which bear witness to this appreciation.[4] Cataloguing the works of the architects is a basic element of this documentation.

Collective biographies of artists have been integral to art history since Giorgio Vasari's *Delle Vite de' più eccelenti pittori, scultori, ed architettori* (1550). Howard Colvin's *A Biographical Dictionary of British Architects 1600-1840* (1954) and the Witheys' *Biographical Dictionary of American Architects (Deceased)* (1956) document the lives of the eminent western architects of recent years. The study of Richardson, Sullivan, and Wright, however, will not explain architecture in Carolina, where, as Carl Lounsbury notes, "the work, practices, and even

---

[1] Other books on South Carolina architecture, from Elias Bull's *Historic Preservation Inventory: Berkeley County* (Charleston: Berkeley-Charleston-Dorchester Council of Governments, 1979) through Mills Lane's *Architecture of the Old South: South Carolina* (Savannah, Georgia: The Beehive Press, 1984) give no serious consideration to post-war buildings. Kenneth Severens [of Charleston!], in *Southern Architecture: 350 Years of Distinctive American Buildings* (New York: E.P. Dutton, 1981) suggests that the South "was largely spared the intrusion of Victorian irregularity, eccentricity, and polychromy, as well as the cheap construction and the shoddy materials and craftsmanship into which the style often degenerated" (p. 148.)

[2] Beyond Mencken's "The Sahara of the Bozarts," there is *American Architecture: Volume 2, 1860-1976* (1983) by Marcus Whiffen and Frederick Koeper, which, purporting to be a comprehensive survey, neglects the South (and other regions and themes) to such extent that it comprises little more than "a history of Anglo-European high-style building along the Atlantic coastal states and selected other cities." See Charlotte Vestal Brown's review in *Winterthur Portfolio*, Vol. 19, No. 4, Winter 1984, pp. 292-295.

[3] Catherine Bishir, in *Early Twentieth-Century Suburbs in North Carolina* (Raleigh: North Carolina Department of Cultural Resources, 1985), observes: ". . . national models for historical and architectural study have focused on the grand works of major architects, the dense concentrations of urban housing, the character of eighteenth and early nineteenth century towns. Having little of these, North Carolinians have slighted the study if not the preservation of what they do have."

[4] Important architectural surveys have recently been published for Biloxi, Mississippi; Birmingham, Alabama; Paducah and McCracken counties, Kentucky; Chesterfield County, Lexington, and Lynchburg, Virginia; and many cities and counties in Maryland and North Carolina. See Don J. Hibbard, "A Survey of Architectural Guidebooks," *Winterthur Portfolio*, Spring 1982, pp. 90-94. Monograph studies have been prepared on southern architects including Frank Milburn, Thomas J. Collins, George Franklin Barber, and Neel Reid. Perhaps the most important analytical study in this field is *Architects and Builders in North Carolina: A History of the Practice of Building*.

identities of most architects and builders have not commanded attention among architectural and social historians."[5] Recent studies, accordingly, are identifying the greater and lesser architects who worked in Tennessee, North Carolina, Georgia, and Virginia, as well as architects of other regions. Joseph Herndon argues that "for the locality and region, these men who have given an identity of time and place are as important if not more so than those men whom art historians have recognized as giants in architectural innovation."[6] Franklin Toker, reviewing the *Biographical Dictionary of Philadelphia Architects 1700-1930*, sees that "the heroes. . . turn out not to be the national stars of the profession but the sturdy foot soldiers: the architects of modest reputation whose restaurants, apartment houses, and churches make up the overall fabric of Philadelphia's streetscapes."[7] South Carolina's architectural heritage, similarly, owes little to the giants.[8]

This data base is compiled, therefore, as a foundation for the evaluation of South Carolina architecture in the period 1885-1935. A biographical dictionary of architects favors the academic and polite architecture, tending to ignore of the substantial body of South Carolina vernacular construction, including most of the speculative housing, the rural tenant houses, and the agricultural structures. Identification of the architects and their works, though, is equally essential for the definition of the regional context and for broadening the basis for comprehension of national architectural patterns.

Within these parameters this survey is intended as comprehensive. Selective surveying, all too often rationalized on a basis of financial and chronological constraints, does not appear adequate for rectifying the pervasive neglect shown for the time and place. While this book is primarily a documentation of the architectural profession, the positive identification of thousands of South Carolina building commissions has great value for the study, interpretation, and appreciation of those sites. Without this data there can be no knowledge.

Range: This study covers the period 1885-1935. The state's cultural and architectural heritage owes less to its heralded antebellum period than to these years. This was South Carolina's great era of industrial development; the era of "The New South," when the old Confederacy essayed a new cultural progressiveness, and factories and schools were built across the region with equal abandon. South Carolina's population increased tremendously in these years, growing from 995,577 in 1880 to 1,738,765 in 1930. Most of the state's cities, including Columbia,

---

[5] Carl Lounsbury, work in progress abstract, "Architects and Builders in North Carolina: A Study of the Building Process," in Camille Wells, editor, *Perspectives in Vernacular Architecture* (Annapolis, Maryland: The Vernacular Architecture Forum, 1982), p. 117. While the Witheys' dictionary includes a number of South Carolina architects, other studies of the type give little or no consideration to the state and region. Lawrence Wodehouse's *American Architects from the Civil War to the First World War*, for example, includes only Frank Milburn among South Carolina practitioners. Wodehouse's "Building Location Index" includes no South Carolina projects, and only 27 projects in the states of the old Confederacy; most of these were the work of Northern designers. The *Macmillan Encyclopedia of Architects* includes no South Carolina architects from the period 1880-1935.

[6] Joseph L. Herndon, *Architects in Tennessee until 1930: A Dictionary* (Masters Thesis, Columbia University, New York, New York, 1975), p. iv.

[7] In *Journal of the Society of Architectural Historians*, December 1986, pp. 424-425.

[8] The "familiar liturgy [of] high-culture architects of the northeast" (Hibbard) had little or no direct impact on South Carolina architecture. Late in his life (and after the study period), Frank Lloyd Wright designed two houses in South Carolina. Thomas Hastings designed a small house for himself in Aiken. Several other New York architects had single projects in South Carolina. But there are no documented works by McKim, Mead & White, or Sullivan, or Richardson, or the Wares, or Burnham, in the state.

Greenville, Spartanburg, Anderson, Sumter, Florence, and Rock Hill, took their modern shapes in this era.[9] South Carolina became a world leader in cotton processing. Between 1880 and 1930 the number of textile mills in the state increased from 14 to 239, and the census of textile workers grew from 2053 to 94,756. Of the state's colleges and universities, Clemson, Winthrop, Converse, Coker, Presbyterian, and South Carolina State were established, and older institutions, including the University of South Carolina and The Citadel Military College, were significantly expanded.

The architectural profession in South Carolina was substantially redefined in this period. Not only did the number of architects multiply, but state laws regulating architectural practice were enacted, the state chapter of the American Institute of Architects was chartered, the first statewide building codes were written, and the state's only architectural education program was created at Clemson College. Many of the most important South Carolina architects, such as Frank Niernsee, Charles C. Wilson, Frank Milburn, William A. Edwards, George E. Lafaye, and Joseph Casey, practiced during the study period.

We have omitted several architects whose work in South Carolina overlaps the study period, arguing that the significant body of their work belongs to earlier or to later periods. John R. Niernsee, J. Crawford Neilson, Samuel Sloan, and Edward B. White are among the architects whose work in South Carolina was concentrated before 1885. These and other early practitioners have been documented elsewhere in considerable detail.

Several architects included in this study, especially Albert Simons, Samuel Lapham, Willis Irvin, James Urquhart, Frank Hopkins, Henry Harrall, and Joseph Sirrine, had careers extending well past 1935. The work of these men beyond the chosen era is given cursory coverage. Architects whose contributions were concentrated in the years after 1935 are not included in this work. Architects belonging to this later period include Wyatt Hibbs, Thomas Harmon, Walter Petty, Herndon Fair, and Alex Dickson. Some of these architects are still alive and their places in the state's architectural pantheon are not so readily determined.

Scope: We have sought to include in this biographical dictionary every man and woman who advertised or practiced as an architect in South Carolina during the chosen period. Not only the major figures who were based in South Carolina, but out-of-state architects who designed South Carolina buildings and the many Carolina designers and near-architects who labored in poverty, obscurity, and/or mediocrity have a place in this forum.

Primary sources often credit contractors, engineers, real estate agents, or property owners with the preparation of plans. A major debate among architects of the period centered on whether such persons could claim the title "architect."[10] This debate, and the associated questions of professional responsibility, led to the legal definition of the profession and the regulation of architects by a state board of registration in 1917. Before that time (indeed, frequently afterwards), anyone could advertise or be described as an ARCHITECT, regardless of training,

---

[9] The major antebellum city, Charleston, was substantially redefined in these years as well. While popular histories and tourist guides maintain that Victorian Charleston was "too poor to paint, and too proud to whitewash," and built nothing substantial during these years, the evidence of the city's surviving buildings and the data in this work indicate otherwise.

[10] Samuel Lapham noted that in the Charleston city directories of the 1870s and 1880s "Civil engineers, surveyors, carpenters, contractors and builders listed themselves as architects and in two extreme cases, a tombstone cutter and a drain pipe manufacturer classified themselves as architects, along with their main activity." The terms "near-architect" and "carpetect" have been used for many years to describe such persons. See Gwendolyn Wright, *Moralism and the Model Home: Domestic Architecture and Cultural Conflict in Chicago 1873-1913* (Chicago: The University of Chicago Press, 1980), pp. 46-55.

experience, or other qualifications.[11] We have not attempted to resolve this question; we have included in this study anyone who claimed to be an architect, or who was credited with providing architectural services. By this measure we hope to include all figures who contributed to South Carolina's architectural heritage during the period.

Even with these liberal standards, there are cases where attributions of design services are not supported. One dubious "architect" was Cummins A. Mebane. In 1905 the *Manufacturers' Record* described A.N. Wood's proposed cotton warehouse building in Gaffney. Construction was to follow "plans and specifications by C.A. Mebane, special agent, Greensboro, N.C." Greensboro city directories identify Mebane as an employee of the Southern Life and Trust Company from 1903 through 1909; he was described variously as clerk, special agent, and acting assistant manager. Did Mebane create the design for Wood's warehouse or was he simply an agent to procure plans from other sources? Standardized plans for warehouses, schools, and other building types were readily available in South Carolina in this period.[12] We have no solid evidence showing that Mebane worked as an architect and we have, accordingly, excluded him from this directory.[13] Several other men, to whom the design of South Carolina buildings has been attributed, are omitted from this directory for comparable lack of evidence.

Depth: How much information should be provided on each architect? Comprehensive biographies on all architects would require many more years (and more justification) than we have. Basic identification and biographical information is provided where it is known; corollary data, quotes, and anecdotes are included where they seemed appropriate; but we have not attempted exhaustive research on most of these figures. There are some architects about whom almost nothing has come to light. Harold Yeatts, for example, is known only through his advertisements in the Darlington newspapers in 1911-1912.[14] In other cases, we have comprehensive biographical information. The lives of Milburn, Sirrine, and Edwards are well documented, and these men are profiled in depth here.

The depth of research and discussion on the out-of-state architects who designed South Carolina buildings also deserves explanation. Where these architects made substantial contributions to the state's building stock, we include longer biographical sketches, with building lists restricted to South Carolina projects. Oliver Duke Wheeler and George Franklin Barber are examples. There were also many out-of-state architects who undertook only one or two South Carolina projects. These architects are discussed in inverse proportion to the degree that their work has been documented. Ernest Flagg, Milton Medary, and other well-documented architects have brief entries here, with reference made to the more complete sources. Still other architects, such as Claude Howell, Alpheus Griffin,

---

[11] Page Ellington, a black bricklayer and builder in Columbia, is an example. Accounts from the early twentieth century bestow the title "architect" on Ellington, evidently because "he could make all of his drawings."

[12] In 1905, architects Wilson & Wendell prepared twenty-nine sets of cotton warehouse plans for the South Carolina Cotton Growers' Association, to be built in the smaller communities of the state. This work is described in the *Manufacturers' Record*, 28 September 1905 and 5 October 1905. In this same year, architects Edwards & Walter prepared sixteen sets of plans for model school buildings for the State Board of Education, ranging in size from one room to ten. Schools based on these plans were built in many South Carolina communities. These plans are illustrated in *Reports and Resolutions of the General Assembly of the State of South Carolina, 1906* (Columbia: Gonzales and Bryan, 1906), Vol. I, pp. 273-338.

[13] All the information we've found on Mebane has been included in this introduction.

[14] There is hope that something can be found on Mr. Yeatts. For several years, we knew of John J. Huddart only through a citation on the Murchison School cornerstone in Bennettsville. Then his connection with Denver, Colorado, was discovered, and extensive information on Huddart's life and work followed.

Walter Tinsley, and Frank Walter, about whose lives little is known and even less has been published, are discussed here at greater length.

Painstaking accuracy is essential in works of this type. Although we have gone to great lengths to insure accuracy, errors will have inevitably crept in. It is certain that further attributions, new names, more precise data, and more complete biographical information will come to light as soon as this volume is published. The authors accept full responsibility for all errors of commission and omission. We welcome all correspondence, corrections, and additions, in the anticipation of including such information in subsequent editions of this work. Questions may be sent to the authors in care of the New South Architectural Press:

New South Architectural Press
P.O. Box 878
Richmond, Virginia 23207

ABRAHAMS, Theodore H. (active 1874-1900) Theodore Abrahams practiced in Charleston in the latter half of the nineteenth century. He was associated with John Seyle (q.v.) as Abrahams & Seyle from 1874 through 1895, after which time he was no longer listed in city directores. Abrahams was admitted to the A.I.A. in 1896. He died in April 1900.

South Carolina projects:

Abrahams & Seyle

1870: C.D. Ahrens & Co. Store Building, 237 King Street, Charleston (*News & Courier,* 3 May 1982.)

1874-1886: Edmonds T. Brown Residence, 179 Rutledge Avenue, Charleston (*News & Courier,* 4 January 1937; 31 August 1981.)

1881: Crafts Elementary School, 67 Legare Street, Charleston (National Register files, S.C. Archives.)

1888: School, Charleston (*MR*, 7 January 1888, p. 978.)

Ca. 1870: Freundschaftsbund Hall, 289 Meeting Street, Charleston (*News & Courier,* 3 May 1982.)

Sources: Charleston city directories; Tony Wrenn, Washington, D.C., unpublished information.

ABRAMS, A.P. (active 1904) A.P. Abrams of Union was identified as the architect for the $8000 W.T. Jones Residence in Santuck, South Carolina, in 1904.

Source: *MR*, 6 October 1904, p. 290.

ADLER, Rudolph S. (active 1919-1927) Adler was a partner in the prominent Atlanta, Georgia, architectural firm, Hentz, Reid & Adler (later Hentz, Adler & Schutze; q.v.) Adler studied architecture at Columbia University in New York City.

South Carolina projects:

See **Hentz, Hal F.** (Hentz, Reid & Adler; Hentz, Adler & Schutze)

Source: *American Art Annual*, Vol. XXI, p. 360.

AIKEN, William Martin (1855-1908) Aiken, a native of Charleston, studied architecture at M.I.T. He worked as a draftsman and designer for Henry Hobson Richardson, and for James McLaughlin of Cincinnati. He had established his own office in New York City by 1886. Aiken served as Supervising Architect of the United States Treasury Department from 1895 to 1897, and he directed the design of many federal buildings across the nation while holding this post. He helped direct the construction of the U.S. Post Office and Courthouse Building in Charleston (John H. Devereux, q.v., designing architect), and he supervised the design of the U.S. Post Office and Courthouse building in Newbern, North Carolina, in 1895.

Aiken maintained an office in New York City in subsequent years. He was allied with Arnold W. Brunner for several years. One of Aiken's prominent New York projects was the Public Baths at East 23rd Street, built in 1906.

A eulogy prepared by Aiken's colleagues in the Supervising Architect's Office praised his contributions:

> He came at a time when Federal architecture was the subject of much public criticism and his constant aim while Supervising Architect was to improve conditions as he found them, and to his credit, long to be remembered, we can testify that a new and better era was dawning with reference to the design and construction of public buildings when he laid down his office.

South Carolina projects:

1881: Monument project, Charleston (*American Architect and Building News*, Vol. IX, #265, 22 January 1881, between pp. 42 & 43.)

2

1881: Aiken County Courthouse project, Aiken (*American Architect and Building News*, Vol. IX, #272, 12 March 1881, p. 127.)

1904: Charleston Medical Society Hospital, Charleston; W.M. Aiken (Aiken & Brunner), Architect (*MR*, 4 August 1904, p. 62; *Southern Architect and Building News*, 4 November 1904, p. 11.)

1906: Improvements, St. Paul's Episcopal Church, Charleston (*MR*, 12 July 1906, p. 732.)

1908: Nurses' Home, Roper Hospital Training School, Charleston; $12,000 (*MR*, 6 February 1908, p. 68; 4 June 1908, p. 70; 11 June 1908, p. 57.)

Sources: *American Architect*, Vol. 94, No. 1722, 1908, p. 215; Francis, p. 11; Herndon, p. 3; Henry-Russell Hitchcock, *The Architecture of H.H. Richardson and His Times* (Revised Edition, Cambridge: The M.I.T. Press, 1961), p. 211; *MR*, various citations; Smith, *The Office of the Supervising Architect*, p. 44; White & Willensky, pp. 124-126; Withey, pp. 11-12; Wodehouse, pp. 21, 29-31.

ANDERSON, D.J. (active 1898-1900) D.J. Anderson was active as an architect and contractor in the Greenville and Greenwood vicinities. His office in 1900 was in Greenville, in Room 6 of the Beattie Building. Anderson was general contractor for buildings at Furman University and at Clemson College in 1900.

South Carolina projects:

1898: Seven Storerooms, Greenwood (*MR*, 22 July 1898, p. 429.)

1898-1899: W.J. Moore Residence, Greenwood; $3500 (*MR*, 14 October 1898, p. 203; 26 May 1899, p. 304.)

1898: Church, Honea Path; $2500 (*MR*, 14 Oct. 1898, p. 203.)

1899: J.W. Brock, L.A. Brock, and Dr. Shirley Business Block, Honea Path; $10,000 (*MR*, 26 May 1899, p. 304.)

1899: J.C. Milford Residence, Honea Path; $2500 (*MR*, 26 May 1899, p. 304.)

1900: Lipscomb & Russell Warehouse, Greenville (*MR*, 26 July 1900, p. 15.)

1900: J.I. Westervelt Residence, Greenville (Greenwood *Index*, 8 February 1900.)

Sources: Greenville city directories; *MR*, various citations.

ANDREWS, Joseph Y. (active 1914-1916) Joseph Y. Andrews of Greenville was a partner of Haskell H. Martin (q.v.)

South Carolina projects:

1914-1916: See **Martin, Haskell Hair** (Martin & Andrews)

ANDREWS, JACQUES & RANTOUL (active 1885-1925) Robert Day Andrews (1857-1928), Herbert Jacques (1857-1916) and Augustus Neal Rantoul (1864-1934) of Boston, Massachusetts, were prominent New England architects with commissions in many states. Their most notable designs were the East and West Wings of the Massachusetts State House, Boston, built in 1895-1913.

South Carolina project:

1908: Thomas Taylor, Jr., Residence, 1503 Senate Street, Columbia (*The State*, 6 May 1979, p. 11-E.)

Sources: Hewitt, p. 267; Withey, pp. 21, 320.

ASBURY, Louis Humbert (1878-1975) Louis Asbury, son of the architect/builder Samuel Jennings Asbury, was educated at Trinity College in Durham. He was first identified as an architect in Charlotte, North Carolina in 1901. Asbury entered the Massachusetts Institute of Technology in the fall of 1901. He worked as a draftsman in New York and Boston for several years, including a term with Cram,

Goodhue & Ferguson. By 1908 he was back in Charlotte.

Asbury was a major figure in North Carolina architecture through the mid-twentieth century. His designs in North Carolina included the $200,000 Auditorium of the National Festival Chorus Club of America at Black Mountain, commissioned in 1916; the five-story, $236,000 Efird Department Store Building in Charlotte, 1922; the Rutherford County Courthouse in Rutherfordton, 1924; the 20-story, $1,000,000 First National Bank Building, Charlotte, 1925 (in association with Lockwood Greene & Co.; q.v.) and the Mecklenburg County Courthouse in Charlotte, 1925-1926.

Asbury was among the first North Carolina members of the American Institute of Architects, and he helped organize the North Carolina chapter of the A.I.A.

South Carolina projects:

1913: J.A. Carroll Residence, S. Johnston Street, Gaffney; $20,000 (*MR*, 10 July 1913, p. 70; 17 July 1913, p. 71.)

1913: Presbyterian Church, Great Falls; $5000 (*MR*, 26 June 1913, p. 68; 3 July 1913, p. 82; 10 July 1913, p. 70.)

1917: Gaffney Hotel Company Hotel, Gaffney; $50,000 (*MR*, 24 May 1917, p. 68.)

1919: Alterations, American State Bank, Gaffney (*MR*, 13 February 1919, p. 101; 6 March 1919, p. 126.)

1929: Efird's Department Store Building, King and Wentworth streets, Charleston (*MR*, 15 August 1929, p. 95.)

1929: Carolina Investment Corp. Apartment Building, E. Main and Alabama streets, Spartanburg; $125,000 (*MR*, 25 April 1929, p. 93.)

Sources: *American Biography: A New Cyclopedia* (New York: American Historical Society, 1930), Vol. XLII, pp. 133-134; Charlotte, North Carolina city directories; Davyd Foard Hood, *The Architecture of Rowan County* (Salisburg, North

Carolina: Rowan County, 1983), pp. 206-207; Peter R. Kaplan, *The Historic Architecture of Cabarrus County, North Carolina* (Concord, N.C.: Historic Cabarrus, Inc., 1981), p. 39; *MR*, various citations.

ATTAWAY, Drew H. (active 1911-1912) Drew H. Attaway advertised as "Attaway the Architect and Builder" in the 1912 Greenville city directory. He appears to have spent no more than a few years in the city.

South Carolina projects:

1911: W.T. Henderson Residence, Greenville; $3000; Attaway, architect and contractor (*MR*, 20 July 1911, p. 70.)

1911: T.F. Floyd Residence, Townes Street, Greenville; $3000; Attaway, contractor (*MR*, 24 August 1911, p. 66.)

1911: A.N. Stall Residence, Greenville; $3000; Attaway, contractor (*MR*, 21 September 1911, p. 67.)

Sources: Greenville city directories; *MR*, various citations.

AYERS, Henry (active 1913-1920) Ayers worked in relative obscurity in Orangeburg. Aside from a listing as an architect in the 1920-1921 Orangeburg City Directory and a single project noted in the *MR* in 1913, Ayers has escaped notice.

South Carolina project:

1913: Morris Mimrow Arcade, Store, Office and Theater Building, Main Street, Summerville; $10,000 (*MR*, 26 June 1913, p. 69; 17 July 913, p. 72.)

BAKER, Leander (active 1896-1926) Leander Baker was a contractor and builder active in Gaffney from ca. 1896 through 1926. He was responsible for the construction of many of the city's buildings of the period and for the design of a considerable number. For many projects, Baker served as contractor and architect. From ca. 1908 through 1915, Baker worked under the firm name Builders' Supply Company. As contractor, he worked with several prominent architects, including Wheeler & Stern of Charlotte; Frank and Joseph Cunningham of Greenville; and Edwards & Walter of Columbia.

South Carolina projects:

1896: J.G. Galloway & Son Business Building, Gaffney; Baker, architect (*MR*, 8 May 1896, p. 255.)

1900: Gaffney Live-Stock Co. Stock Buildings, Gaffney; Baker, contractor (*MR*, 22 November 1900, p. 302.)

1902: Building, Limestone College, Gaffney; $10,000; Baker, contractor (*MR*, 3 July 1902, p. 444.)

1902: Poag Mule Co. Stable, Gaffney; Baker, contractor (*MR*, 4 Dec. 1902, p. 376.)

1903: Cherokee Drug Co. Store Building, Gaffney; Edwards & Walter, architects; Baker, contractor (*MR*, 4 June 1903, p. 410.)

1905: A.N. Wood Cotton Warehouse, Gaffney; Baker, contractor (*MR*, 10 August 1905, p. 100.)

1906: Isaac Turner Furniture Co. Store Building, Gaffney; $7000; Baker, contractor (*MR*, 2 August 1906, p. 69; 9 August 1906, p. 94.)

1906: A.J. Settlinger Store Building, Gaffney; Baker, contractor (*MR*, 9 August 1906, p. 94.)

1907: W.J. and R.M. Wilkins Business Building, Gaffney; $7000; Baker, contractor (*MR*, 6 June 1907, p. 672.)

1907: Joe Spake Office Building, Gaffney; $10,000; Baker, architect (*MR*, 29 August 1907, p. 182.)

1908: Shuford & LeMaster Business Building, Gaffney; $12,000; Baker (Builders' Supply Co.), contractor (*MR*, 16 April 1908, p. 63.)

1908: A.C. Pridmore Residence, Gaffney; $4000; F.H. and J.G. Cunningham, architects; Baker (Builders' Supply Co.),contractor (*MR*, 24 September 1908, p. 59.)

1911: S.B. Crawley Drug Co. Store and Office Building, Gaffney; J.H. Curry and L. Baker, contractors (*MR*, 31 August 1911, p. 66; 21 September 1911, p. 68.)

1911: Limestone College Annex Building, Gaffney; $20,000; Wheeler & Stern, architects; Baker, contractor (*MR*, 28 September 1911, p. 67.)

1912: G.M. Phifer and Isaac Turner Business Building, Gaffney; $5000; Baker, architect (*MR*, 19 September 1912, p. 68.)

1913: Thomas Cole Store Building, Gaffney; Baker, contractor (*MR*, 11 September 1913, p. 66.)

1914: Limestone Baptist Church, Gaffney; $8000; N. Gaillard Walker, architect; Baker (Builders' Supply Co.), contractor (*MR*, 18 June 1914, p. 70.)

1915: Dr. J.N. Nesbitt Store Building, Gaffney; $4000; Wheeler & Stern, architects; Baker, contractor (*MR*, 20 May 1915, p. 60; 3 June 1915, p. 70.)

1915: T.H. Westrope Store, Limestone Street, Gaffney; $2500; Baker, architect and contractor (*MR*, 3 June 1915, p. 70; 10 June 1915, p. 52.)

1915: Repairs, Episcopal Church, Gaffney; Baker, contractor (*MR*, 23 September 1915, p. 58.)

1915: W.K. Davenport Residence, Gaffney; $2500; Baker (Builders' Supply Co.) contractor (*MR*, 7 October 1915, p. 76; 14 October 1915, p. 57.)

1924: Dr. Roby F. Finney Residence, Victoria Avenue, Gaffney; Baker, contractor (*MR*, 10 April 1924, p. 110.)

1924: Dr. J.G. Pittman Business Building, Frederick Street, Gaffney; $10,000; Baker, architect; Builders Supply Co. under supervision of Baker, contractor (*MR*, 21 February 1924, p. 107; 28 February 1924, p. 120.)

1924: Little/Clarkson/Peeler Business Building, Frederick Street, Gaffney; $20,000; Baker, contractor (*MR*, 15 May 1924, p. 127; 26 June 1924, p. 115.)

1925: Sunday School Addition, Goucher Baptist Church, Gaffney vicinity; Baker, architect and contractor (*MR*, 19 February 1925, p. 120.)

1926: Remodeling, Gaffney Manufacturing Co., Gaffney; Baker, contractor (*MR*, 13 May 1926, p. 104.)

1926: Addition, City Hospital, Gaffney; $20,000; Baker, contractor (*MR*, 11 March 1926, p. 118.)

Sources: *MR*, various citations.

BALDWIN, James J. (1888-1955) James J. Baldwin, a native of Ridge Springs, graduated from the University of South Carolina in 1905. He worked as a draftsman for Columbia architect Frank P. Milburn (q.v.) for several years, and relocated with Milburn to Washington, D.C. in 1906. Baldwin moved to Chattanooga, Tennessee, around 1909 to work for prominent architect Reuben Harrison Hunt (q.v.). He returned to South Carolina shortly thereafter and entered a partnership with Christopher Gadsden Sayre (q.v.) in Anderson.

Sayre & Baldwin thrived for several years, with projects in Georgia, South Carolina, and North Carolina. Sayre & Baldwin designed a number of public school buildings in South Carolina in this period. A 1910 article described the Shandon School in Columbia as typical of the firm's work, noting that "a number of [this] type have been erected by the architects, Messrs. Sayre & Baldwin, of Anderson."

The partnership with Sayre was dissolved by 1915 and Baldwin pursued independent practice in Anderson. He opened branch offices in Daytona Beach, Florida, by 1924 and St. Petersburg, Florida, by 1925. Baldwin moved his principal office from Anderson to Asheville, North Carolina, by 1926.

Baldwin's practice included buildings in Tennessee, Florida, and Georgia, as well as the Carolinas.

Baldwin designed a large number of Baptist churches, including at least five in South Carolina and four in Georgia. The $400,000 First Baptist Church in Tampa, Florida, begun in 1922, was among Baldwin's largest commissions. Baldwin was the architect for courthouses in Bleckly, Candler, Bacon, Evans, Lee, Atkinson, and Barrow counties in Georgia, and for the Cherokee County Courthouse in North Carolina. He participated in the design of at least three early skyscrapers as well. A 1920 project for an eleven-story building for the Citizens' National Bank in Anderson appears never to have been built. In 1924 Baldwin, in association with Casey & Fant (q.v.) of Anderson, prepared plans for the eight-story John C. Calhoun Hotel in Anderson, which was (and is) the city's tallest building. The seven-story Cherokee Hotel in Cleveland, Tennessee, was designed by Baldwin in 1927.

Baldwin moved to Washington, D.C. later in his career; he was in Washington at least by 1952. He died in Washington in 1955.

South Carolina projects:

1909-1915: See **Sayre, Christopher Gadsden** (Sayre & Baldwin)

1916: Miss Elizabeth Harrison Residence, Anderson; $3000 (*MR*, 21 September 1916, p. 661.)

1916: W.K. Hudgens Store and Post Office Building, Pelzer; $20,000 (*MR*, 11 May 1916, p. 68; 21 September 196, pp. 66 k, 67.)

1916: W.K. Hudgens Store and Post Office Building, Williamston; $9000 (*MR*, 6 July 1916, pp. 83-84.)

1917-1919: High School, Anderson; $59,937 (*MR*, 19 July 1917, p. 79; 16 January 1919, p. 104.)

1918: School, Fountain Inn; $30,000 (*MR*, 17 January 1918, p. 78.)

1918: Baptist Church, McCormick; $18,000 (*MR*, 18 April 1918, p. 86.)

1919: B.B. Williams Bank Building, Norway; $30,000 (*MR*, 16 January 1919, p. 103.)

1920: Citizens' National Bank Building, E. Whitner and N. Main streets, Anderson; $250,000 (*MR*, 14 October 1920, p. 154 m.)

1920: First Baptist Church, Greer; $100,000 (*Greenville Daily News*, 28 May 1920, p. 3.)

1921: Baptist Church, Great Falls; $50,000 (*MR*, 26 May 1921, p. 92; 2 June 1921, p. 142; 9 June 1921, p. 106.)

1921: School, Lebanon; $18,200 (*MR*, 7 July 1921, p. 114.)

1921: Baptist Church, Taylors; $15,000 (*MR*, 21 July 1921, p. 84, 28 July 1921, p. 91.)

1922: Central Baptist Church, Lloyd and Pinckney streets, Greenville; $150,000 (*MR*, 19 October 1922, p. 90 f.)

1923: Pelzer Manufacturing Co. Gymnasium, Pelzer; $28,000 (*MR*, 14 January 1923, p. 112.)

1923: Pelzer Manufacturing Company School, Pelzer; $65,000 (*MR*, 1 February 1923, p. 119.)

1923: Reconstruction, South Wing, Anderson High School, Anderson; $44,000 (*MR*, 8 February 1923, p. 101.)

1923: High School, Gaffney; $149,401 (*MR*, 12 July 1923, p. 106.)

1923: Grammar School, Gaffney; $70,500 (*MR*, 1 November 1923, p. 130; 22 November 1923, p. 100.)

1924: Negro School, Aiken; $22,500 (*MR*, 3 April 1924, p. 154.)

1924: John C. Calhoun Hotel, N. Main and Sharp streets, Anderson; $325,000; Casey & Fant (q.v.) and James J. Baldwin, architects (*MR*, 12 June 1924, p. 112; 14 August 1924, p. 107; 28 August 1924, p. 113.)

1924: Fairfield County Jail and Jailer's Residence, Winnsboro; $21,500 (*MR*, 21 August 1924, p.118.)

1926: E.H. Drake Residence, River Street, Belton; $10,000 (*MR*, 15 April 1926, p. 113; 22 April 1926, p. 129.)

1927: Women's Building, State Penitentiary, Columbia; $44,500 (*MR*, 18 August 1927, p. 123.)

Sources: Anderson city directories; Herndon, p. 9; Koyl, p. 24; Rudolph E. Lee, "Rural School Improvement," *The Clemson Agricultural College Extension Work Bulletins*, Vol. VI, #3, July 1910; *MR*, various citations; Petty, p. 141; Douglas Swaim, *Cabins & Castles: The History and Architecture of Buncombe County* (Asheville, North Carolina: Historic Resources Commission of Asheville and Buncombe County, 1981.)

BARBER, George Franklin (1854-1915) George F. Barber pursued a career as an order-by-mail architect. From his office in Knoxville, Tennessee, he designed houses which were built in most of the contiguous states. Barber designs have been identified in Oregon, Minnesota, Wisconsin, Illinois, Ohio, and New York, as well as all of the southeastern states. Pattern-books advertising Barber's house designs were widely distributed. When a client responded, Barber would ship the plans, along with the pre-cut and marked raw materials, by rail to the site, where the new homeowner would have the structure built on a prepared foundation.

Barber's designs were generally of the more bizarre and asymmetrical Queen Anne modes. He favored ornate turrets and towers, extensive sawn and turned woodwork, horseshoe arches, rooftop crestings and finials, and similar outlandish touches. In his later years Barber prepared many Colonial Revival style buildings. Barber was associated with Thomas A. Kluttz (q.v.) from 1902 to 1908.

The Foster-Munger Company of Chicago, a mail-order building products house, marketed Barber & Kluttz house designs in 1905. The company's catalogue noted that Barber & Kluttz were chosen:

. . . on account of their long experience, amount of house planning they have done, originality of designs, and their wide experience in furnishing plans for houses in all parts of the country.

South Carolina projects:

1896: N.A. Bull Residence, Orangeburg (*MR*, 10 July 1896, p. 400.)

1896: B.F. Beddingfield Residence, Spartanburg; $2500 (*MR*, 4 September 1896, p. 98.)

Ca. 1896: John Calvin Owings Residence, 787 W. Main Street, Laurens (National Register files, S.C. Archives.)

1897: W.J. Dunn Residence, Camden; $2500 (*MR*, 8 January 1897, p. 417.)

1897: Thos. B. Whitmire Residence, Greenville; $2500 (*MR*, 8 January 1897, p. 47.)

1897: W.D. Arthur Residence, Union; $5000 (*MR*, 8 January 1897, p. 417.)

1897: J.T. Simmons Residence, Greenwood; $5000 (*MR*, 12 February 1897, p. 50.)

1897: C.D. Bobo Residence, Laurens; $3850 (*MR*, 12 February 1897, p. 50.)

1897: S.J. Simpson Residence, Spartanburg; $4000 (*MR*, 12 March 1897, p. 126.)

1897: D.A. Davis Residence, Laurens; $3500 (*MR*, 12 March 1897, p. 126.)

1897: Correll Bros. Store Building, Spartanburg (*MR*, 9 April 1897, p. 195.)

1897: W.F. Beaty Store Building, Union; $4500 (*MR*, 9 April 1897, p. 195.)

1897: N.B. Dial Residence, Laurens; $10,000 (*MR*, 7 May 1897, p. 266.)

1897: W.P. Hall Residence, Greenwood; $6000 (*MR*, 7 May 1897, p. 266.)

1897: R.P. Harry Store Building, Union; $3500 (*MR*, 7 May 1897, p. 267.)

1897: J.A. Fant Store Building, Union; $8500 (*MR*, 7 May 1897, p. 267.)

1897: E. Nicholson Residence, Union; $6000 (*MR*, 7 May 1897, p. 267.)

1897: W.H. Sartor Residence, Union; $6000 (*MR*, 9 July 1897, p. 413.)

1897: T.Y. Williams Building, Lancaster; $4000 (*MR*, 10 September 1897, p. 103.)

1897: Mrs. M.S. Rogers Residence, Bennettsville; $3850 (*MR*, 8 October 1897, p. 167.)

1898: James Powell Residence, Aiken; $4500 (*MR*, 14 January 1898, p. 392.)

1898: Mrs. D. McG. Buck Residence, Glenn Springs; $3500 (*MR*, 6 May 1898, p. 258.)

1898: H.W. Montague Residence, Allendale; $5000 (*MR*, 10 June 1898, p. 332.)

1908: Three Dwellings, Columbia; $3000-$3500 each; Barber & Kluttz, architects (*MR*, 5 March 1908, p. 68.)

1909: Walter Scott Montgomery Residence, 314 S. Pine Street, Spartanburg; $15,000 (*MR*, 25 March 1909, p. 59.)

Sources: George F. Barber & Co., *Modern Dwellings: A Book of Practical Designs and Plans for Those Who Wish To Build or Beautify Their Homes* (Knoxville: S.B. Newman & Co., 1901); *The Foster-Munger Co. Official Catalogue 1905* (Chicago: n.p., 1905), pp. 650-672; James L. Garvin, "Mail-Order House Plans and American Victorian Architecture," *Winterthur Portfolio*, Winter 1981, pp. 309-334; Herndon, p. 12; *MR*, various citations; Michael A. Tomlan, *George F. Barber's The Cottage Souvenir No. 2: A Repository of Artistic Cottage Architecture and Miscellaneous Designs* (Watkins Glen, New York: The American Life Foundation and Study Institute, 1982.)

BARBOT, Decimus Chartrand (1873-1934)
Decimus C. Barbot, a native of Virginia, grew up in Charleston, South Carolina. He studied with his uncle Louis J. Barbot, who was City Engineer for Charleston from 1837 through the 1880s. Decimus Barbot was appointed assistant city surveyor by 1904 and held that post for several years. In 1908 Barbot began independent architectural practice, preparing designs for the Medical College of South Carolina in Charleston.

Among Barbot's more celebrated designs was the 1915 Roman Catholic Church in Florence. The project was described in detail in *The State*:

> The new church will be a magnificent structure built of smooth-faced Pee Dee brick, on lines of pure English Gothic style, the facade being a copy of the parish church at Florence, Italy. The main portal door, 33 feet in height, will be modeled after the western entrance of the church of St. Anthony at Padua, and will be ornamented with five Florentine mosaic panels.

Another Charleston architect, James D. Benson (q.v.) was supervising construction of a residence in Florence across the street from the Roman Catholic Church at this time. Barbot and Benson joined forces shortly thereafter and practiced in Charleston as Benson & Barbot from 1917 through 1926. Both Benson and Barbot were charter members of the South Carolina chapter of the A.I.A., which was founded in 1913.

Barbot spent his last years in Hyattsville, Maryland, where he died on 31 December 1934.

South Carolina projects:

1908: Medical College of South Carolina Building, Charleston; $4000 (*MR*, 20 August 1908, p. 63.)

1909: Catholic Church, Sumter; $30,000 (*MR*, 4 March 1909, p. 78; 11 March 1909, p. 58; 3 June 1909, p. 69.)

1910: Trude Real Estate Co. Apartment and Office Building, Charleston; $14,000 (*MR*, 16 June 1910, p. 69.)

1910: Church of the Holy Rosary, Charleston; $8300 (*MR*, 7 July 1910, p. 81.)

1910: Pastime Amusement Co. Theater, Charleston; $30,000 (*MR*, 15 September 1910, p. 69.)

1912: James F. Condon & Sons Inc. Store Building, 433 King Street, Charleston; $11,000 (*MR*, 30 May 1912, p. 73.)

1913: DuBose Heyward Residence, Charleston; $3500 (*MR*, 30 January 1913, p. 68.)

1913: J.E. Schachte Residence, Charleston; $5000 (*MR*, 22 May 1913, p. 69.)

1913: C.E. Welling Residence, 714 King Street, Charleston; $4000 (*MR*, 31 July 1913, p. 68.)

1915: Roman Catholic Church, Palmetto and Irby streets, Florence; $30,000 (*MR*, 4 March 1915, p. 63; 20 May 1915, p. 59; 30 December 1915, p. 65; *The State*, 1 March 1915, p. 8.)

1916: Dr. H.A. Smathers Residence, Charleston; $3000 (*MR*, 13 April 1916, p.70.)

1917-1926: See **Benson, James D.** (Benson & Barbot)

1927: Addition, James Simons School, King and Moultrie streets, Charleston; $9327 (*MR*, 26 May 1927, p. 109.)

1928: Remodeling, B'rith Sholom Congregation Synagogue, 68 St. Philip Street, Charleston; $20,000 (*MR*, 22 May 1928, p. 85.)

1929: Clubhouse, Charleston Municipal Golf Course, Charleston (*MR*, 31 October 1929, p. 77.)

Sources: Charleston city directories; Francis W. Kervick, *Architects in America of Catholic Tradition* (Rutland, Vermont: Charles E. Tuttle Co., 1962), p. 16; *MR*, various citations; Petty, p. 141; Withey, p. 36.

BARNWELL, John G. (active 1890-1918) John G. Barnwell was a practicing architect in Rome, Georgia, in 1890-1894. He was in Atlanta in 1898. Barnwell took a position with the Columbia, S.C., architectural and engineering firm W.B. Smith Whaley & Co. (q.v.) around 1901. He moved to Chattanooga, Tennessee, around 1903, where he worked for prominent architect W.T. Downing (q.v.) for several years; by 1908 Barnwell had opened his own office in Chattanooga. He was associated with Clarence T. Jones (another architect who had worked in Columbia, South Carolina) as Barnwell & Jones from 1911 through 1914. Bayard L. Barnwell, presumably John's younger brother, joined the firm around 1913, as a representative in Augusta, Georgia; the firm was called Barnwell, Jones & Barnwell this year. From 1915 to 1918 the firm was called Barnwell & Barnwell.

South Carolina project:

1912: James Finlay Store and Office Building, Main and North streets, Greenville; F.H. and J.G. Cunningham (q.v.) and Barnwell & Jones, associated architects (*MR*, 23 May 1912, p. 73.)

Sources: Augusta, Georgia, city directories; Chattanooga, Tennessee, city directories; Columbia city directories; Herndon, p. 14; *MR*, various citations.

BEACH, John F. (active 1905-1909) Beach was a partner of Camden architect Robert W. Mitcham (q.v.) in 1905-1909.

BEACHAM, James Douthit (1891-1956) James D. Beacham was born 9 June 1891 in Greenville. He was educated at Furman University, 1907; at Clemson College, 1909; and at Virginia Polytechnic Institute, 1911. He worked as a draftsman for Joseph E. Sirrine (q.v.), 1911-1914, and 1917-1920; for Hart & Gardner, Chattanooga, Tennessee, 1914-1915; and for H. Olin Jones (q.v.), 1915-1916. Beacham entered independent practice in Greenville in 1921 with Leon LeGrand as partner. LeGrand (q.v.) had also worked in Sirrine's office. The association with LeGrand lasted through 1940.

The firm's largest project in South Carolina was the ten-story Chamber of Commerce Building in downtown Greenville, designed and built in 1924-1925 in association with J.E. Sirrine & Co. The masonry-clad steel frame skyscraper is still a prominent element of the Greenville skyline.

Beacham & LeGrand opened a branch office in Asheville, North Carolina, by 1925. Beacham himself moved to Asheville ca. 1928. For several years Henry Irven Gaines (q.v.) was associated with the firm in Asheville (Beacham, LeGrand & Gaines.) Their major work in North Carolina was the $1,200,000, 14-story New Fleetwood Hotel at Jump-Off Mountain, outside Asheville, commissioned in 1925. The following year, Beacham, LeGrand & Gaines prepared plans for a 15-story Fleetwood of Augusta hotel building in Augusta, Georgia, to cost $1,200,000.

In 1946-1955 Beacham and his brother Eugene W. Beacham were associated in Greenville. James Beacham died in 1956.

South Carolina projects:

Beacham & LeGrand

1919: H. Cleveland Beattie Residence, Greenville; $15,000 (*MR*, 11 September 1919, p. 138 i.)

1920: Salvation Army Hospital, Greenville; $200,000; Beacham & LeGrand and J.E. Sirrine (q.v.), associated architects (*MR*, 8 January 1920, p. 130 m; 15 January 1920, p. 152 j.)

1920: Manufacturers Warehouse Co. Warehouse, Greenville; $250,000 (*MR*, 5 February 1920, p. 176; 12 February 1920, p. 147.)

1921: Planters Savings Bank Building, Greer; $50,000 (*MR*, 3 March 1921, p. 163.)

1921: J.H. Morgan & Associates Business Building, College Street, Greenville (*MR*, 22 September 1921, p. 85.)

1921: J.A. Bull Grocery Co. Building, N. Main Street, Greenville; $15,000 (*MR*, 29 September 1921, p. 89; 6 October 1921, p. 116.)

1921: Enlargement, J.A. Bull Grocery Co. Store Building, Hampton Avenue, Greenville (*MR*, 29 September 1921, p. 89; 6 October 1921, p. 116.)

1921: Fine Arts Building, Greenville Woman's College, Greenville (*MR*, 6 October 1921, p. 116.)

1922: Working Benevolent Society State Grand Lodge Temple Building, Broad and Fall streets, Greenville; $50,000 (Cornerstone; *MR*, 26 January 1922, p. 84; 2 February 1922, p. 104.)

1922: Jones McCrory Store Building, Townes and College streets, Greenville; $35,000 (*MR*, 23 February 1922, p. 74 b.)

1923: Augusta Road School, Greenville; $23,000 (*MR*, 25 January 1923, p. 94.)

1923: C.O. Allen Building, Brown Street, Greenville; $20,000 (*MR*, 22 February 1923, p. 100; 7 June 1923, p. 130-l.)

1923: W.M. Thompson Residence, Greer; $23,000 (*MR*, 26 April 1923, p. 110.)

1923: J.J. McSwain Hotel, Oak Street, Greenville (*MR*, 24 May 1923, p. 109.)

1923: Dr. Fletcher Jordan Library Building, Main and Brown streets, Greenville; $31,000 (*MR*, 12 July 1923, p. 106.)

1923: Girls' Protective Bureau Building, Laurens Road, Greenville $12,000 (*MR*, 13 September 1923, p. 108.)

1924: Holmes Bible School Building, Buncombe Street, Greenville; $15,000 (*MR*, 21 February 1924, p. 105.)

1924: Col. W.H. Keith Store Building, Greenville; $75,000 (*MR*, 27 March 1924, p. 123; 3 April 1924, p. 154.)

1924: Alterations, Majestic Theater, Greenville; $30,000 (*MR*, 17 April 1924, p. 121.)

1924: Piedmont Theater, Greenville; $160,000 (*MR*, 18 September 1924, p. 117; 25 September 1924, p. 118.)

1924-1925: Chamber of Commerce Building, 130 N. Main Street, Greenville; $257,418; Beacham & LeGrand, architects; J.E. Sirrine (q.v.), associated architects and engineers (Cornerstone; *MR*, 28 August 1924, p. 111; 25 September 1924, p. 114; 6 November 1924, p. 127; 4 June 1925, p. 137.)

1925: Col. W.H. Keith Moving Picture House, N. Main Street, Greenville; $150,000 (*MR*, 22 January 1925, p.110.)

1925: Peoples National Bank Building, Laurens and Washington streets, Greenville; $140,000 (*MR*, 5 February 1925, p. 123; 25 June 1925, p. 118.)

1925: Baseball Park Grandstand, Augusta Street, Greenville (*MR*, 26 February 1925, p. 120.)

1925: City Hall, N. First Street, Easley; $11,450 (*MR*, 12 March 1925, p. 117.)

1925: American Bank & Trust Co. Warehouse, Rhett Street, Greenville; $20,000 (*MR*, 16 July 1925, p. 116.)

1926: Burgiss Shrine Hospital for Crippled Children, National Highway, Greenville; $350,000; Hentz, Reid & Adler (q.v.), architects; Beacham & LeGrand, associated architects (*MR*, 20 May 1926, p. 122; 1 July 1926, p. 135; 22 July 1926, p. 111.)

1926: Remodeling, Clarence Gapen Cigar Store (former Peoples National Bank Building), Main and Washington streets, Greenville (*MR*, 3 June 1926, p. 135.)

1927: Dr. Will Fewell Residence, Alta Vista, Greenville; $12,000 (*MR*, 24 November 1927, p. 108.)

1928: H.B. McKoy Residence, 308 McEver Street, Greenville; $12,000 (*MR*, 2 February 1928, p. 120.)

1928: Children of Israel Congregation Synagogue, Buist Circle, Greenville (*MR*, 18 October 1928, p. 98.)

1929: Greenville County Tuberculosis Hospital, Greenville; $150,000 (*MR*, 19 September 1929, p. 97; 26 September 1929, p. 81; 31 October 1929, p. 77.)

1930: School, Anderson Street, Greenville; $26,000 (*MR*, 17 April 1930, p. 85.)

1930: B.S. Phetteplace Residence, Greenville; $13,000 (*MR*, 7 August 1930, p. 80.)

1931: C.B. Martin Duplex, 107 E. Prentiss Avenue, Greenville; $12,000 (*MR*, 2 April 1931, p. 58.)

Sources: Greenville city directories; *The Greenville News*, 20 July 1956, p. 33; Koyl, p. 31; *MR*, various citations; Petty, p. 141; Wallace, p. 51.

BEALER, William P. (active 1924-1928) William P. Bealer was a minor architect practicing in Atlanta, Georgia, in the 1920s. His work has generally escaped notice of historians. He was associated with James J.W. Biggers, Sr. (q.v.) as Bealer & Biggers in 1924.

South Carolina projects:

1924: F. Louise Mayes Memorial Baby Cottage, Thornwell Orphanage, Clinton; $30,000; Bealer & Biggers, architects (*MR*, 5 June 1924, p. 140; 12 June 1924, p. 113.)

1928: President's Residence, Thornwell Orphanage, Clinton; $20,000 (*MR* 23 August 1928, p. 84.)

BEAUCHAMP, H. (active 1924) H. Beauchamp, of Dallas, Texas, was the architect for the $46,000 Seneca Baptist Church Building, at S. Second and Fairplay streets in Seneca, South Carolina. This building was commissioned in 1924. Beauchamp was probably the "Dr. Harry Beauchamp" reported earlier that year in the *MR* as an architect with the Sunday School Board of the Southern Baptist Convention, based in Nashville, Tennessee.

Sources: *MR*, 17 January 1924, p. 106; 14 August 1924, p. 106.

BEEBE, Harwood (active 1926-1928) Harwood Beebe advertised as an architect and engineer, under the firm name The Harwood Beebe Co., in the Spartanburg city directories for 1926 and 1927-1928.

BEERS & FARLEY (active 1919-1950) William Harmon Beers (1891-1949) and Frank Cheney Farley (1880-ca. 1960) were associated as architects in New York City in the period 1919-1950. Beers and Farley both graduated from the Ecole des Beaux Arts in Paris, France. Beers had received prior education at the School of Mines, Columbia University, New York. Farley, a native of Yokohama, Japan, was educated at Harvard University prior to entering the Ecole. Farley worked with Charles A. Platt and with Delano & Aldrich (q.v.) prior to joining Beers.

South Carolina project:

1936: Thomas Archibald Stone Residence (Boone Hall Plantation House), Charleston County (*News & Courier*, 8 November 1936, p. 3-C.)

Sources: Koyl, p. 165; Withey, p. 47.

BELLONBY, Leonard A. (active 1902-1914) L.A. Bellonby was a much-traveled architect active in several southeastern states in the early twentieth century. He was practicing in Ashland, Kentucky, and Charleston, West Virginia, in 1902. He relocated to Rome, Georgia, by 1906. He was active in Augusta, Georgia, in 1911-1913, being associated with Christopher Whaley (q.v.) in 1913. Bellonby & Whaley prepared plans for a $250,000, ten-story Lawrence Hotel in Augusta that year. Bellonby moved to Charlotte, North Carolina, by 1914, where he practiced under the firm name Standard Improvement Company. The Standard Improvement Company provided plans and construction for two South Carolina churches in 1914. Bellonby, true to form, did not remain in Charlotte, disappearing from the city directories by 1915.

South Carolina projects:

1914: [White] Baptist Church, Georgetown; $13,000 (*MR*, 8 January 1914, p. 63.)

1914: [Colored] Baptist Church, Georgetown; $20,000 (*MR*, 8 January 1914, p. 63.)

Sources: Augusta, Georgia city directories; Charlotte, North Carolina city directories; *MR*, various citations.

BENSON, James D. (active 1908-1957) Benson was a partner of Albert W. Todd (q.v.) in Charleston from 1908 to 1915. He associated with fellow Charleston architect Decimus C. Barbot (q.v.) in 1917, and Benson & Barbot practiced in Charleston through 1925. Benson continued practice for several years thereafter.

A greater part of Benson's practice was in school design. He worked with at least seventeen school buildings in Charleston and neighboring communities between 1915 and 1930.

South Carolina projects:

1908-1915: See **Todd, Albert Whitner** (Todd & Benson)

James D. Benson

1915: Mrs. Norma Howle Wysong Residence, Irby and Palmetto streets, Florence; $5000 (*MR*, 16 September 1915, p. 66.)

1915: School, Hemingway; $15,000 (*MR*, 2 September 1915, p. 67; 16 September 1915, p. 67.)

Benson & Barbot

1917: Remodeling, Citizens Bank Building, Charleston (*MR*, 28 June 1917, p. 68.)

1917: School, Ulmers; $7000 (*MR*, 28 June 1917, p. 69.)

1917: High School, Ehrhardt; $12,200 (*MR*, 4 October 1917, p. 94.)

1919: High School, King and Moultrie streets, Charleston; $125,000 (*MR*, 19 June 1919, p. 135.)

1920: Remodeling, James Sottile Residence, Charleston (*MR*, 1 April 1920, p. 185.)

1920: Enlargement, Enterprise Bank, Meeting and Market streets, Charleston; $25,000 (*MR*, 5 August 1920, p. 163; 12 August 1920, p. 144.)

1920: School, Smoaks (*MR*, 23 September 1920, p. 130.)

1921: School, McClellanville; $25,000 (*MR*, 21 July 1921, p. 85.)

1921: School, Sullivan's Island (*MR*, 28 July 1921, p. 90.)

1921: Bishop England High School Building, 205 Calhoun Street, Charleston (*MR*, 14 July 1921, p. 107.)

1921: High School of Charleston, 155 Rutledge Avenue, Charleston; $124,879 (Cornerstone; *MR*, 8 September 1921, p. 90.)

1922-1923: Addition, James Simons School, Charleston; $18,792 (*MR*, 6 July 1922, p. 109; 24 May 1923, p. 110.)

1922: Remodeling, Simonton School, Charleston; $55,465 (*MR*, 6 July 1922, p. 109.)

1922: Remodeling, Bennett School, Charleston; $32,000 (*MR*, 6 July 1922, p. 109.)

1923: Improvements, Memminger School, Charleston; $7437 (*MR*, 19 April 1923, p. 100.)

1924: Addition, Charleston High School, Charleston; $17,242 (*MR*, 22 May 1924, p. 114.)

1925: G.P. Knowles Residence, Sumter (*MR*, 23 April 1925, p. 115.)

James D. Benson

1928: School, Riverland Terrace, James Island; $12,000 (*MR*, 23 August 1928, p. 85.)

1929: School, Moncks Corner; $46,700 (*MR*, 9 May 1929, p. 104.)

1929: St. Andrews Elementary School, Charleston; $64,046 (*MR*, 1 August 1929, p. 98.)

Sources: Charleston city directories; *MR*, various citations; Petty, pp. 140-141.

BENTON, Charles Collins (1888-1960) Benton, a graduate of the Massachusetts Institute of Technology, was active as an architect in Wilson, North Carolina, from 1907. His brother Frank Benton (q.v.) joined the office ca. 1916, and the firm Benton & Benton was active until 1935. Charles Benton was later associated with his sons Henry Benton and Charles Benton Jr. Two South Carolina theaters, including the marvelous Riveria Theater in Charleston, were designed by Benton.

South Carolina projects:

1929-1930: Hamrick Theater, 306 N. Limestone Street, Gaffney; Benton & Benton, architects (*MR*, 31 October 1929, p. 78; Naylor, p. 114.)

1939: Riveria Theater, 225 King Street, Charleston; Charles C. Benton, architect (Naylor, p. 112.)

Sources: Robert C. Bainbridge and Kate Ohno, *Wilson Historic Buildings Survey, Wilson, North Carolina* (1980: City of Wilson, North Carolina), p. 234; *MR*, various citations; David Naylor, *Great American Movie Theaters* (Washington, D.C.: The Preservation Press, 1987.)

BENTON, Frank Warthall (active 1915-1960) Frank Benton was associated with his brother Charles C. Benton (q.v.) in Wilson, North Carolina, from 1915 to 1935.
Sources: Robert C. Bainbridge and Kate Ohno, *Wilson Historic Buildings Survey, Wilson, North Carolina* (1980: City of Wilson, North Carolina), p. 234; *MR*, 31 October 1929, p. 78, and various other citations.

BERG, Gustavus Theodore (ca. 1823-1905) Gustavus Theodore Berg, a native of Konigsberg, Germany, was educated in engineering and architecture at an unidentified European polytechnic school. He emigrated to the United States ca. 1850 and came to Baltimore, where he took a position with John R. Niernsee, architect. Niernsee and Berg came to South Carolina in 1856 to design the new State Capitol building in Columbia.

Berg remained in Columbia through the course of the Civil War; he was present in 1865 when the city was burned by General William T. Sherman's army. From this time until the turn of the century, Berg practiced architecture in Columbia; he was one of the very few architects active in the state in this period.

South Carolina projects:

1867: Masonic Temple and Firehouse Building, Main and Washington streets, Columbia (*The State*, 24 March 1906, p. 8.)

Ca. 1870-1874: Ebenezer Lutheran Chapel, Columbia (National Register files, S.C. Archives.)

Ca. 1880: Robertson-Hutchinson House, 419 N. Main Street, Abbeville (National Register files, S.C. Archives.)

1880-1882: North Wing, South Carolina Lunatic Asylum, Columbia (*Reports and Resolutions 1880-1881* (Columbia: James Woodrow, State Printer, 1882), pp. 299-300, 360-379, 386-387.)

Sources: 1860 Census, Richland District, South Carolina, p. 82; Columbia city directories; Petty, p. 8; *Reports and Resolutions 1903* (Columbia: The State Printing Company, 1903), pp. 1173-1176; *The State*, 16 June 1905, p. 5.

BERRYMAN, George R. (1884-1957) Berryman was born in Surry County, Virginia, and educated at George Washington University School of Architecture. He worked as a draftsman for the U.S. Government in the early twentieth century. Around 1920 Berryman entered the office of Charles Coker Wilson (q.v.) in Columbia, South Carolina. He became a full partner in the firm in 1923. The firm's principal offices were in Columbia. Branch offices in North Carolina were maintained in Gastonia and Wilson, and later, in Raleigh and Charlotte. Berryman had an independent practice in Raleigh after 1926.

During the Great Depression Berryman worked for the WPA. He resumed private practice in Raleigh in 1946, and he retired in 1952. Berryman designed two courthouses at his home, Surry County, Virginia; one in 1907 (while working in Washington, D.C.,) and a second courthouse in 1923, after the first building was destroyed by fire.

South Carolina projects:

1923-1926: See **Wilson, Charles Coker** (Wilson & Berryman; Wilson, Berryman & Kennedy)

1928: Marlboro County Hospital, Bennettsville; $53,000; George R. Berryman, architect; Henry D. Harrall (q.v.), associated architect (*MR*, 19 July 1928, p. 93.)

Sources: Columbia city directories; Koyl, p. 41; *MR*, various citations; National Register files, Virginia Department of Historic Resources, Richmond, Virginia; Tony Wrenn, Washington, D.C., unpublished research.

BETELLE, James O. (1879-1954) James O. Betelle of Newark, New Jersey, was a nationally prominent designer of school buildings. He studied architecture at the School of Industrial Arts in Philadelphia, and with Philadelphia architects Cope & Stewardson. Later Betelle studied with Cass Gilbert, Donn Barber, and John Russell Pope. He entered a partnership with Ernest F. Guilbert in Newark in 1910-1916.

Over 800 school buildings were designed by Betelle in the Middle Atlantic states, representing over $100 million in construction costs. One hundred twenty-five of Betelle's schools were built in Delaware, the gift of Pierre S. duPont. Betelle served as consulting architect for the school boards of Scranton, Pennsylvania; Berkeley, California; and Charleston, South Carolina.

Betelle was consulting architect for the 1920 Buist Grade School in Charleston, South Carolina (David B. Hyer, q.v., designing architect.)

Sources: Betelle, James O., *Architectural Styles as Applied to School Buildings* (Milwaukee, Wisconsin: Reprinted from the American School Boards Journal, n.d.); *MR*, 3 June 1920, p. 183; *Newark Evening News*, 5 June 1954; Newark Public Library, Newark, New Jersey.

BETSWORTH, Walter W. (active 1920-1929) Walter W. Betsworth worked for the Brissey Lumber Company in Anderson in the 1920s. He was variously described as a bookkeeper, an estimator, and an architect with the firm. Betsworth is identified as the architect of two buildings in Anderson in the 1920s.

South Carolina projects:

1920: F.J. Rhody Residence, Anderson; $15,000 (*MR*, 26 February 1920, p. 147.)

1926: Remodeling, J. Dexter Brown Store and Office Building, N. Main and W. Benson streets, Anderson; $15,000 (*MR*, 11 February 1926, p. 106; 18 February 1926, p. 128.)

Sources: Anderson city directories; *MR*, various citations.

BETTON, William L. (active 1901) Betton was identified as an architect and contractor in the 1901-1902 Greenville city directory.

BIGGERS, James W. (b. 1893) Biggers, a ca. 1915 graduate of Georgia Tech, was active in Georgia and Florida in the mid-twentieth century. He was associated with William P. Bealer (q.v.) as Bealer & Biggers in 1924. From ca. 1926 through 1928, he was associated with a man named Greer as Greer & Biggers, with offices in Jacksonville, Florida, and Valdosta, Georgia. Biggers was living in Columbus, Georgia, in later years.

Biggers was active in Georgia and Florida from 1924 through 1932.

South Carolina project:

1924: See **Bealer, William P.** (Bealer & Biggers)

Sources: Jacksonville, Florida city directories; *MR*, various citations; *Architects and Builders in Georgia*.

BIRCH, Mahlon T. (active 1909-1918) Mahlon T. Birch was an instructor in drawing at Clemson College from 1909 through 1918. He spent the years 1917-1918 on leave and was not listed in the Clemson College catalogues in subsequent years.

South Carolina project:

1916: G.M. Crum Residence, Clemson; $3000 (*MR*, 20 July 1916, p. 68.)

Sources: Clemson College catalogues, 1909-1918.

BLACK, Albert W. (active 1900-1921) A.W. Black of St. Louis, Missouri, was an architect, contractor, and builder active in the early twentieth century. He advertised as architect and builder of cold storage houses, beef houses, and warehouses in 1902; and in 1903 he was identified as an architect and as superintendent of the Frostline Construction Company. Black provided plans for the Armour Packing Company cold storage warehouse on Gervais Street, Columbia, South Carolina, in 1900.

Black's firm was called A.W. Black & Son from 1908 through 1921.

Sources: St. Louis, Missouri, city directories; *The State*, 1 December 1900, p. 8.

BLACK, Edgar Otho (1872- ca. 1950) Edgar O. Black was an entrepreneur and businessman active in Columbia in the early twentieth century. In partnership with J.C. Coulter through 1912, Black helped develop several housing projects in Columbia. Black & Coulter were variously described as developers, contractors, realtors, or architects.

Black was identified as a banker by 1920. He served as president of the Equitable Building & Loan Association in Columbia from 1928 through the 1940s.

South Carolina projects:

1901: Three Residences, Elmwood Avenue, Columbia (*The State*, 20 March 1901, p. 8.)

1901: Residence, Pendleton Street and Elmwood Avenue, Columbia; $3200 (*The State*, 20 March 1901, p. 8.)

1907-1908: Forty-Eight Residences, Columbia; $1000 to $2000 each (*MR*, 19 December 1907, p. 62; 2 January 1908, p. 106.)

1909: W. Banks Dove Residence, Columbia; $4000; J. Coulter, architect; Coulter & Black, contractors (*MR*, 4 January 1909, p. 56.)

Sources: Columbia city directories; *MR*, various citations; Wallace, IV, p. 854.

BLACK, Fingal Conway (active 1900-1937) Fingal C. Black, a Spartanburg native, entered South Carolina College around 1885. He practiced architecture for a short time in Charlotte, North Carolina, and he later worked as a civil engineer for the City of Columbia under supervision of Charles C. Wilson (q.v.) Black and several associates, perhaps because of a disagreement with Wilson, lobbied against Wilson's bid for a seat on Columbia City Council in 1910, with no discernable impact.

Black worked as a civil engineer and realtor in Columbia from 1920 until his retirement ca. 1930. He died ca. 1947.

South Carolina projects:

1900: Thirteen Residences, Columbia; $1200 each (*MR*, 12 July 1900, p. 426.)

Sources: Columbia city directories; Moore, p. 38; *The State*, 29 April 1910, p. 12; 30 April 1910, p. 1; 1 May 1910, p. 3; 3 May 1910, p. 12; 4 May 1910, pp. 1, 4; 5 May 1910, p. 4.

BLACK, H.C. (active 1894-1895) H.C. Black was listed as an architect working in Orangeburg and in Greenville in several regional architects' directories. In 1896, Black's Orangeburg business was called H.C. Black & Son. An H.C. Black was identified as the architect of the Gulfport, Mississippi, City Hall in 1905, in the *MR*; this may have been the same H.C. Black.

Source: *MR*, 22 June 1905, p. 535.

BLACKWOOD, E.S. (active 1896) Blackwood, of Greenville, was identified as an architect in the 1895-1896 Comstock directory of architects.

BLANCHE, John H. (active 1929-1956) Blanche was a student of mechanical engineering at South Carolina State College in Orangeburg in the late 1920s. He prepared plans for the Dukes Gymnasium Building at S.C. State in 1929 as a graduation thesis, under the direction of Professor Miller F. Whittaker (q.v.), the state's first registered black architect. The Dukes Gymnasium was constructed according to Blanche's plans in 1931.

Blanche was appointed instructor at S.C. State by 1938. He became an associate professor by 1940, and remained at the college through 1956.

Sources: Cornerstone, Dukes Gymnasium, Orangeburg; Dedication Program, Dukes Gymnasium, 26 May 1931; National Register files, S.C. Archives; Orangeburg city directories.

BONFOEY, Fred L. (active 1909-1932) Fred L. Bonfoey was a minor architect practicing in Charlotte, North Carolina, and vicinity in the early twentieth century. His work was primarily residential; many houses in Charlotte's suburbs were Bonfoey designs. He prepared plans for several speculative housing developments as well, including nine bungalows on Worthington Avenue in Charlotte for the Charlotte Consolidated Construction Co. in 1918, and twenty bungalows in Myers Park for the Henderson & King Home Building Company in 1919.

South Carolina projects:

1917: Parsonage, Flint Hill Baptist Church, Fort Mill; $2500 (*MR*, 15 March 1917, p. 74.)

1922: W.H. Lowrance Residence, Saluda Street, Chester (*MR*, 9 March 1922, p. 84; 16 March 1922, p. 90.)

Sources: Charlotte, North Carolina, city directories; *MR*, various citations.

BONITZ, Henry Emil Julius (1872-1921) Bonitz, a graduate of the North Carolina State College of Agriculture and Engineering, began his architectural career as a draftsman for James F. Post in Wilmington, North Carolina, around 1893. He opened his own office soon thereafter. Bonitz worked in Wilmington and nearby communities for more than twenty years, designing over one hundred buildings in Wilmington. The "Lumina" Pavilion at Wrightsville Beach was prominent among Bonitz's designs. His work was described in contemporary accounts variously as "Eastlake," "Renaissance," "Old English," and "Spanish mission."

South Carolina projects:

1899-1900: T.B. Gibson Hotel, McColl; $7000 (*MR*, 23 November 1899, p. 308; 22 March 1900, p. 153.)

1904: Conway & Seacoast Railway Co. Hotel, Conway; $7000 (*MR*, 28 January 1904, p. 33.)

1904: Remodeling, Conway & Seacoast Railway Co. Building, Conway; $3000 (*MR*, 28 January 1904, p. 33.)

1904-1906: Burroughs School, Conway (*MR*, 4 August 1904, p. 62; 2 February 1905, p. 58; 23 March 1905, p. 206; *Southern Architect and Building News*, 12 August 1904, p. 11; plaque in building.)

1905: Bank of Conway Building, Conway; $15,000 (*MR*, 23 November 1905, p. 498; 30 November 1905, p. 525.)

1906: Baptist Church, Conway; $10,000 (*MR*, 12 July 1906, p. 733.)

1906: St. James Lutheran Church, Florence; $6000 (*MR*, 12 July 1906, p. 733.)

1911: Page's Mill Public School, Page's Mill (Cornerstone.)

Sources: Bisher, *North Carolina Architecture*, p. 380; Charlotte Brown, Raleigh, N.C., unpublished research; *MR*, various citations; Tony P. Wrenn, Washington, D.C., unpublished research.

BRADFORD, Jules L. (active 1904-1906) Bradford was employed as a draftsman with the Seaboard Air Line Railway in Portsmouth, Virginia, from 1904 to 1906. In 1906 Bradford drew plans for the railway's $7000 passenger depot in Greenwood, South Carolina.

Sources: *MR*, 8 March 1906, p. 210; 15 March 1906, p. 237; Portsmouth, Virginia, city directories.

BRANNAN, Raymond O. (1892-1974) Ray O. Brannan, a native of Greenville, Tennessee, was employed by the Lynchburg Foundry Company in Lynchburg, Virginia, in 1912-1915. He was identified variously as a clerk, a chemist, and finally a manager of the foundry. By 1920 Brannan was secretary-treasurer of the Virginia Ores Corporation. Stanhope S. Johnson (q.v.), a Lynchburg architect, was vice-president of the Virginia Ores Corporation at this time. Brannan became an associate in Johnson's architectural office by 1925, and by 1928 the firm was called Johnson & Brannan. Brannan commenced independent architectural practice in Lynchburg later that year.

South Carolina projects:

1928: See **Johnson, Stanhope S.** (Johnson & Brannan)

1928: Dr. George R. Wilkinson Residence, Cleveland Park, Greenville; $25,000 (*MR*, 9 August 1928, p. 88.)

1932: Berkeley County Hospital, Moncks Corner; $84,326; Roy O. Brannan and F. Arthur

Hazard (q.v.) architects (*MR*, 17 March 1932, p. 30; 14 July 1932, p. 30.)

Sources: Lynchburg Architectural Archive, Jones Memorial Library, Lynchburg, Virginia; Lynchburg, Virginia city directories; *MR*, various citations.

BREEDING, Harry D. (active 1896-1923) Harry D. Breeding, son of architect John C. Breeding, trained in his father's architectural office in Chattanooga, Tennessee. He was a full partner in his father's office by 1896. He moved to Greenville ca. 1901 and worked for a short time in South Carolina before relocating to Birmingham, Alabama. Breeding pursued a career in Birmingham through 1923.

South Carolina project:

1901: Dormitory, Sans Souci Home School, Greenville; $5000 (*MR*, 1 July 1901, p. 473.)

Sources: Greenville city directories; Herndon, p. 27; *MR*, various citations.

BRENDON, Charles (active 1888-1918) Charles Brendon, a native of England, practiced in New York City from ca. 1888 through 1918. He advertised a specialty in the design of apartment houses.

South Carolina project:

Ca. 1918: Restoration, Mulberry Plantation, Berkeley County (Samuel Gaillard Stoney, Albert Simons, and Samuel Lapham, Jr., *Plantations of the Carolina Low Country* (Charleston: The Carolina Art Association, 1938; rev. 1955, 1964), p. 51.)

Source: Francis, p. 18.

BRITE, James (1864-1942) James Brite of New York City, an alumnus of the McKim, Mead & White offices, was the architect of the first skyscraper in South Carolina, the ten-story National Loan & Exchange Bank Building of 1901-1903, in addition to several other South Carolina projects. Brite studied architecture in Europe before entering McKim's office. He and fellow MM&W alumnus Henry

Bacon (1866-1924) formed their own office, Brite & Bacon, in 1897 and the partnership lasted until 1902.

South Carolina projects:

Brite & Bacon

Ca. 1898: E.W. Robertson Residence, "Laurel Hill," Laurel and Assembly streets, Columbia (*The State*, 18 October 1903, p. 23; Work Projects Administration, *South Carolina: A Guide to the Palmetto State* (New York: Oxford University Press, 1941), p. 235.)

1901-1903: Robertson Office Building (National Loan & Exchange Bank Building), Main and Washington streets, Columbia; $325,000 (*MR*, 7 February 1901, p. 53; 14 February 1903, p. 73; 14 November 1901, p. 291; 10 April 1902, p. 213; *The State*, 18 October 1903, p. 23.)

1902: Robertson & Co. Apartment House, Columbia (*MR*, 9 October 1902, p. 216.)

1910: Equitable Real Estate Co. Arcade Building, Main and Washington streets, Columbia; $135,000 (*MR*, 20 January 1910, p. 65; 17 November 1910, p. 72.)

James Brite

1924: E.W. Robertson Residence, Seneca and Edisto avenues, Columbia; James Brite, architect; Lafaye & Lafaye (q.v.), supervising architects (*MR*, 24 April 1924, p. 111.)

Sources: Francis, p. 18; Hewitt, p. 269; Moore, p. 328; Withey, p. 77; Wodehouse, p. 29.

BROCK, W.H. (active 1886) W.H. Brock (or Brook) of Modoc was listed as an architect in *The South Carolina State Gazetteer and Business Directory for 1886-1887.*

BROWN, Anthony Ten Eyck (1878-1940) A. Ten Eyck Brown was born in Albany, New York. He was a graduate of the Architectural School of Design, New York. After working as draftsman for J.E.R. Carpenter in Nashville, Tennessee, 1900-1902,

Brown took a position with the Supervising Architect's Office in Washington, D.C., and then had a private practice in Norfolk, Virginia. Brown went to Atlanta, Georgia, in 1906, where he was associated early with Philip Thornton Marye (q.v.) before resuming independent practice.

Brown contributed to the design of many major buildings in the southeastern states. His work in Georgia included the twenty-seven story Realty Trust Co. office building (1910); the Fulton County Courthouse (1911-1914, with Morgan & Dillon); the Federal Reserve Bank Building (1917); and the Citizens and Southern National Bank Building; all in Atlanta. He also prepared plans for the New Orleans Courthouse; the Dade County Courthouse and City Hall in Miami, Florida (with August Geiger); the Birmingham Terminal Station, Alabama; and the Federal Reserve Bank Branch, Nashville, Tennessee (1922, with Marr & Holman.)

South Carolina projects:

1910-1911: Enlargement and Remodeling, Laurens County Courthouse, Laurens; $40,951; A. Ten Eyck Brown and Proffitt & Hampton (q.v.), architects (*MR*, 3 February 1910, p. 81; 10 August 1911, p. 69.)

1911: Union County Courthouse, W. Main and Herndon streets, Union; $75,000 (Cornerstone; *MR*, 8 June 1911, p. 72.)

1913: J.S. Bailey Office Building, Greenwood; $62,000 (*MR*, 30 January 1913, p. 68; 6 February 1913, p. 79.)

1913: Oregon Hotel, Greenwood; $93,900; A. Ten Eyck Brown, architect; Luther D. Proffitt (q.v.), supervising architect (*MR*, 30 January 1913, p. 68; 6 February 1913, p. 80.)

1919: Commercial Trust Company Bank and Office Building, Greenwood; $167,484 (*MR*, 18 September 199, p. 136 j.)

1922-1923: Federal Land Bank Building, Hampton and Marion streets, Columbia; $132,850 (*MR*, 28 December 1922, p. 86; 11 January 1923, p. 110 f; 4 June 1925, p. 105.)

Sources: *The Atlanta Constitution*, 9 June 1940, p. 1; Herndon, p. 29; *MR*, various citations; Morgan, pp. 93-161; *Architects and Builders in Georgia*; Withey, p. 80.

BROWN, A.W. (active 1929) A ten-story office building project was proposed by the Anderson Building Corporation for Anderson, South Carolina, in 1929. The architect was identified as A.W. Brown, of the Philadelphia, Pennsylvania, engineering firm Meigs, Long & Beale. Meigs may have been John Meigs, but no further information on Long, Beale, or A.W. Brown has been found to date. The structure is not standing and does not appear ever to have been built.

Sources: *MR*, 21 February 1929, p. 81; Sandra Tatman, The Athenaeum, Philadelphia, Pa., to John E. Wells, 2 January 1985.

BRUCE, Alexander Campbell (1835-1927) Alexander C. Bruce was, by all accounts, among the foremost architects working in the southeastern United States. He was born in Fredericksburg, Virginia, in 1835, and learned the building trades with his father, Robert C. Bruce. He studied architecture with H.M. Ackeroid, an English architect working in Nashville, Tennessee. Bruce practiced architecture in Knoxville, Tennessee, from 1869 to 1879, and then moved to Atlanta, Georgia, where he worked with William Parkins (q.v.) for several years. He was associated in Atlanta with Thomas H. Morgan (q.v.) as Bruce & Morgan from 1882 to 1904. Bruce practiced independently for several years after parting with Morgan. He was associated with A.F.N. Everett (q.v.) in Atlanta from 1907 to 1908.

Bruce & Morgan were major architects in the southeast, with projects in Florida, Georgia, Alabama, Tennessee, North Carolina, and South Carolina. Their work spanned the stylistic spectrum, including Queen Anne, Romanesque Revival, Second Empire, Gothic Revival, and Renaissance Revival themes. Bruce & Morgan designed commercial buildings, residences, schools, colleges, churches, and public buildings; they made a specialty of county courthouses.

South Carolina projects:

Bruce & Morgan

1890-1893: Tillman Hall, Clemson College, Clemson; $40,000 (*MR*, 19 April 1890, p. 44; 3 May 1890, p. 46; 31 May 1890, p. 43; 18 October 1890, p. 42.)

1890-1891: Main Building, Converse College, Spartanburg (*MR*, 9 January 1892, p. 38; 16 January 1892, p. 36; 30 January 1892, p. 32; *Sandlapper*, Columbia, South Carolina, December 1976, p. 31.)

1890-1891: School, Newberry; $12,000 (*MR*, 16 August 1890, p. 43; 30 August 1890, p. 40; 21 February 1891, p. 38; 7 March 1891, p. 43; 14 March 1891, p. 41.)

1891: Y.M.C.A. Building, Anderson; $7500 (*MR*, 7 March 1891, p. 43; 14 March 1891, p. 41.)

1891: R.S. Hill Building, Anderson (*MR*, 14 March 1891, p. 41.)

1891: Graham Male & Female College Building, Graham; $15,000 (*MR*, 7 March 1891, p. 42; 14 March 1891, p. 41.)

1893-1895: Tillman Building, Winthrop Normal College, Rock Hill (*MR*, 23 June 1893, p. 302; 18 August 1893, p. 53; 25 August 1893, p. 71; 3 November 1893, p. 242; "Existing Facilities Study.")

Ca. 1893: Harris Residence, Abbeville (original blueprints preserved on property.)

1894: Reconstruction, Tillman Hall, Clemson College, Clemson; $23,393 (*MR*, 1 June 1894, p. 302; 8 June 1894, p. 317; 6 July 1894, p. 382.)

1894-1895: Margaret Nance Building (North Dormitory), Winthrop College, Rock Hill ("Existing Facilities Study.")

1895: McBryde Cafeteria Kitchen, Winthrop College, Rock Hill ("Existing Facilities Study.")

1896: Crawford Health Center, Winthrop College, Rock Hill ("Existing Facilities Study".)

Bruce & Everett

1907: Art and Auditorium Building, Greenville Female College, Greenville (*MR*, 4 July 1907, p. 805; 11 July 1907, p. 837; 1 August 1907, p. 82.)

1908: Baptist Church, Latta; $15,000 (*MR*, 30 January 1908, p. 58; 2 April 1908, p. 69.)

Sources: "Existing Facilities Study, Winthrop College, Rock Hill, South Carolina," Triad Architectural Associates, Columbia, S.C., 1980; Anne Harman and Janice Hardy, "Alexander Campbell Bruce," in *Dictionary of Georgia Biography*, pp. 126-128; Elizabeth A. Lyon, "Thomas Henry Morgan," in *Dictionary of Georgia Biography*, pp. 726-728; *The National Cyclopedia of American Biography* (1893), Vol. 3, p. 361; Withey, p. 84.

BRUNSON, J.C. (active 1911-1924) J.C. Brunson of Hartsville advertised as a civil engineer, architect, surveyor, mapper, and municipal engineer in the Darlington *News & Press* in 1911-1912. James P. Brunson, perhaps the same man, was president and treasurer of the Daniel Lumber Company in Darlington in 1924.

Sources: Darlington *News & Press*, 14 December 1911, 4 January 1912, 8 November 1912; 1924-1925 Darlington city directory, p. 109.

BRYAN, Andrew J. (active 1894-1913) Andrew J. Bryan was architect for many county courthouses in the southeastern states. He was a partner of Willis F. Denny in Atlanta, Georgia, in 1894. Bryan pursued independent practice in Atlanta, 1895-1900; in Jackson, Mississippi, 1902; in New Orleans, Louisiana, 1904-1907; and in Louisville, Kentucky, ca. 1913. Bryan designed courthouses in Abbeville, Clarksville, Columbus, Douglasville, Hawkinsville, Homerville, Lumpkin, Morganton, and Moultrie, Georgia; St. Francisville, Louisiana; Booneville, Brookhaven, Forest, Indianola, Kosciusko, and Macon, Mississippi; as well as two courthouse projects in South Carolina.

South Carolina projects:

1896: Berkeley County Courthouse, Moncks Corner; $6000 (*MR*, 29 May 1896, p. 303; 21 August 1896, p. 65.)

1898: Dillon County Courthouse and Jail, Dillon (*MR*, 15 April 1898, p. 212.)

Sources: *MR*, various citations; *Architects and Builders in Georgia*.

BRYANT, Charles K. (1869-1933) Bryant, a native of Powhatan County, Virginia, studied for several years with architect Marion J. Dimmock in Richmond, Virginia. He began independent practice in Richmond ca. 1892, in association with William Poindexter. Bryant prepared plans for several commercial buildings in Richmond. The John Marshall High School in Richmond was prominent among Bryant's designs. A number of buildings in North Carolina were also designed by Bryant.

South Carolina projects:

1914: Anderson Development Co. Theater and Office Building, Anderson; $40,000 (*MR*, 30 July 1914, p. 67; 1 October 1914, p. 71.)

1917: McNeel Memorial Sunday School Building, First Presbyterian Church, York (*MR*, 7 June 1917, p. 95.)

1919: J.S. Machorell (Mackorell) Residence, York; $28,000 (*MR*, 22 May 1919, p. 118; 29 May 1919, p. 129.)

Sources: *MR*, various citations; Andrew Morrison, editor, *The City on the James: Richmond, Virginia* (Richmond, Virginia: George W. Englehardt, 1893), p. 58; Richmond, Virginia city directories; Robert P. Winthrop, *Architecture in Downtown Richmond* (Richmond, Virginia: Historic Richmond Foundation, 1982,) p. 238; Withey, p. 86.

BRYANT, Virgil F. and William D. (active 1920) Virgil F. Bryant and his brother William D. Bryant of Orangeburg practiced architecture, civil engineering, and surveying under the firm name Bryant Engineering Company.

Sources: Orangeburg city directories.

BUDD, KATHERINE COTHEAL (1860- ca. 1932) Kate Cotheal Budd of New York City, born in 1860, was architect for a number of Y.W.C.A.-sponsored "hostess houses" at military camps in the Southeast during World War I. She was active as an architect by 1899, and she joined the New York chapter of the A.I.A. in 1916. Budd registered for professional practice in Georgia in 1920.

South Carolina projects:

1918: Y.W.C.A. National War Work Council Colored Hostess-House, Fort Jackson, Columbia (*MR*, 20 June 1918, p. 81.)

1918: Y.W.C.A. National War Work Council Hostess-House, Spartanburg (*MR*, 31 October 1918, p. 78.)

Sources: Francis, p. 19; *MR*, various citations; Judith Paine, "Pioneer Women Architects," in Susana Torre, ed., *Women in American Architecture: A Historic and Contemporary Perspective* (New York: Whitney Library of Design, 1977), p. 69; Susan Hunter Smith, "Women Architects in Atlanta, 1895-1979," *The Atlanta Historical Journal*, Vol. XXIII, No. 4, Winter 1979/1980, p. 86; Withey, p. 538.

BULLARD & BULLARD (active 1890-1948) Bullard & Bullard of Springfield, Illinois, (the firm was also called Bullard & Son) prepared plans for a $10,000 Baptist Church in St. Matthews in 1908. George W. Bullard (1855-1935) and S.A. Bullard were the first partners; S.A. Bullard was architect for the First Baptist Church in Carbondale, Illinois, built in 1902-1903. Roger C. Bullard (died 1948) and Clark W. Bullard were also members of the firm.

Sources: *MR*, 5 March 1908, p. 68; 12 March 1908, p. 58; Susan E. Maycock, *An Architectural History of Carbondale, Illinois* (Carbondale and Edwardsville, Illinois: Southern Illinois University Press, 1983), p. 29; Withey, p. 93.

BURDEN, Henry S. (active 1908-1940) Burden was an associate of Henry F. Walker (q.v.) in Charleston from 1910 through 1919. Burden worked as a draftsman for architect Rutledge S. Holmes (q.v.) in 1898-1899, and later at the Charleston navy yard for several years prior to joining Walker's firm. He took a position as superintendent of construction for the Charleston Engineering and Contracting Company around 1920 and held this job for several years. By 1931 Burden had resumed his architectural practice in Charleston.

Burden resumed work as a draftsman at the Charleston Navy Yard by 1934, evidently because of the Great Depression. He was able to re-establish his architectural practice in Charleston by 1938. Constance F. Burden, widow of H.S. Burdon, lived in Charleston in 1958.

South Carolina projects:

1910-1919: See **Walker, Henry F.** (Walker & Burden)

Sources: Charleston city directories; *MR*, various citations.

BURGESS, W.C. (active 1935) W.C. Burgess, of 2024 S. Racine Ave., Chicago, Illinois, prepared plans for improvements to the operatives' houses and boiler plant of the Burton Dixie Corporation in Blacksburg, South Carolina, in 1935.

Source: *MR*, August 1935, p. 50.

BURNHAM & BLEISNER (active 1904) Franklin P. Burnham (died 1909) of Los Angeles, California, and his partner _____ Bleisner designed the Kennedy Free Library at 122 Magnolia Street, Spartanburg, South Carolina, in 1904. Burnham was an associate of Willoughby J. Edbrooke in Chicago ca. 1884-1893 and with Edbrooke designed the Georgia State Capitol building in Atlanta. Burnham went to California around 1900. Prominent among Burnham's California works were the 1903-1904 Riverside County Courthouse in Riverside and the 1909 First Church of Christ Scientist in Pasadena.

Sources: David Gebhard and Robert Winter, *A Guide to Architecture in Los Angeles and Southern California* (Salt Lake City: Peregrine Smith, Inc., 1982), pp. 341, 373, and 404; Herndon, pp. 36, 65; Elizabeth A. Lyon, Atlanta, Georgia, "Images and Origins of a New South City: The Central Business District of Atlanta," (unpublished typescript, 1975); *MR*, 10 March 1904, p. 7; 31 March 1904, p. 239; and 20 October 1904, p. 337; *Southern Architect and Building News*, 12 August 1904, p. 11; Withey, p. 100.

BURRELL, Seymour (active 1909-1921) Seymour Burrell of New York City was company architect for the S.H. Kress & Co. dime store chain from ca. 1909 through 1921. Burrell prepared plans for Kress store buildings across the nation during this period. Kress stores in Salisbury, Fayetteville, Durham, Charlotte, High Point, and Winston-Salem, North Carolina; Athens and Albany, Georgia; Roanoke, Virginia; Helena, Arkansas; and Johnson City, Tennessee, among other southeastern cities, were designed or remodeled by Burrell.

South Carolina project:

1917: S.H. Kress & Co. Store Building, Sumter; $24,000 (*MR*, 4 January 1917, p. 81.)

Sources: *MR*, various citations.

BURTON, Ralph F. (active 1915-1917) Ralph F. Burton was a contractor in Charleston in 1915-1916. Burton was an associate of Lebon W. Garner (q.v.) in 1917.

Sources: Charleston city directories.

BUSCH, E.H. (active 1909) E.H. Busch of Aiken prepared plans for the 1909 Lutheran Church in Aiken. The project, described in the *MR* on 18 February 1909, p. 67, was contracted at $3000.

CAIN, Herbert Levi (1888- ca. 1960) Herbert L. Cain, a prominent church architect during the early twentieth century, prepared designs for religious buildings in many eastern states. Cain was born in Harrington, Delaware, on 29 June 1888. He studied architecture through International Correspondence School courses, while receiving practical experience as a draftsman for John D. Allen & Co. of Philadelphia (1907), Charles G. Fisher of Milford, Delaware (1908), and Scarborough & C.K. Howell (q.v.) of Richmond, Virginia (1908-1909.)

Cain was a junior associate of D. Wiley Anderson in Richmond in 1909; he opened his own practice in Richmond by 1912. He maintained this office through the 1950s. From 1924 to 1929 Cain had a branch office in Philadelphia. In 1955 Cain was registered as an architect in Florida, North Carolina, Virginia, and West Virginia.

Cain's practice was restricted to church work from 1927. Two church projects in South Carolina are included among Cain's designs.

South Carolina projects:

1920: Citadel Square Baptist Church Sunday School Building and Remodeling of Auditorium, 328 Meeting Street, Charleston; $100,000 (*MR*, 1 July 1920, p. 172; 8 July 1920, p. 125.)

1928-1929: First Presbyterian Church Sunday School Building and Remodeling of Main Building, W. Washington and Coffee streets, Greenville; $125,000 (Cornerstone; *MR*, 11 November 1928, p. 105.)

Sources: Koyl, pp. 78-79; *MR*, various citations; Richmond, Virginia, city directories; Tatman/Moss, p. 125.

CARLISLE, Aiken R. (active 1922-1936) Aiken R. Carlisle began practice as a consulting engineer in Spartanburg around 1922. He also ran a business providing architectural and engineering blueprints. Carlisle was preparing plans for small buildings in Spartanburg by 1923. From 1922 to 1928, the blueprint business was Carlisle's primary concern.

Carlisle had associated with Robert A. Freeman by 1929. The architects Carlisle & Freeman pursued a modest practice and dissolved with the onset of the Great Depression. In 1934, Carlisle had resumed his blueprint business and had also taken a position as architect with the Spartanburg County Emergency Relief Administration. He was able to resume his independent architectural practice by 1936.

South Carolina projects:

1923: School District # 12 Building, Spartanburg (*MR*, 26 July 1923, p. 107.)

1924: S.J. Dupre Residence, Glendalyn Avenue, Spartanburg (*MR*, 15 May 1924, p. 125.)

1927: Three Store Buildings, East Main Street Development Co., Spartanburg (*MR*, 28 July 1927, p. 106; 18 August 1927, p. 126.)

1927: Dr. S.B. Moore Store Building, Spartanburg (*MR*, 22 December 1927, p. 93.)

Carlisle & Freeman

1929: Administration Building, Textile Industrial Institute, Spartanburg (*MR*, 18 July 1929, p. 99.)

1930: C.C. McMillen Residence, Fingerville (*MR*, 27 March 1930, p. 83.)

1930: Auditorium Remodeling and Sunday School Addition, Central Methodist Church, Spartanburg; **Charles W. Fant**, architect, and Carlisle & Freeman, associated architects (*MR*, 26 June 1930, p. 79.)

Sources: *MR*, various citations; Spartanburg city directories.

CARSON, John (active 1902) John Carson was identified as an architect in the 1902 Charleston city directory. He was not listed in other directories of the period.

CARTER, Avery (1863- ca. 1920) Avery Carter was born in North Carolina in February 1863. He received a technical education in Baltimore and by 1899 was working as superintendent of the planing mills of the Morgan Iron Works in Spartanburg, South Carolina.

Carter described himself as an architect in the 1900 federal census. He established a partnership with L.P. Epton to pursue architecture and real estate marketing. Carter and Epton had their offices in rooms 13-15 of the Cleveland Building in Spartanburg; they arranged their pursuits under the firm names of Avery Carter & Co., Architects, and L.P. Epton & Co., Real Estate. Thomas Keating (q.v.) was a draftsman working for Carter. The firm designed a number of small buildings in Spartanburg and upstate South Carolina in 1903.

Carter left Spartanburg late in 1903 to associate with architect James H. Sams (q.v.) in Columbia. Sams & Carter were active until March of 1905, when the partnership was dissolved. Several commercial and institutional buildings in central South Carolina were designed by Sams & Carter, including two buildings for Benedict College in Columbia.

Immediately after leaving Sams, Carter formed a partnership with the young architect Robert S. Pringle (q.v.) Carter & Pringle pursued a modest practice from 1905 to 1906. Six school buildings around the state are attributed to the firm. The 1906 Carnegie Dormitory at the Due West Female College was among their most important work.

The partnership with Pringle was dissolved by 1907. Carter was listed as an architect in the 1909 Columbia city directory, but no projects dating to this period have been identified.

Carter had moved to Nashville, Tennessee by 1910. Prominent architect Clarence K. Colley, who employed Carter as a draftsman, designed a house for Carter at 1715 Blair Boulevard in 1912. Carter worked in Colley's office for several years, and around 1915 he associated with South Carolina native Russell E. Hart. Hart & Carter were active in Nashville through 1917. Avery Carter was listed in the 1918 Nashville directory as an architect.

South Carolina projects:

1903: Science Hall, Wofford College, Spartanburg; $15,000 (*MR*, 12 March 1903, p. 164.)

1903: School, Anderson (*MR*, 26 March 1903, p. 204; 23 April 1903, p. 285; 11 June 1903, p. 428.)

1903: Two Dwellings, Presbyterian College, Clinton; $3500 (*MR*, 11 June 1903, p. 429.)

1903: John Ferguson Residence, Spartanburg; $4000 (*MR*, 11 June 1903, p. 429.)

1903: A.J. Dillard Residence, Spartanburg; $12,000 (*MR*, 11 June 1903, p. 429.)

1903: Alumni Building, Converse College, Spartanburg; $10,000 (*MR*, 11 June 1903, p. 429; 6 August 1903, p. 53.)

1903: W.S. Glenn Business Block, Spartanburg; $6000 (*MR*, 11 June 1903, p. 429.)

1903: John Q. Little Store and Office Building, Spartanburg; $5000 (*MR*, 11 June 1903, p. 429.)

1903: Y.M.C.A. Building, Spartanburg (*MR*, 11 June 1903, p. 429.)

1903: School, Westminster; $9000 (*MR*, 11 June 1903, p. 429.)

1903: School, Easley (*MR*, 23 July 1903, p. 15.)

1903: School, Pickens; $8150 (*MR*, 27 August 1903, p. 106.)

1903-1904: See **Sams, James Hagood** (Sams & Carter)

Carter & Pringle

1905: School, Jefferson; $6100 (*MR*, 6 April 1905, p. 256; 11 May 1905, p. 384.)

1905: Hotel, Jonesville; $5000 (*MR*, 20 April 1905, p. 309.)

1905: School, Kershaw; $10,000 (*MR*, 6 April 1905, p. 256.)

1905: School, Liberty; $10,000 (*MR*, 6 April 1905, p. 256.)

1905: Fire Department House, Rock Hill; $8500 (*MR*, 30 March 1905, p. 229; 6 April 1905, p. 256.)

1905: Municipal Building, Rock Hill; $5140 (*MR*, 3 August 1905, p. 77; 10 August 1905, p. 101.)

1905: School, Whitmire; $5500 (*MR*, 6 April 1905, p. 256.)

1906: Carnegie Dormitory, Due West Female College, Due West; $30,000 (*MR*, 26 July 1906, p. 43; 23 August 1906, p. 143.)

1906: School, Mullins (*MR*, 1 March 1906, p. 183.)

Sources: 1900 Census, South Carolina, Vol. 46, Enumeration District 108, Sheet 10; Columbia city directories; *Directory of Historic American Architectural Firms*, p. 14; Herndon, p. 40; Kline, p. 11; *MR*, various citations; Nashville, Tennessee city directories; Spartanburg city directories; *The State*, 5 March 1905, 7 March 1905.

CARTER, T.T. (active 1904-1918) Architect T.T. Carter of Bluefield, West Virginia prepared plans for the W.H. Greever residence at 1616 Bull Street, Columbia, South Carolina, in 1908.

Source: *MR*, 24 December 1908, p. 67.

CASEY, Joseph Huntley (1875-1928) Casey, a native of Binghamton, New York, studied architecture through the International Correspondence School. He worked for the Buffalo architectural firms Green & Wicks and Lansing & Beierel for several years before coming to Anderson, South Carolina, around 1900. He formed a partnership with Charles W. Fant (q.v.) around 1913, and the firm of Casey & Fant practiced in Anderson until Casey's death in Baltimore in 1928.

Casey won a great number of ecclesiastical projects, especially Baptist churches, during his career. He designed Carnegie Library buildings in Anderson (1905-1907) and Honea Path (1907.)

Casey's son Huntley F. Casey worked as a draftsman for Casey & Fant ca. 1925-1927.

South Carolina projects:

1904: Dr. D.S. Watson Hotel, Anderson (*MR*, 24 March 1904, p. 216; *The State*, 20 March 1904, p. 1.)

1905: Anderson Real Estate & Investment Co. Hotel, Anderson; $10,000 (*MR*, 27 July 1905, p. 50.)

1905-1907: Carnegie Free Library, 405 N. Main Street, Anderson (*MR*, 2 November 1905, p. 412; 16 August 1906, p. 117; 21 March 1907, p. 291; 28 March 1907, p. 323; Norryce, *A General Sketch of Anderson*; Withey, p. 114; George S. Bobinski, *Carnegie Libraries: Their History and Impact on American Public Library Development* (Chicago: American Library Association, 1969), p. 208.)

1906: Anderson Banking & Trust Co. Building, Anderson; $8000 (*MR*, 16 August 1906, p. 117; 30 August 1906, p. 168.)

1906: Judge W.F. Cox Residence, Anderson; $12,000 (*MR*, 16 August 1906, p. 117; 23 August 1906, p. 143.)

1906: J. Reid Garrison Residence, Denver; $6000 (*MR*, 16 August 1906, p. 118.)

1906: Thomas C. Jackson Residence, Iva; $10,000 (*MR*, 16 August 1906, p. 118.)

1906: Dr. C.L. Guyton Residence, Williamston (*MR*, 16 August 1906, p. 119.)

1906: C.W. Bauknight Residence, Walhalla; $5000 (*MR*, 16 August 1906, p. 119.)

1907: Anderson Hospital Association Hospital, Anderson; $17,500 (*MR*, 14 February 1907, p. 136; 21 February 1907, p. 167; 23 May 1907, p. 603.)

1907-1910: St. John's Methodist Church, Anderson; $50,000 (*MR*, 16 May 1907, p. 572; 9 April 1908, p. 57; 16 April 1908, p. 62; 10 February 1910, p. 62; Withey, p. 114.)

1907: Oakwood Baptist Church, Brogan Mills, Anderson (*MR*, 1 August 1907, p. 81.)

1907: People's Furniture Co. Warehouse, Anderson (*MR*, 1 August 1907, p. 81.)

1907: Union Church, Glenwood Mills, Easley (*MR*, 1 August 1907, p. 82.)

1907: Carnegie Library, Honea Path; $5000 (*MR*, 9 May 1907, p. 538; 16 May 1907, p. 574; 23 May 1907, p. 605; George S. Bobinski, *Carnegie Libraries: Their History and Impact on American Public Library Development* (Chicago: American Library Association, 1969), p. 221.)

1907-1909: School, Iva; $6000 (*MR*, 16 May 1907, p. 574; 6 June 1907, p. 672; 20 June 1907, p. 737; 1 August 1907, p. 82; 29 October 1908, p. 67; 17 December 1908, p. 69; 14 January 1909, pp. 58-59.)

1907: Addition, Pickens County Courthouse, Pickens; $6000 (*MR*, 18 July 1907, p. 22; 1 August 1907, p. 83.)

1908: B.F. Kramer Residence, Anderson; $6000 (*MR*, 12 March 1908, p. 58.)

1908: Frank Hall Residence, Anderson; $5000 (*MR*, 12 March 1908, p. 58.)

1908: Mrs. Chenault Residence, Anderson; $6000 (*MR*, 12 March 1908, p. 58.)

1908: W.W. Sullivan Residence, Anderson; $8000 (*MR*, 12 March 1908, p. 58.)

1908: J. Dexter Brown Residence, Anderson; $10,000 (*MR*, 14 May 1908, p. 58; 28 May 1908, p. 65.)

1908: B.T. Armnock, Jr. Residence, Anderson; $4000 (*MR*, 18 June 1908, p. 62.)

1908: Mulkey, Ramsey & Trammell Store Building, Anderson; $20,000 (*MR*, 2 July 1908, p. 69; 9 July 1908, p. 56; 16 July 1908, p. 58.)

1908: Mrs. W.Q. Hammond Residence, Anderson; $5000 (*MR*, 29 October 1908, p. 66.)

1908-1909: Paul Crowther Residence, Anderson (*MR*, 5 November 1908, p. 70; 12 November 1908, p. 61; 4 February 1909, p. 76.)

1908: Sullivan Hardware Co. Warehouse, Anderson; $15,000 (*MR*, 31 December 1908, p. 61.)

1908: School, Belton; $12,500 (*MR*, 21 May 1908, p. 63; 18 June 1908, p. 64; 2 July 1908, p. 70.)

1908: Bank of Calhoun Falls Building, Calhoun Falls; $5000 (*MR*, 29 October 1908, p. 65.)

1908: School, Fountain Inn; J.H. Casey and C.H. Choate (q.v.), architects (*MR*, 2 April 1908, p. 91; 2 July 1908, p. 70.)

1908: Presbyterian Church, Fountain Inn; $7000 (*MR*, 5 November 1908, p. 69.)

1908: Dr. J.F. Shirley Residence, Honea Path; $7000 (*MR*, 12 March 1908, p. 58.)

1908: School, Seneca; $10,720 (*MR*, 26 March 1908, p. 60; 16 April 1908, p. 64; 2 July 1908, p. 70; 16 July 1908, p. 59.)

1908: Addition, Bank of Williamston Building, Williamston; $2500 (*MR*, 29 October 1908, p. 65.)

1909: H.R. Wells Residence, Anderson; $3000 (*MR*, 14 January 1909, p. 56; 4 February 1909, p. 76.)

1909: Associate Reformed Presbyterian Church, Anderson; $5000 (*MR*, 18 February 1909, p. 67.)

1909: C.W. McGee Residence, Anderson (*MR*, 4 March 1909, p. 78; 18 March 1909, p. 63.)

1909: O.G. Burriss Residence, Anderson (*MR*, 18 March 1909, p. 63.)

1909: J.F. McClure Residence, Anderson (*MR*, 18 March 1909, p. 63.)

1909: Sunday School Building, First Baptist Church, Anderson; $8000 (*MR*, 22 April 1909, p. 60; 13 May 1909, p. 60; 5 August 1909, p. 71.)

1909: G.F. Tolley and Son Store Building, 131 E. Whitner Street, Anderson (*MR*, 18 March 1909, p. 64; Norryce, *A General Sketch of Anderson.*)

1909: J.R. Chamblee Apartment House, Anderson (*MR*, 19 August 1909, p. 59; 26 August 1909, p. 55.)

1909: Addition, City Hospital, Anderson; $40,000 (*MR*, 30 September 1909, p. 67; 4 November 1909, p. 78.)

1909: Leroy A. Wertz Business Building, Belton (*MR*, 5 August 1909, p. 72; 28 October 1909, p. 126.)

1909: Baptist Church, Clinton; $15,000 (*MR*, 5 August 1909, p. 71; 7 October 1909, p. 79.)

1909: Mrs. H.E. Pressley Residence, Due West (*MR*, 5 August 1909, p. 71.)

1909: W.M. Hagood Residence, Easley (*MR*, 5 August 1909, p. 71.)

1909: Luther Townsend, Four Store Buildings, Iva (*MR*, 5 August 1909, p. 72.)

1909: W.F. McGee Store Building, Iva (*MR*, 5 August 1909, p. 72.)

1909: Red Bank Baptist Church, Saluda; $10,000 (*MR*, 11 November 1909, p. 64; 9 December 1909, p. 64.)

1909: F.S. Holleman Residence, Seneca; $7000 (*MR*, 18 March 1909, p. 63; 29 April 1909, p. 70.)

1909: Methodist Church, Walhalla (*MR*, 5 August 1909, p. 71.)

1909: Blue Ridge Railway Depot, Walhalla (*MR*, 5 August 1909, p. 72.)

1909: Auditorium Addition, School, Westminster; $5000 (*MR*, 25 February 1909, p. 63; 17 June 1909, p. 69.)

1909: W.H. Pepper Store, Whitney (*MR*, 5 August 1909, p. 72.)

1909: A.G. Pinckney and W.A. Hammond Store Building, Williamston; $8000 (*MR*, 5 August 1909, p. 72.)

1909: Williamston Mills Store, Williamston; $3500 (*MR*, 9 September 1909, p. 58.)

1910: Addition, County Hospital, Anderson; $8000 (*MR*, 27 January 1910, p. 65.)

1910: H.G. Anderson Residence, Anderson; $6000 (*MR*, 26 May 1910, p. 65.)

1910: Anderson Hardware Co. Store, Anderson; $8000 (*MR*, 16 June 1910, p. 70.)

1910: W.R. Hayne Residence, Belton; $6000 (*MR*, 20 January 1910, p. 66; 24 March 1910, p. 66.)

1910: Baptist Church, Belton; $15,000 (*MR*, 13 October 1910, p. 67.)

1910: Baptist Church, Johnston; $15,000 (*MR*, 3 February 1910, p. 80; 10 February 1910, p. 62; 9 June 1910, p. 65.)

1910: M.B. Glenn Residence, Liberty; $3500 (*MR*, 24 March 1910, p. 66.)

1910: M.C. Smith Residence, Pickens; $4000 (*MR*, 24 March 1910, p. 66.)

1911: J.M. Sullivan Residence, Anderson (*MR*, 13 July 1911, p. 72.)

1911: Administration Building and Two Dormitories, Anderson College, Anderson; Joseph H.

Casey, architect; Shand & Lafaye (q.v.), associated architects (*MR*, 31 August 1911, p. 66; *The State*, 2 May 1928, p. 9; Withey.)

1911: S.N. Gilmer Residence, Anderson (*MR*, 21 September 1911, p. 67.)

1913: Kennedy Street School, Anderson (*MR*, 11 September 1913, p. 66.)

1913: G.W. Rush Residence, Greenwood; J.H. Casey and S.N. Vance (q.v.), architects (*MR*, 3 April 1913, p. 82.)

1913: Bailey Military Institute Building, Greenwood; J.H. Casey and S.N. Vance (q.v.), architects (*MR*, 10 April 1913, p. 74; 1 May 1913, p. 84.)

1913: D.A.G. Ouzts Residence, Greenwood; J.H. Casey and S.N. Vance (q.v.), architects (*MR*, 24 April 1913, p. 74.)

1913: Parsonage, First Baptist Church, Laurens (*MR*, 26 June 1913, p. 69.)

Casey & Fant

1913: Farmer's Bank Building, Iva (*MR*, 18 December 1913, p. 73; 25 December 1913, p. 64.)

1914: Ligon & Ledbetter Store and Office Building, Anderson (*MR*, 18 June 1914, p. 72; 25 June 1914, p. 59.)

1914: President's Residence, Anderson College, Anderson (*MR*, 16 July 1914, p. 70.)

1914: Methodist Church, Clinton (*MR*, 16 July 1914, p. 69.)

1915: City Barn, Anderson (*MR*, 8 April 1915, p. 56; 15 April 1915, p. 57.)

1915: J.H. Anderson Store Building, Anderson; Casey & Fant, and J.B. and W.D. Simpson (q.v.), architects (*MR*, 17 June 1915, p. 60.)

1915: Mrs. N.B. Sullivan Residence, Anderson (*MR*, 22 July 1915, p. 60.)

1915: W. Frank McGee Warehouse and Store, Iva (*MR*, 22 July 1915, p. 61.)

1915: Dr. C.S. Breeding Hospital, Anderson (*MR*, 5 August 1915, pp. 70-71.)

1915: Mrs. L.A. Earle Store and Office Building, Anderson (*MR*, 23 September 1915, p. 59; 7 October 1915, p. 76.)

1915: Mrs. J.B. Sanders Residence, Anderson (*MR*, 9 December 1915, p. 68.)

1916: Lee G. Holleman Residence, Anderson (*MR*, 27 January 1916, p. 62; 3 February 1916, p. 80.)

1916: J.H. Anderson/M.M. Mattison Office Building, Anderson (*MR*, 1 June 1916, pp. 81-82.)

1916: A.M. McFall Residence, Anderson (*MR*, 10 August 1916, p. 66.)

1916: John R. Anderson Residence, Anderson (*MR*, 21 September 1916, p. 66l.)

1916: W.D. McLean Residence, Anderson (*MR*, 2 November 1916, p. 84; 9 November 1916, p. 69.)

1916: J.D. Bell Residence, Clinton (*MR*, 1 June 1916, p. 82.)

1916: School, Lowndesville (*MR*, 27 July 1916, p. 66.)

1916: Methodist Church, Lowndesville (*MR*, 5 October 1916, p. 86.)

1916: Williamston Mills Church, Williamston (*MR*, 2 November 1916, p. 84.)

1917: H.P. Hunter Residence, Anderson (*MR*, 22 March 1917, p. 71.)

1917: Parsonage, First Baptist Church, Anderson (*MR*, 29 March 1917, p. 72.)

1917: Additions, Dormitories, Anderson College, Anderson (*MR*, 10 May 1917, p. 72; 17 May 1917, p. 76.)

1917: Community Building, Equinox Mills, Anderson (*MR*, 20 September 1917, p. 86; 27 September 1917, p. 75.)

1918: Remodeling, Sullivan Hardware Co. Building, Anderson (*MR*, 4 April 1918, p. 95.)

1918: Leopold Geisberg Residence, Anderson (*MR*, 2 May 1918, p. 92; 9 May 1918, p. 78.)

1918: W. Frank McGhee Residence, Anderson (*MR*, 23 May 1918, p. 77.)

1918: Repairs, W. Frank McGhee Store, Iva (*MR*, 28 November 1918, p. 82.)

1918: Remodeling, Grace Methodist Episcopal Church South, Union (*MR*, 21 March 1918, p. 79; 28 March 1918, p. 79.)

1919: Annex, Anderson Hospital, Anderson (*MR*, 27 February 1919, p. 114.)

1919: Harry Geisberg Residence, Anderson (*MR*, 14 August 1919, p. 124.)

1920: J. Dexter Brown Theater, Anderson; $25,000 (*MR*, 19 February 1920, p. 149.)

1920: Dormitory, Anderson College, Anderson; $175,000 (*MR*, 20 May 1920, p. 142.)

1920: Residence, Belton; $12,000 (*MR*, 15 January 1920, p. 152 i.)

1920: Residence, Westminster; $15,000 (*MR*, 15 January 1920, p. 152 i.)

1920: W.E. Cheswell Theater, Store and Office Building, Westminster (*MR*, 13 May 1920, p. 127.)

1921: Masonic Temple, Clifton (*MR*, 3 November 1921, p. 112.)

1921: Methodist Church, Hartsville (*MR*, 30 June 1921, p. 103.)

1921: Baptist Church, Lockhart (*MR*, 31 March 1921, p. 116.)

1922: Boys' High School, Anderson (*MR*, 2 November 1922, p. 118 i.)

1922: High School, Belton (*MR*, 20 April 1922, p. 91.)

1923: Addition, Dining Hall, Presbyterian College, Clinton (*MR*, 2 August 1923, p. 150.)

1923: High School, Due West (*MR*, 1 November 1923, p. 130.)

1923: St. John's Methodist Episcopal Church South, Rock Hill (Cornerstone; *MR*, 8 November 1923, p. 111.)

1923: Sunday School Annex, Methodist Church, Seneca (*MR*, 6 December 1923, p. 126.)

1923-1924: Sunday School, First Presbyterian Church, Union (*MR*, 4 October 1923, p. 124; 18 October 1923, p. 117; 21 February 1924, p. 105.)

1924: Addition, Anderson County Hospital, Anderson (*MR*, 5 June 1924, p. 139.)

1924-1925: John C. Calhoun Hotel, Anderson; Casey & Fant and James J. Baldwin (q.v.), architects; $325,000 (*MR*, 14 August 1924, p. 107; 28 August 1924, p. 113; Withey, p. 114.)

1924: Methodist Church, Clemson College, Clemson (*MR*, 31 January 1924, p. 111; 7 February 1924, p. 147.)

1924: Thomas Smyth Dormitory, Presbyterian College, Clinton (*MR*, 10 January 1924, p. 120.)

1924: Easley Loan & Trust Co. Building, Easley (*MR*, 27 March 1924, p. 119; 3 April 1924, p. 150.)

1924: High School, Honea Path (*MR*, 15 May 1924, p. 126.)

1924: Addition, First Baptist Church Sunday School Building, Inman (*MR*, 10 April 1924, p. 109.)

1924: Samuel Krass Store Building, Union (*MR*, 10 April 1924, p. 112.)

1924: School, Clinton (*MR*, 23 October 1924, p. 109; 16 October 1924, p. 109.)

1924: Sunday School Addition and Remodeling of Auditorium, Buford Street Methodist Church, Gaffney (*MR*, 9 October 1924, p. 117.)

1924: Sunday School, First Baptist Church, Gaffney (*MR*, 25 September 1924, p. 114.)

1925: Methodist Church, Clinton Mills, Clinton (*MR*, 4 June 1925, p. 137.)

1925: A.R.P. Church, Due West (*MR*, 9 April 1925, p. 104; 16 April 1925, p. 113.)

1925: Wolf Creek Baptist Church, Landrum (*MR*, 24 September 1925, p. 96; 8 October 1925, p. 107.)

1925: Second Presbyterian Church, Spartanburg (*MR*, 5 November 1925, p. 129.)

1926: Remodeling, Oakwood Baptist Church, Anderson (*MR*, 15 April 1926, p. 112.)

1926: Addition, East Whitner School, Anderson (*MR*, 27 May 1926, p. 113; 3 June 1926, p. 135.)

1926: Addition, Glenn School, Anderson (*MR*, 27 May 1926, p. 113; 3 June 1926, p. 135.)

1926: Boys' High School, Anderson (*MR*, 29 July 1926, p. 96; 5 August 1926, p. 125; 6 October 1926, p. 115; 13 October 1926, p. 115.)

1927: Remodeling, Sunday School, St. John's Methodist Church, Anderson; $23,000 (*MR*, 6 October 1927, p. 115; 13 October 1927, p. 115.)

1927: Sunday School Building, Central Presbyterian Church, Anderson; $13,000 (*MR*, 24 November 1927, p. 107; 1 December 1927, p. 108.)

1927: Sunday School Building, Washington Street Methodist Church, Columbia; Casey & Fant and Lafaye & Lafaye (q.v.), associated architects; $100,000 (*MR*, 24 November 1927, p. 107; 1 December 1927, p. 108; 8 December 1927, p. 110.)

1927: School, Seneca; $50,000 (*MR*, 7 April 1927, p. 121.)

1928: Addition, North Anderson School, Anderson (*MR*, 6 September 1928, p. 91.)

1928: Addition, High School, Clinton (*MR*, 24 May 1928, p. 90; 31 May 1928, p. 80.)

Sources: Anderson city directories; *MR*, various citations; C.W. Norryce, ed., *A General Sketch of Anderson, S.C.* (Anderson: Roper Printing Co., 1909), n.p.; *The State*, 2 May 1928, p. 9; Withey, p. 114.

CATHCART, Samuel M. (active 1920-1963) Samuel Cathcart was employed as a draftsman by Gadsden Sayre (q.v.) in Anderson in 1920-1922. He opened his own architectural office by 1927. Cathcart served on the State Board of Architectural Examiners from 1938 to 1947.

South Carolina projects:

1928: Addition, Southside School, Anderson (*MR*, 6 September 1928, p. 91.)

1928: Addition, North Fant Street School, Anderson (*MR*, 6 September 1928, p. 91.)

1928: Addition, Glenn Street School, Anderson (*MR*, 6 September 1928, p. 91.)

1928: A.F.A.M. Building, Clemson; $20,000 (*MR*, 10 May 1928, p. 91.)

1929: County Home, Anderson; $50,000 (*MR*, 2 May 1929, p. 99; 4 July 1929, p. 96.)

1930: City Hall and Fire Department Building, Honea Path; $17,000 (*MR*, 10 July 1930, p. 76.)

1935: Junior High School, Anderson; $70,670; C.W. Fant (q.v.) and Samuel Cathcart, architects (*MR*, June 1935, p. 32.)

1939: Addition, Anderson City Hall, Anderson; C.W. Fant (q.v.) and Samuel Cathcart, architects (Plaque on building.)

1947: Agricultural Building, W. Market and Tower streets, Anderson; $270,100 (*Construction*, November 1947, p. 69.)

Sources: Anderson city directories; Petty, pp. 119-191, 133.

CHAPMAN, Hugh R. (1894- ca. 1950) Hugh R. Chapman, a native of Liberty, worked as a draftsman for Joseph E. Sirrine (q.v.) in Greenville in 1924. He opened his own architectural office in Greenville ca. 1928. The venture was unsuccessful, and by 1931 Chapman was reduced to a draftsman, working for architect Haskell H. Martin (q.v.)

Chapman worked later as an engineer and superintendent with the Piedmont Print Works in Greenville.

Sources: Greenville city directories; *The Official Roster of South Carolina Soldiers, Sailors and Marines in the World War, 1917-1918* (n.p.: Joint Committee on Printing, General Assembly of South Carolina, ca. 1929), Vol. 1, p. 269.

CHOATE, Charles E. (1866-1929) Choate was working in the architectural office of Joseph C. Turner (q.v.) of Augusta, Georgia, in 1902. He had begun independent practice in Augusta by 1903. Choate relocated to Atlanta around 1909, and he pursued a modest practice in that city until his death in 1929.

South Carolina projects:

1903-1904: School, Greenville (*MR*, 9 July 1903, p. 511; 15 October 1903, p. 251; 28 January 1904, p. 33; 18 February 1904, p.97.)

1908: School, Fountain Inn; Joseph H. Casey (q.v.) and Charles E. Choate, architects (*MR*, 2 April 1908, p. 71; 2 July 1908, p. 70.)

1909: Second Presbyterian Church Edifice and Manse, Greenville; $26,500 (*MR*, 4 February 1909, pp. 76-77; 25 March 1909, p. 59.)

Sources: Atlanta, Georgia, city directories; Augusta, Georgia, city directories; *MR*, various citations; Morgan, pp. 98, 99, 162; *Architects and Builders in Georgia*.

CHUNN, Charles H. (active 1909-1924) Chunn, a minor North Carolina architect based in West Asheville, designed a $2260 bungalow for Roy P. Whitelock in Lansdowne, South Carolina, in 1913. Chunn was designer of the Methodist Episcopal Church South in West Asheville, N.C., in 1909.

Sources: *MR*, 27 February 1913, p. 70, and various other citations.

CLARK, Lloyd A. (active 1917-1940) Lloyd A. Clark was identified as a bookkeeper in the 1912 Greenville city directory. By 1917 he was listed as an architect. Clark worked in obscurity in Greenville for many years. He held certification number 1 from the South Carolina State Board of Architectural Examiners, a body established by law in 1917.

South Carolina projects:

1922: Addition, Dr. R.E. Houston Professional Building, Greenville; $15,000 (*MR*, 17 August 1922, p. 85.)

1922: C.M. McGee Residence, Earle Street, Greenville; $12,000 (*MR*, 7 September 1922, p. 113.)

Sources: Greenville city directories; *MR*, various citations; 1940 Registered Architects in South Carolina.

CLINTON, Charles Kenneth (1889-1976) Charles K. Clinton was associated with a man named Russell from 1920 through 1940 in New York City. Among the firm's works in the southeast were the 1921 Humble Oil & Refining Company Building in Houston, Texas, and the 1923 State & City Bank & Trust Company Building in Richmond, Virginia. Clinton designed two major residences in South Carolina for New York clients. For the Richmond Plantation House, a massive Baronial structure, Clinton incorporated architectural fragments salvaged from various European buildings.

South Carolina projects:

1930: George A. Ellis Residence and Outbuildings, Richmond Plantation, Cordsville vicinity (Original blueprints preserved at property; National Register files, S.C. Archives; Koyl.)

1930: H.P. Bingham Hunting Lodge, Cotton Hall Plantation, Yemassee vicinity; Russell & Clinton, architects; Henry S. Burden (q.v.), supervising architect (*MR*, 14 August 1930, p. 81; Koyl.)

Sources: Koyl, p. 99; *MR*, various citations.

COLLINS, J. Frank (active 1911-1936) Collins was identified as an architect in Spartanburg city directories from 1911 through 1936. He was associated with Joseph B. Simpson (q.v.) as Collins & Simpson in 1923-1926.

Collins won commissions for many important institutional buildings in Spartanburg and neighboring communities. Prominent among his work was the 1927 Masonic Temple in Spartanburg, a heroic edifice with a colossal colonnade in the Greek Doric order. He was also architect for three projects for the Spartanburg General Hospital, and for two other hospital projects in the region. Nine school projects by Collins have also been identified.

South Carolina projects:

J. Frank Collins

1913-1914: Y.M.C.A. Building, Spartanburg; J. Frank Collins and **Shattuck & Hussey**, architects; $70,000 (*MR*, 6 November 1913, p. 75; 2 April 1914, p. 76.)

1919: Community Building, Drayton Mills (*MR*, 13 March 1919, p. 17; 20 March 1919, p. 114.)

1919: Building, Spartanburg General Hospital, Spartanburg; $200,000 (*MR*, 31 July 1919, p. 124.)

1921: School, Clifton Manufacturing Company, Clifton; $58,000 (*MR*, 14 April 1921, p. 116.)

1921: School, Pacolet Manufacturing Company, Pacolet; $150,000 (*MR*, 6 January 1921, p. 166; 13 January 1921, p. 128.)

1921: Colored School, Henry Street, Spartanburg; $27,310 (*MR*, 15 September 1921, p. 89.)

1922: Remodeling and Additions, Community Building, Spartan Mills, Spartanburg; $15,000 (*MR*, 12 October 1922, p. 89.)

1923: Sunday School Building, Bethel M.E. Church, Lee Street, Spartanburg; $15,000 (*MR*, 1 February 1923, p. 118.)

1923: Dr. B.O. Hutchinson Residence, Woodburn Hills, Spartanburg; $10,000 (*MR*, 30 August 1923, p. 106.)

Collins & Simpson

1923: Earnest Burwell Residence, Connecticut Avenue, Spartanburg; $18,000 (*MR*, 27 September 1923, p. 105; 4 October 1923, p. 125.)

1923: Nurses' Home, Spartanburg General Hospital, Spartanburg; $73,700 (*MR*, 1 November 1923, p. 129.)

1924: Community House, Spartan Mills, Spartanburg (*MR*, 29 May 1924, p. 114.)

1924: Addition, Southside School, Spartanburg; $45,000 (*MR*, 5 June 1924, p. 140.)

1924: Greer Drug Co. Store Building, Magnolia Street, Spartanburg; $24,420 (*MR*, 3 April 1924, p. 154; 10 April 1924, p. 112.)

1926: City Stadium, Duncan Park, Spartanburg; $30,946 (*MR*, 4 February 1926, p. 134.)

J. Frank Collins

1925: A.B. Vogel Residence, Spartanburg (*MR*, 8 October 1925, p. 108.)

1926: Residence, Woodburn Hills, Spartanburg; $30,000 (*MR*, 26 August 1926, p. 102.)

1926: Addition, Fremont School, Spartanburg (*MR*, 10 June 1926, p. 111.)

1926: Negro School, Cummings Street, Spartanburg; $52,450 (*MR*, 19 August 1926, p. 110.)

1927: Clifton Methodist Church Building, Clifton; $12,000 (*MR*, 28 July 1927, p. 103; 11 August 1927, p. 110.)

1927: Masonic Temple, Spartanburg; $94,000 (*MR*, 21 April 1927, p. 100.)

1927: Sunday School Building, First Baptist Church, Spartanburg; $110,000 (*MR*, 28 April 1927, p. 11.)

1927: Office and Shop Building, Spartanburg Water Works, W. Main Street, Spartanburg; $27,998 (*MR*, 7 April 1927, p. 119; 8 September 1927, p. 107.)

1927: James F. Byrnes Residence, Otis Boulevard and Mills Avenue, Spartanburg; $20,000 (*MR*, 21 July 1927, p. 119.)

1927: Gymnasium, Spartanburg; $48,307 (*MR*, 29 September 1927, p. 97.)

1929: Spartanburg County Tuberculosis Sanitarium, County Farm, Spartanburg County; $175,000 (*MR*, 21 November 1929, p. 85; 28 November 1929, p. 76.)

1929: Field House, Wofford College, Spartanburg; $40,000 (*MR*, 21 February 1929, p. 83.)

1929: Additions and Remodeling, Dormitory, Converse College, Spartanburg (*MR*, 4 July 1929, p. 98.)

1930: Negro Hospital, Catawba Street, Spartanburg; $60,000 (*MR*, 6 March 1930, p. 109.)

1930: Outpatient Clinic, Spartanburg General Hospital, Spartanburg; $36,690 (*MR*, 13 March 1930, p. 94.)

Sources: *MR*, various citations; Petty, p. 141; Spartanburg city directories.

COMES, John T. (1873-1922) John T. Comes of Pittsburgh, Pennsylvania, devoted his architectural career to the service of the Roman Catholic Church, designing buildings for the Church in many states. Charles D. Maginnis, a contemporary, described Comes as a man dedicated to his mission:

A man of strong faith and unusually developed mystical nature, the beauty of the material temple was a positive passion with him. He rejoiced that his art made him an instrument in achieving it.

Comes, who worked in the office of Rutan & Russell early in his career, was fluent in most of the medieval-inspired styles of the period. He designed buildings in Byzantine, Lombardic, Romanesque, and Gothic revival styles, as well as Spanish Renaissance Revival.

South Carolina project:

1914: St. Mary's Catholic Church Building, 1725 Lyttleton Street, Camden; $13,000 (*MR*, 22 January 1914, p. 66.)

Sources: Charles D. Maginnis, "The Work of John T. Comes," *The Architectural Record*, January 1924, pp. 93-101; James D. Van Trump and Arthur P. Zeigler, Jr., *Landmark Architecture of Allegheny County Pennsylvania* (Pittsburgh: Pittsburgh History & Landmarks Foundation, 1967); Withey, p. 133.

COOKE, William Wilson (1871- ca. 1945) William W. Cooke, a native of Greenville, was a pioneer black architect in South Carolina and the nation. He was the first black architect with professional qualifications to practice in the state. Cooke worked as a carpenter in Greenville in the 1880s, and enrolled at Claflin University in Orangeburg, one of the state's black colleges, in 1888. From 1894 to 1897 Cooke was the Superintendent of Mechanic Arts at Georgia State College, Savannah; and from 1897-1907 he was Superintendent of Vocational Training at Claflin. After taking courses at M.I.T. and at Columbia University in New York, Cooke was awarded a Bachelor of Science in Technology degree in 1902.

The Freedmen's Aid Society and the Woman's Home Missionary Society enlisted Cooke as architect from 1901 to 1907. During this time Cooke prepared plans for several Claflin University buildings. Tingley Hall, the Claflin College administration building designed in 1907, was Cooke's South Carolina masterwork; it is an elegant essay in Palladian composition and detailing.

Cooke was active as a contractor, builder, and architect in Greenville ca. 1906-1908. In 1907, Cooke passed the Civil Service exam and subsequently entered the Supervising Architect's office in the Department of the Treasury, Washington, D.C., as a senior architectural designer. He was the first black man to hold this office. Cooke worked in field operations, as Superintendent of Construction of Federal Buildings in Pennsylvania, Ohio, Illinois, and West Virginia. From 1918 to 1920 Cooke served in the War Department as director of Vocational Guidance and Training. He later pursued private practice in Gary, Indiana, and Chicago, Illinois. In 1930 Cooke returned to the Supervising Architect's office.

South Carolina projects:

1903: Major John Hammond Fordham House, 415 Boulevard, Orangeburg; $1326 (Robinson, "Looking Homeward.")

1907-1908: Tingley Memorial Hall, Claflin University, Orangeburg; $85,000 (Fitchett, "The Role of Claflin College.")

Sources: *Christian Educator: A Magazine of Facts Relating to the Education Work of the*

34

Methodist Episcopal Church in the South, No. 22 (February 1912), pp. 8-9; E. Horace Fitchett, "The Role of Claflin College in Negro Life in South Carolina," *Journal of Negro Education* 12 (Winter 1943), pp. 42-68; Greenville city directories; Eugene Robinson, "Looking Homeward at Four Generations: The house my great-grandfather built resonates amid a discordant world," *The Washington Post*, 13 December 1981, pp. C1, C4.

CORSE, Henry (1886-1949) Henry Corse, a native of Saugerties, New York, practiced architecture in New York City for many years. He designed several buildings in Hobe Sound, Florida, in addition to his work in the north.

South Carolina project:

1929: H.K. Hudson Residence, Stables, and Overseer's Dwelling, Beaufort (*MR*, 28 March 1929, p. 88.)

Source: *The New York Times*, 13 August 1949, p. 12.

COTHRAN, James Sproull (1869- ca. 1911) James S. Cothran graduated from South Carolina College in 1890 with a mechanical engineering degree. He taught "shopwork" at the college for several years afterwards, and then entered Cornell University to earn an M.E. He worked later as a mill engineer and architect.

Source: Moore.

COTHRAN, Thomas W. (active 1902-1940) Thomas Cothran, architect, contractor, and engineer, worked in Greenwood and neighboring communities during the early twentieth century. He was a member of the first class of Clemson College, graduating in 1896. Cothran worked for several years as an engineer and architect for the Seaboard Air Line Railway, designing depots and freight stations in Georgia, Alabama and Virginia, as well as in the Carolinas.

From 1908 to 1911 Cothran was associated with Willie M. Cothran in Greenwood, as Cothran &

Cothran, architects and engineers. Thomas Cothran served as City Engineer and Building Inspector for Greenwood in 1911. He was active as a contractor in the period 1911-1920; among his work was the 1915 Y.M.C.A. Building at Clemson College, which was designed by Rudolph E. Lee (q.v.)

South Carolina projects:

1902: Seaboard Air Line Freight Station, Gervais Street, Columbia (*Greenwood, S.C.*)

Cothran & Cothran

1908-1909: City Hall, Greenwood; $5000 (*MR*, 5 November 1908, p. 71; 10 December 1908, p. 68; 18 February 1909, p. 69.)

1908: C.W. Graham Residence, Greenwood (*MR*, 12 November 1908, p. 61.)

1909: L.W. Stansell Residence, Greenwood; $6500 (*MR*, 23 September 1909, p. 60; 30 September 1909, p. 66; *Greenwood, S.C.*)

1909: Mrs. L.M. Barr Residence, Greenwood; $10,000 (*MR*, 18 February 1909, p. 68; *Greenwood, S.C.*)

1909: B.T. McKellon (or McKellor) Residence, Greenwood; $7500 (*MR*, 25 February 1909, p. 60; *Greenwood, S.C.*)

1909: Home and Industrial Training School Buildings, Connie Maxwell Orphanage, Greenwood (*MR*, 5 August 1909, p. 73.)

1909: D.H. Counts Residence, Laurens; $10,000 (*MR*, 22 July 1909, p. 60; *Greenwood, S.C.*)

1909: J.D. Watts Residence, Laurens; $8000 (*MR*, 22 July 1909, p. 60; *Greenwood, S.C.*)

1910: Grier & Park Store and Office Building, Greenwood; $40,000 (*MR*, 6 January 1910, p. 165; 7 April 1910, pp. 82-83; *Greenwood, S.C.*)

1910: Addition, Oregon Hotel, Greenwood; $45,000 (*MR*, 6 January 1910, p. 166; 7 April 1910, p. 83; *Greenwood, S.C.*.)

1910: Dr. T.J. Crymes Apartment House, Greenwood; $14,000 (*MR*, 5 May 1910, p. 82; 26 May 1910, p. 64; *Greenwood, S.C.*)

1911: Episcopal Church, Greenwood; $7000 (*MR*, 6 October 1911, p. 78.)

1911: W.C. Collins Warehouse, Greenwood; $6000 (*MR*, 2 March 1911, p. 81.)

1911: Dormitory, Lander College, Greenwood; $24,025 (*MR*, 8 June 1911, pp. 72-73.)

1911: School, Greenwood; $14,438 (*MR*, 7 December 1911, p. 87.)

Ca. 1911: J.P. Jennings Building, Greenwood (*Greenwood, S.C.*)

Ca. 1911: Rush Brothers Building, Greenwood (*Greenwood, S.C.*)

Ca. 1911: H.B. Ellis Residence, Greenwood (*Greenwood, S.C.*)

Ca. 1911: R.N. McLeod Residence, Greenwood (*Greenwood, S.C.*)

Ca. 1911: G.E. Banister Residence, Greenwood (*Greenwood, S.C.*)

Ca. 1911: J.M. Simmons Residence, Mountville (*Greenwood, S.C.*)

Thomas W. Cothran

1916: Remodeling, E.K. Snead Building, Greenwood; $4000 (*MR*, 26 October 1916, p. 65; 2 November 1916, p. 84.)

1917: John I. Chipley Residence, Greenwood (*MR*, 18 January 1917, p. 72.)

1917: Remodeling, R.R. Tolbert Residence, Greenwood; $12,000 (*MR*, 4 October 1917, p. 94.)

1917: K.C. Self Residence, Greenwood; $20,000 (*MR*, 4 October 1917, p. 94; 22 November 1917, p. 77.)

1917: Peoples Bank of McCormick Bank, Store, and Office Building, McCormick; $7000 (*MR*, 5 July 1917, p. 92.)

1920: H.V.R. Schrader Residence, Greenwood (*MR*, 26 February 1920, p. 147.)

1920: G.C. Bowen Residence, Greenwood (*MR*, 26 February 1920, p. 147.)

1920: H.C. Tillman Residence, Greenwood (*MR*, 26 February 1920, p. 147.)

1920: H.S. Hartzog Residence, Greenwood (*MR*, 26 February 1920, p. 147.)

1920: Addition, Lander College, Greenwood; $100,000 (*MR*, 15 April 1920, p. 143.)

Sources: Greenwood city directories; *Greenwood, South Carolina* (Greenwood, S.C.: n.p., n.d., ca. 1911), p. 53; Greenwood *Index*, 19 January 1911, p. 1; *MR*, various citations; Darlington *News & Press*, 10 July 1915, supplement.

COTHRAN, Willie M. (active 1908-1911) Willie M. Cothran of Greenwood was associated with Thomas W. Cothran (q.v.) as architect and engineer in 1908-1911.

South Carolina projects:

See **Cothran, Thomas W.** (Cothran & Cothran)

Sources: Greenwood city directories; *Greenwood, South Carolina* (Greenwood, S.C.: n.p., n.d., ca. 1911), p. 53.

CRAMER, Eugene (active 1894-1900) Eugene Cramer of Columbia was listed as an architect in Comstock's 1894 *Architects Directory*. He was described as a scenic artist in the 1899 Columbia city directory.

CRICHTON & HARRISON (active 1898) Crichton & Harrison were listed as contractors and architects in Aiken in the 1898 South Carolina State Gazetteer. They were the contractors, and possibly the architects, for Miss M.A. Andrews' $5200 Queen Anne style residence on Hayne Avenue in Aiken in 1898.

Source: *The Southern Architect*, June 1898, p. 461.

CUNNINGHAM, Frank H. (active 1907-1928) Frank Cunningham graduated from Clemson College in 1903 with a degree in Textile Engineering. He was associated with his brother Joseph G. Cunningham (q.v.) in Greenville as Cunningham & Cunningham from 1908 through 1928.

The seven-story Imperial Hotel in Greenville, begun in 1911, was among the firm's largest and most important projects. The building has a steel skeleton frame carrying much of the load of the floors, but the walls are load-bearing masonry, not fully integrated with the skeleton frame.

South Carolina projects:

Cunningham & Cunningham

1908: A.C. Pridmore Residence, Gaffney; $4000 (*MR*, 24 September 1908, p. 59.)

1908: W.C. Cleveland Office Building, Greenville; $60,000 (*MR*, 17 September 1908, p. 67; 24 September 1908, p. 59.)

1908: Edward J. Gage Residence, Greenville; $6000 (*MR*, 15 October 1908, p. 72; 22 October 1908, p. 58.)

1908: Harry H. Harris Residence, Greenville; $7000 (*MR*, 15 October 1908, p. 72; 22 October 1908, p. 58.)

1908: W.W. Stover Apartment Building, Greenville (*MR*, 26 November 1908, p. 64.)

1908: Charles Allen Residence, Greenville; $3200 (*MR*, 26 November 1908, p. 65.)

1908: E.B. Patterson Residence, Greenville; $4000 (*MR*, 26 November 1908, p. 65.)

1909: J.D. Rast Residence, Anderson; $2600 (*MR*, 14 January 1909, p. 56.)

1909: St. Paul's Methodist Church, Greenville; $15,000 (*MR*, 8 July 1909, p. 62; 15 July 1909, p. 65.)

1910: Remodeling, W.L. Maudlin Office Building, Greenville (*MR*, 24 March 1910, p. 65.)

1910: Remodeling, Blue Ridge Inn, Greenville (*MR*, 24 March 1910, p. 66.)

1910: J.B. Rasor Residence, Greenville; $10,000 (*MR*, 24 March 1910, p. 66.)

1910: George Brunson Residence, Greenville; $3800 (*MR*, 24 March 1910, p. 66.)

1910: Mrs. M.E. Cleveland Store and Office Building, Greenville; $15,000 (*MR*, 8 September 1910, p. 62.)

1911: Addition and Remodeling, First Presbyterian Church, Greenville; $16,000 (*MR*, 22 June 1911, p. 69; 29 June 1911, p. 70.)

1911: Dr. A.B. Wardlaw Residence, Greenville; $2300 (*MR*, 31 August 1911, p. 66; 7 September 1911, p. 77.)

1911: T.O. Lawton Residence, Greenville; $6000 (*MR*, 21 September 1911, p. 67.)

1911: Imperial Hotel, Washington and Richardson streets, Greenville; $45,000 (*MR*, 16 November 1911, p. 75; 14 December 1911, p. 67.)

1911: Oakland Avenue School, Spartanburg; $31,500 (*MR*, 25 May 1911, p. 74; 29 June 1911, p. 70; 5 October 1911, p. 82.)

1912: Two Residences, Messrs. Cleveland and Williams, Greenville; $5500 (*MR*, 28 March 1912, p. 67.)

1912: W.M. Jordan Residence, N. Main Street, Greenville (*MR*, 16 May 1912, p. 74.)

1912: James Finlay Store and Office Building, Main and North streets, Greenville; $50,000; Barnwell & Jones (q.v.), architects; F.H. and J.G. Cunningham, associate architects (*MR*, 23 May 1912, p. 73.)

1912: W.A. Bates Residence, Greenville (*MR*, 13 June 1912, p. 71.)

1912: Henry T. Mills Residence and Barn, Greenville (*MR*, 25 July 1912, p. 72.)

1912: W.T. Henderson and Associates Arcade Building, N. Main Street, Greenville; $15,500 (*MR*, 15 August 1912, p. 69.)

1913: Five Warehouses, Greenville, Spartanburg & Anderson Railway, McBee Avenue, Greenville; $30,000 (*MR*, 18 September 1913, p. 73.)

1914: W.N. Watson Business Building, Brown and Coffee streets, Greenville (*MR*, 30 April 1914, p. 66.)

1914: David Jennings Residence, Greenville; $5000 (*MR*, 14 May 1914, p. 65.)

1914: J.B. Rasor Store Building, Greenville; $3500 (*MR*, 11 June 1914, p. 63; 18 June 1914, p. 72.)

1914: Seven Warehouses, Piedmont & Northern Railway Co., McBee and Piedmont avenues, Greenville; $30,000 (*MR*, 16 July 1914, p. 71; 23 July 1914, p. 58.)

1914: Science Building, Converse College, Spartanburg; $25,000 (*MR*, 25 June 1914, p. 59.)

1915: High School, Orangeburg; $21,000 (*MR*, 16 September 1915, p. 67.)

1915: Citizens' Bank of Taylors Building, Taylors; $2000 (*MR*, 15 April 1915, p. 57; 22 April 1915, p. 53.)

1916: School, Gaffney; $18,388 (*MR*, 29 June 1916, p. 69.)

1916: Improvements, Beattie Building, Greenville; $2500 (*MR*, 10 February 1916, p. 64.)

1916: Sullivan-Markley Hardware Co. Store Building, Warehouse, and remodeling of Main Street Building, Greenville; $16,000 (*MR*, 13 April 1916, p. 70.)

1916: Baptist Church, Jonesville; $6100 (*MR*, 21 December 1916, p. 71.)

1917: Addition, Imperial Hotel, Greenville; $150,000 (*MR*, 18 January 1917, p. 72.)

1917: Remodeling, Colonial Auditorium, Greenville (*MR*, 30 August 1917, p. 74.)

1917: Repairs, Scoville Block, Orangeburg; $8000 (*MR*, 1 March 1917, p. 79.)

1919: A.H. Monteith Apartment House, Cagle Park, Greenville; $25,000 (*MR*, 17 July 1919, p. 126.)

1922: High School, Bamberg; $31,000 (*MR*, 30 November 1922, p. 92 g.)

1923: Methodist Episcopal Church Building, Fountain Inn (*MR*, 12 July 1923, p. 104.)

1923: Dr. J.W. Jervey Eye, Ear, Nose & Throat Hospital, Greenville; $20,000 (*MR*, 15 March 1923, p. 100.)

1923: Remodeling, Building, Greenville; $13,500 (*MR*, 19 July 1923, p. 122.)

1923: School, Wilton Street, Greenville; $44,000 (*MR*, 11 October 1923, p. 113.)

1923: Two Wings, Orangeburg High School, Orangeburg; $27,375 (*MR*, 10 May 1923, p. 109.)

1923: Auditorium Addition, Mellichamp School, Orangeburg; $42,000 (*MR*, 10 May 1923, p. 109; 24 May 1923, p. 110.)

1924: F.H. and J.G. Cunningham Office Building, Coffee and Spring streets, Greenville (*MR*, 8 May 1924, p. 110.)

1924: School, Pendleton; $40,000 (*MR*, 14 August 1924, p. 108.)

1924: High School, St. Matthews; $32,800 (*MR*, 20 March 1924, p. 112.)

1925: School, Easley; $10,000 (*MR*, 16 July 1925, p. 116.)

1925: School, Woodruff; $50,000 (*MR*, 14 May 1925, p. 116; 30 July 1925, p. 121.)

1926: Marion B. Leach Storage Warehouse, Rhett Street, Greenville; $25,000 (*MR*, 19 August 1926, p. 111.)

1926: School, Paris; $20,000 (*MR*, 22 July 1926, p. 112.)

1927: Repairs, Palmetto Building, Greenville; $20,000 (*MR*, 14 April 1927, p. 103; 5 May 1927, p. 114.)

1927: Bush River Consolidated High School, Newberry County; $26,000 (*MR*, 19 May 1927, p. 112; 30 June 1927, p. 106.)

1927: High School, Prosperity; $20,685 (*MR*, 30 June 1927, p. 106.)

1927: Forty-four residences, Mills Mill No. 2, Woodruff (*MR*, 7 July 1927, p. 113.)

1928: Pickens County Jail, Pickens; $20,000 (*MR*, 24 May 1928, p. 88.)

Sources: *The Clemson Agricultural College Record, Directory of Graduates, 1896-1940*, New Series, Vol. XV, October 1940, No. 5, p. 50; Greenville city directories; *MR*, various citations; Petty, p. 142.

CUNNINGHAM, Joseph Gilbert (active 1909-1956) Joseph G. Cunningham, brother of Frank H. Cunningham (q.v.), was associated with his brother in Greenville from 1908 through 1928. Joseph

Cunningham received a Textile Engineering degree from Clemson College in 1903, and he worked as a textile engineer for Joseph E. Sirrine (q.v.) in Greenville before embarking on his architectural career.

South Carolina projects:

1908-1928: See **Cunningham, Frank H.** (Cunningham & Cunningham)

1928: School, Tumbling Shoals (*MR*, 16 August 1928, p. 104.)

1929: Beth Israel Congregation Building, Townes Street, Greenville (*MR*, 6 June 1929, p. 107.)

1929: School, Pickens; $18,000 (*MR*, 19 December 1929, p. 90.)

1930: Anna M. Moore, Six Stores, McBee Avenue and Richardson Street, Greenville (*MR*, 13 February 1930, p. 88.)

1930: Remodeling, School, Jonesville (*MR*, 19 June 1930, p. 82.)

1930: High School, Jonesville; $45,000 (*MR*, 19 June 1930, p. 82.)

1930: School, Travelers Rest; $15,000 (*MR*, 21 August 1930, p. 77.)

1930: High School, Travelers Rest; $26,000 (*MR*, 6 November 1930, p. 84.)

1932: Monoghan Baptist Church, Greenville; $11,117 (*MR*, 12 May 1932, p. 38.)

Sources: *The Clemson Agricultural College Record*, Directory of Graduates, 1896-1940, New Series, Vol. XV, October 1940, No. 5, p. 50; Greenville city directories; *MR*, various citations.

CUSACHS, Philip Alain (1888-1931) Cusachs, a New Orleans native, practiced architecture in New York City in the early twentieth century. He was educated at Tulane University and studied architecture at the Ecole des Beaux-Arts in Paris. His work included a number of large estates built in the South for northern clients.

Cusachs was associated for several years in New York with his brother-in-law Raymond F. Almirall. Cusachs was also connected with the Beaux Arts Institute of Design in New York. He died in 1931.

South Carolina projects:

1929: Remodeling, Solomon R. Guggenheim Residence (Roper House), 9 East Battery, Charleston; $48,000 (*MR*, 4 July 1929, p. 97.)

1930: House, Yemassee vicinity; $100,000 (*MR*, 24 July 1930, p. 78.)

Sources: *MR*, various citations; Withey, pp. 155-156.

DALLIS, Park A. (1873-1947) Park A. Dallis was a mill architect and engineer. He was city engineer in Greenville in 1901-02. Dallis worked for Joseph E. Sirrine (q.v.) in 1906-1907. He opened his own practice in Atlanta ca. 1907. Dallis designed the 1915 Hillside Cotton Mill complex in Lagrange, Georgia, which included one hundred twenty-two operatives' houses. His conventional architectural practice included a number of modest projects in Georgia and at least two in South Carolina.

South Carolina projects:

1912: R.I. McDavid Residence, Greenville; $10,000 (*MR*, 8 February 1912, p. 68.)

1912: Dr. J.L. Anderson Residence, Greenville; $3500 (*MR*, 11 July 1912, p. 70.)

Sources: Atlanta, Georgia, city directories; *MR*, various citations; *Architects and Builders in Georgia*.

DEAL, Fred R. (active 1915-1924) Fred R. Deal was associated with J.H. Johnson (q.v.) in Sumter in 1915-1921.

South Carolina projects:

1915-1921: See **Johnson, James Herbert** (Johnson & Deal)

Sources: *American Art Annual*, Vol. 21, p. 387; Petty, p. 142.

DECAMPS, Christopher J.B. (active 1907-1925) DeCamps was a partner in DeCamps & Cunningham, Architects and Engineers, in Anderson from 1907 to 1908. His associate may have been Frank H. Cunningham (q.v.) DeCamps continued his architectural practice through 1912.

DeCamps was city engineer of Anderson in 1913. He associated with Jonathan Frank as Frank & DeCamps Realty Co. around this time. From 1917 through 1925, DeCamps was identified variously as a civil engineer and as a realtor.

South Carolina projects:

DeCamps & Cunningham

1907: J.M. Evans Business Building, Anderson; $10,000 (*MR*, 13 June 1907, p. 699.)

1907: Westminster Farmers' Warehouse Co. Standard Warehouse, Westminster (*MR*, 1 August 1907, p. 83.)

1908: J.M. Hubbard Store Building, Anderson; $10,000 (*MR*, 28 May 1908, p. 66.)

Sources: Anderson city directories; *MR*, various citations.

DELANO & ALDRICH (active 1903-1949) The New York City firm of William Adams Delano and Chester Holmes Aldrich was nationally prominent in the first half of the twentieth century. Their work included the 1914 Knickerbocker Club in New York; the 1932 Japanese Embassy in Washington, D.C.; the U.S. Chancellery in Paris, 1932; and the Yale Divinity School, 1933. In South Carolina, the firm designed a winter residence at Wando Plantation, Charleston County, for Mrs. Edward V. Hartford. This project was contracted at $100,000 in 1931.

Sources: Koyl, p. 131; *MR*, 16 April 1931, p. 59; White & Willensky, various citations; Withey, pp. 13-14.

DENNIS, Fred (active 1900) Fred Dennis, a native of Lousiana, was born in 1871. He was working in Columbia in 1900 as an architect. He shared an address with Joe Stone (q.v.) and George Lafaye (q.v.) in that year. Lafaye was also from Louisiana, and Dennis may have come to Columbia in association with Lafaye.

Source: 1900 Federal Census, Richland County, South Carolina.

DEVEREUX, John Henry (1840-1920) John H. Devereux, a native of Ireland, came to the United States about 1843. His family settled in Charleston. By 1860 John H. and James W. Devereux were ssociated as Devereux & Brothers, "plasterers." The firm soon expanded its services to include general contracting and lumbering. N.F. Devereux joined the firm by 1874.

John Devereux served as a cavalry captain in the Civil War, and he began practice as an architect by 1867. He spent his entire career in Charleston, and he won great respect for his work in the city. His obituary noted:

> His opinion was looked upon as par excellence in connecting with any and every subject relating to architecture. Old Charlestonians of the past sought his advice in remodeling their homes and much of the taste for which these homes are now noted found a birthplace in his productive mind.

Devereux entered government service in 1885, and for many years he worked in Charleston as superintendent of repairs of Government buildings. Devereux's daughter Dorothy C. Devereux worked in his office as a draftsman in 1904-1905, and again in 1912-1921; in 1908-1910 she was identified in the city directories as a bookkeeper.

Devereux's greatest achievement was the United States Courthouse and Postoffice at the corner of Meeting and Broad streets, Charleston. This three-story granite edifice was designed and constructed under the nominal direction of the supervising architect of the United States Treasury Department. Four men--James H. Windrim, Willoughby J. Edbrooke, Charles E. Kemper, and Charleston native William Martin Aiken (q.v.)--held this office during the construction of the Charleston building, 1890-1896. The actual design and the supervision of the construction are attributed to Devereux.

Ravenel described something of the man Devereux:

> The architect is recalled as a stout, jolly man. Fond of rowing boats, he spent his summers on Sullivan's Island, where his gateway was formed of a whale's jawbones, and a wooden lady, once the figurehead of a ship, presided over the garden.

South Carolina projects:

1867-1872: St. Matthew's German Lutheran Church, 405 King Street, Charleston (Ravenel.)

1868-1873: Stella Maris Roman Catholic Church, Sullivan's Island ("John H. Devereux Has Passed Away.")

Ca. 1869: Academy of Music Building, King and Market streets, Charleston (Ravenel.)

Ca. 1870: Remodeling, Col. Richard Lathers Residence, 20 South Battery, Charleston (Stockton.)

Ca. 1870: Remodeling, George Cook Residence, 24 South Battery, Charleston (National Register files, S.C. Archives.)

1870-1872: Masonic Hall, 270 King Street, Charleston (Ravenel; "Building at King and Wentworth Once was Held to Be Place for Devil Worship. Cost $35,000 to Build in 1872," *News and Courier*, 17 March 1935.)

1872: St. Agatha's Chapel, St. Lawrence Cemetery, Charleston (Stockton.)

1872: Stonewall Fire Company Hall, Charleston (Stockton.)

1874: Roman Catholic Church, Florence (Stockton.)

1875-1878: St. Mark's Protestant Episcopal Church, 14 Thomas Street, Charleston (Stockton.)

Ca. 1885: William M. Bird Residence, 152 Broad Street, Charleston (Stockton.)

1888: Completion, North Pier, Custom-House Wharf, Charleston; $138,000 (*MR*, 23 June 1888, p. 27.)

1890: Improvements, Hotel Charleston, Charleston; $15,000 (*MR*, 16 August 1890, p. 42.)

1890-1896: Federal Court House and Post Office, Broad and Meeting streets, Charleston (Plaque on building; Ravenel; *MR*, 1 March 1890, p. 39; 28 March 1891, p. 45; 20 June 1891, p. 42; 25 July 1891, p. 42; 8 February 1895, p. 29; 11 October 1895, p. 173.)

1891: Emanuel African Methodist Episcopal Church, Calhoun Street, Charleston; $40,000 (*MR*, 23 May 1891, p. 42.)

1908: Improvements, Custom-House Building, East Bay Street, Charleston (*MR*, 9 July 1908, p. 56.)

1912: Improvements, James Island Quarantine Station, Charleston; $5000 (*MR*, 25 April 1912, p. 70.)

Sources: Charleston city directories; "John H. Devereux Has Passed Away," *News and Courier*, 17 March 1920; *MR*, various citations; Ravenel, *Architects of Charleston*, 2nd edition, pp. 265-266; Robert P. Stockton, "Devereux Dominated His Architectural Era," *News and Courier*, 26 October 1981.

DEVEREUX, Leslie W. (active 1924) Leslie Devereux of New York City was the architect for the Dr. R.H. Wilds Residence at 739 Hayne Avenue, Aiken, South Carolina, in 1924. The Tudor Revival style building was contracted at $40,600. Willis Irvin (q.v.) was supervising architect for the Wilds project. Aiken was a popular resort town for wealthy north-

erners in this era, and many buildings in the city were designed by architects from New York.

Sources: *MR*, 12 June 1924, p. 111; 19 June 1924, p. 116.

DICKENSON, Mahlon H. II (active 1891-1929) Mahlon H. Dickenson, a Philadelphia architect, prepared plans for a hotel in Columbia, South Carolina, in 1901, in association with C.S. Dickenson. The building has not been positively identified, and it may never have been built.

Source: Tatman/Moss, pp. 209-210.

DINGLE, James Hervey (active 1894-1938) James H. Dingle was City Engineer of Charleston from 1894 through 1938. In this capacity he was connected with several city building projects, including the 1903 Gibbes Art Gallery. He is presumed to have prepared plans for the 1909 Engine House No. 8 in Charleston, though the sources are not clear. In 1900 the firm Dingle & Barbot, of Charleston, was active; this was probably James Dingle and Decimus C. Barbot (q.v.)

South Carolina projects:

1898: Remodeling, City Hall, Charleston; $10,000 (*MR*, 10 June 1898, p. 332; *The Bricklayer and Mason*, Vol. I, No. 1, 20 July 1898, p. 30.

1900: Sisters of St. Francis Convent, Florence; $5000; **Dingle & Barbot**, architects (*MR*, 1 November 1900, p. 252; *The State*, 27 October 1900, p. 2.)

1909: Engine House No. 8, Charleston; $7500 (*MR*, 18 March 1909, p. 65.)

1911: J.H. Dingle Residence, Charleston; $7000 (*MR*, 17 August 1911, p. 68.)

Sources: Charleston city directories; Charleston city year books; *MR*, various citations.

DINKELBERG, Frederick Philip (1861-1935) Dinkelberg, a native of Pennsylvania, began architectural practice in New York City by 1882. He worked for a period with D.H. Burnham in Chicago, and he is also believed to have had an office in Philadelphia. Dinkelberg prepared plans for a three-story, $200,000 hotel on South Battery in Charleston, South Carolina, in 1893.

Sources: Francis, p. 26; *MR*, 24 February 1893, p. 79; Withey, pp. 174-175.

DOUDEN, William (1869-1946) William Douden, a native of Allentown, Pennsylvania, pursued a career in Washington, D.C., from 1922 to 1946. In 1919-1920 Douden lived and practiced in Union, South Carolina, with an office in the Nicholson Bank & Trust Company Building. He was registered for practice in South Carolina at least through 1929.

Douden's work in Washington included the eight-story J.L. Dillard Hotel at 110 Third Street, contracted in 1932.

Sources: *MR*, 21 January 1932, p. 40; Petty, p. 142; Union city directories; Withey, p. 180.

DOWNING, Walter Thomas (1865-1918) Walter Downing was one of Atlanta's leading architects in the late nineteenth and early twentieth centuries. He established his practice in 1891 after an apprenticeship with Lorenzo B. Wheeler and William H. Parkins (q.v.) In association with Morgan & Dillon (q.v.), Downing designed several of Atlanta's larger business buildings, including the 1913 Healey Building. Downing was noted for the many residences he built in Atlanta, and for the Oglethorpe University buildings designed in 1916 in collaboration, again, with Morgan & Dillon.

South Carolina project:

1901: Major J.A. Fant Residence, Union; $15,000 (*MR*, 16 May 1901, p. 318.)

Sources: Elizabeth A. Lyon, "Walter Thomas Downing," in *Dictionary of Georgia Biography*, pp. 268-269; *MR*, various citations; Morgan, pp. 103-104, 148.

DOZIER, Henrietta Cuttino (1872-1947) Henrietta Dozier, a pioneer female architect, studied at the Pratt Institute in New York and at the Massachusetts Institute of Technology. Her unexecuted designs for the Woman's Building of the 1895 Cotton States and International Exposition in Atlanta helped to establish her career. She practiced in Atlanta through 1916, relocating to Jacksonville, Florida, in that year.

An unverified reference in a Seneca, South Carolina, newspaper described the 1898 G.W. Gignilliat residence in that city, stating that "the architect was a woman from Atlanta." This is presumed to have been Dozier, the only identified woman architect in Atlanta at the time.

. . . Her work followed no particular style and often reflected highly personalized, if not inventive, qualities. She is remembered for always wearing trousers on her work sites and for listing her name as "H.C. Dozier," underscoring her competitiveness in a male-dominated profession.

South Carolina project:

1898: G.W. Gignilliat Residence, Seneca (*Journal-Tribune*, Seneca, Centenniel Edition, 8 August 1973.)

Sources: Jacksonville, Florida city directories; Susan Hunter Smith, "Henrietta Cuttino Dozier," in *Dictionary of Georgia Biography*, pp. 269-270; Susan Hunter Smith, "Women Architects in Atlanta, 1895-1979," *The Atlanta Historical Journal*, Vol. XXIII, Number 4, Winter 1979-1980, pp. 85-90; *MR*, various citations; Wayne W. Wood, *Jacksonville's Architectural Heritage: Landmarks for the Future* (Jacksonville, Florida: University of North Florida Press, n.d., ca. 1985), p. 9.

DRUMMOND, E. Lynn (active 1914-1940) Drummond studied architecture at Georgia Tech and in the office of Hyman W. Witcover (q.v.) Drummond worked also with Augusta architects Scroggs & Ewing (q.v.), Henrik Wallin (q.v.), and Harrison S. McCrary Jr. He designed many residences in Savannah's Ardsley Park and Chatham Crescent neighborhoods.

South Carolina project:

1931: Mrs. Lloyd Richards Residence, Aiken; $30,000 (*MR*, 30 April 1931, p. 62.)

Sources: Augusta, Georgia city directories; National Register files, S.C. Archives.

DUNNE, Edwin J. (active 1884-1912) Edwin J. Dunne, the son of an Irish immigrant, was born in Connecticut ca. 1850. He came to South Carolina around 1884 and pursued a career as contractor and builder. From 1909 to 1912 Dunne and his son William K. Dunne (q.v.) were active as architects in the Sumter area. They designed a number of small churches, schools, and residences in central South Carolina. A high school in North Carolina and an academy building in Georgia were also designed by the Dunnes.

South Carolina projects:

Dunne & Dunne

1909: Remodeling, Methodist Church Parsonage, Bamberg; $3500 (*MR*, 27 May 1909, p. 67.)

1909: Henry Copeland Residence, Bamberg; $2500 (*MR*, 10 June 1909, p. 66; 22 July 1909, p. 60.)

1909: Remodeling, Mrs. Charles Booker Residence, Bamberg; $2500 (*MR*, 22 July 1909, p. 60.)

1909: School, Cameron; $10,000 (*MR*, 18 March 1909, p. 65; 15 April 1909, p. 66; 27 May 1909, p. 68.)

1909: School, Eastover; $5500 (*MR*, 15 April 1909, p. 66; 13 May 1909, p. 63; 27 May 1909, p. 68.)

1909: Methodist Church, Elloree; $8000 (*MR*, 10 June 1909, p. 65.)

1909: School, Hyman; $4000 (*MR*, 24 June 1909, p. 65.)

1909: M.J. Spears Residence, Lamar; $5000 (*MR*, 20 May 1909, p. 62.)

1909: Merchants and Planters Bank Building, Lamar; $8000 (*MR*, 26 August 1909, p. 55.)

1909: School, Lamar (*MR*, 26 August 1909, p. 57; 23 September 1909, p. 61.)

1909: School, Little Mountain; $7000 (*MR*, 3 June 1909, p. 71.)

1909: W.A. Counts Residence, Little Mountain; $3500 (*MR*, 24 June 1909, p. 58.)

1909: Baptist Church, Pinewood; $6000 (*MR*, 26 August 1909, p. 55.)

1909: Lincoln School (Colored), Sumter; $5000 (*MR*, 10 June 1909, p. 68; 1 July 1909, p. 72.)

1909-1910: School, Paxville; $11,300 (*MR*, 27 May 1909, p. 69; 28 July 1910, p. 68.)

1911: M.J. Sapis Office and Postoffice Building, Lamar (*MR*, 8 June 1911, p. 71.)

1911: R.J. Mayes Store Building, Mayesville; $5000 (*MR*, 13 April 1911, p. 71; 20 April 1911, p. 74.)

1912: Bultman & Bultman Store Building, Sumter; $12,000 (*MR*, 14 November 1912, p. 68.)

Sources: 1910 Federal Census, Sumter County, South Carolina, Enumeration District 122, p. 20; *MR*, various citations.

DUNNE, William K. (active 1909-1913) William K. Dunne, son of architect-builder Edwin J. Dunne (q.v.), was born in South Carolina in 1884. He worked with his father as Dunne & Dunne, architects, from 1909 to 1912.

South Carolina projects:

1909-1912: See **Edwin J. Dunne** (Dunne & Dunne)

1913: Perry Moses, Two Store Buildings, Sumter; $20,000 (*MR*, 17 April 1913, p. 74.)

DURANG, F. Ferdinand (1884-1966) Ferdinand Durang, son of architect Edwin Forrest Durang, succeeded his father in "one of the most successful ecclesiastical architectural practices in Philadelphia of the late 19th and early 20th centuries." He was educated at Drexel Institute and the Pennsylvania Museum & School of Industrial Art. Durang was primarily involved with Catholic church and institutional projects. His work in the South included the 1920 St. Joseph's Infirmary in Atlanta, Georgia.

South Carolina project:

1923-1925: St. Francis Xavier Infirmary and Sanitarium Hospital Building (Sisters of Mercy Hospital), Calhoun Street and Ashley Avenue, Charleston; $161,000; F. Ferdinand Durang, architect; John D. Newcomer (q.v.), associated architect (Tatman/Moss, p. 235; *MR*, 8 January 1925, p. 116; 2 July 1925, p. 130; 9 July 1925, p. 122.)

Sources: *MR*, various citations; Tatman/-Moss, pp. 234-237.

EDBROOKE, Willoughby J. (1843-1896) Edbrooke held the position of Supervising Architect of the United States Department of the Treasury from 1891 to 1893. He had supervision over the design and construction of the United States Courthouse and Post Office Building in Charleston during this period. John H. Devereux (q.v.) was the primary architect of the building.

South Carolina projects:

1891: United States Courthouse and Post Office, Broad and Meeting streets, Charleston; W.J. Edbrooke, supervising architect; John H. Devereux (q.v.), architect (*MR*, 20 June 1891, p. 42.)

1891: Repairs, United States Customs House, East Bay Street, Charleston (*MR*, 8 August 1891, p. 37; 5 September 1891, p. 44.)

Sources: *Macmillan Encyclopedia*, Vol. II, pp. 6-7; *MR*, various citations; Smith, *The Office of the Supervising Architect*, p. 44.

EDENS, Allen W. (active 1896-1903) Allen W. Edens was listed as an engineer and architect in the Greenville city directories from 1896 to 1903. He was city engineer in 1896 and 1901.

EDWARDS, William Augustus (1866-1939) William Augustus Edwards was one of the most important architects of educational buildings in the Southeast in the early twentieth century. Edwards, a native of Darlington, was educated at South Carolina College in Columbia, earning a degree in Mechanical Engineering in 1889. He sought to establish a brick works at Palmetto, South Carolina, in 1891. Around 1893 Edwards went to Roanoke, Virginia, to work as a draftsman for fellow Darlington County native Charles Coker Wilson (q.v.) Edwards went with Wilson to Lynchburg, Virginia, in 1895; and when Wilson returned to South Carolina later the same year, he opened an office in Columbia with Edwards as his associate.

The young architects Wilson & Edwards prospered in Columbia. Edwards directed the firm's business in 1900, while Wilson was touring Europe and studying at the Ecole des Beaux-Arts. In 1901 Wilson & Edwards were appointed supervising architects for the South Carolina College Mess Hall, while Walter & Legare (q.v.) were chosen as designing architects. Edwards left Wilson's office soon afterwards and associated with Frank C. Walter, and the firm of Edwards & Walter pursued a thriving business in Columbia through 1908.

South Carolina was commencing a statewide program of public school construction in the first decade of the twentieth century, and Edwards was a major factor in this program. With his partner Walter, he prepared a series of sixteen standard public school designs for the State Board of Education in 1902-1905. These designs, ranging from simple one-room buildings to formal ten-room, two-story buildings with indoor plumbing and auditoriums, were adapted in many South Carolina communities, including Laurens, Union, Belton, Pelzer, Greenville, Greer, and Walhalla. The Taylor School in Columbia, designed by Edwards & Walter and built in 1904-1905, was described by Professor Rudolph Lee (q.v.) as "the first of the modern school buildings to be erected for the graded school system of buildings in the City of Columbia."

Edwards and Walter moved to Atlanta, Georgia, in 1908. They were briefly associated with a man named Parnham (or Parham.) The firm lasted through 1911, when Walter left to pursue his own practice. Edwards maintained a profitable practice in Atlanta until his death in 1939. He established a partnership with William J. Sayward (q.v.) in 1915. Joseph Leitner (q.v.) was connected with the firm in 1919.

Prominent among the designs of Edwards in South Carolina were the buildings at Winthrop Normal College in Rock Hill, especially the magnificent Withers Training School (1910-1912.) Edwards designed twelve buildings for the Winthrop campus between 1909 and 1930. Edwards designed seven buildings for the South Carolina School for the Deaf & Blind, Spartanburg County, and several buildings at Clemson College and at the University of South Carolina.

Among Edwards's collegiate works in Florida were the campus of the University of Florida in Gainesville, including the $1,000,000 Administration Building in 1923; the campus of the Florida State School for the Deaf & Blind, St. Augustine; and the campus of the Florida State College for Women in Tallahassee. In Georgia Edwards designed several buildings at the Georgia State Women's College in Valdosta; at the Columbia Theological Seminary in Decatur; and at the Georgia State College.

Edwards also won distinction as a designer of county courthouses in South Carolina. He designed courthouses for Darlington County (1903), Kershaw County (1904-1905), Sumter County (1905-1906), Abbeville County (1907-1908), Lee County (1907-1909), Dillon County (1911), Calhoun County (1913), York County (1914), and Jasper County (1914-1915.) Edwards appears to have had a monopoly on county courthouse design in South Carolina in these years. All of these buildings except the Darlington and Kershaw Courthouses are still standing.

The W.C. Heath Residence in Columbia, designed by Edwards in 1914 and called Heathwood

Hall, was a splendid and arrogant private residence with a superfluity of coupled Corinthian columns.

South Carolina projects:

1895-1901: See **Wilson, Charles Coker** (Wilson & Edwards)

Edwards & Walter

1902: Church and School Building, Belton Mills, Belton (*MR*, 8 May 1902, p. 286; "School Improvement," p. 323.)

1902: School, Clinton (*MR*, 7 August 1902, p. 52; "School Improvement," p. 326.)

1902: Dr. L.B. Owens Business Block, Columbia (*MR*, 27 February 1902, p. 101.)

1902: Dr. O.J. Harris, Six Cottages, Columbia (*MR*, 8 May 1902, p. 286.)

1902: Hospital Building, Limestone College, Gaffney (*MR*, 28 August 1902, p. 105.)

1902: Church and School Buildings, F.W. Poe Manufacturing Co., Greenville (*MR*, 28 August 1902, p. 105; "School Improvement," p. 323.)

1902: Graded School, N. Broad and College streets, Walhalla (*MR*, 27 February 1902, p. 101; 8 May 1902, p. 287; "School Improvement," pp. 326-330.)

Ca. 1902: School, Monarch Mills, Union ("School Improvement," p. 323.)

1902-1903: Grace Episcopal Church, Anderson (*MR*, 22 May 1902, p. 325; 30 April 1903, p. 310.)

1903-1904: Agricultural Building, Clemson College, Clemson; $50,000 (*MR*, 18 June 1903, p. 447; 27 August 1903, p. 106; 1 October 1903, p. 219; 15 October 1903, p. 251; *Southern Architect and Building News*, 12 August 1904, p. 12.)

1903: F.H. Hyatt Dairy Barn, Columbia (*MR*, 26 February 1903, p. 123.)

1903: Six Residences, Darlington Manufacturing Co., Darlington (*MR*, 28 May 1903, p. 390.)

1903: Darlington County Courthouse, Darlington; $45,000 (*MR*, 4 June 1903, p. 410; 1 October 1903, p. 219.)

1903: A.N. Wood Bank Building, Gaffney (*MR*, 4 June 1903, p. 410.)

1903: Cherokee Drug Co. Store Building, Gaffney (*MR*, 4 June 1903, p. 410.)

1903: Rutherford Street Baptist Church, Greenville; $7000 (*MR*, 19 February 1903, p. 103; 28 May 1903, p. 390.)

1903: C.F. Dill Business Block, Greenville; $25,000 (*MR*, 4 June 1903, p. 410.)

1903: Graded School, Honea Path (*MR*, 18 June 1903, p. 447; "School Improvement," p. 326.)

1903: Rectory, Episcopal Church, Laurens (*MR*, 4 June 1903, p. 410.)

1903: School, Laurens Cotton Mills, Laurens (*MR*, 4 June 1903, p. 410; 30 July 1903, p. 32; "School Improvement," p. 334.)

1903: Watts Cotton Mills Store, Laurens (*MR*, 4 June 1903, p. 410.)

1903: W.P. Roof Store Building, Lexington (*MR*, 26 February 1903, p. 123.)

1903: Lutheran Parsonage, Newberry (*MR*, 26 February 1903, p. 123.)

1903: School and Auditorium, Pelzer Manufacturing Co., Pelzer (*MR*, 26 February 1903, p. 123; "School Improvement," p. 323.)

1903: Prof. D.B. Johnson School Building, Rock Hill (*MR*, 26 February 1903, p. 123.)

1903: C.H. Ellison Hotel, Seneca (*MR*, 26 March 1903, p. 205; 4 June 1903, p. 410.)

1903: Associate Reformed Presbyterian Church, Winnsboro (*The State*, 8 November 1903, p. 17; *MR*, 26 February 1903, p. 123.)

1903: Mrs. C.G. Parrish Hotel, Yorkville (*MR*, 4 June 1903, p. 410.)

1903-1904: J. Caldwell Robertson Business Block, Columbia (*MR*, 4 June 1903, p. 409; *Southern Architect and Building News*, 29 January 1904, p. 8.)

1904: L.T. Villepique Residence, Camden (*Southern Architect and Building News*, 29 January 1904, p. 8.)

1904: G. Duncan Bellinger Residence, Columbia (*Southern Architect and Building News*, 29 January 1904, p. 8.)

1904: Maynard Spigener Residence, Columbia (*Southern Architect and Building News*, 29 January 1904, p. 8.)

1904: Robert Coggeshall Residence, Darlington (*Southern Architect and Building News*, 29 January 1904, p. 8.)

1904: Henry Crum Residence, N. Palmetto Avenue, Denmark (*Southern Architect and Building News*, 29 January 1904, p. 8.)

1904: J. Speigel and D.M. Speigel Residence, Greenwood (*Southern Architect and Building News*, 5 February 1904, p. 8.)

1904: School, Victor Manufacturing Company, Greer (*Southern Architect and Building News*, 5 February 1904, p. 8; "School Improvement," p. 323.)

1904: Lyceum Building, Victor Manufacturing Company, Greer (*Southern Architect and Building News*, 5 February 1904, p. 8.)

1904: Two Churches, Victor Manufacturing Company, Greer (*Southern Architect and Building News*, 5 February 1904, p. 8.)

1904: Gymnasium and Library, Laurens Cotton Mills, Laurens (*Southern Architect and Building News*, 29 January 1904, p. 8.)

1904: L.W. Floyd Residence, Newberry (*Southern Architect and Building News*, 18 March 1904, p. 12.)

1904: Sunday School Building, Pelzer Manufacturing Co., Pelzer (*Southern Architect and Building News*, 29 January 1904, p. 8.)

1904: First Baptist Church, Union (*MR*, 10 March 1904, p. 167; *Southern Architect and Building News*, 11 March 1904, p. 10.)

1904: P.E. Fant Residence, Union; $8000 (*MR*, 31 March 1904, p. 239; 7 April 1904, p. 267.)

1904-1905: Trinity United Methodist Episcopal Church, E. Railroad Avenue, Bamberg; $9000 (*MR*, 5 May 1904, p. 358; 12 May 1904, p. 383; 7 July 1904, p. 569.)

1904-1905: Kershaw County Courthouse, Camden (*The State*, 9 June 1904, p. 3; *MR*, 17 November 1904, p. 441; 24 November 1904, p. 459; 5 January 1905, p. 619; 16 February 1905, p. 100; 16 March 1905, p. 184; Withey, p. 191.)

1904-1905: Taylor Street School, Columbia; $42,000 (*MR*, 29 September 1904, p. 265; 20 October 1904, p. 337; 19 January 1905, p. 16; 16 February 1905, p. 100; 16 March 1905, p. 184.)

1905: School, Bowman (*MR*, 9 November 1905, p. 438.)

1905: Oneale Street Methodist Church, Newberry; $4000 (*MR*, 2 March 1905, pp. 144-145.)

Ca. 1905: Southern Express Building, 1112 Lady Street, Columbia (*Merchantile and Industrial Review*, p. 49.)

Ca. 1905: Remodeling, Sylvan's Building, Columbia (*Merchantile and Industrial Review*, p. 49.)

Ca. 1905: M.A. Malone's Music House, Columbia (*Merchantile and Industrial Review*, p. 49.)

Ca. 1905: William Augustus Edwards Residence, Columbia (*Merchantile and Industrial Review*, p. 49.)

1905-1906: Sumter County Courthouse, Sumter; $85,000 (*MR*, 18 May 1905, p. 416; 27 July 1905, p. 52; 8 March 1906, p. 211; 12 April 1906, p. 363; 24 May 1906, p. 534; 28 June 1906, p. 681.)

1906: Bamberg Banking Co. Bank Building, Bamberg (*MR*, 10 May 1906, p. 168.)

1906: Improvements, F.D. Kendall Residence, Columbia; $20,000 (*MR*, 30 August 1906, p. 168.)

1906: Church of the Holy Comforter, Sumter (*MR*, 19 April 1906, p. 388.)

1906-1907: City Hall and Theatre/Opera House, Abbeville; $46,100 (*MR*, 3 January 1906, p. 209; 10 January 1907, p. 692; 30 May 1907, p. 640; 20 June 1907, p. 736.)

1907: Farmers' Bank, Abbeville; $10,000 (*MR*, 8 August 1907, p. 110.)

1907-1908: School, Laurens; $30,000 (*MR*, 4 April 1907, p. 356; 25 April 1907, p. 457; 2 May 1907, p. 488; 20 February 1908, p. 58.)

1907-1908: Abbeville County Courthouse, Abbeville; $56,000 (*MR*, 3 January 1907, p. 667; 7 March 1907, p. 227; 30 May 1907, p. 640; 20 June 1907, p. 736; plaque on building.)

1907-1909: Lee County Courthouse, 123 Main Street, Bishopville; $65,000 (*MR*, 14 March 1907, p. 260; 11 April 1907, p. 389; 25 April 1907, p. 456; 11 July 1907, p. 836; 1 August 1907, p. 81; 27 February 1908, p. 57; 12 March 1908, p. 58.)

Edwards, Walter & Parnham

1907-1908: Hartsville Graded School, Hartsville; $25,000 (J.L. Coker, *HARTSVILLE. Its Early Settlers. The Growth of the Town with Sketches of its Institutions and Enterprises.* (n.p., n.p., 1911), p. 45; *MR*, 21 May 1908, p. 63.)

1908: School, Manning (*The State*, 8 July 1908, p. 3; 12 July 1908, p. 3.)

Edwards & Walter

1909: Dining Hall and Kitchen Addition, Tillman Building, Winthrop Normal College, Rock Hill; $32,000 (*MR*, 8 April 1909, p. 62; 27 May 1909, p. 69; 17 June 1909, p. 69.)

1909: Joseph Norwood Residence, 1927 Pendleton Street, Columbia (*American Architect and Building News*, 2 June 1909.)

1909-1910: McMaster School (Senate Street School), Columbia; $40,000 (*MR*, 1 April 1909, p. 71; 28 October 1909, p. 127; 4 November 1909, p. 78; 25 November 1909, p. 66; 9 December 1909, p. 66; 3 February 1910, p. 83.)

1909-1910: J.W. Smith Residence, 1801 Pendleton Street, Columbia (*American Architect and Building News*, 12 May 1909.)

1910-1911: Withers Training School, Winthrop Normal College, Rock Hill; $125,000 (*MR*, 13 January 1910, p. 61; 20 January 1910, p. 65; 12 November 1911, p. 85.)

William Augustus Edwards

1911: Sunday School Addition, First Baptist Church, Columbia; $19,000 (*MR*, 5 October 1911, p. 81.)

1911: Dillon County Courthouse, 1303 W. Main Street, Dillon; $75,149 (*MR*, 18 May 1911, p. 76.)

1911-1912: First Baptist Church, Darlington (*MR*, 2 November 1911, p. 85; *News & Press*, Darlington, 18 January 1912, p. 5.)

1912-1914: Union National Bank Building, 1200 Main Street, Columbia; $175,000 (*MR*, 21 March 1912, p. 72.)

1912: Building, Winthrop Normal College, Rock Hill (*MR*, 10 October 1912, p. 65.)

1913: Calhoun County Courthouse, S. Railroad Avenue, St. Matthews; $19,000 (*MR*, 27 March 1913, p. 70.)

1914: Heathwood Hall (W.C. Heath Residence), Columbia; $100,000 (*The State*, 3 October 1914; 3 September 1978, p. 8-E; Maxey, p. 36.)

1914: Johnson Hall, Winthrop Normal College, Rock Hill; $9947 (*MR*, 28 May 1914, p. 62.)

1914: City Hall and Jail, Spartanburg; $30,000 (*MR*, 14 September 1914, p. 62.)

1914: York County Courthouse, York; $74,000 (*MR*, 29 January 1914, p. 68; 5 February 1914, p. 78; 26 March 1914, p. 68; Withey, p. 191.)

1914-1915: Primary Building, South Carolina School for the Deaf & Blind, Cedar Springs; $48,000 (*MR*, 2 July 1914, p. 79; 24 September 1914, p. 62; 15 April 1915, p. 57.)

1914-1915: Jasper County Courthouse, Russell Street, Ridgeville (*MR*, 30 July 1914, p. 65; 13 August 1914, p. 63; 15 April 1915, p. 57; *The State*, 10 April 1915, p. 5.)

Edwards & Sayward

1915: Addition, School, St. Matthews (*MR*, 17 June 1915, p. 59.)

1917: Remodeling, Administration Building, South Carolina School for the Deaf & Blind, Cedar Springs; $20,000 (*MR*, 17 May 1917, p. 76; 24 May 1917, p. 69.)

1917-1919: Law School Building (Currell College), University of South Carolina, Columbia; $40,000 (*MR*, 6 September 1917, p. 95; 27 December 1917, p. 81; 31 January 1918, p. 87.)

1917: Thomas F. McDow Residence, York (*MR*, 26 July 1917, p. 74; 9 August 1917, p. 73.)

1918: Laundry & Boiler House Building and Central Heating Plant, South Carolina School for the Deaf & Blind, Cedar Springs; $34,000 (*MR*, 30 May 1918, p. 81.)

1919: Dormitory, Winthrop Normal College, Rock Hill; $100,000 (*MR*, 2 January 1919, p. 171.)

Edwards, Sayward & Leitner

1919: Student Activities Building, Winthrop Normal College, Rock Hill; $110,000 (*MR*, 2 January 1919, p. 171; 28 August 1919, p. 123; 11 September 1919, p. 138 i.)

Edwards & Sayward

1921: Auditorium and Dining Hall Annex, Administration Building, South Carolina School for the Deaf & Blind, Cedar Springs; $66,645 (*MR*, 26 May 1921, p. 93.)

1921: Superintendent's Residence, South Carolina School for the Deaf & Blind, Cedar Springs; $13,969 (*MR*, 11 October 1921, p. 93.)

1921: Addition, School, York; $77,665 (*MR*, 17 November 1921, p. 92.)

1922: School, North (*MR*, 2 February 1922, p. 105.)

1923: High School, Chester; $125,000 (*MR*, 26 April 1923, p. 111.)

1923: Teachers' Dormitory, Winthrop Normal College, Rock Hill; $75,000 (*MR*, 16 August 1923, p. 116.)

1923: Dormitory, Winthrop Normal College, Rock Hill; $100,000 (*MR*, 15 November 1923, p. 116.)

1924: Infirmary Building, South Carolina School for the Deaf & Blind, Cedar Springs; $30,000 (*MR*, 18 September 1924, pp. 115-116; 25 September 1924, p. 116.)

1924: High School and Public School, Laurens; $135,915 (*MR*, 5 June 1924, p. 140.)

1925: High School, McColl; $65,000 (*MR*, 24 September 1925, p. 98; 1 October 1925, p. 131.)

1926: Teachers' Dormitory Building, Winthrop Normal College, Rock Hill; $63,500 (*MR*, 17 June 1926, p. 110.)

1927: Girls' Dormitory, South Carolina School for the Deaf & Blind, Cedar Springs; $34,450 (*MR*, 28 April 1927, p. 113.)

1929: Classroom Building, Winthrop Normal College, Rock Hill; $113,280; Edwards & Sayward, architects; Robert B. Logan, associate architect (*MR*, 6 June 1929, p. 108; 13 June 1929, p. 89.)

1929: Residence, Winthrop Normal College, Rock Hill; $25,000; Edwards & Sayward, architects; Robert B. Logan, associate architect (*MR*, 24 October 1929, p. 85.)

1930: Addition, Dormitory, Winthrop Normal College, Rock Hill; $80,000 (*MR*, 13 February 1930, p. 88.)

1931: Addition, Dining Hall, Winthrop Normal College, Rock Hill; $35,000 (*MR*, 9 July 1931, p. 55.)

Sources: *Alumni Directory, University of South Carolina* (Columbia: Bureau of Publications, University of South Carolina, 1926), p. 11; *American Art Annual*, Vol. 21, p. 393; *Architectural Forum*, May 1938, pp. 410-411; Atlanta, Georgia, city directories; *Atlanta Constitution*, Atlanta, Georgia, 31 March 1939, p. 3; Columbia city directories; Rudolph E. Lee, "Rural School Improvement," *The Clemson Agricultural College Extension Work Bulletins*, Vol. VI, #3, July 1910; *MR*, various citations; Russell Maxey, *Historic Columbia Yesterday and Today in Photographs* (Columbia: The R.L. Bryan Co., 1980), pp. 36, 151, 213, 338; *Merchantile and Industrial Review of Columbia and Richland Conty, South Carolina* (Portsmouth, Virginia: Seaboard Air Line Railway, n.d., ca. 1908), pp. 9, 49; "School Improvement," *Reports and Resolutions of the General Assembly of the State of South Carolina, 1906* (Columbia: Gonzales and Bryan, 1906), pp. 273-338; Withey, pp. 190-191, 412, 537-538.

EICHBERG, Alfred S. (active 1882-1895) Alfred Eichberg was a student of William H. Parkins (q.v.)

of Atlanta in the early 1880s, and took further training in Heidelberg, Germany. He was associated with Calvin Fay in Atlanta in 1882. Eichberg moved to Savannah, Georgia, around 1886.

South Carolina project:

1892: Synagogue, Sumter; $5000 (*MR*, 11 November 1892, p. 308; 18 November 1892, p. 329.)

Sources: *MR*, various citations; Morgan, pp. 142, 146; *Architects and Builders in Georgia*; Withey, p. 667.

EISENSCHMIDT, Robert C. (active 1909-1941) Robert Eisenschmidt practiced architecture in Fayetteville and Charlotte, North Carolina, from 1909 to 1914, designing sundry small buildings. He moved to Columbia and worked as a draftsman for George E. Lafaye (q.v.) in 1916-1920.

Eisenschmidt pursued his own modest architectural practice in Columbia from 1921 until his death in 1941.

South Carolina projects:

1921: Sunday School Building, Shandon Baptist Church, Columbia; $10,000 (*MR*, 21 July 1921, p. 84.)

1921: J.C. Townsend Residence, Columbia; $12,500 (*MR*, 13 October 1921, p. 95.)

1921: J.H. Fair Residence, St. Matthews; $15,000 (*MR*, 15 September 1921, p. 88.)

1922: W.H. Henderson Residence, Columbia; $22,500 (*MR*, 25 May 1922, p. 91.)

1922: Mrs. M.A. Coleman Residence, Columbia; $11,500 (*MR*, 24 August 1922, p. 84.)

1923: Annex, Lutheran Church of the Redeemer, Newberry; $27,500 (*MR*, 17 May 1923, p. 108.)

1928: Addition, James L. Tapp Store Building, Columbia; $50,000 (*MR*, 19 January 1928, p. 108.)

Sources: Charlotte, North Carolina city directories; Columbia city directories; *MR*, various citations.

ELLINGTON, Page (active 1875-1912) Page Ellington was a black bricklayer and builder in Columbia. Some sources refer to Ellington as an architect. J.F. Williams stated of Ellington:

> Page was a brick layer. He was a hard student and kept up with the affairs of the day for many years. He was employed at the State Hospital to look after the building. He was a good architect and could make all of his drawings.

Sources: Columbia city directories; Helen Kohn Hennig, ed., *Columbia Capital City of South Carolina 1786-1936* (Columbia: The Columbia Sesqui-Centennial Commission, 1936), p. 307; J.F. Williams, *Old and New Columbia* (Columbia: Epworth Orphanage Press, 1929.)

EPTON, Leland P. (active 1896-1911) For most of his career Leland P. Epton was listed as a real estate agent in the Spartanburg city directories. He was briefly associated with architects Avery Carter (q.v.) and Thomas Keating (q.v.) in 1903-1905. Carter, an enterprising young architect and builder, joined forces with Epton around 1903 in a joint architecture-real estate practice. The firm was listed under the dual names "L.P. Epton & Co., Real Estate" and "Avery Carter & Co., Architects." Keating was a draftsman for the firm.

Carter left Spartanburg late in 1903, and Epton associated with Keating to continue the architectural practice. Epton & Keating completed the Science Hall at Wofford College (begun under Carter's direction), designed several residences in Spartanburg. The firm was dissolved by 1905, and Epton continued work as a real estate agent.

South Carolina projects:

Epton & Keating

1904: School, Greer; $9000 (*MR*, 10 March 1904, p. 166; 8 September 1904, p. 189; 6 October 1904, p. 289.)

1904: Julia Smith Residence, Spartanburg (*Spartanburg of Today.*)

1904: Jno. A. Walker Residence, Spartanburg (*Spartanburg of Today.*)

1904: Charles H. Henry Residence, Spartanburg (*Spartanburg of Today.*)

1904: Dr. O.W. Leonard Residence, Spartanburg; $3000 (*Southern Architect and Building News*, 22 January 1904, p. 10; *Spartanburg of Today.*)

1904: Dr. Baer Residence, Spartanburg (*Spartanburg of Today.*)

1904: Alterations, Edgar L. Bomar Residence, Spartanburg; $1200 (*Southern Architect and Building News*, 22 January 1904, p. 0.)

1904: Jno. D. Wood Residence, Woodruff; $2000 (*Southern Architect and Building News*, 22 January 1904, p. 10.)

1904: T.J. Willard Residence, Spartanburg; $2500 (*Southern Architect and Building News*, 29 January 1904, p. 8.)

1904: F.M. Sheridan Residence, Greenwood; $2000 (*Southern Architect and Building News*, 12 August 1904, p. 8.)

1904: Parsonage, Spartanburg (*Southern Architect and Building News*, 12 August 1904, p. 8.)

1904: John G. Garlington Residence, Spartanburg; $6000 (*Southern Architect and Building News*, 12 August 1904, p. 8.)

1904: School, Fair Forest; $3000 (*Southern Architect and Building News*, 12 August 1904, p. 8.)

1904: James L. Parker Residence, Spartanburg; $2500 (*Southern Architect and Building News*, 12 August 1904, p. 8.)

1904: Improvements, J.M. Elford Residence, Spartanburg; $1500 (*Southern Architect and Building News*, 12 August 1904, p. 8.)

1904: Addition, J.B. Martin Residence, Spartanburg; $3500 (*Southern Architect and Building News*, 12 August 1904, p. 8.; *Spartanburg of Today*)

Sources: *MR*, various citations; Spartanburg city directories; *Spartanburg of Today: The Progressive City of the Piedmont* (n.p., n.p., n.d., ca. 1904).

ETTER, William (active 1898-1900) William Etter advertised in 1898 as "William Etter, Architect and Superintendent, Spartanburg, S.C. / Estimates cheerfully furnished on application."

Sources: *South Carolina State Gazetteer 1898*, p. 439; Spartanburg city directories.

EVANS, Alfred F. (active 1900-1929) Alfred F. Evans of New York City provided plans for the remodeling of the W.T. Grant Co. store building, Greenville, South Carolina, in 1923. Evans also prepared plans for remodeling of a W.T. Grant building in Atlanta, Georgia, in 1924, and for a W.T. Grant Store in Danville, Virginia, in 1929.

Sources: Francis, p. 29; *MR*, 20 December 1923, p. 103; 8 May 1924, p. 113; and various other references.

EVERETT, Alex F.N. (1880-1937) Alex F.N. Everett was associated with senior architect Alexander C. Bruce (q.v.) in Atlanta from 1902 to 1908. The firm designed two buildings in South Carolina. Everett continued his career in Atlanta after Bruce's retirement.

South Carolina projects:

1907-1908: See **Bruce, Alexander Charles** (Bruce & Everett)

Sources: Atlanta, Georgia, city directories; *MR*, various citations; *Architects and Builders in Georgia.*

EWING, Whitley Lay (active 1915-1955) Whitley Ewing was a draftsman in the office of G. Lloyd Preacher (q.v.) in 1915-1917. He associated with Philander Pearsall Scroggs (q.v.), another veteran of Preacher's office, in Augusta in 1919. The firm designed a number of buildings in South Carolina, including many large residences in Aiken.

South Carolina projects:

1920-1929: See **Scroggs, Philander** (Scroggs & Ewing)

Sources: Augusta, Georgia, city directories; Koyl, p. 495; *Architects and Builders in Georgia.*

FANT, Charles William (1886-1956) Fant, a native of Anderson, was educated at Clemson College and at Columbia University in New York. He joined the office of prominent Anderson architect Joseph H. Casey (q.v.) and became an associate of the firm by 1913. Fant managed the office after Casey's death in 1928, in association with his sons Albert Reese Fant and Charles W. Fant Jr.

South Carolina projects:

1913-1928: See **Casey, Joseph Huntley** (Casey & Fant)

1929: Sunday School Annex, First Baptist Church, Anderson; $38,958 (*MR*, 7 February 1929, p. 111.)

1930: Sunday School Addition, Central Methodist Church, Newberry; $22,000 (*MR*, 7 August 1930, p. 80.)

1930: Sunday School Addition and Remodeling of Auditorium, Central Methodist Church, Spartanburg; Charles W. Fant, architect; Carlisle & Freeman (q.v.), associated architects (*MR*, 26 June 1930, p. 79.)

1931: Remodeling, Abbeville County Memorial Hospital Building, Abbeville; $26,500 (*MR*, 27 August 1931, p. 43.)

1931: Alterations and Enlargement, Fort Hill Presbyterian Church, Clemson; $20,000 (*MR*, 2 July 1931, p. 54.)

1935: Junior High School, Anderson; $70,670; Charles W. Fant and Sam Cathcart (q.v.), architects (*MR*, June 1935, p. 32.)

1948: Henry Laurens Hotel, Laurens; $250,000 (*Construction*, January 1948, p. 57.)

n.d.: Anderson Memorial Hospital, Anderson (*South Carolina Magazine*, Vol. 13, No. 1, January 1950, p. 48.)

n.d.: Belk Presbyterian Church, uAnderson (*South Carolina Magazine*, Vol. 13, No. 1, January 1950, p. 49.)

n.d.: A.J. Cromer Residence, Anderson (*South Carolina Magazine*, Vol. 16, No. 1, January 1952, p. 24.)

n.d.: W.J. Erwin Residence, Ware Shoals (*South Carolina Magazine*, Vol. 16, No. 1, January 1952, p. 29.)

n.d.: Young Memorial Associate Reformed Presbyterian Church, Anderson (*South Carolina Magazine*, Vol. 16, No. 1, January 1952, p. 68.)

Sources: Koyl, p. 164; *MR*, various citations; Petty, p. 142.

FERGUSON, John R. (active 1929-1930) John Ferguson was listed as an architect in the Spartanburg city directories for 1929 and 1930.

FLAGG, Ernest (1857-1947) Ernest Flagg of New York City, the distinguished Beaux-Arts trained architect, was mentioned in connection with a hotel project in Aiken, South Carolina, in 1898. A number of resort hotels catering to wealthy northern patrons were being built in Aiken at this time. It is not known whether the Flagg project was ever carried out.

Sources: Mardges Bacon, *Ernest Flagg, Beaux-Arts Architect and Urban Reformer* (Cambridge, Massachusetts: The M.I.T. Press, 1985); Hewitt, p. 273; *Macmillan Encyclopedia*, Vol. II, pp. 87-89; *MR*, 13 May 1898, p. 273; Withey, pp. 211-212; Wodehouse, pp. 65-66.

FOGARTY, James (active 1920) Fogarty was a partner of prominent Charleston architect Albert W. Todd (q.v.) in 1920.

South Carolina projects:

1920: See **Todd, Albert Whitner** (Todd & Fogarty)

Sources: Charleston city directories.

FOGETTE, E. (active 1880-1894) E. Fogette (also spelled Foggette, or Foggett) was an architect and contractor active in Gaffney and Spartanburg, and in Asheville, North Carolina, in the late nineteenth century.

South Carolina project:

1885: Sacred Heart Catholic Church, 128 N. Main Street, Abbeville, South Carolina (*The Press and Banner*, Abbeville, 28 October 1885.)

FORT, O.M. (active 1905-1918) Architect O.M. Fort of Camden was listed in several architects directories, including the 1918 *Hendricks' Commercial Register*, but no information about his life and work has been identified to date.

FOULK, Sidney W. (active 1889-1905) Sidney W. Foulk maintained a practice in New Castle, Pennsylvania, in the 1890s. He designed several large buildings in the Southeast, including the Buena Vista Hotel (1890) and the DeHart Hotel (1891) in Rockbridge County, Virginia, and the 1904 Greensboro Female College in Greensboro, North Carolina.

Foulk had a branch office in Richmond, Virginia in 1892. Around 1904 Foulk relocated to Greensboro, North Carolina. His son Frank H. Foulk maintained the New Castle office, while Ralph P. Foulk (another son?) worked as a draftsman in the Greensboro office. In 1905 Foulk advertised "Church architecture a specialty."

Foulk's 1889 Y.M.C.A. Building in Charleston, South Carolina, is a splendid brick, stone, and terra-cotta building in the Romanesque Revival mode.

South Carolina projects:

1889: Y.M.C.A. Building, King Street, Charleston; $21,000 (*MR*, 26 January 1889, p. 23.)

1891: Sumter Hotel Co. Hotel, Sumter (*MR*, 27 June 1891, p. 45.)

1894: Charleston Hotel, Charleston; $25,000 (*MR*, 15 June 1894, p. 334.)

Sources: *Architectural Drawing in Lexington, 1779-1926* (Lexington, Virginia: Washington and Lee University, 1978), pp. 33-34; Lauren Batte, "S.W. Foulk, Victorian Architecture and the Main Hall of Southern Seminary Junior College," unpublished paper, Washington and Lee University, Lexington, Virginia, 1989; Greensboro, North Carolina, city directories; Royster Lyle, Jr., and Pamela Hemenway Simpson, *The Architecture of Historic Lexington* (Charlottesville, Virginia: The University Press of Virginia, 1977), pp. 39, 40, 43; *MR*, various citations; Richmond, Virginia, city directories.

FREEMAN, George A. Jr. (1850-1934) George A. Freeman, Jr., was a New York City architect active from the 1880s to the early twentieth century. He was educated at the Massachusetts Institute of Technology, and he established his practice in New York City by 1880. In 1883 Freeman was associated with noted architect Bruce Price.

Freeman prepared designs in 1897 for the enlargement and renovation of Joye Cottage in Aiken, South Carolina, for William C. Whitney. The contract for the work was let in August 1897. The expanded Joye Cottage was a sprawling suburban residence with a full range of support buildings, including a squash court. Freeman later designed buildings for Whitney on October Mountain in Lenox, Massachusetts (ca. 1898), and in Newport and Westbury.

Freeman relocated to Sarasota, Florida, sometime after 1918, where he had his offices in the Blackburn Building. He died on 24 November 1934.

Sources: Francis, pp. 32, 63; *The Journal and Review*, Aiken, 25 August 1897; *MR*, 31 July 1930, p. 71; "Mr. Whitney's Southern Home," *The New York Times Illustrated Magazine*, 16 January 1898, p. 14; Withey, p. 221.

FREEMAN, Robert A. (active 1924-1942) Robert A. Freeman worked as a draftsman for J. Frank Collins (q.v.) in Spartanburg in 1924-1927. He set up his own architectural office in 1927, and in 1929 he associated with Aiken R. Carlisle (q.v.) Carlisle & Freeman pursued a modest practice into the 1940s.

South Carolina projects:

1929-1930: See **Carlisle, Aiken R.** (Carlisle & Freeman)

Sources: Spartanburg city directories.

FRERET, Will A. (active 1888-1889) Freret, Supervising Architect of the United States Department of the Treasury from 1888 to 1889, had nominal supervision of the extension and completion of the granite wharf at the Charleston Customs-House in 1888.

Sources: *MR*, 24 November 1888, p. 23; Smith, *The Office of the Supervising Architect*, p. 44; Wodehouse, p. 269.

FREUND, John Jr. (active 1906-1930) John Freund Jr. of Baltimore, Maryland, was the architect for the $4000 Methodist Episcopal Church in Blacksburg, South Carolina, in 1906.

Sources: *MR*, 25 January 1906, p. 48; 3 May 1906, p. 446; 17 May 1906, p. 506.

FULLER, Rex G. (active 1922-1929) Rex G. Fuller was listed as an architect in the Charleston city directories from 1922 through 1929.

Sources: Charleston city directories; Petty, p. 142.

GABLER, Herman (active 1888) Gabler advertised and was listed as an architect in the 1888 Greenville city directory.

GAINES, Henry Irven (active 1922-1940) Henry I. Gaines, of Central, South Carolina, received a B.S. degree in engineering from Clemson College in 1922. He worked with established architects James D. Beacham and Leon LeGrand (q.v.) in Asheville, North Carolina in 1925-1926, and established his own office in Asheville by 1929.

South Carolina project:

1930: Major R.J. Ramer Residence, Anderson; $50,000 (*MR*, 1 May 1930, p. 91.)

Sources: *The Clemson Agricultural College of South Carolina, Annual Catalogue* (1922-1923), pp. 177-179; *MR*, various citations; Douglas Swaim, Talmage Powell and John Ager, *Cabins & Castles: The History & Architecture of Buncombe County, North Carolina* (Asheville, North Carolina: Historic Resources Commission of Asheville and Buncombe County, 1981), pp. 92, 96.

GAISFORD, John (1876-1918) John Gaisford, a native of Warminster, England, was educated in architecture at Warminster National School and at Birkbeck Institute in London. He came to the United States in 1901, and after working in Pittsburgh for four years, located in Memphis, Tennessee, in 1905. Gaisford designed a large number of buildings in Tennessee and the Southeast, including many church buildings. It is not known how he came to design a building in the village of North, South Carolina.

South Carolina project:

1917: Methodist Episcopal Church, North; $13,000 (*MR*, 31 May 1917, p. 69.)

Sources: Herndon, p. 76; *MR*, various citations.

GALLOWAY, Theophilis Spurgeon (active 1913-1917) Galloway worked as a carpenter and contractor in Charleston. He is believed to have been the "M.S. Galloway" identified as architect for the James F. Condon store building commissioned at Warren and King streets, Charleston, in 1914.

Sources: Charleston city directories; *MR*, 5 March 1914, p. 75.

GARNER, Lebon W. (active 1915-1917) Garner was listed as a contractor in Charleston city directories of 1915-1916. He was associated with Ralph F. Burton (q.v.) in 1917.

South Carolina project:

Garner & Burton

1917: P.M. Clement Store Building, King Street, Charleston; $20,000; Garner & Burton, contractors and architects (*MR*, 22 March 1917, p. 72.)

Sources: Charleston city directories.

GASSAWAY, Minnie Quinn (died 1965) Minnie Quinn Gassaway, wife of textile baron Walter Lewis Gassaway (1865-1930), is believed to have designed the couple's palatial estate in Greenville, the $150,000 "Isaqueena" at 106 DuPont Drive. The house, built in 1919-1924, is now called Gassaway Mansion. Mrs. Gassaway is said to have taken a correspondence course in architecture, and to have based the design of Isaqueena on her favorite historic themes. This may account for the bizarre composition, which features a colossal pedimented Tuscan portico fronting a pseudo-medieval stone keep.

Sources: *Greenville Daily News*, 30 May 1920, p. 13; *MR*, 10 June 1920, p. 127; 24 June 1920, p. 125; National Register files, S.C. Archives.

GEBHARDT, A. Paul (active 1909) Gebhardt is identified as an architect in Charleston in the 1909 edition of Comstock's *The Architects' Directory*. He is not listed, however, in Charleston city directories of the period.

GIBBES, Lewis R. (active 1886-1888) Gibbes and Edward E. Jenkins, Jr. (q.v.) were associated as architects and civil engineers in Charleston in 1886. Gibbes was listed as an architect in the 1887 Charleston city directory. In 1888 he was described as a professor at the College of Charleston.

Sources: Charleston city directories.

GILBERT, Bradford Lee (1853-1911) Bradford L. Gilbert of New York City was the Architect-in-Chief for the South Carolina Interstate and West Indian Exposition, held in Charleston in 1901-1902. He was responsible for the overall design of the fair and for the design of several of the buildings, including the Agricultural Palace.

Gilbert had a comparable position in Georgia in 1894-1895, serving as architect for The Cotton States & International Exposition in Atlanta. Eight buildings at this fair were designed under Gilbert's supervision. In addition to his work for the fair, Gilbert designed the Southern Railway Passenger Depot (1895); the $200,000, 12-story Mutual Building Co. Office Building (1896), and the $225,000, 13-story English-American Loan & Trust Company Office Building (1897) in Atlanta.

Gilbert was born in Watertown, New York, and learned the profession in the office of J. Cleveland Cady. He worked for the New York, Lake Erie and Western Railroad in 1876. He opened his New York office around 1882 and pursued a profitable business in that city. Gilbert's 1887-1889 Tower Building in New York was among the earlier skyscrapers in the nation. His 1903 Engine Company 258 Building in New York City was described as a "robust multistory firehouse with stepped super-Dutch gable." Gilbert was also the architect for the 1899-1900 alterations to the Tower Building at Grand Central Station.

South Carolina projects:

1901: Andrew Simonds Hotel, Charleston (*MR*, 7 February 1901, p. 53.)

1901-1902: South Carolina Interstate and West Indian Exposition, Charleston ("The Exposition"; *MR*, 4 April 1901, p. 207; Withey.)

Sources: Charleston city directories; "The Exposition," Vol. 1, #6, May 1901 (copy in National Register files, S.C. Archives); Francis, p. 34; *Macmillan Encyclopedia*, Vol. II, p. 201; *MR*, various citations; White & Willensky, p. 503; Winston Weisman, "A New View of Skyscraper History," in *The Rise of an American Architecture* (New York: Praeger Publishers, Inc., 1970), pp. 142-143; Withey, p. 233; Wodehouse, p. 270.

GILCHRIST, Alfred D. (active 1913-1940) Alfred D. Gilchrist was working in Rock Hill as manager of the Rock Hill office of (Charles C.) Hook & Rogers, Architects (q.v.) in 1913. He opened his own office by 1920 and maintained an unspectacular practice in Rock Hill through 1940.

Many of the small rural and town schools built in north central South Carolina in the 1920s were designed by Gilchrist. Sixteen such projects are identified in the *MR* building notices.

South Carolina projects:

1920: Church, Baldwin Cotton Mills, Chester; $40,000 (*MR*, 7 October 1920, p. 193.)

1920: School, Rock Hill; $40,000 (*MR*, 27 May 1920, p. 127.)

1921: Church, Fort Mill; $18,000 (*MR*, 17 February 1921, p. 130 b; 24 February 1921, p. 128.)

1921: Ebenezer Avenue Grammar School, Rock Hill; $55,500 (*MR*, 27 January 1921, p. 136 e.)

1922: Sunday School Building, First Baptist Church, Chester; $29,000 (*MR*, 9 March 1922, p. 83; 16 March 1922, p. 90.)

1922: Manse, Purity Presbyterian Church, Chester; $11,998 (*MR*, 25 May 1922, p. 91.)

1922: Sunday School Building, First Presbyterian Church, Rock Hill; $42,000 (*MR*, 30 March 1922, p. 89; 6 April 1922, p. 124.)

1922: Addition, Grammar School, Rock Hill (*MR*, 17 August 1922, p. 87.)

1922: Addition, High School, Rock Hill (*MR*, 17 August 1922, p. 87.)

1922: Mt. Zion School, Winnsboro; $60,000 (*MR*, 20 July 1922, p. 84.)

1923: Second Methodist Episcopal Church, Baldwin Mill Village, Chester; $16,000 (*MR*, 26 April 1923, p. 110.)

1923: Gymnasium, Presbyterian College, Clinton; $85,000 (*MR*, 25 October 1923, p. 145.)

1923: York Wilson Residence, Rock Hill; $20,000 (*MR*, 11 October 1923, p. 112.)

1924: H.L. Schlosburg Store, Gadsden and Wylie streets, Chester; $35,000 (*MR*, 24 January 1924, p. 108; 31 January 1924, p. 113.)

1924: Associate Reformed Presbyterian Church, Chester; $30,000 (*MR*, 23 October 1924, p. 107; 30 October 1924, p. 90.)

1924: Wellridge School, Chester County; $9000 (*MR*, 27 November 1924, p. 98; 4 December 1924, p. 123.)

1924: First National Bank Building, Main Street, Fort Mill; $21,149 (*MR*, 28 August 1924, p. 111; 11 November 1924, p. 104.)

1924: Presbyterian Church, Great Falls; $30,000 (*MR*, 14 February 1924, p. 103.)

1924: Julian Sanders Residence, Hagood (*MR*, 4 September 1924, p. 128.)

1924: North Side School, Rock Hill; $26,778 (*MR*, 12 June 1924, p. 114.)

1925: R.S. Mebane, Jr., Residence, Great Falls; $14,000 (*MR*, 22 January 1925, p. 108.)

1925: Negro School, Winnsboro; $17,890 (*MR*, 28 May 1925, p. 103.)

1926: Sunday School, Bethel Methodist Episcopal Church, Chester; $32,795 (*MR*, 2 September 1926, p. 135.)

1926: Grammar School, Great Falls; $75,000 (*MR*, 25 February 1926, p. 104; 4 March 1926, p. 141.)

1926: P.A. Pappas and James Dionisopoulos Store Bulding, Rock Hill; $14,665 (*MR*, 19 August 1926, p. 111.)

1927: Assembly Room, Everett School, Winnsboro; $15,890 (*MR*, 11 August 1927, p. 112; 18 August 1927, p. 125.)

1928: Additions, Chester County Courthouse, Chester (Cornerstone; *MR*, 19 April 1928, p. 84.)

1928: Stadium, Presbyterian College, Clinton; $10,500 (*MR*, 23 August 1928, p. 85.)

1928: Auditorium, Great Falls High School, Great Falls; $29,302 (*MR*, 27 December 1928, p. 73.)

1928: High School, Monticello; $36,000 (*MR*, 19 July 1928, p. 94.)

1928: High School, Salem's Crossing; $36,000 (*MR*, 2 August 1928, p. 103.)

1929: Remodeling, Chester City Hall, Chester; $25,000 (*MR*, 17 October 1929, p. 95.)

1929: Associate Reformed Presbyterian Church Building, Rock Hill; $65,000 (*MR*, 16 May 1929, pp. 84-85; 23 May 1929, p. 96.)

1929: York Furniture Company Store Building, Oakland Avenue and Southern Street, Rock Hill; $12,500 (*MR*, 22 August 1929, p. 81.)

1930: Baron DeKalb High School, Camden; $27,850 (*MR*, 26 June 1930, p. 80.)

1930: School, Red River (*MR*, 3 July 1930, p. 85.)

1930: Belk Brothers Store, Main Street, Rock Hill; $100,000 (*MR*, 31 July 1930, p. 72.)

1930: Addition, District 14 School, Winnsboro (*MR*, 14 August 1930, p. 82.)

1931: S.R. Latham Residence, Chester (*MR*, 5 February 1931, p. 66.)

1931: Alterations, Library, Rock Hill; $12,400 (*MR*, 9 April 1931, p. 58.)

1937-1939: Winthrop Auditorium, Winthrop Normal College, Rock Hill; James B. Urquhart (q.v.) and Alfred D. Gilchrist, architects ("Existing Facilities Study," p. 26.)

1939: Conservatory of Music, Winthrop Normal College, Rock Hill; James B. Urquhart (q.v.) and Alfred D. Gilchrist, architects ("Existing Facilities Study," p. 30.)

Sources: *American Art Annual*, Vol. 21, p. 401; *MR*, various citations; Petty, p. 142; Rock Hill city directories; Triad Associates, "Existing Facilities Study: Winthrop College," Columbia, 1980.

GOLUCKE, James Wingfield (1857-1907) James W. Golucke of Atlanta, Georgia, had an extensive architectural practice in the years 1890-1907, with buildings and projects in many southeastern states, including Georgia, the Carolinas, and Alabama.

Golucke, a native of Crawfordville, Georgia, had no formal architectural training. He worked as a carpenter, woodworker and machinist in his younger years. He had begun architectural practice in Atlanta by 1891, and he formed a partnership with George Wilson Stewart (q.v.) in 1893. Golucke & Stewart designed county courthouses for Johnson, Emanuel and Pike counties in Georgia in 1894. More than twenty Georgia county courthouses were designed by Golucke. Stewart left the firm in 1900.

In 1907 Golucke was jailed on a misappropriation of funds charge. After an unsuccessful suicide attempt, he died in prison in October 1907.

South Carolina projects:

Golucke & Stewart

1894: School, Orangeburg; $16,000 (*MR*, 20 April 1894, p. 197.)

1899: First Presbyterian Church, Spartanburg; $15,000 (*MR*, 3 March 1899, p. 98; 14 April 1899, p. 201.)

Sources: Anne Harman and Janice Hardy, "James Wingfield Golucke," in *Dictionary of Georgia Biography*, Vol. 1, pp. 351-352; *Architects and Builders in Georgia*.

GOODRICH, Lewis F. (1848-ca. 1917) Lewis F. Goodrich practiced architecture in Augusta, Georgia and neighboring communites in Georgia and South Carolina from 1889 to 1916. He was president of the short-lived Southern Chapter of the American Institute of Architects in 1893. Goodrich's early designs, especially the 1891 Aiken Institute and the 1895 Morrah Residence, are characteristic of the late Victorian period in their picturesque asymmetry, varying rooflines, and material polychromy.

Goodrich designed the Screven County Courthouse in Sylvania, Georgia, in 1897.

South Carolina projects:

1891: Aiken Institute, Aiken (Cornerstone; *MR*, 17 January 1891, p. 38.)

1892: Opera House, Aiken; $12,000 (*MR*, 27 May 1892, p. 45.)

1895: Morrah Residence, Mount Carmel (National Register files, S.C. Archives.)

1908: North Augusta Baptist Church, North Augusta; $8500 (*MR*, 19 March 1908, p. 59; 2 April 1908, p. 69.)

1909: Repairs, Aiken County Courthouse, Aiken; $4837 (*MR*, 29 July 1909, p. 60; 19 August 1909, p. 60.)

1909: P.F. Henderson Residence, Aiken; $4000 (*MR*, 19 August 1909, p. 60.)

1909: Toole & Woodward Livery Stable, Aiken; $2500 (*MR*, 19 August 1909, p. 60.)

1911: Improvements, Farmers and Merchants Bank Building, Aiken; $10,000 (*MR*, 27 April 1911, p. 70.)

1911: High School, North Augusta; $11,000 (*MR*, 31 August 1911, p. 66; 7 September 1911, p. 78.)

Sources: Augusta, Georgia, city directories; *MR*, various citations; *Architects and Builders in Georgia*.

GOURDIN, John K. (active 1867-1895) Gourdin was associated with Edwin J. White (q.v.) in Charleston in 1867; they were described as civil engineers and surveyors. Gourdin assumed the title "architect" by 1886.

Sources: Charleston city directories; Ravenel, p. 263.

GREEN, James M., Jr. (active 1920-1923) James Green was a draftsman for Columbia architect Charles C. Wilson (q.v.) in 1920-1922. He was listed as an architect in private practice in the 1923 Columbia city directory.

Sources: Columbia city directories.

GREEN, J. Perry (active 1915-1920) J. Perry Green (or **Greene**) of Atlanta, Georgia, was identified as architect for two bank projects in South Carolina.

South Carolina projects:

1915: Remodeling, Bank of Spartanburg Building, Main and Wall streets, Spartanburg; $6000 (*MR*, 20 May 1915, p. 59.)

1920: Norwood National Bank Building, Greenville; $50,000 (*MR*, 25 March 1920, p. 150 b; 20 May 1920, p. 140.)

Sources: *MR*, various citations.

GRIFFIN, Alpheus M. (active 1911-1925) Alpheus M. Griffin was employed as an architect for the Atlantic Coast Line Railway in the 1920s. Working from the railway's office building in Wilmington, North Carolina, Griffin designed freight and passenger depots, warehouses, office buildings, and other projects for the A.C.L. in the Carolinas and Alabama. Prior to working with the A.C.L., Griffin worked in Nashville, Tennessee. He was employed in 1918 as an architect for the N & C Railway in Nashville.

South Carolina projects:

1921: Atlantic Coast Line Railway Freight Station, Bishopville; $30,000 (*MR*, 8 September 1921, p. 90.)

1925: Addition, Atlantic Coast Line Railway Y.M.C.A. Building, Florence; $85,000 (*MR*, 2 April 1925, p. 133.)

Sources: Robert C. Bainbridge and Kate Ohno, *Wilson Historic Buildings Inventory, Wilson, North Carolina* (Wilson, North Carolina: City of Wilson, 1980), pp. 74, 235; Herndon, p. 83; *MR*, various citations; Nashville, Tennessee, city directories.

GRUBE, A. (active 1898) Grube prepared plans for residences for C.E. Graham and F.F. Capers in Greenville in 1898. He is not identified in the Greenville city directories of the period.

Source: *The Southern Architect*, May 1898, p. 438.

HAHN, F.W. (active 1879) Hahn was associated with Albert W. Todd (q.v.) in Anderson in 1879.

Source: Zach Watson Rice, New York, New York, unpublished research.

HAIR, Nell Roper (active 1919-1941) Nell Roper, a Columbia schoolteacher, married attorney Thomas E. Hair around 1922. The couple operated the Realty & Investment Company in Columbia for several years; Thomas Hair was the president, and Nell Roper Hair was the secretary and treasurer. The firm was active in development of the Shandon suburb of Columbia. Thomas Hair commissioned three bungalows at 2219-2223 Blossom Street in Columbia in 1924, and he proposed seventeen further residences at Ingleside Terrace in Columbia at the same time; Nell Roper Hair was identified as the architect for this work. In 1930 Nell Roper Hair contracted with J.C. Wallace and Sons, Contractors, to build a $75,000 apartment building at 700-714 Pickens Street in Columbia; she may have provided architectural plans for this building as well.

Sources: Columbia city directories; *MR*, 10 January 1924, p. 119; 21 August 1930, p. 76.

HAMBY, Arthur Williams (active 1897-1934) Hamby, a native of Columbia, worked as a draftsman for Charles C. Wilson (q.v.) in Columbia from ca. 1897 through 1904. He had opened his own office in Columbia by 1905.

Hamby was associated with his brother Thomas C. Hamby (q.v.) from 1907 through 1910. The firm advertised as architects and engineers. A ca. 1910 publication noted that Hamby & Hamby made "a specialty of surveying re-inforce and concrete constructions" [sic].

Pennsylvania native Edwyn Grant Rorke (q.v.) came to Columbia around 1912 and associated with Hamby in 1913. The firm of Hamby & Rorke won several important commissions in the state in 1913; these appear to have been Hamby's most successful times. Rorke left in 1914 to establish his own practice in Pennsylvania, and Hamby assumed an independent career.

Hamby's surviving work shows general competence and limited artistic vision. His church designs followed the prevailing conservative fashions; the 1911 First Baptist Church in St. Matthews and the 1913 St. Timothy Episcopal Church in Columbia are straightforward Gothic Revival compositions. The 1927 First Church of Christ Scientist in Columbia is an interesting Roman temple-form building with a Roman Doric portico and uncoursed stone veneer. The 1923 Town Theatre Building in Columbia has an innovative facade with a triumphal arch and broad ogee parapet; but it is suggested that a Chicago architect named Harry Jenkins composed this facade, and that Hamby's work was limited to the remainder of the building.

South Carolina projects:

1905-1906: Dr. H.T. Lykes Building, Columbia (*MR*, 30 November 1905, p. 525; 8 March 1906, p. 210.)

1906: La Coste Evans Residence, Cheraw (*MR*, 15 March 1906, p. 237.)

1906: Mrs. R.S. Desportes Residence, 1311 Gervais Street, Columbia (*MR*, 15 March 1906, p. 237; *Merchantile & Industrial Review*.)

1906: W.B. Guimarin Residence, Columbia (*MR*, 15 March 1906, p. 237.)

1906: Nurses' Home, Columbia Hospital, Columbia (*MR*, 15 March 1906, p. 237.)

1906: Athol H. Miller Residence, 1208 Senate Street, Columbia (*MR*, 28 June 1906, p. 680; *Merchantile & Industrial Review*.)

1906: Dr. LeGrand Guerry Office Building, Columbia (*MR*, 28 June 1906, p. 680; *Merchantile & Industrial Review*.)

1906: S.A. Blackmon Store Building, Holly Hill (*MR*, 15 March 1906, p. 237.)

1906: S.J. Watson Residence, Johnston; $6000 (*MR*, 15 March 1906, p. 237; 22 March 1906, p. 262.)

1906: John F. Weekly Residence, Ulmers (*MR*, 15 March 1906, p. 238.)

1907: Baptist Church, Camden; $11,500 (*MR*, 7 March 1907, p. 227; 16 May 1907, p. 573.)

Hamby & Hamby

1907: Remodeling, James L. Tapp Co. Store Building, Columbia (*MR*, 23 May 1907, p. 604.)

1907: Lewis W. Haskell Residence, 1605 Main Street, Columbia; $4250 (*MR*, 23 May 1907, p. 604; 6 June 1907, p. 672; *Merchantile & Industrial Review*.)

1907: B. Lucas Webb Residence, 1523 Plain Street, Columbia (*MR*, 23 May 1907, p. 604; *Merchantile & Industrial Review*.)

1907: Annex, Georgetown County Courthouse, Georgetown; $10,000 (*MR*, 21 February 1907, p. 167; 28 February 1907, p. 199; 18 April 1907, p. 423; 23 May 1907, p. 605.)

1907: Herman Schenk Residence, Georgetown (*MR*, 23 May 1907, p. 605.)

1907: L.S. Ehrich Residence, Georgetown; $10,000 (*MR*, 23 May 1907, p. 605.)

1907: School, St. Matthews; $10,000 (*MR*, 16 May 1907, p. 575; 23 May 1907, p. 606; 6 June 1907, p. 674.)

1907: Methodist Church, Winnsboro; $12,000 (*MR*, 21 February 1907, p. 169; 14 March 1907, p. 262; 6 June 1907, p. 674.)

1907: William R. Rabb Residence, Winnsboro (*MR*, 23 May 1907, p. 607.)

1907: Mrs. John F. Davis Residence, Winnsboro (*MR*, 23 May 1907, p. 607.)

1907: Enterprise Building Association Office and Store Building, Winnsboro; $25,000 (*MR*, 13 June 1907, p. 703; 27 June 1907, p. 773; 4 July 1907, p. 806; 22 August 1907, p. 160.)

1908: Charles H. Barringer Hotel, Florence; $10,000 (*MR*, 5 March 1908, p. 68; 9 July 1908, p. 56; 6 August 1908, p. 67; 29 October 1908, p. 66.)

1908-1909: Presbyterian Church, Bishopville; $15,000 (*MR*, 6 August 1908, p. 66; 12 August 1909, p. 58.)

1909: Carolina National Bank Store and Office Building, Columbia; $7000 (*MR*, 4 March 1909, p. 77.)

1909: Consolidated Holding Company Store and Apartment Building, Columbia; $12,000 (*MR*, 4 March 1909, p. 79.)

1909: Dr. E.C.L. Adams Residence, Columbia (*MR*, 8 April 1909, p. 60.)

1909: Consolidated Holding Company Business and Knights of Pythias Lodge Building, Columbia; $16,000 (*MR*, 8 April 1909, p. 61; 22 July 1909, p. 61.)

1909: T.B. Stackhouse Residence, Columbia; $18,000 (*MR*, 22 July 1909, p. 60.)

1909: O.P. Bourke Residence, Georgetown; $4000 (*MR*, 22 July 1909, p. 60.)

1909: Joseph Kaminski Residence, Georgetown; $6000 (*MR*, 22 July 1909, p. 60.)

1909: School, Rosemary (*MR*, 8 July 1909, p. 64.)

1909: School, St. Matthews; $18,000 (*MR*, 28 January 1909, p. 61; 22 July 1909, p. 62.)

1910: Consolidated Holding Co. Southern Express Office and Storage Building, Columbia; $15,000 (*MR*, 18 August 1910, p. 68.)

Arthur W. Hamby

1910: Wesley Methodist Episcopal Church, Columbia; $13,000 (*MR*, 18 August 1910, p. 68.)

1910: S.T. Carter Residence, Columbia; $6000 (*MR*, 18 August 1910, p. 68.)

1910: Mrs. L.E. Rivers Store and Apartment Building, Columbia; $9000 (*MR*, 22 December 1910, p. 64; 29 December 1910, p. 65.)

1911: Mrs. T.W. Bouchier Store Building, Columbia; $17,000 (*MR*, 7 September 1911, p. 78.)

1911: Fire Station, Georgetown; $9500 (*MR*, 6 April 1911, p. 85; 1 June 1911, p. 91.)

1911: E.E. Carnes Store and Armory Building, Hartsville; $6000 (*MR*, 13 April 1911, p. 71.)

1911: First Baptist Church, St. Matthews (Cornerstone; *MR*, 6 April 1911, p. 85; 13 April 1911, p. 70.)

Hamby & Rorke

1913: Consolidated Holding Company Store and Apartment Building, Columbia (*MR*, 27 March 1913, p. 71.)

1913: Richland County Jail, Columbia; $42,475 (*MR*, 3 April 1913, p. 81; 11 September 1913, p. 65.)

1913: St. Timothy Protestant Episcopal Church, Lincoln and Calhoun streets, Columbia (*The State*, 30 May 1913, p. 10; *MR*, 5 June 1913, p. 84.)

1913: Dr. C.L. Kibler Residence, Columbia; $8000 (*MR*, 10 July 1913, p. 70.)

1913: Carnegie Library, Gaffney; $7500 (*MR*, 30 October 1913, p. 71; George S. Bobinski, *Carnegie Libraries: Their History and Impact on American Public Library Development* (Chicago: American Library Association, 1969), p. 218.)

Arthur W. Hamby

1914: Chester County Jail, Chester; $24,715 (*MR*, 18 June 1914, p. 70.)

1915: Ridgeland School, Ridgeland (*The State*, 9 April 1915, p. 3; *MR*, 22 April 1915, p. 54.)

1916: W.J. McGhee Residence, Columbia (*MR*, 27 April 1916, p. 66.)

1917: Sunday School, Baptist Church, Beaufort; $5000 (*MR*, 22 February 1917, p. 118; 1 March 1917, p. 78.)

1923: Addition, Associate Reformed Presbyterian Church, Columbia (*MR*, 24 May 1923, p. 108.)

1924: Town Theatre, 1020 Sumter Street, Columbia; $20,200 (*MR*, 3 July 1924, p. 139; 24 July 1924, p. 129; 31 July 1924, p. 118.)

1925: Remodeling, Agricultural Building, Columbia; $11,575 (*MR*, 14 May 1925, p. 117.)

1925: National Guard Camp, Camp Jackson, Columbia (*MR*, 25 July 1925, p. 120.)

1927: First Church of Christ Scientist Building, Columbia; $25,000 (*MR*, 9 June 1927, p. 112.)

1927: Assistant Superintendent's Residence and Addition to Women's Infirmary, South Carolina State Hospital, Columbia; $7450 and $9445 (*MR*, 28 July 1927, p. 104; 4 August 1927, p. 117.)

1929: Women's Infirmary, State Park Tuberculosis Sanatorium; $35,000 (*MR*, 10 October 1929, p. 94.)

1931: Nurses' Home, Physician's Home, and Dairyman's Cottage, South Carolina Sanatorium; $15,276 (*MR*, 20 August 1931, p. 47.)

Sources: Columbia city directories; *MR*, various citations; *Merchantile and Industrial Review of Columbia and Richland County, South Carolina* (Portsmouth, Virginia: Seaboard Air Line Railway, n.d., ca. 1908), p. 42; *A Proclamation with Illustrated Views of Columbia, The Capital City of South Carolina, The Gem of the South The Pride of the Palmetto State* (Augusta, Georgia: Wolfe & Lombard, n.d., ca. 1910), p. 21.

HAMBY, Thomas C. (active 1907-1910) Thomas C. Hamby, a civil engineer, was associated with Arthur W. Hamby (q.v.) in Columbia from 1907 through 1910. An article in *The State* described Hamby's work in 1908:

Mr. T.C. Hamby of the firm of Hamby & Hamby . . . goes to Marion today to commence a survey of the county. . . Before coming to Columbia, [Mr. Hamby] was one of the engineers on the. . . railroad over an arm of the sea to Key West.

South Carolina projects:

See **Hamby, Arthur W.** (Hamby & Hamby)

Sources: Columbia city directories; *MR*, various citations; *The State*, 8 August 1908, p. 2.

HAMPTON, Martin Luther (active 1908-1932) Martin Luther Hampton, a descendent of General Wade Hampton, was born ca. 1889 in Laurens. He was educated at Columbia University in New York, and he studied architecture in several *ateliers* there. Hampton commenced architectural practice by 1908 in Gastonia, North Carolina, where he provided plans for a city fire station.

Hampton was renting a room in Laurens in 1910. He was associated with Luther Proffitt (q.v.) in Spartanburg in 1911. Proffitt & Hampton, Architects, prepared plans for the enlargement and remodeling of the Laurens County Courthouse in 1911, in association with Atlanta architect A. Ten Eyck Brown (q.v.)

In 1914 Hampton opened an architectural office in Miami, Florida. He pursued a profitable career in Florida, designing buildings in the Spanish Colonial Revival and Moorish styles. For several years he was associated with E.H. Ehmann in Miami. Prominent among Hampton's Miami commissions were the Granada Apartment House, 1922; the Miami Beach City Hall, 1927-1928; and the Warren Wright Winter Residence, 1932. In 1924 Hampton & Ehmann prepared plans for a 15-story office building for the Miami Realty Board, to be clad in "Florentine Gothic type" terra cotta.

Hampton opened a branch office in Lenoir, North Carolina, in 1928, where he provided plans for the remodeling of the Caldwell County Courthouse. He maintained his office in Miami at least through 1932.

South Carolina projects:

1911: See **Proffitt, Luther** (Proffitt & Hampton)

Sources: 1910 Federal Census, Laurens County, South Carolina; H.G. Cutler, *History of Florida Past and Present* (Chicago and New York: The Lewis Publishing Co., 1923), Vol. 2, p. 26; *From Wilderness to Metropolis: The History and Architecture of Dade County, Florida, 1825-1940* (Miami, Florida: Metropolitan Dade County, 1982), pp. 32, 77, 79; *MR*, various citations; Spartanburg city directories; Withey, p. 192.

HARDER, Julius F. (active 1894-1930) Julius Harder of New York City designed two of South Carolina's earliest and most elegant skyscrapers. No "skyscrapers" were built in South Carolina until the ten-story National Loan and Exchange Bank Building in Columbia went up in 1901-1903. Over the next thirty years, some forty high-rise buildings were planned and built in the state. Two of these buildings, the Palmetto Building in Columbia and the Chapman Building in Spartanburg, were designed by Harder. These buildings dominated their respective cities; the Palmetto Building is still one of Columbia's most-admired structures. The two Harder buildings were built with steel skeleton frames and masonry sheathing.

Harder was associated with Charles Henry Israels in New York from 1894 through 1911.

South Carolina projects:

1912-1913: Palmetto National Bank, Main and Lady streets, Columbia; $300,000; Julius Harder, architect; Wilson & Sompayrac (q.v.), supervising architects (*The State*, 6 February 1912, p. 10; *MR*, 15 February 1912, pp. 56, 71; *The Columbia Record*, Palmetto Building Supplement, 21 December 1913.)

1913: Chapman Building, Morgan Square, Spartanburg; $200,000 (*MR*, 13 February 1913, p. 69; 13 March 1913, p. 64.)

Sources: *The Columbia Record*, 21 December 1913, Palmetto Building supplement, p. 2;

Francis, pp. 37, 43; *MR*, various citations; Withey, p. 316.

HARPER, Arthur L. (active 1929-1936) Harper was associated with Florence architect Walter D. Harper (q.v.) in W.D. Harper & Co., Architects, in 1929. Arthur Harper was listed as a building contractor in the 1936 Florence city directory.

Sources: Florence city directories.

HARPER, Walter D. (active 1913-1948) Walter D. Harper of Florence had an unspectacular practice in eastern South Carolina during the early and middle decades of the twentieth century. He was associated with an unidentified brother in 1914; with Leon Hicks (q.v.) in 1916-1917; and with Arthur D. Harper in 1929. In the 1940s Harper's firm was called W.D. Harper & Sons.

South Carolina projects:

W.D. Harper & Brother

1914: W.M. Waters Undertaking Establishment and Store Building, Florence; $31,000 (*MR*, 19 March 1914, p. 69; 26 March 1914, p. 69.)

1914: P.J. Maxwell Merchantile Building, Florence; $11,000 (*MR*, 4 June 1914, p. 81.)

1914: John M. Timmons Store and Office Building, S. Dargan Street, Florence; $12,000 (*MR*, 13 August 1914, p. 64.)

1914: Isaac Sulzbacher Residence, 9 S. McQueen Street, Florence; $4000 (*MR*, 20 August 1914, p. 62; 1 October 1914, p. 70; 14 September 1914, p. 62.)

1916-1917: See **Hicks, Leon McDuff** (Hicks & Harper)

W.D. Harper

1917: Dr. F.H. McLeod Residence, Florence; $20,000 (*MR*, 20 September 1917, p. 86.)

1920: Dr. B.G. Gregg and Morrison Investment Co. Store and Office Building, Florence; $25,000 (*MR*, 14 October 1920, p. 154 c.)

1922: Graded School, Nichols; $18,500 (*MR*, 4 May 1922, p. 106.)

1923: High School, Chesterfield; $22,000 (*MR*, 30 August 1923, p. 106; 6 September 1923, p. 125.)

1923: School, Lane; $16,300 (*MR*, 8 November 1923, p. 112.)

1923: High School, Mullins; $38,000 (*MR*, 18 January 1923, p. 83.)

1924: Addition, Bishopville High School, Bishopville; $18,887 (*MR*, 10 July 1924, p. 106.)

1924: B.P. Sandlin Apartment Building, S. Coit and Evans streets, Florence; $20,000 (*MR*, 27 November 1924, p. 98.)

1924: High School, Kingstree; $44,000 (*MR*, 14 February 1924, p. 106; 22 May 1924, p. 114.)

1924: High School, Lakeview; $32,400 (*MR*, 28 August 1924, p. 115.)

1924: Municipal Building, Mullins; $10,000 (*MR*, 6 November 1924, p. 127.)

1927: Nurses' Home, Mullins Hospital, Mullins; $30,000 (*MR*, 11 August 1927, p. 111.)

W.D. Harper & Co.

1929: Dr. S.R. Lucas Store Building (Montgomery Ward & Co. Store Building), Florence; $60,000 (*MR*, 28 February 1929, p. 91.)

1930: High School, Loris; $35,000 (*MR*, 3 April 1930, p. 98.)

W.D. Harper & Sons

1948: Negro School, Georgetown; $192,573 (*Construction*, January 1948, p. 61.)

1948: Howard School, Georgetown; $125,663 (*Construction*, January 1948, p. 61.)

Sources: Florence city directories; *MR*, various citations.

HARRALL, Henry Dudley (1878-1959) Henry Harrall, a native of Greenville, maintained an architectural practice in Bennettsville for more than four decades. Harrall was educated at The Citadel Military College in Charleston, and he worked with the Army Corps of Engineers at Fort Caswell, North Carolina, as a draftsman in 1898-1899. In 1899 Harrall took a draftsman's position with the architectural and engineering firm W.B. Smith Whaley & Co. (q.v.) in Columbia. Harrall went with Whaley to Boston in 1903, and later worked in New York before establishing his Bennettsville office in 1915.

Harrall began his architectural career with a flourish, as described in *The State*:

> Mr. Henry Harrall, a native of this town, a Citadel student, now of New York city, is an architect and designer. He is a member of Bennettsville Presbyterian Church . . . [Harrall] has offered to furnish gratuitously plans and specifications for the modern structure. The building committee has accepted his liberal and generous proposition.

Harrall established an architectural office in Bennettsville around 1920. He pursued a modest practice over the next forty years, with projects concentrated in the state's northeastern counties. Harrall was president of the South Carolina chapter of the A.I.A. in 1939-1940.

South Carolina projects:

1906: Bennettsville Presbyterian Church, Bennettsville; $10,000 (*MR*, 8 March 1906, p. 210; 15 March 1906, p. 237; *The State*, 5 March 1906, p. 5.)

1917: Main Street Methodist Church, Greenwood; $45,000; J.E. Summer (q.v.) and H.D. Harrall, architects (*MR*, 5 April 1917, p. 92.)

1920: Agricultural High School, McColl; $50,000 (*MR*, 19 February 1920, p. 148.)

1924: School, Dillon; $12,475 (*MR*, 15 May 1924, p. 126; 15 October 1924, p. 114.)

1925: Sunday School Building, Methodist Episcopal Church South, Bennettsville; $28,300 (*MR*, 25 June 1925, p. 119.)

1928: Colored Elementary School, Bennettsville; $91,000 (*MR*, 21 June 1928, p. 97.)

1928: Marlboro County Hospital, Bennettsville; $53,000; George R. Berryman (q.v.), architect; H.D. Harrall, associate architect (*MR*, 19 July 1928, p. 93.)

1929: Baptist Church, Society Hill; $25,000 (*MR*, 18 April 1929, p. 104.)

1930: J.E. Phillips Hotel, Darlington (*MR*, 15 May 1930, p. 81.)

1930: J.E. Phillips, Five Store Buildings, Darlington; $15,000 (*MR*, 8 May 1930, p. 98.)

1951: Lee County Memorial Hospital, Bishopville (Koyl; *South Carolina Magazine*, June 1956, p. 47.)

1952: Remodeling, Marlboro County Courthouse, Bennettsville (Koyl; *South Carolina Magazine*, April 1955, p. 37.)

n.d.: Manse, Presbyterian Church, Bennettsville (*South Carolina Magazine*, January 1950, p. 33.)

n.d.: Dr. Randolph C. Charles Residence, Bennettsville (*South Carolina Magazine*, January 1952, p. 36.)

n.d.: Shiloh Baptist Church, Bennettsville (*South Carolina Magazine*, January 1952, p. 60.)

n.d.: Marlboro County Public Library, Bennettsville (*South Carolina Magazine*, January 1952, p. 67.)

n.d.: T.C. Coxe, Jr. Residence, Mont Clare (*South Carolina Magazine*, April 1955, p. 63.)

n.d.: Methodist Church, Moncks Corner (*South Carolina Magazine*, June 1956, p. 45.)

Sources: Koyl, p. 229; Petty, pp. 138, 139, 143; *The State*, 5 March 1906, p. 5; *MR*, various citations.

HART, John (active 1898-1900) Hart, a Spartanburg contractor and builder, prepared plans for the Mt. Zion Church in Spartanburg in 1898.

Source: *The Southern Architect*, August 1898, p. 523.

HARTMANN, Charles Conrad (1889- ca. 1975) Charles C. Hartmann, a native of New York City, was educated at New York University. He worked in the offices of architects C.E. Berge and W.L. Stoddart (q.v.) through 1920. Stoddart was designing major hotels in many states, and Hartmann worked as his southern representative. He came to Greensboro, North Carolina around 1917 to supervise construction of Stoddart's O. Henry Hotel at Elm and Bellemeade streets.

Hartmann established his own office in Greensboro in 1920. He designed many large hotels and office buildings in North Carolina in the 1920s. His major projects included the seventeen-story Jefferson Standard Life Insurance Co. Bank and Office Building at Elm and W. Market streets, Greensboro, contracted at $2,000,000 in 1922.

South Carolina projects:

1924-1925: Citizens Bank and Trust Co. Building, E. Main and Caldwell streets, Rock Hill; $110,000 (*MR*, 6 November 1924, p. 127; 1 January 1925, p. 131 g; cornerstone.)

1925: Remodeling and Addition, Peoples National Bank Building, Rock Hill; $70,000 (*MR*, 1 January 1925, p. 131 g; 8 January 1925, p. 114; 22 January 1925, p. 107; 5 February 1925, p. 123.)

Sources: Robert C. Bainbridge and Kate Ohno, *Wilson Historic Buildings Inventory, Wilson, North Carolina* (Wilson, North Carolina: City of Wilson, 1980), p. 235; Ruth Little-Stokes, *An Inventory of Historic Architecture, Greensboro, N.C.* (Greensboro and Raleigh, North Carolina: City of Greensboro and North Carolina Department of Cultural Resources, 1976), pp. 16, 36, 38, 55; *MR*, various citations; *Who's Who in the South*, 1927, p. 337.

HASTINGS, Thomas (1860-1929) Thomas Hastings, the distinguished New York City architect and partner in Carrere & Hastings, designed a small resort house for himself in 1929, in the popular society retreat of Aiken, South Carolina. The house, located at 324 Newberry Street, is called "Horse Haven."

Sources: Hewitt, p. 275; *Macmillan Encyclopedia*, Vol. I, pp. 387-388; H.J. Whigham, "A Small House by a Great Architect," *Home and Field*, July 1930, pp. 11-17; Withey, pp. 269-271; Wodehouse, pp. 42-44, 87-88.

HAWES, Edward Jr. (active 1911) The W.G. Bryant commercial building in Orangeburg, contracted at $6000 in 1911, was designed by one Edward Hawes, Jr. The project was described in the *MR*, 14 September 1911, p. 64.

HAY, E.J. (active 1890-1894) Hay was listed as an architect in Camden in national architects' directories in 1890 and 1894. No further information on Hay has been found.

HAYDEN, Luke (active 1892-1901) Hayden was associated with Oliver Duke Wheeler (q.v.) in Atlanta, Georgia from 1896 to 1899. L.E. Schwend joined the firm around 1899. The firm relocated to Charlotte, North Carolina around 1900. Prominent among the firm's designs in Charlotte was the 1901 Presbyterian College Building.

The 1899 Main Street Methodist Episcopal Church in Columbia was one of the firm's largest South Carolina commissions. The church has been radically altered, but photographs show the original building as a well-composed late Gothic Revival design with asymmetrical towers.

Wheeler established his own office in Charlotte in 1901, while Hayden and Schwend disappeared.

South Carolina projects:

Hayden & Wheeler

1897: John L. Agurs Building, Chester (*MR*, 13 August 1897, p. 42.)

1897: Jos. A. Walker Store Building, Chester; $4500 (*Southern Architect and Building News*, July 1897, p. 200; *MR*, 13 August 1897, p. 42.)

1897: Associate Reformed Presbyterian Church, Chester; $10,000 (*Southern Architect and Building News*, July 1897, p. 202; *MR*, 13 August 1897, p. 42.)

1897: M.E. Church, Chester; $12,000 (*MR*, 13 August 1897, p. 42.)

1898-1899: Second Methodist Episcopal Church, Gaffney (*MR*, 22 July 1898, p. 429; 9 June 1899, p. 340; 28 July 1899, p. 15.)

1899: Main Street Methodist Episcopal Church, 1830 Main Street, Columbia (*MR*, 9 June 1899, p. 340.)

1899: First Baptist Church, Gaffney (*MR*, 9 June 1899, p. 340; 30 June 1899, p. 391.)

Hayden, Wheeler & Schwend

1900: City Hall and Opera House, Florence; $17,315 (*MR*, 1 March 1900, p. 102; 10 May 1900, p. 273.)

1901: Jacob's Hotel, Florence (*MR*, 24 January 1901, p. 15.)

1901: First Methodist Church School Building and Church, Darlington; $10,000 (*MR*,

24 January 1901, p. 15; 21 February 1901, p. 96; 18 April 1901, p. 245.)

Sources: Charlotte, North Carolina, city directories; *MR*, various citations.

HAZARD, Frank Arthur (1890- ca. 1960) Arthur Hazard, a native of Georgetown, studied engineering at The Citadel in Charleston. He worked as a specifications writer for Scroggs & Ewing (q.v.) in 1929-1930. He established his own office in Augusta, Georgia in 1930. In 1955 Hazard was registered for practice in Florida, Georgia, North Carolina, and South Carolina.

South Carolina projects:

1931: Mrs. Albert Goodwyn Residence, Charleston (*MR*, 16 April 1931, p. 59.)

1931: Robert A. Easterling & Associates Hotel, Walterboro; $70,000 (*MR*, 8 October 1931, p. 44.)

1932: Berkeley County Hospital, Moncks Corner; $84,326; F. Arthur Hazard and Roy O. Brannon (q.v.), architects (*MR*, 28 January 1932, p. 38; 17 March 1932, p. 40; 14 July 1932, p. 30.)

1953: First Baptist Church, Conway (Koyl.)

1954: High School, Williston (Koyl.)

Sources: Augusta, Georgia, city directories; Koyl, p. 237; *MR*, various citations.

HEATON, Roy K. (active 1908) Roy K. Heaton & Co. of Spartanburg were described as architects for the Methodist Episcopal Church South edifice at Clemson College. The building was contracted at $12,000 in 1908.

Sources: *MR*, 30 January 1908, p. 58; 6 February 1908, p. 67; 3 December 1908, p. 76.

HEISTER, Michael (active 1903-1927) Michael Heister worked with Frank P. Milburn (q.v.) in

Columbia and in Washington, D.C. Heister is identified as the architect of the St. Peter's Roman Catholic Church in Columbia (1902-1906) in some of the project references. In Milburn's 1903 *Book of Designs*, Heister was called "designer and manager of draughting department."

South Carolina projects:

1903-1907: See **Milburn, Frank P.** (Milburn, Heister & Co.)

Sources: Columbia city directories; *MR*, various citations; Frank P. Milburn, *Designs from the Work of Frank P. Milburn, Architect, Columbia, South Carolina 1903* (Columbia: The State Company, 1903.)

HEMPHILL, James Calvin Sr. (1889- ca. 1961) Hemphill, a native of Abbeville, was educated at the College of Charleston. He studied architecture at Harvard University Summer School and through night classes at the Boston Architectural Club. Hemphill worked as a draftsman for Lockwood, Greene & Co. (q.v.) in Boston and in Greenville, S.C.; he later worked with Warren & Smith in Boston. He was established in Greenwood by 1913. In 1916-1917 Hemphill was associated with J. Ernest Summer (q.v.) in Greenwood.

Hemphill worked in association with Charles C. Wilson (q.v.) in 1925-1929 on five public school projects in Greenwood, including the massive Greenwood High School.

Hemphill worked with the Historic American Buildings Survey during the Depression; he drew the HABS plans of the Ainsley Hall House (Robert Mills House) in Columbia in 1934.

James Calvin Hemphill Jr., born in 1920, worked in his father's office and became an associate by 1947. Lawrence W. Cobb became an associate of Hemphill, Sr. in 1956.

South Carolina projects:

1916-1917: See **Summer, J.E.** (Summer & Hemphill)

1918: Kerr Residence, 313 Greenville Street, Greenwood (Survey files, S.C. Archives.)

1919: Geo. W. Hart Store Building, Greenwood (*MR*, 15 May 1919, p. 120.)

1919: C.C. Wharton Residence, Greenwood; $11,000 (*MR*, 3 July 1919, p. 157; Snowden & Cutler.)

1920: Community Building, Abbeville Cotton Mills, Abbeville; $40,000 (*MR*, 11 November 1920, p. 130; 2 December 1920, p. 175.)

1920: C.C. Wharton Dry Goods Department Store Building, Greenwood (*MR*, 6 May 1920, p. 201.)

1920: Abraham Rosenberg Residence, 424 E. Cambridge Avenue, Greenwood (Survey files, S.C. Archives.)

Ca. 1920: Abbeville County Memorial Hospital, Abbeville (Snowden & Cutler.)

Ca. 1920: Dr. W.A. Barnett Residence, Greenwood (Snowden & Cutler.)

Ca. 1920: W.H. Mays Residence, Greenwood (Snowden & Cutler.)

Ca. 1920: J.B. Walton Residence, Greenwood (Snowden & Cutler.)

1921: Negro School, Newberry; $25,000 (*MR*, 1 December 1921, p. 105 f; 8 December 1921, p. 84 e.)

1921: Addition, High School, Newberry (*MR*, 1 December 1921, p. 105 f.)

1922: School, Central; $20,000 (*MR*, 29 June 1922, p. 80; 6 July 1922, p. 109.)

1922: Annex, High School, Easley; $30,000 (*MR*, 14 September 1922, p. 82; 21 September 1922, p. 93.)

1922: Addition, Greenwood Hospital, Greenwood; $22,000 (*MR*, 27 July 1922, p. 78; 3 August 1922, p. 100; Snowden & Cutler.)

1923: Negro Hospital, Brewer Normal Institute, Greenwood; $26,887; Holmes & Von Schmid (q.v.), architects; J.C. Hemphill, associated architect (*MR*, 15 February 1923, p. 109.)

1924: Municipal Fire Department and Water & Light Company Building, Abbeville (*MR*, 31 January 1924, p. 111.)

1924: School, Calhoun Falls; $36,000 (*MR*, 19 June 1924, p. 118.)

1924: Sunday School Annex, First Presbyterian Church, Greenwood; $25,000 (*MR*, 20 March 1924, p. 109.)

1924: Associate Reformed Presbyterian Church, Calhoun Avenue and Lander Street, Greenwood; $30,000 (*MR*, 28 August 1924, p. 112; 18 September 1924, p. 114.)

1924: Dormitory, Lander College, Greenwood; $61,000; James C. Hemphill and Rudolph E. Lee (q.v.), associated architects (*MR*, 12 June 1924, p. 114.)

1924: Newberry County Hospital, Newberry; $38,395 (*MR*, 12 June 1924, p. 112; 10 July 1924, p. 105.)

1925: Sunday School Annex, Methodist Episcopal Church, Abbeville; $32,000 (*MR*, 29 January 1925, p. 99; 5 February 1925, p. 123.)

1925: Greenwood High School, Greenwood; $151,310; James C. Hemphill and Wilson, Berryman & Kennedy (q.v.), associated architects (*MR*, 2 July 1925, p. 131.)

1925: South Greenwood School, Greenwood; $17,691; James C. Hemphill and Wilson, Berryman & Kennedy (q.v.), associated architects (*MR*, 2 July 1925, p. 131.)

1925: West Side School, Greenwood; $40,635; James C. Hemphill and Wilson, Berryman & Kennedy (q.v.), associated architects (*MR*, 2 July 1925, p. 131.)

1925-1926: School, Ninety Six Cotton Mill, Ninety Six; $40,000 (*MR*, 8 October 1925, p. 109; 20 May 1926, p. 123; 27 May 1926, p. 113.)

1927-1928: Clyde D. Keller Residence, 511 E. Cambridge Avenue, Greenwood; $15,000 (*MR*, 21 April 1927, p. 101; 5 May 1927, p. 116; Survey files, S.C. Archives.)

1929: Classroom and Gymnasium Addition, Greenwood High School, Greenwood; Charles C. Wilson (q.v.), architect; James C. Hemphill, associated architect (*MR*, 7 November 1929, p. 101.)

1929: Classroom and Auditorium Addition, Grammar School, Greenwood; Charles C. Wilson (q.v.), architect; James C. Hemphill, associated architect (*MR*, 7 November 1929, p. 101.)

1932: Church of the Resurrection, Greenwood (Koyl; *South Carolina Magazine*, January 1950, p. 45.)

1947: Alterations and Additions, Vocational Building Cafeteria, Greenwood; $100,000 (*Construction*, July 1947, p. 67.)

1948: Abbeville County Jail, Abbeville (Koyl.)

1948: Young Men's Christian Association Building, Greenwood (Koyl; *South Carolina Magazine*, October 1950, p. 25.)

1950: Self Memorial Hospital, Greenwood (Koyl; *South Carolina Magazine*, January 1950, p. 46.)

1951: Mathews Elementary School, Greenwood (Koyl; *South Carolina Magazine*, April 1955, p. 27.)

1955: West Side Baptist Church, Greenwood (Koyl.)

Ca. 1956: H.K. Thayer Residence, Greenwood (*South Carolina Magazine*, June 1956, p. 69.)

Ca. 1956: E.W. Milford Residence, Greenwood (*South Carolina Magazine*, June 1956, p. 69.)

Ca. 1956: Mrs. J.W. Lever Residence, Columbia (*South Carolina Magazine*, June 1956, p. 76.)

Ca. 1956: Raymond W. Sifley Residence, Orangeburg (*South Carolina Magazine*, June 1956, p. 77.)

n.d.: C.Y. Thomason Residence, Greenwood (*South Carolina Magazine*, January 1952, p. 21.)

n.d.: J.W. Pickens Residence, Greenwood (*South Carolina Magazine*, January 1952, p. 29.)

n.d.: Brewer High School and Gymnasium, Greenwood (*South Carolina Magazine*, January 1952, p. 77.)

n.d.: Alterations, Ware Shoals Methodist Church, Ware Shoals (*South Carolina Magazine*, April 1955, p. 35.)

n.d.: Henry Thayer, Jr. Residence, Greenwood (*South Carolina Magazine*, April 1955, p. 73.)

n.d.: L.R. Smith Residence, Orangeburg (*South Carolina Magazine*, April 1955, p. 74.)

Sources: Crawford, *Who's Who in South Carolina*, pp. 81-82; Greenwood city directories; Koyl, p. 241; *MR*, various citations; Snowden & Cutler, *History of South Carolina*, 1920, Vol. 5, pp. 43-44.)

HENTZ, Hal Fitzgerald (1883-1972) Hal F. Hentz was the senior partner of the prestigious and successful Atlanta, Georgia firms of Hentz, Reid & Adler and Hentz, Adler & Schutze. Hentz, a native of City Point, Florida, was educated at Emory University. He was described as superintendent of construction for the landmark Candler Building in Atlanta (George Murphy and George Stewart, architects; 1904-1906.) Joseph Neel Reid (q.v.) met Hentz around this time, and the two men went together to Columbia University in New York, and then to the Ecole des Beaux-Arts in Paris, France. Hentz worked with Kirby, Petit & Green in New York in 1908-1909 before joining the office of Gottfried L. Norrman (q.v.) in Atlanta. When Norrman died in 1909, Hentz assumed leadership of the office. He completed his education with a degree from Columbia University, New York, in 1912. Neel Reid and Rudolph S. Adler (q.v.) were partners in the firm. When Reid died in 1926, Philip Trammell Schutze (q.v.) became a partner.

Prominent among the firm's designs were the ten-story, $200,000 Georgia Life Insurance Co. Building at Macon, built in 1911; the eight-story, $500,000 George Muse Clothing Company Building in Atlanta, begun in 1920; and the twelve-story, $1,000,000 Tampa Terrace Hotel in Tampa, Florida, built in 1924. The firm also had projects in Tennessee, North Carolina, Alabama, and New York.

Hentz called himself Supervising Architect for the Shriners Hospitals in 1921-1936. Hentz, Reid & Adler designed at least six Shriners Hospitals for Crippled Children around the nation; these were in Springfield, Massachusetts (1923-1924), Shreveport, Louisiana (1923-1924), Chicago, Illinois (1925), Lexington, Kentucky (1925), Portland, Oregon (1925), and Greenville, South Carolina (1926-1927.)

Hentz served on the commission which rewrote the Atlanta Building Code in the 1920s. He was chief and supervising architect for the Federal Housing Administration in Georgia. He retired in 1943.

South Carolina projects:

Hentz & Reid

1912: Mrs. Clarence E. Breeden Residence, Bennettsville (Grady, p. 199.)

Hentz, Reid & Adler

1919: Geo. L. Snowden Residence, Converse Heights, Spartanburg; $14,000 (*MR*, 26 June 1919, p. 140; Grady, p. 199.)

1924: Science Building, Benedict College, Columbia; Hentz, Reid & Adler, architects; J.B. Urquhart (q.v.), associate architect (*MR*, 13 November 1924, p. 111.)

1925-1926: Alterations and Additions, J.B. Clark Residence, Ridgeland (Grady, p. 199.)

1926-1927: Burgiss Shrine Hospital for Crippled Children, National Highway, Greenville; $350,000; Hentz, Reid & Adler, architects; Beacham & LeGrand (q.v.), associate architects (*MR*, 20 May 1926, p. 122; 1 July 1926, p. 135; 22 July 1926, p. 111; 10 February 1927, p. 107; Grady, p. 199.)

Hentz, Adler & Schutze

1938-1939: Southern Bell Telephone Exchange, 18 St. Philip Street, Charleston (Charleston *Post*, 12 May 1938; *News and Courier*, 9 February 1939.)

Sources: *American Art Annual*, Vol. XXI, pp. 360, 409; Atlanta, Georgia city directories; James Grady, *Architecture of Neel Reid in Georgia* (Athens, Georgia: University of Georgia Press, 1973); Koyl, p. 242; *MR*, various citations; *Who's Who in the South*, 1927, p. 349.

HEWITT & ASH (active 1917-1924) The firm of William Dempster Hewitt (1847-1924) and Percy Ash (1863-1933) was active in Philadelphia, Pennsylvania from 1917 to 1924. In collaboration with Norman Hulme (q.v.), Hewitt & Ash prepared plans for the Hampton Terrace Hotel in North Augusta, South Carolina, in 1921. It is not clear whether this building was ever built.

Source: Tatman/Moss, pp. 14-15, 375-377.

HIBBS, Henry Clossen (1882-1949) Hibbs, a native of New Jersey, designed major buildings for many southern colleges during the mid-twentieth century. He studied architecture at the University of Pennsylvania, and he worked in the offices of Frank Miles Day, George B. Post, and Ludlow & Peabody (q.v.) Hibbs opened his own architectural practice in Nashville, Tennessee in 1916. He designed buildings for Davidson College, Mary Baldwin College, Vanderbilt, Fisk, and other universities in the south. His 1939-1940 McKissick Library Building at the University of South Carolina is a ponderous domed edifice dominating the historic campus.

South Carolina project:

1939-1940: McKissick Library, University of South Carolina, Columbia (Plaque on building.)

Sources: Herndon, pp. 93-94; Withey, pp. 284-285.

HICKS, Leon McDuff (active 1913-1935) Leon McD. Hicks was practicing architecture in Florence by 1913, in association with William J. Huggins (q.v.) The partnership was dissolved by 1914, and Hicks pursued independent practice until 1916, when he associated with Walter D. Harper (q.v.) This firm, Hicks & Harper, was discontinued by 1920. Hicks designed houses, schools, and other small buildings in eastern South Carolina through the 1920s. John Hicks, probably a relative, worked as a draftsman for Hicks in 1915.

The Saunders Memorial Hospital in Florence, contracted in 1920 at $100,000, was among Hicks's largest projects. He also designed a hospital building in Mullins in 1924.

Hicks died ca. 1935. He was survived by his widow, Allie Hicks.

South Carolina projects:

1914: School, Poston (*MR*, 19 November 1914, p. 64.)

1915: School, Bannockburn (*MR*, 7 October 1914, p. 76.)

1915: J.P. Matthews Co. Store Building, Lake City; $7000 (*MR*, 29 July 1915, p. 59.)

1915: J.L. Richardson Residence, Lake City; $3000 (*MR*, 12 August 1915, p. 59.)

Hicks & Harper

1916: School, Hebron; $8000 (*MR*, 1 June 1916, p. 83.)

1916: School, Leo; $4000 (*MR*, 18 May 1916, p. 74.)

1916: School, Furman; $7500 (*MR*, 7 September 1916, p. 78.)

1917: T.C. Perrin Residence, Bishopville; $5000 (*MR*, 19 April 1917, p. 74 n.)

L. McD. Hicks

1920: Saunders Memorial Hospital, Florence; $100,000 (*MR*, 16 September 1920, p. 139.)

1921: Parish House, St. John's Episcopal Church, Florence; $20,000 (*MR*, 20 October 1921, p. 100.)

1922: High School, Timmonsville; $26,500 (*MR*, 22 June 1922, p. 86.)

1923: Tans Bay School, Florence; $20,713 (*MR*, 3 May 1923, p. 130.)

1924: Remodeling, Times Building, Florence; $26,075 (*MR*, 6 November 1924, p. 129.)

1924: B.G. McClam Residence, Lake City; $35,000 (*MR*, 5 June 1924, p. 138.)

1924: Mullins Hospital, Mullins; $33,355 (*MR*, 8 September 1924, p. 116.)

1925: A.F.A.M. Lodge Building, Mullins; $19,465 (*MR*, 10 September 1925, p. 107; 17 September 1925, p. 113.)

1929: High School, St. Stephens; $28,000 (*MR*, 23 May 1929, p. 98.)

Sources: Florence city directories; *MR*, various citations.

HOFFMAN, Francis Burrall Jr. (1882-1980) Burrall Hoffman, Jr., native of New Orleans and a graduate of the Ecole des Beaux-Arts in Paris, designed the Dibble Memorial Library in Aiken, South Carolina in 1926. The project, on Laurens Street, was contracted at $10,000. Among Hoffman's other southern projects was the $500,000 James Deering villa at Miami, Florida, begun in 1912. Hoffman worked in the offices of Carrere & Hastings (q.v.) before commencing his own practice.

Sources: Hewitt, p. 275; *MR*, 30 April 1914, p. 50; 29 April 1926, p. 107; 6 May 1926,

p. 132; Noffsinger, pp. 108, 114; White & Willensky, p. 237; Wodehouse, p. 89.

HOLMAN, Arthur E. (active 1909-1956) Holman was a partner of Geoffrey Lloyd Preacher (q.v.) in Augusta, Georgia in 1909. He commenced an engineering career in Anderson, South Carolina, by 1920, when he was working for Brogan Mills. He worked in later years for Toxaway, Riverside, and Gossett Mills in Anderson. A school at Williamston Mills in Williamston, South Carolina, was designed by Holman in 1923. This building was contracted at $17,000.

Sources: Anderson city directories; *MR*, 16 August 1923, p. 116; 30 August 1923, p. 107; and various other citations.

HOLMES, Rutledge (1866-1929) Rutledge Holmes practiced as an architect and civil engineer in Charleston from ca. 1895 through 1902. Samuel Lapham (q.v.) wrote that, among Charleston architects at the end of the nineteenth century, Holmes was "the one most deserving the title from his manner of practice." Holmes was associated with S. Lewis Simons (q.v.) in 1895, and with St. James Alison Lawton (q.v.) in 1901-1902. Holmes & Lawton won several commissions in Jacksonville, Florida, in 1901 and 1902, including a $67,000 courthouse; and in 1902 Holmes relocated to Jacksonville. He was active in that city through 1924. Holmes committed suicide in his office in Quincy, Florida, in 1929.

South Carolina projects:

1898: Charleston Industrial School Building, Charleston (*MR*, 13 May 1898, p. 273.)

Holmes & Lawton

1901: Remodeling of "Mills House" to Apartment House, Charleston; $40,000 (*MR*, 21 February 1901, p. 96; 11 July 1901, p. 473.)

Sources: Charleston city directories; Jacksonville, Florida, city directories; *MR*, various citations; Petty, p. 7; Wayne W. Wood, *Jacksonville's Architectural Heritage: Landmarks for the Future*

(Jacksonville: University of North Florida Press, n.d., ca 1985), p. 10.

HOLMES & VON SCHMID (active 1921-1923) Arthur Brautigam Holmes (born 1888), a graduate of Cornell, served as supervising architect for the American Missionary Association from 1916 to 1921. He was associated with _____ Von Schmid from 1921 to 1923. He worked out of Montclair, New Jersey, and New York, New York.

South Carolina project:

1923: Negro Hospital, Brewer Normal Institute, Greenwood; $26,887; Holmes & Von Schmid, architects; James C. Hemphill (q.v.), associate architect (*MR*, 15 February 1923, p. 109.)

Source: Koyl, p. 254.

HOOK, Charles Christian (1869-1938) Charles C. Hook was among the most prominent and productive architects of Charlotte, North Carolina, in the late nineteenth and early twentieth centuries. He was born at Wheeling, West Virginia, in 1869, and educated at Wheeling Business College and at Washington University in St. Louis, Missouri. Hook established his architectural office in Charlotte by 1891. Frank M. Sawyer (q.v) was associated with Hook in Charlotte from 1898 through 1905. Willard G. Rogers (q.v.) was Hook's partner in 1905-1915. His son Walter W. Hook, who entered the office as draftsman in 1923, became an associate in the firm by 1932.

Hook designed a vast number of residences, commercial buildings, churches, and other small projects in central North Carolina in the 1890s. City halls in Monroe (1893) and Salisbury (1895) were among Hook's important early commissions. The seven-story Piedmont Realty Company office building in Charlotte, designed by Hook, and contracted in 1901, was among North Carolina's first skyscrapers. Hook's practice expanded greatly in the first decade of the twentieth century, and he won commissions for schools, banks, libraries, hospitals, and larger commercial buildings in both North and South Carolina in these years.

Hook designed buildings for many colleges, including Davidson, Guilford, North Carolina State, St. Mary's, and the State Normal College in North Carolina, and Converse, Winthrop, Erskine, and Limestone College in South Carolina. He was architect for most of the buildings at Trinity College (Duke University) in Durham, built between 1898 and 1923, including the $175,000 Southgate Memorial Dormitory, commissioned in 1921. Hook also designed several Masonic buildings, including the neo-Egyptian temple in Charlotte (1913-1914.)

The Piedmont & Northern Railway, which operated an electric rail line in North and South Carolina, employed Hook & Rogers in 1911 to design their freight and passenger depots. The firm's buildings were similarly detailed, varying in size according to the importance of the station; they were of red and yellow brick, with clay tile roofs. The Piedmont & Northern rail line from Greenwood to Belton in South Carolina is relatively intact, and the stations at Hodges, Shoals Junction, Donalds, Honea Path, and other communities are standing.

Hook's practice continued to prosper after the First World War. He specialized in public school design. Hook also was architect for the Richmond County Courthouse in Rockingham (1922) and the Courthouse and Municipal Buildings in Charlotte, which were contracted at $488,000 in 1924.

South Carolina projects:

1892: School, Florence; $10,000 (*MR*, 15 July 1892, p. 41.)

1895: Bank Building, Spartanburg; $6000 (*MR*, 22 February 1895, p. 61.)

1895: J.H. Montgomery Office Building, Spartanburg (*MR*, 1 March 1895, p. 77.)

1896: Dormitory, Erskine College, Due West (*MR*, 3 July 1896, p. 386.)

1896: Laurens Cotton Mills Store Building, Laurens (*MR*, 27 March 1896, p. 152.)

1896: Reece Harry Store Building, Union (*MR*, 27 March 1896, p. 152.)

1896: M.F. Farr Bank and Office Building, Union (*MR*, 10 April 1896, p. 185.)

1898: A.N. Wood Store Building, Gaffney (*MR*, 22 April 1898, p. 228.)

1898: O.S. Poe Residence, Rock Hill (*MR*, 15 April 1898, p. 212.)

1898-1899: Twitchell Auditorium, Converse College, Spartanburg (National Register files, S.C. Archives.)

Hook & Sawyer

1898: R. Lee Kerr Residence, Rock Hill (*MR*, 9 December 1898, p. 345.)

1899: Auditorium and Library Building, Limestone College, Gaffney; $15,000 (*MR*, 23 June 1899, p. 374.)

1899: W.C. Whitner Residence, Rock Hill (*MR*, 22 September 1899, p. 162.)

1900: J.A. Bailey Residence, Clinton (*MR*, 15 February 1900, p. 65.)

1900: J.A. Copeland Store, Office, and Opera House Building, Clinton (*MR*, 15 February 1900, p. 65.)

1900: Hon. A.N. Wood Residence, Gaffney (*MR*, 22 March 1900, p. 152.)

1900: Col. T.B. Butler Residence, Gaffney (*MR*, 29 March 1900, p. 171.)

1901: Star Theater and Office Building, Gaffney (*MR*, 20 June 1901, p. 417; 27 June 1901, p. 437; 1 August 1901, p. 31; 10 October 1901, p. 201.)

Hook & Rogers

1905: Southern Power Company Hotel, Catawba Falls; $6500 (*MR*, 17 August 1905, p. 121.)

1908: T.L. Nichols Residence and Camphouse, Chester (*MR*, 26 March 1908, p. 59.)

1908: W.J. Lunney Residence, Seneca (*MR*, 19 March 1908, p. 60.)

1911: Louis Wood Moving Picture Theater, Limestone Street, Gaffney; $5000 (*MR*, 17 August 1911, p. 69.)

1911: Remodeling, Carolina Hotel, Rock Hill; $10,000 (*MR*, 20 July 1911, p. 71.)

1911: Arts and Science building, Winthrop Normal College, Rock Hill; $60,000 (*MR*, 2 November 1911, p. 85.)

1911: Oakland Avenue Presbyterian Church, Rock Hill; $25,000 (*MR*, 30 November 1911, p. 72; 7 December 1911, p. 86.)

Ca. 1911: Piedmont & Northern Railway freight and passenger stations, Greenwood-Greenville-Charlotte Line (Fetters and Swanson.)

1912: W.J. Rodney Residence, Rock Hill; $20,000 (*MR*, 20 June 1912, p. 76.)

1912: Two Warehouses, Victoria Cotton Mills, Rock Hill; $5300 (*MR*, 22 August 1912, p. 68; 29 August 1912, p. 66.)

1912: Building, Winthrop Normal College, Rock Hill (*MR*, 3 October 1912, p. 85; 10 October 1912, p. 65.)

1913: Conservatory of Music, Women's College, Due West; $25,000 (*MR*, 5 June 1913, p. 85.)

1913: Southern Power Company Hotel, Great Falls; $7000 (*MR*, 21 August 1913, p. 71.)

1913: Addition, Central School, Rock Hill; $17,800 (*MR*, 22 May 1913, p. 70.)

Sources: *Directory of Historic American Architectural Firms*, p. 11; Thomas T. Fetters and Peter W. Swanson, Jr., *Piedmont and Northern: The Great Electric System of the South* (San Marino, California: Golden West Books, 1974); Thomas W. Hanchett, Charlotte, North Carolina, unpublished research; Koyl, p. 255; *MR*, various citations; Claudia P. Roberts et.al., *The Durham Architectural*

and Historic Inventory (Durham, North Carolina: City of Durham, 1982), pp. 175-176; *Who's Who in the South* (1927), p. 365.

HOPKINS, Alfred H. (1870-1941) Alfred H. Hopkins of New York City prepared plans for a hotel in Aiken, South Carolina, for the Aiken Hotel & Improvement Company in 1903. He was best known in New York for designing penitentiaries and other correctional institutions. President Franklin D. Roosevelt appointed Hopkins a delegate to the 1935 International Prison Conference in Berlin. He studied architecture at the Ecole des Beaux-Arts.

Sources: Hewitt, p. 275; *MR*, 5 March 1903, p. 146; 12 March 1903, p. 163; Withey, p. 299.

HOPKINS, Frank Vincent (active 1924-1964) Hopkins was associated with William J. Wilkins (q.v.) in Florence from 1924 through 1932. He practiced in Florence from that time through 1964. William W. Baker was associated with Hopkins by 1936. The firm was later called Hopkins, Baker & Gill.

South Carolina projects:

1924-1932: See **Wilkins, William J.** (Wilkins & Hopkins)

Hopkins & Baker

1935: Alterations and additions, Florence County Courthouse, Florence; $98,000 (*MR*, May 1935, p. 70.)

Hopkins, Baker & Gill

1942: Shop Building, Poynor School, Florence (GWW, List.)

1950: Cafeteria Building, Poynor School, Florence (GWW, List.)

1951: Carver School, Florence (GWW, List.)

1951: Six classrooms, Harllee School, Florence (GWW, List.)

1954: Savannah Grove School, Florence (GWW, List.)

1954: Addition, Wallace Gregg School, Florence (GWW, List.)

1954: Willow Creek Elementary School, Florence (GWW, List.)

1954: Mars Bluff Elementary School, Florence (GWW, List.)

1956: Moore Junior High School, Florence (GWW, List.)

1956: Wilson School, Florence (GWW, List.)

1957: Gymnasium addition, McClenaghan School, Florence (GWW, List.)

1957: Delmae School, Florence (GWW, List.)

1964: Science wing, McClenaghan School, Florence, (GWW, List.)

n.d.: Horry County Memorial Library, Conway (*South Carolina Magazine*, January 1950, p. 42.)

n.d.: Winthrop Senior Hall, Winthrop Normal College, Rock Hill (*South Carolina Magazine*, January 1950, p. 42.)

n.d.: Winthrop Home Economics Building, Winthrop Normal College, Rock Hill (*South Carolina Magazine*, January 1950, p. 43.)

n.d.: St. Luke's Evangelical Lutheran Church, Florence (*South Carolina Magazine*, October 1950, p. 21.)

n.d.: Clemson College Chemistry Building, Clemson (*South Carolina Magazine*, October 1950, p. 21; January 1952, p. 79.)

n.d.: Marion Coca-Cola Bottling Company Building, Conway (*South Carolina Magazine*, January 1952, p. 47.)

n.d.: Barnwell County Court House and Office Building, Barnwell (*South Carolina Magazine*, January 1952, p. 64.)

n.d.: Presbyterian Church, Myrtle Beach (*South Carolina Magazine*, January 1952, p. 78.)

Sources: Florence city directories; Gill, Wilkins & Wood, List of school projects in Florence County, S.C., copy in National Register files, S.C. Archives; *MR*, various citations.

HOPPIN & KOEN (1894-1923) The firm of Francis Laurens Vinton Hoppin (1867-1941) and Terence A. Koen (1856-1923) designed three large houses in the popular "winter colony" at Aiken, South Carolina. Hoppin, who studied at Brown, M.I.T., and the Ecole des Beaux-Arts, worked for several years for McKim, Mead & White in New York. In private practice, he was noted as a designer of police stations, firehouses, and private estates. Koen was another alumnus of McKim, Mead & White.

The three Aiken estates are large Colonial-Revival style buildings situated on substantial suburban plots. Sandhurst has a colossal Corinthian entrance portico.

South Carolina projects:

Ca. 1902: "Sandhurst," W.H. Sands Residence, Aiken (*The Architectural Review*, Vol. IV, 1902.)

Ca. 1902: "Hopelands," C. Oliver Iselin Residence, Aiken (*The Architectural Review*, Vol. IV, 1902.)

Ca. 1902: F.S. Taylor Residence, Aiken (*The Architectural Review*, Vol. IV, 1902.)

Sources: Francis, pp. 40, 47; Hewitt, p. 275; *Macmillan Encyclopedia*, Vol. II, p. 419; *The National Cyclopedia of American Biography*, Vol. XXXI (New York: James T. White & Company, 1944), p. 163; White & Willensky, pp. 49, 134, 188, 223; Withey, pp. 300, 353.

HOWE, Gadsden E. (active 1880-1882) Howe was associated with S. Lewis Simons (q.v.) in Charleston as civil engineers, surveyors, and architects.

Sources: Charleston city directories.

HOWE, William B.W. Jr. (active 1883-1911) Howe, son of Right Reverend William Bell White Howe, worked in Charleston in 1883-1891, before relocating to Knoxville, Tennessee. He worked in Knoxville from 1892 to 1894, and had established an engineering and architectural practice in Spartanburg, South Carolina, by 1898. A.C. Olney (q.v.) was associated with Howe from 1898 to 1899.

South Carolina projects:

1883: Vestry Room, St. Michael's Church, Charleston (*News & Courier*, 28 December 1981.)

1884-1885: Charles H. Drayton Residence, 25 East Battery, Charleston (*News & Courier*, 28 December 1981.)

1891: Poppenheim Commercial Building, 363 King Street, Charleston (*News & Courier*, 23 March 1892; 28 December 1981.)

Howe & Olney

1898: C.M. Hinkle Residence, Aiken; $10,000 (*MR*, 10 June 1898, p. 332.)

1898: C.M. Drake Residence, Charleston; $10,000 (*MR*, 10 June 1898, p. 332.)

W.B.W. Howe

1901: School, Spartanburg; $12,000 (*MR*, 13 June 1901, p. 399; 15 August 1901, p. 64.)

1901: T.S. Lease Residence, Spartanburg (*MR*, 13 June 1901, p. 399.)

1901: C.L. O'Neal Residence, Spartanburg (*MR*, 13 June 1901, p. 399.)

1901: H.M. Grimbale Residence, Spartanburg (*MR*, 13 June 1901, p. 399.)

1902: Episcopal Church, Darlington (*MR*, 12 June 1902, p. 385; 19 June 1902, p. 409.)

1902: Merchants' and Farmers' Bank, Spartanburg (*MR*, 29 May 1902, p. 348; 12 June 1902, p. 395.)

1905: Montgomery & Crawford Warehouse, Spartanburg (*MR*, 13 April 1905, p. 282.)

1905: School, Spartanburg; $22,000 (*MR*, 25 May 1905, p. 439; 13 July 1905, p. 612; 20 July 1905, p. 26; 7 September 1905, p. 201.)

1907: Rev. R.S. Nettles, three residences, Spartanburg; $9000 (*MR*, 21 November 1907, p. 63; 28 November 1907, p. 57.)

1908: Fielder & Brown Warehouse, Spartanburg; $10,000 (*MR*, 2 July 1908, p. 71.)

1909: C.H. Buckley Residence, Spartanburg; $3300 (*MR*, 18 February 1909, p. 68.)

Sources: Charleston city directories; Herndon, p. 98; *MR*, various citations; *News & Courier*, 28 December 1981; Spartanburg city directories.

HOWELL, Claude K. (active 1904-1940) Howell was active in the early twentieth century, specializing in the design of theaters. He was described in a 1916 notice as "architect for the Keith Circuit." Theaters designed by Howell have been identified in Richmond, Lynchburg, and Danville, Virginia; in Greensboro, North Carolina; in Thomasville, Americus, Atlanta, Augusta, and Athens, Georgia; and in Charleston and Fort Moultrie, South Carolina. The Towne Theater, a Renaissance-Revival movie palace in Richmond, Virginia (1922) is among Howell's more noteworthy buildings.

Howell's home in these years was variously listed as Charlottesville, Richmond, Savannah, and Atlanta. He was identified as an architect in Richmond by 1904. Howell was associated with Francis W. Scarborough in Richmond in 1908-1912.

South Carolina projects:

1918: Garden Theater, 371 King Street, Charleston; Claude K. Howell and David B. Hyer (q.v.), architects (David Naylor, *Great American Movie Theaters* (Washington, D.C.: The Preservation Press, 1987), p. 112.)

1926: Gloria Theater, King and George streets, Charleston; Claude K. Howell, architect; John D. Newcomer (q.v.), associate architect (*MR*, 20 May 1926, p. 124.)

1928: Theater, Fort Moultrie; $12,000 (*MR*, 26 January 1928, p. 90.)

Sources: Koyl, p. 78; *MR*, various citations; Richmond, Virginia city directories; *Architects and Builders in Georgia.*

HUDDART, John J. (1857- ca. 1918) John J. Huddart, a native of England, had a thriving architectural practice in Denver, Colorado, from ca. 1882 until the early twentieth century. Huddart had traveled in Brazil and Australia, and he began architectural work in Jacksonville, Florida in the 1880s before going to Denver. His work in Denver was primarily in the polychrome Ruskinian Gothic Revival and Richardsonian Romanesque modes. Representative works include the Kinneavy Terrace Building (1889) and the Creswell House (1889) in Denver, and the Swift Building in Pueblo, Colorado (1890.) Huddart was the architect for the 1902 Murchison School, a symmetrical Romanesque-Revival brick building in Bennettsville, South Carolina.

South Carolina project:

1902: Murchison School, Bennettsville; $32,000 (*MR*, 21 April 1902, p. 307; 1 May 1902, p. 269; Cornerstone.)

Sources: Richard R. Brettell, *Historic Denver: The Architects and The Architecture 1858-1893* (Denver, Colorado: Historic Denver, Inc., 1973), pp. 128-135; Langdon E. Morris, Jr., *Denver Landmarks* (Denver, Colorado: Charles W. Cleworth, 1979), pp. 218-219.

HUGER, Frank P. (active 1889-1892) Huger was an associate of S. Lewis Simons (q.v.) in Charleston in 1889-1891. He was identified as a civil engineer in the 1892 Charleston city directory.

South Carolina projects:

See **Simons, S. Lewis** (Simons & Huger)

Sources: Charleston city directories; *MR*, various citations.

HUGGINS, Henry Hartwell (1864-1912) Henry H. Huggins, a native of Darlington, was educated at South Carolina College in civil engineering. He worked as a surveyor and civil engineer in South Carolina and Alabama for several years. In 1891 Huggins joined fellow Darlington County native Charles C. Wilson (q.v.) in opening an architectural office in Roanoke, Virginia. Neither man had substantial architectural education or experience at the time, but they won a number of important commissions. They advertised a specialty in hotels and public buildings.

The partnership with Wilson was dissolved in 1893, and Huggins pursued independent practice in Roanoke. He found a thriving trade, and remained in Roanoke until his mysterious death in 1912. He was found to have been living an alternate life in Richmond, with an alternate name (Johnston) and an alternate wife.

Huggins advertised freely in Roanoke city directories in the later nineteenth and early twentieth centuries. Beneath a picture of the new Hollins Institute Building in the 1900 directory, Huggins paid for the caption "Hollins Institute's fine new building by me. You ought to see this building when finished." In the same directory, he boasted "Roanoke is proud of her school buildings. I planned the four best ones. How's that?" In 1909, the brash Huggins advertised "HURRAH! Roanoke has over 40,000 people, and more of them live in Huggins' designed buildings than in buildings designed by any other twelve architects. A bold assertion, but I can prove it."

South Carolina projects:

1892: See **Wilson, Charles Coker** (Wilson & Huggins)

Sources: *MR*, various citations; Roanoke, Virginia, city directories; Minnie King Thomas, "H.H. Huggins, Early Roanoke's Most Prominent Architect" (unpublished paper, Roanoke, Virginia, 1981); W.L. Whitwell and Lee W. Winborne, *The Architectural Heritage of the Roanoke Valley* (Charlottesville, Virginia: The University Press of Virginia, 1982), pp. 98, 134, 139, 142.

HUGGINS, William J. (active 1911-1913) Huggins was a contractor active in eastern South Carolina. He was identified as an architect on several occasions; and in 1913 he was a partner of architect Leon Hicks (q.v.) in Florence.

South Carolina project:

1911: Dr. W.V. Brockington Residence, Kingstree; $5000 (*MR*, 5 October 1911, p. 81.)

Sources: Florence city directories; *MR*, various citations.

HULME, Norman (1887-1964) Philadelphia architect Norman Hulme, in collaboration with Hewitt & Ash (q.v.), designed the Hampton Terrace Hotel in North Augusta, South Carolina, in 1921. This project, a reconstruction of a burned earlier building, does not appear to have been carried out.

Source: Tatman/Moss, pp. 398-399.

HUNT, Reuben Harrison (1862-1937) Reuben Harrison Hunt was among the region's most prolific architects. He designed churches, courthouses, commercial buildings, and schools across the Southeast, and in many other states. Hunt designs have been identified in all the states of the Confederacy, as well as in Oklahoma and Walla Walla, Washington. He also designed projects in Brazil and in China. Eleven projects by Hunt have been identified in South Carolina.

Hunt was born in Elbert County, Georgia. He worked as a builder, contractor, and carpenter in 1876-1881, studying architecture meanwhile. He moved to Chattanooga, Tennessee, in 1882 and began the practice of architecture in 1885. Hunt pursued a profitable career in Chattanooga over the next fifty years. After 1930 Hunt maintained offices in Dallas, Texas, as well as in Chattanooga. His contributions to Chattanooga were extensive:

> At the time of his death in 1937, most of Chattanooga's public buildings were his designs, including four of the city's five then existing skyscrapers, the City Hall, the Courthouse, the Carnegie Library, the Tivoli Theater, and numerous churches and schools.

Hunt's designs showed great stylistic diversity; his buildings have been categorized as "Gothic Revival, Romanesque Revival, Beaux Arts Classicism, Neo-Classicism, Georgian Revival, and Art Deco." Many of his South Carolina projects, including the Newberry and Greenwood churches and the Magnolia School in Greenwood, are in the Richardsonian Romanesque style.

South Carolina projects:

1894-1901: Central United Methodist Church, Newberry; $12,000 (*MR*, 10 June 1892, p. 45; 2 June 1893 p. 335; 2 March 1894, p. 78; Clifton Graham, *A History of Central United Methodist Church, Newberry, South Carolina* (Newberry: n.p., 1970), p. 4.)

1896-1897: Greenwood County Courthouse, Greenwood (*MR*, 11 December 1896, p. 332; 23 April 1897, p. 232; "R.H. Hunt Architect.")

1898: Presbyterian Church, Greenwood (*Greenwood Index*, 3 February 1898; "R.H. Hunt Architect.")

1903: Magnolia School, Greenwood; $20,000 (*MR*, 9 April 1903, p. 244; 21 May 1903, p. 372; 18 June 1903, p. 447; *Greenwood Index*, 30 April 1903; "R.H. Hunt Architect.")

1903: Williamston Female College Building, Greenwood; $30,000 (*MR*, 21 May 1903, p. 372; 18 June 1903, p. 447; "R.H. Hunt Architect.")

1913: Sunday School Building and repairs to Present Building, First Baptist Church, Greenville;

R.H. Hunt, architect; H. Olin Jones (q.v.), supervising architect (*MR*, 25 December 1913, p. 64.)

1924-1925: Sunday School Building, remodeling of Smith Memorial Chapel, and remodeling of Main Auditorium, First Presbyterian Church, Marion Street, Columbia; $250,000; R.H. Hunt, architect; Lafaye & Lafaye (q.v.), supervising architects (*MR*, 30 October 1924, p. 90; 27 November, p. 96; 2 July 1925, p. 128; 6 August 1925, p. 121.)

n.d.: Methodist Church, Laurens ("R.H. Hunt Architect.")

n.d.: Graded School, Spartanburg ("R.H. Hunt Architect.")

n.d.: Duncan Business Block, Spartanburg ("R.H. Hunt Architect.")

n.d.: Y.M.C.A. Building, Columbia (Biography File, Chattanooga Public Library.)

Sources: Biography File, Chattanooga-Hamilton County Bicentennial Library, Chattanooga, Tennessee; M.A. Carver, "Buildings in Hamilton County Designed by R.H. Hunt," National Register Nomination, Chattanooga-Hamilton County Regional Planning Commission, Chattanooga, 1979; Chattanooga city directories; Herndon, pp. 99-100; "R.H. Hunt, Widely Known Architect, Dies," *The Chattanooga News*, 28 May 1937; "R.H. Hunt Architect," (list of works,) *Chattanooga Star*, 31 August 1909; *MR*, various citations; Withey, pp. 309-310.

HUNTER, James E. Jr. (active 1920-1932) James E. Hunter Jr. was first listed in the Columbia city directories in 1918, as a member of the U.S. Marines. He was a draftsman with architect J. Carroll Johnson (q.v.) from 1920-1921, and with Harold Tatum (q.v.) from 1922 through 1929. He was described as an architect from 1925 through 1929, and he was registered as an architect in 1929.

In 1930 Hunter was identified as a draftsman with the Columbia Blue Print Company. He returned to Johnson's office in 1931. In later years Hunter was clerk of the State House of Representatives.

Sources: Columbia city directories; Julie Turner, S.C. Department of Archives & History, Columbia, to John E. Wells, 8 September 1988.

HUNTER, Leonard LeGrande (active 1903-1926) Hunter was a partner of James M. McMichael (q.v.) in Charlotte, North Carolina, in 1903-1904. He was later associated with S. Luther Vaughan (1907-1908), with Franklin Gordon (1909-1918), and with Nat G. Walker (q.v.) (1925-1926.)

South Carolina projects:

1903-1904: See **McMichael, James M.** (McMichael & Hunter)

Hunter & Vaughan

1908: Associate Reformed Presbyterian Church, Spartanburg; $8000 (*MR*, 23 July 1908, p. 55; 13 August 1908, p. 58.)

L.L. Hunter

1921: R.S. Lipscomb Residence, Petty Street and Rutledge Avenue, Gaffney; $14,000 (*MR*, 3 November 1921, p. 112.)

Sources: Charlotte, North Carolina city directories; *MR*, various citations.

HYER, David B. (active 1905-1942) David B. Hyer practiced as a civil engineer in Charleston in 1905. He was employed as a superintendent of construction at the Charleston Navy Yard in 1908, and afterwards worked for the Simons-Mayrant Company (q.v.) Hyer joined the firm of Todd & Benson, Architects (q.v.) by 1912, and he opened his own architectural practice in Charleston later that same year.

Hyer's practice was concentrated in Charleston, and included the remodeling of several existing buildings. The $180,000 vocational school building on Chisholm Street, contracted in 1922, was among Hyer's largest projects.

Hyer evidently opened a branch office in Orlando, Florida, in the 1920s. He was still listed in the Charleston city directories in these years. Buildings designed by Hyer in Winter Haven and Orlando, Florida, were described in the *MR* in 1929.

Hyer's widow, Sally Hyer, is listed in the 1948 Charleston city directory.

South Carolina projects:

1912: Addition, Southern Fruit Company Building, Charleston; $7000 (*MR*, 6 June 1912, p. 90.)

1912: Southeastern Warehouse Company Warehouse, Concord and Hasell streets, Charleston; $40,000 (*MR*, 4 July 1912, p. 87; 1 August 1912, p. 86.)

1913: Oriole W. Nohrden two-family residence, Charleston; $5000 (*MR*, 20 March 1913, p. 70.)

1914: W.B. Cohen Residence, Charleston; $10,000 (*MR*, 17 December 1914, p. 57.)

1915: Remodeling and addition, Crafts School, Legare Street, Charleston; $27,000 (*MR*, 13 May 1915, p. 62; 3 June 1915, p. 69.)

1915: J.A. Storfer, two residences, Gibbes Street, Charleston (*MR*, 18 November 1915, p. 66.)

1916: Pastime Amusement Co. Moving-Picture Theater, King Street, Charleston; $100,000 (*MR*, 2 March 1916, p. 77.)

1916: Remodeling, I. Silver & Brother Co. Building, King Street, Charleston; $20,000 (*MR*, 2 March 1916, p. 77; 9 March 1916, p. 70; 16 November 1916, p. 70; 30 November 1916, p. 66.)

1916: Remodeling, Old Library Building, Charleston; $3674 (*MR*, 9 March 1916, p. 69.)

1916: A. Kroeg, Jr. Residence, Charleston; $7500 (*MR*, 11 May 1916, p. 67.)

1916: Addition, General Asbestos & Rubber Company Building, 27 Cumberland Street, Charleston; $7500 (*MR*, 16 November 1916, p. 69.)

1916: Silver Brothers Store, Columbia; $19,000 (*MR*, 16 November 1916, p. 70; 30 November 1916, p. 66.)

1917: Mrs. Emma Bohlen Residence, Charleston; $6500 (*MR*, 22 March 1917, p. 71.)

1917: Rutledge Avenue Baptist Church, Charleston; $22,000 (*MR*, 20 September 1917, p. 86.)

1917: Kiawato Club Clubhouse, Seabrook Island; $6000 (*MR*, 6 September 1917, p. 95; 13 September 1917, p. 77.)

1918: Victory Housing Corp., eighteen residences, Charleston; $71,250 (*MR*, 5 September 1918, p. 99.)

1918: Y.W.C.A. Building, Society Street, Charleston; $91,000 (*MR*, 19 September 1918, p. 94; 19 December 1918, p. 84.)

1918: Garden Theater, 371 King Street, Charleston; David B. Hyer and Claude K. Howell (q.v.), architects (David Naylor, *Great American Movie Theaters* (Washington, D.C.: The Preservation Press, 1987), p. 112.)

1919: Reconstruction, Grace Episcopal Church, Charleston (*MR*, 14 August 1919, p. 124.)

1919: H.J. Harby Apartment Building, Sumter; $80,000 (*MR*, 4 December 1919, p. 173.)

1920: Farmers' and Merchants' Bank Building, Andrews (*MR*, 15 January 1920, p. 152 i.)

1920: Kerrison Dry Goods Store Building, Charleston (*MR*, 19 February 1920, p. 148.)

1920: Parish House, St. John's Lutheran Church, Charleston (*MR*, 26 February 1920, p. 147.)

1920: Jas. F. Condon & Son Building, Charleston (*MR*, 3 June 1920, p. 183.)

1920: Remodeling, Y.W.C.A. Building, Charleston (*MR*, 3 June 1920, pp. 181-182.)

1920: Remodeling, Mercy Maternity Hospital, Charleston (*MR*, 3 June 1920, p. 182.)

1920: Buist Grade School, Calhoun Street, Charleston; $100,000; D.B. Hyer, architect; James Betelle (q.v.), consulting architect (*MR*, 3 June 1920, p. 183.)

1920: S. Hirschman & Son Warehouse, East Bay Street, Charleston (*MR*, 5 August 1920, p. 165.)

1920: Addition, Medical College, Locust and Mills streets, Charleston; $55,000 (*MR*, 19 August 1920, p. 138.)

1920: W.J. Condon Residence, Charleston; $50,000 (*MR*, 4 November 1920, p. 184.)

1920: Port City Bank Building, North Charleston (*MR*, 11 March 1920, p. 147.)

1921: St. Barnabas Lutheran Church Building, Rutledge Avenue and Moultrie Street, Charleston (*MR*, 3 March 1921, p. 163.)

1921: Remodeling, Commercial National Bank, Charleston (*MR*, 15 September 1921, p. 88.)

1922: A. Marion Stone Residence, South Battery and Rutledge Avenue, Charleston; $12,900 (*MR*, 19 January 1922, p. 76 g.)

1922: Vocational School, Chisholm Street, Charleston; $180,000 (*MR*, 21 September 1922, p. 93.)

1922: First National Bank, Holly Hill; $25,000 (*MR*, 6 April 1922, p. 123.)

1922: School, North Charleston; $46,000 (*MR*, 13 April 1922, p. 78.)

1923: Improvements, Crafts School, Legare Street, Charleston; $7237 (*MR*, 19 April 1923, p. 100.)

1923: Janitor's Lodge, Vocational School, Chisholm Street, Charleston (*MR*, 4 October 1923, p. 125.)

1923: Six Units at Home for Aged Presbyterian Women, Meeting and Huger streets, Charleston; $46,000 (*MR*, 2 August 1923, p. 150.)

1923: School, Georgetown; $50,000 (*MR*, 8 November 1923, p. 112.)

1941: Addition, Charleston County Courthouse, Broad and Meeting streets, Charleston (*News & Courier*, 30 November 1981, pp. 1-B, 12-B.)

Sources: *American Art Annual*, Vol. 21, p. 416; Charleston city directories; *MR*, various citations.

IRVIN, Willis (1890-1950) Willis Irvin of Augusta, Georgia won regional acclaim as a designer of elegant rural estates in the mid-twentieth century. His obituary stated that Irvin "is best known for his designing of some of the magnificent estates of South Carolina's tidewater area in the state's lowcountry."

Irvin was born at Washington, Georgia, and studied architecture at Georgia Tech. He worked as a draftsman for architects Harry Leslie Walker of Atlanta; Hyman W. Witcover of Savannah (q.v.); and G. Lloyd Preacher of Augusta (q.v.) In 1917 Irvin was associated with Haralson Bleckley in Augusta.

Irvin's daughter Helen Stuart Irvin Dowling joined his office in the 1940s. She continued the practice after her father's death.

South Carolina projects:

1920-1921: High School, Graniteville (*MR*, 30 December 1920, p. 92; *Selections from the Work.*)

1922: Addition, Highland Park Hotel, Aiken (*MR*, 20 July 1922, p. 83; 27 July 1922, p. 78.)

1923: Aiken County Jail, Aiken; $25,259 (Cornerstone; *MR*, 14 June 1923, p. 113 m.)

1923: Sunday School Building, St. Thaddeus Episcopal Church, Aiken (*MR*, 16 August 1923, p. 115.)

1923: High School, Clio; $42,000 (*MR*, 29 March 1923, p. 102; 5 April 1923, p. 122.)

1924: Dr. R.H. Wildes Residence, Hayne Avenue, Aiken; $40,600; Leslie W. Devereux (q.v.), architect; Willis Irvin, supervising architect (*MR*, 12 June 1924, p. 111; 19 June 1924, p. 116.)

1924: Baptist Church, Williston; $40,000 (*MR*, 28 February 1924, p. 118; 15 May 1924, p. 124; 19 June 1924, p. 115; 26 June 1924, p. 111.)

1924: First Presbyterian Church, Aiken; $38,000 (*MR*, 10 July 1924, p. 103.)

1925: Consolidated High School, Williston; $52,500 (*MR*, 30 April 1925, p. 125.)

1925: Baptist Church, Barnwell; $40,000 (*MR*, 17 December 1925, p. 106.)

1925: School, Blacksburg; $72,000 (*MR*, 22 October 1925, p. 104.)

1926: Miss Sara Peet Residence, Aiken; $20,000 (*MR*, 1 April 1926, p. 130.)

1926: School, Allendale; $71,000 (*MR*, 12 August 1926, p. 98.)

1926: Addition, Eugene Grace Residence, Barnwell (*MR*, 17 June 1926, p. 109.)

1927: C.M. Bishop Residence, S. Boundary Street, Aiken; $30,000 (*MR*, 18 August 1927, p. 123.)

1927: Mrs. M.E. Chaffee Residence, Whiskey Road, Aiken; $35,000 (*MR*, 18 August 1927, p. 123.)

1927: Judge J. Henry Johnson Residence, Allendale (*MR*, 11 August 1927, p. 111.)

1927: Baptist Church, Bamberg; $60,000 (*MR*, 24 February 1927, p. 105.)

1927: Solomon Blatt Residence, Barnwell (*MR*, 11 August 1927, p. 111; 18 August 1927, p. 123.)

1927: Two overseers' residences, Graniteville Manufacturing Co., Graniteville; $14,000 (*MR*, 19 May 1927, p. 111.)

1928: S.G. Flagg Residence, Aiken; $25,521 (*MR*, 3 May 1928, p. 118.)

1928: "Whitehall," Col. Robt. R. McCormick Residence, Aiken; $60,000 (*MR*, 17 May 1928, p. 93; *Selections from the Work*.)

1928: William Zeigler Residence, Aiken; $100,000 (*MR*, 14 June 1928, p. 103; *Selections from the Work*.)

1928: Addition and remodeling, J. Oscar Williams Residence, Aiken; $15,698 (*MR*, 19 July 1928, p. 93.)

1928: Remodeling, Julian B. Salley Residence, Aiken (*MR*, 2 August 1928, p. 101; *Selections from the Work*.)

1929: Mrs. R.S. Linsley Residence, Aiken; $36,500 (*MR*, 20 June 1929, p. 91.)

1929: Hotel Henderson, Aiken; $150,000 (*MR*, 13 June 1929, p. 88; *Selections from the Work*.)

1929: Jas. G. Campbell Hunting Lodge, Allendale (*MR*, 18 July 1929, p. 98.)

1929: H.N. Forrester Residence, Sumter; $25,000 (*MR*, 19 September 1929, p. 97.)

1930: First Presbyterian Church, Clinton; $63,000 (*MR*, 26 June 1930, p. 79; *Selections from the Work*.)

1930: Aiken County Hospital, Aiken (*Selections from the Work*.)

Ca. 1930: W.R. Comfort Residence, Aiken (*Southern Architect and Building News*, January 1930.)

Ca. 1930: William Dominick Residence, Yemassee (*Southern Architect and Building News*, January 1930.)

1931: Mrs. Gustavo L.F.G. di Rosa Residence, Aiken; $50,000 (*MR*, 16 April 1931, p. 59.)

1931: Richard Howe Residence, Aiken; $75,000 (*MR*, 16 July 1931, p. 51; 30 July 1931, p. 52; *Selections from the Work*.)

1934: Remodeling, Aiken County Courthouse, Aiken (National Register files, S.C. Archives.)

1946-1949: Remodeling, Rose Hill Plantation House (John Sturgeon Residence), Bluffton (National Register files, S.C. Archives.)

n.d.: High School, Aiken (*Selections from the Work*.)

n.d.: Bayard Dominick Residence, Coosawatchie (*Selections from the Work*.)

n.d.: Henry W. Corning Residence, Grays Hill (*Selections from the Work*; "Gold Seeds Planted.")

n.d.: A.H. Caspary Residence, Ritter (*Selections from the Work*.)

n.d.: John S. Williams Residence, Yemassee (*Selections from the Work*.)

n.d.: James L. Coker Residence, Hartsville (*Selections from the Work*.)

n.d.: C.K. Dunlap Residence, Hartsville (*Selections from the Work*.)

Sources: Augusta, Georgia, city directories; Willis Irvin, Jr., "Gold Seeds Planted in 1865 Germinate in South Today," *Southern Antiques and the Southeast Trader*, Lake City, Florida, February 1985, pp. 1, 10-A; Willis Irvin, Sr., *Selections from the Work of Willis Irvin, Architect, Augusta, Georgia* (New York: Architectural Catalog Co., Inc., 1937); "Willis Irvin, Sr., Architect of Aiken, Dies," *The State*, 9 August 1950, p. 11-A; *MR*, various citations; *Southern Architect and Building News*, January 1930, pp. 36-43; *Who's Who in the South*, 1927, p. 384.

JEFFREYS, J.E. (active 1891) J.E. Jeffreys was described as the architect of the Yorkville Enquirer Building in Yorkville in 1891.

Source: *MR*, 2 May 1891, p. 45.

JENKINS, Edward E. Jr. (active 1886) Edward E. Jenkins Jr. was associated with Lewis R. Gibbes (q.v.) in Charleston. The firm advertised as architects and civil engineers in the 1886 Charleston city directory.

JOHANNSEN, Heinrich H. (active 1898-1918) Heinrich H. Johannsen, an architect, engineer, and contractor, was active in Georgia and South Carolina in the late 19th and early 20th centuries. He was associated with Joseph F. Leitner (q.v.) in Augusta, Georgia, in 1898. Johannsen located in Charleston, South Carolina, in 1902; and by 1911 he had moved his practice to Orangeburg. Johannsen was architect and contractor for the 1911 Exhibition Building at the Orangeburg County Fair. This structure, which includes a sheltered grandstand, is distinguished by its curvilinear parapets.

South Carolina projects:

1911: Orangeburg County Fair Exhibition Building, U.S. Highway 21, Orangeburg; $8000 (*MR*, 7 September 1911, p. 77; *Times and Democrat*, Orangeburg, 19 September 1911.)

1912: School, Norway; $8000 (*MR*, 12 September 1912, p. 67)

Sources: Augusta, Georgia, city directories; Charleston city directories; *MR*, various citations.

JOHNSON, John Carroll (1882-1967) J. Carroll Johnson practiced architecture in Columbia for over fifty years. He maintained a small office for most of his career, concentrating on residential work. Aside from his work for the University of South Carolina, Johnson rarely won major commissions.

Johnson was born in Christianstad, Sweden, on 9 November 1882. He came to the United States at age 3. He worked in the architectural office of Jenny & Mundie in Chicago for two years before entering the Armour Institute of Technology in Chicago; he received a B.S. degree in 1906. Johnson accepted a position with the Washington, D.C., architects Wood, Donn & Deming in 1906. He pursued his architectural education at the University of Pennsylvania in these years as well, earning a second degree in 1908. Johnson worked with the Taft Inaugural Decoration Committee in 1908-1909, and he is said to have designed the inaugural stand.

In 1910 Johnson came to Columbia, South Carolina, and entered the office of Charles Coker Wilson (q.v.), Edwin D. Sompayrac (q.v.), and James Burwell Urquhart (q.v.) Johnson was chief designer for the firm from 1910 to 1912.

Urquhart left Wilson's office in 1910 to open his own office in Columbia. In 1912 Johnson became Urquhart's partner, and the firm enjoyed a period of prosperity which lasted until the First World War. The partnership was dissolved in 1917, and both Urquhart and Johnson pursued independent practice in Columbia.

Johnson maintained his practice in Columbia from 1918 into the 1960s. James E. Hunter, Jr. (q.v.) worked for Johnson as a draftsman in 1920-1921 and again in 1931. From 1938 to 1942 Johnson was associated with Jesse W. Wessinger (q.v.) in Columbia as Wessinger & Johnson.

Wyatt Hibbs, an architect active in Columbia in 1935-1940, described Johnson in this period:

> J. Carroll Johnson was a capable architect-designer. . . I do not believe he profited from the prosperity most of the architects enjoyed from the distribution of government funded projects. . . [Johnson] had a miserable office with an iron stove for heating, on the second floor over a Main Street store.

Johnson designed several buildings at the University of South Carolina between 1924 to 1952, and he served as university architect from 1944 through 1956. Johnson had done earlier work at the University in 1910-1912 as chief designer for Charles C. Wilson, the university architect in those years.

South Carolina projects:

1912-1917: See **Urquhart, James Burwell** (Urquhart & Johnson)

1917: Mrs. William S. Hendley Residence, 1803 Catawba Avenue, Columbia (Johnson.)

1917: E.S. Mather Residence, 136 Edisto Avenue, Columbia (Johnson.)

1918: State Industrial School for Girls, Columbia; Ludlow & Peabody (q.v.), architects; J. Carroll Johnson, associate architect (*MR*, 3 October 1918, p. 107.)

1918: John T. Stevens Residence, 225 W. Richland, Kershaw (Koyl; Johnson.)

1919: W.T. Derieux Residence, Columbia; $11,000 (*MR*, 31 July 1919, p. 124.)

1919: R.C. Shane Residence, 1820 Seneca Avenue, Columbia (Johnson.)

1920: First Presbyterian Church, Richland and Cleveland streets, Kershaw (Johnson.)

1922: Mill Village Graded School, Negro School, and High School, Lancaster; $158,000 (*MR*, 21 September 1922, p. 93.)

1923: J.M. Herron Residence, Bishopville; $40,000 (*MR*, 22 November 1923, p. 99.)

1923: Sunday School, Presbyterian Church, Camden; $12,911 (*MR*, 21 June 1924, p. 122.)

1924: Addition, Taylor Street School, Columbia; $45,963 (*MR*, 27 March 1924, p. 122.)

1924: Alterations and Repairs, Gymnasium and Harper College, University of South Carolina, Columbia (*MR*, 19 June 1924, p. 118.)

1924: J. Carroll Johnson Residence, 102 Southwood Drive, Columbia (Johnson.)

1925: Reconstruction, Lebanon Methodist Church, Columbia (*MR*, 2 April 1925, p. 134.)

1926: Field House, University of South Carolina, Columbia; $30,000 (*MR*, 16 September 1926, p. 121; Johnson.)

1927: Physics and Engineering Departments Classroom Building (Sloan College), University of South Carolina, Columbia; $75,000 (*MR*, 6 January 1927, p. 143; Johnson.)

1928: Addition and Remodeling, South Caroliniana Library, University of South Carolina, Columbia; $30,000 (*MR*, 12 July 1928, p. 93; Johnson.)

1928: Melton Observatory, University of South Carolina, Columbia (Johnson.)

1928: Robert W. Cain Residence, 105 Saluda Avenue, Columbia (Johnson.)

1929: Dr. Robert Emmett Seibels Residence, 21 Heathwood Circle, Columbia; $40,000 (*MR*, 10 January 1929, p. 115; Johnson.)

1931: Wardlaw College, University of South Carolina, Columbia; $300,000 (*MR*, 1 January 1931, p. 52.)

1931: University High School, Columbia (Johnson; Koyl.)

1938-1942: See **Wessinger, Jesse W.** (Wessinger & Johnson)

1945: Seibels Residence, Columbia (Koyl.)

1948: West End Elementary School, Union; $106,741 (*Construction*, January 1948, p. 61.)

1950: Petigru College, University of South Carolina, Columbia; Simons & Lapham (q.v.), architects; J. Carroll Johnson, supervising architect (Johnson.)

1950: Ramsing Residence, Salem Cross Roads (Johnson.)

1951: Rutledge L. Osborne Administration Building, University of South Carolina, Columbia (Johnson; plaque on building.)

1952: LeConte College, University of South Carolina, Columbia (Johnson; plaque on building.)

1955: Engineering Building, University of South Carolina, Columbia; Lyles, Bissett, Carlisle & Wolfe, architects; J. Carroll Johnson, associate architect (Johnson.)

1959: Jack S. Graybill Residence, 4334 Chicora, Columbia (Johnson.)

1961: J.J. Baker Residence, Mohawk Street and Saluda River Drive, Columbia (Johnson.)

1961: S. Taylor Garnett Residence, 2 Heathwood Circle, Columbia (Johnson.)

1961: J. Bruce Green Residence, Lake Murray, South Carolina (Johnson.)

1961: Dwight Grimsley Residence, Ridge Lane, Columbia (Johnson.)

1962: Bert Arnold Residence, Overcreek Road, Columbia (Johnson.)

n.d.: Ridgewood Club (Geddings.)

n.d.: First National Bank, Camden (Geddings.)

n.d.: Dr. L.W. Blackmon Residence, 9 Glenlake Road, Columbia (Johnson.)

n.d.: Darnall W. Boyd Residence, 1609 Milford Road, Columbia (Johnson.)

n.d.: Charles J. Cate Residence, 1828 Green Street, Columbia (Johnson.)

n.d.: W.H. Caughman Residence, 1809 Heyward Street, Columbia (Johnson.)

n.d.: Stanley Donen Residence, Wales Garden, Columbia (Johnson.)

n.d.: Dr. Hugh H. DuBose Residence, 5001 Courtney Road, Columbia (Johnson.)

n.d.: Frank N. Erlich Residence, 2330 Terrace Way, Columbia (Johnson.)

n.d.: R. Beverley Herbert, Jr., Residence, 329 Edisto Avenue, Columbia (Johnson.)

n.d.: Mrs. Elizabeth Hicklin Residence, 2920 Gervais Street, Columbia (Johnson.)

n.d.: H.W. Hoefer Residence, 1429 Adger Road, Columbia (Johnson.)

n.d.: Arthur L. Humphries Residence, 3631 Devereaux Road, Columbia (Johnson.)

n.d.: Jeff Hunt Residence, 142 Edisto Avenue, Columbia (Johnson.)

n.d.: Shepherd Jones Residence, 3704 Linwood Street, Columbia (Johnson.)

n.d.: Irwin Kahn Residence, 3811 Kilbourne Road, Columbia (Johnson.)

n.d.: Mrs. D.A. Macaulay Residence, 2300 Wheat Street, Columbia (Johnson.)

n.d.: Dr. Neil W. Macaulay Residence, 12 Clement Road, Columbia (Johnson.)

n.d.: Carl J. Niggel Building, 4130 Blossom Street, Columbia (Johnson.)

n.d.: Carl J. Niggel Building, 20 Woodhill Circle, Columbia (Johnson.)

n.d.: Mrs. Niggel Residence, 830 Cross Hill Road, Columbia (Johnson.)

n.d.: Dean Norwood Residence, 811 Albion Road, Columbia (Johnson.)

n.d.: G. Trezevant Pressley Residence, 915 Gregg Street, Columbia (Johnson.)

n.d.: George B. Rawls Residence, 224 S. Gregg Street, Columbia (Johnson.)

n.d.: Dr. Robert Emmett Seibels Residence, 2818 Canterbury Road, Columbia (Johnson.)

n.d.: Scott C. Strohecker and Frank C. Robinson Residence, 1722 Hollywood Drive, Columbia (Johnson.)

n.d.: Robert L. Sumwalt Residence, 1420 Belmont Drive, Columbia (Johnson.)

n.d.: Benjamin F. Taylor Residence, 1619 Green Street, Columbia (Johnson.)

n.d.: Charles Todd Residence, 1306 Greenhill Road, Columbia (Johnson.)

n.d.: John S. Walker Residence, 1415 Heatherwood Road, Columbia (Johnson.)

n.d.: Joseph Walker Residence, Saluda Avenue, Columbia (Johnson.)

n.d.: Dr. C. Tucker Weston Residence, 1548 Kathwood, Columbia (Johnson.)

n.d.: Dr. James F. Williamson Residence, 720 Albion Road, Columbia (Johnson.)

n.d.: John Bollin et.al. Building, 1834 Heyward Street, Columbia (Johnson.)

n.d.: James L. Coker Residence, 210 E. Home Avenue, Hartsville (Johnson.)

n.d.: William Coxe Residence, 110 N. Myrtle, Darlington (Johnson.)

n.d.: John Ray Efird Residence, N. Ocean Drive and 33rd Avenue, Myrtle Beach (Johnson.)

n.d.: Philip Washington Fairey/Joseph Fairey Jr. Residence, Calhoun County (Johnson.)

n.d.: Floyd's Brace Co., Inc. Building, 243 Calhoun Street, Charleston (Johnson.)

n.d.: Miss Etta B. Skipper Residence, 303 W. Dunlap Street, Lancaster (Johnson.)

n.d.: Methodist Parsonage, Orangeburg (Johnson.)

n.d.: Eugene Moses Residence, Sumter (Johnson.)

n.d.: Pergola, T. English McCutcheon Residence, Bishopville (Johnson.)

Sources: Columbia city directories; *The Columbia Record*, Columbia, 21 December 1913, p. 6; Geddings, pp. 92-93; Wyatt Hibbs, Norfolk,

Virginia, to John E. Wells, 19 October 1983; Dorothy C. Johnson, Columbia, South Carolina, unpublished research; Koyl, p. 279; *MR*, various citations.

JOHNSON, James Herbert (active 1907-1957)

James H. Johnson pursued a modest architectural practice in South Carolina and Florida in 1907-1957. Little is known of his early life. An architectural firm called Timmons & Johnson was active in Sumter in 1907; James H. Johnson is believed to have been a partner in this firm. He is first positively identified in 1910, as the architect of two store buildings in Sumter.

Johnson designed a number of residences, stores, and public buildings in central South Carolina in the ensuing years. He worked in association with Rock Hill architect Nat G. Walker (q.v.) on three large projects in 1915-1916. In the years 1915-1921 Johnson was the partner of Fred H. Deal (q.v.)

Around 1923 Johnson relocated to Bradenton, Florida. His Florida practice appears to have been lucrative. One large project was the "Spanish type" Palma Sola Country Club Building in Bradenton, which was contracted at $60,000 in 1924.

Johnson returned to South Carolina around 1930, making his home at Aiken, where he was still active in 1955.

South Carolina projects:

1907: See _____ **Timmons** (Timmons & Johnson)

1910: Wilson & Rowland, Two Store Buildings, Sumter (*MR*, 23 June 1910, p. 71.)

1911: William M. Reid Residence, 201 W. Ridge Street, Bishopville; $4500 (*MR*, 24 August 1911, p. 66; 31 August 1911, p. 66.)

1912: Realty Holding Co. Store Building, Sumter; $9000 (*MR*, 6 June 1912, p. 90; 13 June 1912, p. 72.)

1915: Girls' High School and Auditorium, W. Liberty Street, Sumter; Nat G. Walker (q.v.) and James Herbert Johnson, associated architects; $21,650 (*MR*, 16 September 1915, p. 67; 30 September 1915, p. 59.)

1916: E.W. Tisdale Residence, 529 N. Main Street, Bishopville; $18,000 (*MR*, 26 October 1916, p. 66.)

Johnson & Deal

1916: Neill O'Donnell Store Building, Sumter; Nat G. Walker and Johnson & Deal, associated architects; $25,175 (*MR*, 30 March 1916, p. 67; 6 April 1916, p. 83.)

1916: Carnegie Library, Sumter; Nat G. Walker (q.v.) and Johnson & Deal, associated architects; $7500 (*MR*, 22 June 1916, p. 68; 13 July 1916, p. 65; George S. Bobinski, *Carnegie Libraries: Their History and Impact on American Public Library Development* (Chicago: American Library Association, 1969), p. 237.)

1917: T.E. McCutcheon Residence, 120 S. Heyward Street, Bishopville (*MR*, 19 April 1917, p. 74 n.)

1917: W.G. Deschamps Residence, Bishopville; $3000 (*MR*, 19 April 1917, p. 74 n.)

1917: School, Bishopville; $20,000 (*MR*, 11 October 1917, p. 78.)

1918: Sunday School Building, First Presbyterian Church, Sumter (*MR*, 8 August 1918, p. 78.)

1921: School, Clyde; $11,000 (*MR*, 15 September 1921, p. 89; 22 September 1921, p. 85.)

James Herbert Johnson

1928: Henry W. Busc Residence, Aiken (*MR*, 13 December 1928, p. 109.)

1930: School, Windsor; $27,000 (*MR*, 30 January 1930, p. 76; 6 February 1930, p. 100.)

Sources: Koyl, p. 279; *MR*, various citations; Petty, p. 143.

JOHNSON, Stanhope S. (1882-1973) Stanhope S. Johnson was a prominent architect of Lynchburg, Virginia, and the designer of many buildings in Georgia, Florida, and the Carolinas during a long practice. He was born in Lynchburg in 1882, and was working for Lynchburg architect Edward B. Frye at age 17. Johnson became a partner in the firm of McLaughlin, Pettit & Johnson by 1909, and he commenced independent architectural practice in 1917. For a short period in the late 1920s he was allied with Ray O. Brannan (q.v.) in Lynchburg.

Johnson's primary architectural language was Georgian Revival, but he was also fluent in the Art Deco and Art Moderne of the 1920s and 1930s. His Allied Arts Building in Lynchburg, built in 1929-1931, is a 17-story modernist skyscraper comparable to the Hugh Ferris and Eliel Saarinen compositions. Johnson's *oeuvre* includes several large hotels in North Carolina, South Carolina, and Virginia, built in the 1920s.

The 1928-1929 Ocean Forest Hotel, designed by Johnson & Brannan and built in Myrtle Beach, was the firm's greatest work in South Carolina. The ten-story building, described as "Georgian-Colonial" in contemporary notices, had some two hundred twenty guest rooms. It dominated the Atlantic shoreline for many years before its demolition in the 1970s.

South Carolina projects:

Johnson & Brannan

1928: Myrtle Beach Estate Clubhouse (Ocean Forest Clubhouse), Myrtle Beach; $130,000 (*MR*, 10 May 1928, p. 94; Chambers, unpublished research.)

1928-1929: Ocean Forest Hotel, Myrtle Beach; $1,200,000 (*MR*, 21 June 1928, p. 96; 9 August 1928, p. 58; Chambers, unpublished research.)

1928: Dr. George R. Wilkinson Residence, Cleveland Park, Greenville; $25,000 (*MR*, 9 August 1928, p. 88; Chambers, unpublished research.)

Sources: S. Allen Chambers, Jr., *Lynchburg: An Architectural History* (Charlottesville,

Virginia: The University Press of Virginia, 1981), pp. 359, 412, 432, 440-444; S. Allen Chambers, Jr., Washington, D.C., unpublished research; Lynchburg Architectural Archive, Jones Memorial Library, Lynchburg, Virginia; *MR*, various citations.

JOHNSON, U.H. (active 1904) U.H. Johnson of Wilmington, North Carolina, was identified as the architect for the $10,000 Atlantic Coast Line Railway passenger station in Marion, South Carolina, in 1904. The A.C.L. had its headquarters in Wilmington, and it is presumed that Johnson was a railroad employee.

Sources: *MR*, 4 August 1904, p. 62; 11 August 1904, p. 84.

JONES, Clarence T. (1879-1951) Clarence Jones, a native of Frankfort, Kentucky, studied electrical engineering at the University of Cincinnati and at Ohio Mechanical Institute. He worked as a draftsman for Samuel Hannaford & Sons in Cincinnati for several years. Jones came to Columbia, South Carolina, about 1903 to work for architect Frank Pierce Milburn (q.v.). Jones entered the office of Gadsden Shand and George Lafaye (q.v.) in 1905 and remained with this firm for five years.

Jones moved to Chattanooga, Tennessee, in 1910, where he associated with John G. Barnwell (q.v.). Barnwell had also worked in Columbia, South Carolina, in the early 1900s. Barnwell & Jones, working in association with F.H. and J.G. Cunningham (q.v.), designed the James Finlay Store and Office Building in Greenville, South Carolina, in 1912. The partnership with Barnwell ended in 1915, and Jones pursued a profitable architectural practice in Chattanooga until his death in 1951.

Astronomy was the architect's avocation; he was one of the best-known amateur astronomers in the nation. He designed observatory buildings at Vanderbilt and at the University of Tennessee, Chattanooga; the latter is now called the Clarence T. Jones Observatory.

Sources: Zella Armstrong, *The History of Hamilton County and Chattanooga, Tennessee* (Chattanooga: Lookout Publishing Co., 1940), Vol. II, pp. 229-231; Chattanooga, Tennessee, city directories; *Chattanooga Times*, Chattanooga, Tennessee, 30 January 1924, p. 4; 31 July 1951, p. 1; Columbia city directories; Philip M. Hamer, *Tennessee, A History, 1673-1932* (New York: American Historical Society, Inc., 1933), Vol. 4, p. 760; Herndon, p. 104; *MR*, various citations; *Who's Who in the South*, 1927, p. 400.

JONES, H. Olin (1880-1941) Henry Olin Jones, son of William Baylis and Mary Josephine Jones, was born 30 October 1880 at Elberton, Georgia. He was educated at Emory College in Atlanta, graduating in 1901. Jones was working as an engineer in Greenville, South Carolina, by 1909.

Jones secured a position in the Greenville office of Joseph Emory Sirrine (q.v.) by 1912. He opened his own office in Greenville the next year. Jones pursued a moderately successful career in Greenville and the surrounding communities until 1941. From 1921 to 1926 Henry R. Trott (q.v.) was an associate of Jones; the firm was called Jones & Trott, Inc. Trott established his own practice in Greenville by 1929.

Prominent among Jones's designs were the central building of the Greenville City Hospital, 1918-1919, and the five-story Fair Forest Hotel in Union, 1923-1926. The Fair Forest still dominates Union's Main Street. In 1916-1917 Jones was the supervising architect for the new Greenville County Courthouse, working under the direction of prominent Atlanta architect Philip Thornton Marye (q.v.)

When the South Carolina Board of Architectural Examiners was created by legislative action in 1917, Governor Richard Ira Manning appointed Jones and four other architects to the Board. Walter Petty described the curious circumstances of Jones's departure from the Board:

> Mr. H. Olin Jones, an original Board member, who had served continuously since 1917, suddenly disappeared from the State shortly after the July, 1941 meeting, and all efforts to locate his whereabouts proved of no avail.

South Carolina projects:

1913: School, Greenville; $5000 (*MR*, 16 October 1913, p. 68 c.)

1913: Sunday School Building and repairs to Auditorium, First Baptist Church, Greenville; $33,000; R.H. Hunt (q.v.), architect; H. Olin Jones, supervising architect (*MR*, 25 December 1913, p. 64.)

1914: Dr. W.M. Burnett Residence, Park Avenue, Greenville; $3800 (*MR*, 1 October 1914, p. 70.)

1915: Greenville Amusement Co. Moving Picture Theater, Greenville; $14,000 (*MR*, 27 May 1915, p. 52.)

1916: U.Z. Ellis Apartment House, Greenville; $6500 (*MR*, 7 December 1916, p. 84.)

1916-1917: Greenville County Courthouse, Greenville; P. Thornton Marye (q.v.), architect; H. Olin Jones, supervising architect; $110,000 (Cornerstone; *MR*, 24 February 1916, p. 66; 5 April 1916, p. 88; 4 April 1917, p. 92.)

1917: Mills District School Building, Greenville; $20,000 (*MR*, 26 April 1917, p. 71; 10 May 1917, p. 72.)

1917: A. Adams Residence, Greenville; $2000 (*MR*, 25 October 1917, p. 76.)

1917: Methodist Church, Simpsonville (*MR*, 16 August 1917, p. 72.)

1918: Mrs. Charlotte R. Smith Store Building, Greenville; $35,000 (*MR*, 14 February 1918, p. 79.)

1918-1919: Central Building, Greenville City Hospital, Greenville; $125,000 (*MR*, 19 September 1918, p. 95; 20 March 1919, p. 114.)

1919: Professional Building Co. Office Building, Greenville; F.G. Rogers (q.v.), architect; H. Olin Jones, supervising architect; $20,000 (*MR*, 26 June 1919, p. 139; 3 July 1919, p. 156.)

Jones & Trott

1922: Earle Street Baptist Church, Greenville; $50,000 (*MR*, 27 July 1922, p. 77.)

1922: Remodeling, J.H. Morgan, Jr., Store, Greenville (*MR*, 27 July 1922, p. 79.)

1922: School, Mauldin; $15,000 (*MR*, 6 July 1922, p. 109.)

1923: School, Westminster; $33,000 (*MR*, 11 October 1923, p. 113; 25 October 1923, p. 144.)

1923-1924: Fair Forest Hotel, Union (*Union Progress*, Union, 22 August 1923, 12 September 1923, 23 January 1924, 13 February 1924, 17 July 1924; *MR*, 10 January 1924, p. 119; 17 January 1924, p. 107.)

1924: Union-Buffalo Mills Co. School, Buffalo; $60,000 (*MR*, 15 May 1924, p. 126; 29 May 1924, p. 114.)

1926: Central Baptist Church, Pinckney and Lloyd streets, Greenville; $85,000 (*MR*, 21 October 1926, p. 101.)

1927: Addition, Woodside Cotton Mills School, Greenville; $30,000 (*MR*, 19 May 1927, p. 112.)

1927: School, Taylors; $30,000 (*MR*, 5 May 1927, p. 117.)

1928: School, Laurel Creek; $20,000 (*MR*, 26 July 1928, p. 91.)

1928: Sixty residences, Piedmont Print Works, Inc., Taylors; J.E. Sirrine & Co. (q.v.), engineers; Jones & Trott, architects and construction superintendents (*MR*, 8 March 1928, p. 97.)

H. Olin Jones

1931: A.F. Cannon Residence, 104 W. Earle Street, Greenville; $14,000 (*MR*, 7 May 1931, p. 59.)

Sources: Geddings, pp. 92-93; Greenville city directories; *MR*, various citations; Petty, p. 120.

KEATING, Thomas (active 1903-1915) Thomas Keating was active as a contractor and builder in the late nineteenth century. He worked as a draftsman for Avery Carter (q.v.) in 1903. Around 1904 he entered professional practice as the partner of Leland P. Epton (q.v.) in Spartanburg. In 1905 Keating was associated with Luther D. Proffitt (q.v.) in Spartanburg.

Keating left Spartanburg around 1906 and opened an architectural office in Greer, where he was working as late as 1915.

South Carolina projects:

1904: See **Epton, Leland P.** (Epton & Keating)

1904: Fire Department Engine House, Spartanburg; $6000 (*MR*, 8 December 1904, p. 512; 15 December 1904, p. 538.)

1904: School, Duncan; $3000 (*Southern Architect and Building News*, 4 November 1904, p. 13.)

1904: W.C. Routh Residence, Spartanburg (*Southern Architect and Building News*, 4 November 1904, p. 13.)

1904: J.W. Wood Residence, Duncan (*Southern Architect and Building News*, 4 November 1904, p. 13.)

1904: Alterations, Dr. G. DeFoix Wilson Residence, Spartanburg; $3500 (*Southern Architect and Building News*, 4 November 1904, p. 13.)

1904: E.W. Johnson Residence, Spartanburg; $2000 (*Southern Architect and Building News*, 4 November 1904, p. 13.)

1904: School, Greer; $9000 (*Southern Architect and Building News*, 4 November 1904, p. 13.)

1904: L.P. Sims Store Building, Spartanburg; $4000 (*Southern Architect and Building News*, 4 November 1904, p. 13.)

1904: Julius Jones Residence, Spartanburg; $2000 (*Southern Architect and Building News*, 4 November 1904, p. 13.)

Keating & Proffitt

1905: Baptist Church, Greer (*MR*, 5 October 1905, p. 301; 19 October 1905, p. 354.)

1905: Graded School, Landrum (*MR*, 4 May 1904, p. 355.)

1905: Fitting-School Department Building, Wofford College, Spartanburg (*MR*, 16 March 1905, p. 185; 29 June 1905, p. 560.)

1906: Lutheran Church, Spartanburg (*MR*, 8 February 1906, p. 104.)

Thomas Keating

1910: R.L. Marchant Business Building, Greer; $8500 (*MR*, 20 October 1910, p. 73.)

1913: Thomas Keating Residence, 213 N. Main Street, Greer (Survey files, S.C. Archives.)

1915: Marvin R. Rees Store and Office Building, Trade Street, Greer; $3500 (*MR*, 7 October 1915, p. 76; 4 November 1915, p. 77; 11 November 1915, p. 64.)

Sources: *MR*, various citations; Spartanburg city directories; *Spartanburg of Today: The Progressive City of the Piedmont* (n.p., n.p., n.d., ca. 1905; copy in National Register files, S. C. Archives.)

KEELY, Patrick Charles (1816-1896) Keely, a native of Kilkenny, Ireland, learned the profession in his father's office. He emigrated to the United States in 1841, and was established in Brooklyn, New York, by 1850. Much of Keely's work was for the Roman Catholic Church; over six hundred Keely projects for the Church have been described. Keely's projects included English Gothic Revival, Romanesque Revival, and Second Empire designs.

Keely designed three churches in Charleston, including the Cathedral of St. John the Baptist, begun in 1888. The monumental cathedral was built on the site of an earlier Keely edifice, the Cathedral of St. John and St. Finbar, which was destroyed by fire in 1861. The new cathedral was completed in 1907.

South Carolina projects:

1850-1854: Cathedral of St. John and St. Finbar, 122 Broad Street, Charleston; $103,000 (Ravenel, p. 255.)

1886-1887: St. Patrick's Catholic Church, 136 St. Philip Street, Charleston (National Register files, S.C. Archives; Ravenel, p. 255.)

1888-1907: Roman Catholic Cathedral of St. John the Baptist, 122 Broad Street, Charleston (Church Records, Cathedral of St. John the Baptist, Charleston; *MR*, 3 November 1888, p. 27; 9 June 1904, p. 479; Ravenel, p. 255.)

Sources: Francis, pp. 8, 91; *Macmillan Encyclopedia*, Vol. II, pp. 556-557; Ravenel, *Architects of Charleston*, pp. 254-257; Withey, p. 333.

KEBBON, Eric (1890- ca. 1956) Eric Kebbon of New York was educated at the Massachusetts Institute of Technology, and he worked with Welles Bosworth before establishing his own architectural office in 1921 in New York City. From 1935 to 1937 Kebbon worked with the office of the Supervising Architect of the United States Treasury Department in Washington, D.C. Federal buildings in Tallahassee, Florida, and Greenville, South Carolina, were among his works in this period.

South Carolina project:

1936: Federal Building and Courthouse, 300 E. Washington Street, Greenville; Eric Kebbon, architect; Louis Simon (q.v.), supervising architect (Cornerstone; Koyl, p. 291.)

Sources: Koyl, p. 291; White & Willensky, pp. 196, 319.

KEITH COMPANY (active 1899-1931) The Keith Company of Minneapolis, Minnesota, had a widespread mail-order house design business in the early twentieth century. Max Le Roy Keith was senior in the firm, which also included J.W. Lindstrom and Walter Jewett Keith, the author of *Historic Architecture for the Homebuilder* (1905). The company advertised its designs in catalogs and booklets, including *Keith's Beautiful Homes Magazine* (published under various titles, 1899-1931), *Keith's Book of Bungalows*, *Keith's Attractive Homes*, *Keith's Attractive Garages*, and *Keith's Twenty Wonder Houses* (1919). The Keith Company advertised hundreds of house patterns, including variations of Tudor Revival, Colonial Revival, foursquare, and bungalow styles. Plans for these buildings could be purchased for $15 to $40, and the company suggested that most of the houses could be built for between $3500 and $7000. Among the more expensive designs was No. K-1279, a Prairie-School influenced house estimated to cost $25,000.

As an added service, the Keith Company would prepare "personal" designs from a prospective homeowner's sketches: "Your own Original Ideas Worked into a Bright, Original, Attractive Home."

South Carolina project:

1910: Floyd L. Liles Residence, Spartanburg; $10,000 (*MR*, 10 February 1910, p. 63; 17 February 1910, p. 71.)

Sources: Gowans, *The Comfortable House*, pp. 24, 45-46, 231; *Keith's Artistic Homes* (Minneapolis, Minnesota: M.L. Keith, n.d.); *Keith's Attractive Homes*, Vol. IV (Minneapolis, Minnesota: Max L. Keith, n.d.)

KELLOGG, Fay (active 1915-1918) Fay Kellogg of New York City, one of very few female architects in practice, designed a number of Y.W.C.A. "hostess houses" at United States military facilities during the First World War. Kellogg projects have been identified in Charlotte, North Carolina, and Chattanooga, Tennessee, as well as in Greenville and Charleston, South Carolina.

South Carolina projects:

1917: Y.W.C.A. National War Council Hostess House, Camp Sevier, Greenville; $12,120 (*MR*, 25 October 1917, p. 75; 1 November 1917, p. 85.)

1918: Y.W.C.A. Building, Navy Yard, Charleston; $75,000 (*MR*, 24 January 1918, p. 73.)

Sources: *MR*, various citations; Withey, p. 538.

KEMPER, Charles C. (active 1894-1908) Charles C. Kemper, acting supervising architect of the United States Department of the Treasury in 1894-1895 and again in 1897-1898, had nominal charge of the construction of the United States Courthouse and Post Office in Charleston (John H. Devereux, designing architect) in 1895. Kemper remained with the office at least through 1908 as assistant to the supervising architect.

Sources: *The American Architect*, Vol. 94, No. 1722, 1908, p. 214; *MR*, 8 February 1895, p. 29; Smith, *The Office of the Supervising Architect*, p. 44.

KENNEY, John (active 1881) John Kenney was proprietor of Kenney's Concrete Drain Pipe and Kaolin Boiler Covering Works in Charleston. He was also listed as an architect in the Charleston city directory in 1881. Samuel Lapham (q.v.), decrying the unrestricted use of the title "architect" in the late nineteenth century, noted that "a drain pipe manufacturer" and various other tradesmen "classified themselves as architects, along with their main activity" in city directories. Kenney was evidently the object of Lapham's scorn. Whether he ever worked as an architect is not known.

Sources: Charleston city directories; Petty, p. 6.

KILHAM & HOPKINS (active 1900-1926) Walter H. Kilham (1868-1948) and James C. Hopkins of Boston, Massachusetts, were employed by the Pacific Mills in Columbia between 1918 and 1922 for a number of projects. Kilham described the work thus:

The work for the Pacific Mills at Columbia, South Carolina, began in March 1918 when Mr. Edwin Farnham Greene telephoned and asked me to go down there and look the place over, which I did for a few days. The mills were making a great deal of money and income taxes were going to take a lot of it, but what they put into improvements they would save in taxes. In the next three or four years I built a swimming pool building, twenty or thirty houses and plans for more, studies for new street layouts and all sorts of miscellaneous buildings, mill stables, community barns and plans for a new mill office which never got built. The slump in cotton in 1922 brought this work to an end.

The Pacific Mills Group was based in Lawrence, Massachusetts; they had purchased the South Carolina mills in 1915-1916.

South Carolina projects:

1918: Pacific Mills, nineteen residences, Whaley Street, Columbia; $70,500 (*MR*, 8 August 1918, p. 78; Candee.)

1919: Pacific Mills, remodeling of Y.M.C.A. Building, Columbia; $18,000 (*MR*, 23 October 1919, pp. 125, 127.)

1919: Pacific Mills, Store and Lodge Building, Columbia; $48,000 (*MR*, 23 October 1919, pp. 125, 127.)

1920: Pacific Mills, eight residences, Columbia; $44,000 (*MR*, 4 March 1920, p. 181.)

Sources: Alvin W. Byars, *Olympia Pacific: The Way It Was 1895-1970* (Columbia: Alvin W. Byars, 1981); Richard M. Candee, York, Maine, unpublished research; *MR*, various citations; Withey, pp. 342-343.

KING, Harvey Marinus (1894- ca. 1960) Harvey M. King, a native of Minnesota, was educated at the University of Minnesota and at the Massachusetts Institute of Technology. He worked as consulting architect for the Methodist Episcopal Church South from 1924 to 1942. Through the Architectural Department of the Board of Extension of the M.E. Church South, based in Louisville, Kentucky, King designed buildings for the Methodist Church in many southern states. King also wrote extensively on religious architecture; his works included *A Guide to Church Planning* (1952.)

South Carolina projects:

1924: Methodist Church Building, Swansea; $25,000 (*MR*, 23 October 1924, p. 107.)

1927: Sunday School Building, Buncombe Street Methodist Episcopal Church South, Greenville; $100,000 (*MR*, 17 February 1927, p. 117; 24 February 1927, p. 105.)

Sources: Koyl, p. 300; *MR*, various citations.

KLUTTZ, Thomas A. (active 1886-1908) Kluttz was practicing architecture in Augusta, Georgia, in 1886, as a partner in Kluttz & Norrell. From 1902 to 1908, Kluttz was associated with George F. Barber (q.v.) as Barber & Kluttz, Architects, in Knoxville, Tennessee.

South Carolina projects:

See **Barber, George Franklin** (Barber & Kluttz)

Sources: Augusta, Georgia, city directories; Herndon, pp. 12, 110; *MR*, various citations.

KOETH, Lawrence A.H. (active 1904-1913) L.A.H. Koeth was a minor architect in Wilmington, North Carolina. He designed a number of residences, churches, and commercial buildings in that city.

South Carolina project:

1904: R.M. Richardson Hotel, Seneca; $20,000 (*MR*, 21 January 1904, p. 14.)

Sources: *MR*, various citations; Tony P. Wrenn, Washington, D.C., unpublished research.

KUYKENDALL, Clarence (active 1934-1936) Clarence Kuykendall is listed as an architect in the Rock Hill city directories for 1934-1936.

LADSHAW, George Edward (1850-1926) George Ladshaw was active as an engineer and architect in North and South Carolina in the early twentieth century. Ladshaw was born in Drummondville, Canada, and served an architectural and civil engineering apprenticeship with his grandfather John Ladshaw. He was established in Spartanburg by 1894, in association with his brother Thomas, as Ladshaw & Ladshaw. The firm advertised primarily as civil and hydraulic engineers.

Ladshaw designed and built several mill complexes in North Carolina. He was chief designing and consulting engineer for the Henrietta Mills in Rutherford County, and he designed buildings for Haynes Mills in Avondale in 1917. George Ladshaw's widow Joanna was listed in the 1927 Spartanburg city directory.

South Carolina projects:

1901: Improvements, Jonesville Knitting Mills, Jonesville; $25,000 (*MR*, 30 May 1901, p. 345.)

n.d.: Hydraulic Plant, Pacolet Manufacturing Company No. 1 Mill, Pacolet (Garlington.)

n.d.: Hydraulic Plant, Whitney Manufacturing Company, Whitney (Garlington.)

Sources: Garlington, *Men of the Time*, pp. 250-251; *MR*, various citations; Spartanburg city directories.

LADSHAW, Thomas D. (active 1894-1910) Thomas Ladshaw was associated with his brother George Ladshaw (q.v.) as an engineer and architect in Spartanburg from 1894 through 1910.

Sources: Spartanburg city directories.

LAFAYE, George Eugene (1878-1939) George E. Lafaye was among the most important architects practicing in South Carolina in the early twentieth century. He was born in New Orleans, Louisiana, and was educated at Jesuit College. He worked as a draftsman in New Orleans before coming to Columbia around 1900. Lafaye was an architectural design-

er for W.B. Smith Whaley & Co. from 1900 to 1903. A 1904 account described Lafaye's work with the company:

> . . . He has for the past four years been in charge of the draughting department. . . . Under his personal supervision have been designed almost all of the buildings erected by that firm in the vicinity of Columbia, and the chapels in the mill district, the Palmetto Bank and Trust company's building, and the homes of Mr. F.H. Weston, Mr. G.E. Shand, and Mr. Jno. P. Thomas, Jr., are from his designs.

When the Whaley firm was dissolved in 1903, Lafaye and senior architect Gadsden Shand (q.v.) associated as Shand & Lafaye, Architects and Engineers, in Columbia.

Shand retired from architectural practice in 1912, and Lafaye continued the office under his own name. In 1919 his brother Robert S. Lafaye (q.v.) became an associate in the firm, which was then called Lafaye & Lafaye.

Lafaye was among the state's most respected and most successful architects. Architect Wyatt Hibbs, who worked in Columbia from 1935 to 1942, described the Lafaye firm:

> George E. Lafaye (Sr.) was living when I arrived in Columbia. The office of Lafaye (George) and Lafaye (Bob), I considered to be the number one architectural office in Columbia when I joined Mr. Urquhart, whom I considered to be number two.

Lafaye secured several profitable state contracts. As architect for the expansion program at the South Carolina State Hospital for the Insane in Columbia, Lafaye was responsible for the renovation of the hospital's existing campus and for the construction of several new buildings between 1915 and 1929. He was also architect for the State Training School for the Feeble-Minded in Clinton, designing nine buildings for the campus between 1919 and 1929. Lafaye was appointed to the South Carolina Board of Architectural Examiners by Governor Manning when the board was created in 1917, serving in 1917-1919 and again in 1933-1938.

Lafaye's National Loan and Exchange Bank Annex in Columbia, built in 1925, is a distinctive Neoclassical design, with a colossal Tuscan order defining its facade. The firm's 1929-1930 Township Auditorium in Columbia is an impressive Georgian Revival composition, encompassing most of a city block. The 1935 Community Building in Hartsville, a dominant building in the town's business sector, has a full-blown Art Deco facade.

South Carolina projects:

1903-1912: See **Shand, Gadsden E.** (Shand & Lafaye)

1912: Shore, Manning, Rowland and Weber, Three Store Buildings, Sumter (*MR*, 18 July 1912, pp. 78-79.)

1913: Walter A. Keenan Business Building, Sumter Street, Columbia; $15,000 (*The State*, 13 June 1913, p. 6.)

1913: Lorick & Lowrance Building, 1523 Main Street, Columbia; $45,000 (*MR*, 18 September 1913, p. 73.)

1914: Fidelity Real Estate & Trust Co. Hotel, Aiken; $45,369 (*MR*, 14 May 1914, p. 65.)

1914: School, Devine Street and Garner's Ferry Road, Columbia; $8000 (*MR*, 20 August 1914, p. 63.)

1915: Shandon Methodist Episcopal Church, Preston and Maple streets, Columbia; $6000 (*MR*, 25 March 1915, p. 54.)

1915: Alterations, Senate Chamber, South Carolina State House, Columbia (*The State*, 9 April 1915, p. 10.)

1915: Dairy Barn, State Hospital for the Insane, Columbia; $12,500 (*MR*, 19 August 1915, p. 63.)

1915: School, Marion Street, Columbia; $26,000 (*MR*, 2 December 1915, p. 74.)

1916: Olympia School, Columbia; $20,000 (*MR*, 12 October 1916, p. 66.)

1917: Dr. W.T.C. Bates Residence, Columbia; $10,500 (*MR*, 1 November 1917, p. 70.)

1917: Shandon Annex Co., three residences, Columbia; $3500 each (*MR*, 23 August 1917, p. 70.)

1918: B.B. Kirkland Apartment House, Columbia; $40,000 (*MR*, 16 May 1918, p. 83; 23 May 1918, p. 77.)

1919: Remodeling, Bank of Camden, Camden; $30,000 (*MR*, 5 June 1919, p. 148.)

1919: Two Cottages, State Training School for the Feeble-Minded, Clinton; $24,000 (*MR*, 14 August 1919, p. 125; 21 August 1919, p. 129.)

1919: Dairy Barn, South Carolina State Sanitarium, Columbia (*MR*, 5 June 1919, p. 149.)

1919: Remodeling, Rutledge College, University of South Carolina, Columbia; $25,000 (*MR*, 3 July 1919, p. 158; 10 July 1919, p. 120 h.)

Lafaye & Lafaye

1919: Thomas & Howard Company Warehouse, Columbia; $15,000 (*MR*, 9 October 1919, p. 134 m.)

1919: Dixie Highway Hotel Co. Hotel, Edgefield; $70,000 (*MR*, 4 December 1919, p. 174.)

1920: Remodeling, State Hospital for the Insane, Columbia (*MR*, 15 January 1920, p. 152 j.)

1920: Building, Columbia Hospital, Columbia; $100,000 (*MR*, 3 June 1920, p. 182.)

1920: Manning Hotel Company Hotel, Manning; $40,000 (*MR*, 19 February 1920, p. 148.)

1921: Main Building, Camden Hospital, Camden; $38,500 (*MR*, 4 August 1921, p. 104.)

1921: Mrs. F.W. Bratton Residence, Columbia; $28,000 (*MR*, 17 February 1921, p. 130 b.)

1921: W.H. Cary Apartment House, College and Henderson streets, Columbia (*MR*, 23 June 1921, p. 91.)

1921: Improvements, Imperial Hotel, Columbia; $15,000 (*MR*, 13 October 1921, p. 95.)

1921: Wm. F. Prioleau Residence, Columbia; $12,500 (*MR*, 8 December 1921, p. 84 d.)

1921: Jones-Germany Warehouse Co. Warehouse, Columbia (*MR*, 29 December 1921, p. 80.)

1922: Dormitory, Carlisle Fitting School, Bamberg; $26,000 (*MR*, 27 April 1922, p. 86; 4 May 1922, p. 106.)

1922: Main Street Methodist Church Building, Columbia (*MR*, 19 January 1922, p. 76 g.)

1922: Sunday School Building, Green Street Methodist Church, Columbia (*MR*, 2 February 1922, p. 104.)

1922: J.R. Cain Residence, University Place and Pickens Street, Columbia (*MR*, 14 December 1922.)

1922: S.A. Nettles Hotel, Manning; $40,000 (*MR*, 27 July 1922, p. 78.)

1923: Addition, First National Bank, Batesburg (*MR*, 7 June 1922, p. 130 l.)

1923: C.R. Dreher Residence, Batesburg (*MR*, 7 June 1923, p. 130 l.)

1923: C.D. Boling Apartment House, Laurens and Pendleton streets, Columbia; $10,000 (*MR*, 10 May 1923, p. 107.)

1923: Two Cottages, State Hospital, Columbia (*MR*, 24 May 1923, p. 109.)

1923: East Wing, Woodrow College, University of South Carolina, Columbia; $51,875 (*MR*, 5 July 1923, p. 119; 29 November 1923, p. 101.)

1923: Ward No. 2, State Hospital, Columbia; $150,000 (*MR*, 19 July 1923, p. 120.)

1923: Two Physicians' Residences, State Hospital, Columbia (*MR*, 9 August 1923, p. 111.)

1923: Salvation Army Citadel, Lady Street, Columbia; $20,487 (*MR*, 23 August 1923, p. 106.)

1923: Shandon Graded School, 705 Maple Street, Columbia; $50,000 (*MR*, 15 November 1923, p. 116.)

1923: Mrs. O.A. Burnside Residence, Columbia (*MR*, 22 November 1923, p. 99.)

1924: Three Dormitories, State Training School, Clinton; $55,890 (*MR*, 26 June 1924, p. 114.)

1924: Standard Building & Loan Association Office Building, Washington Street, Columbia; $25,000 (*MR*, 12 June 1924, p. 110.)

1924: E.W. Robertson Residence, Seneca and Edisto avenues, Wales Garden, Columbia; James Brite (q.v.), architect; Lafaye & Lafaye, supervising architects (*MR*, 24 April 1924, p. 111.)

1924-1925: Remodeling, Mrs. P.C. Lorick Residence, Hampton and Barnwell streets, Columbia (*MR*, 26 June 1924, p. 112; 23 April 1925, p. 115.)

1924: Alterations, Residences of Professors Davis and McCutcheon, University of South Carolina, Columbia; $14,000 (*MR*, 26 June 1924, p. 112.)

1924: Fire Escapes, Dormitories, University of South Carolina, Columbia (*MR*, 3 April 1924, p. 154.)

1924: Restoration, Davis College, University of South Carolina, Columbia; $20,880 (*MR*, 10 April 1924, p. 112.)

1924: W.M. Burney Store and Office Building, Columbia; $40,000 (*MR*, 24 April 1924, p. 113; 1 May 1924, p. 156.)

1924: Rectory, St. Francis de Sales Roman Catholic Church, Columbia (*MR*, 19 June 1924, p. 116.)

1924: Christian Church, Columbia; $19,095 (*MR*, 30 October 1924, p. 90.)

1924-1925: Sunday School Building, Remodeling Smith Memorial Chapel, and Enlarging Main Auditorium, First Presbyterian Church, Columbia; $250,000; R.H. Hunt (q.v.), Architect; Lafaye & Lafaye, supervising architects (*MR*, 30 October 1924, p. 90; 27 November 1924, p. 96; 2 July 1925, p. 128; 6 August 1925, p. 121.)

1924: W.H. Carey Apartment Building, 1603 College Street, Columbia (*MR*, 25 September 1924, p. 116; 2 October 1924, p. 142.)

1924: High School Building and Improvements, School Building, Summerville; $62,693 (*MR*, 17 July 1924, p. 117.)

1924: Geo. D. Levy Residence, Sumter; $18,000 (*MR*, 20 November 1924, p. 111; 27 November 1924, p. 97.)

1925: National Loan & Exchange Bank Annex, 1208 Washington Street, Columbia; $150,000 (*MR*, 14 May 1925, p. 114; 21 May 1925, p. 116; 25 June 1925, p. 118.)

1925: Medical Building, Marion Street, Columbia; $22,440 (*MR*, 11 June 1925, p. 16.)

1925: Storefront, New York Waist House Building, Columbia (*MR*, 7 May 1925, p. 141.)

1925: Addition and Remodeling, National Bank of Newberry, Newberry (*MR*, 2 February 1925, p. 118.)

1925: W.P. Stroman Residence, Orangeburg (*MR*, 26 March 1925, p. 116.)

1925: Laundry Building and Two Residences, State Training School, Clinton; $13,300 (*MR*, 16 July 1925, pp. 115-116.)

1925: R.H. Jennings, Jr., Residence, Orangeburg (*MR*, 9 July 1925, p. 122.)

1925: Bank of Prosperity Building, Prosperity; $15,000 (*MR*, 24 September 1925, p. 95.)

1925: George L. Ricker Residence, Sumter; $23,000 (*MR*, 22 October 1925, p. 103; 29 October 1925, p. 97.)

1925: Remodeling, Hampton County Courthouse, Hampton (National Register files, S.C. Archives.)

1926: Additions, School, Cameron (*MR*, 17 June 1926, p. 110.)

1926: St. John's Protestant Episcopal Church, Columbia (*MR*, 21 January 1926, p. 104.)

1926: Building No. 3, State Park, Columbia; $121,600 (*MR*, 5 August 1926, p. 124.)

1926: Grandstand, South Carolina State Fair, Columbia; $12,500 (*MR*, 1 July 1926, p. 136.)

1926: Bank of Kershaw Bank and Office Building, Kershaw; $21,250 (*MR*, 19 August 1926, p. 107.)

1926: Dr. E.O. Horger Residence, Ellis Avenue and N. Boulevard, Orangeburg; $25,000 (*MR*, 23 December 1926, p. 97.)

1926: High School, Swansea; $38,984 (*MR*, 10 June 1926, p. 111.)

1927: Incarnation Lutheran Church, Columbia; $25,000 (*MR*, 3 October 1927, p. 115.)

1927: Sunday School Building, Washington Street Methodist Episcopal Church, Columbia; Casey & Fant (q.v.), architects; Lafaye & Lafaye, associated architects (*MR*, 24 November 1927, p. 107; 1 December 1927, p. 108; 8 December 1927, p. 110.)

1927: George E. Lafaye Residence, 1716 College Street, Columbia (*MR*, 20 October 1927, p. 112.)

1927: Alterations, Parker Building, State Hospital, Columbia; $31,000 (*MR*, 25 August 1927, p. 98.)

1927: Shandon School, Columbia; $50,400 (*MR*, 6 January 1927, p. 143.)

1927: Two Ward Buildings, South Carolina State Hospital, Columbia (*MR*, 18 August 1927, p. 124; 25 August 1927, p. 98.)

1928: Dr. J.L. Claussen, Seven Residences, Florence; $40,000 (*MR*, 1 March 1928, p. 102.)

1928: Mrs. G.A. Lemmon Store Building, Main Street, Sumter; $43,300 (*MR*, 13 September 1928, p. 96.)

1928: Bethel Methodist Episcopal Church, Walterboro; $30,000 (*MR*, 23 February 1928, p. 91.)

1929: School, State Training School, Clinton; $26,165 (*MR*, 23 May 1929, p. 98.)

1929-1930: Columbia Township Auditorium, 1703 Taylor Street, Columbia; $300,000 (*MR*, 17 October 1929, p. 95; 20 March 1930, p. 80; Cornerstone.)

1929: A.F. Spigner Residence, 400 Harden Street, Columbia; $15,000 (*MR*, 3 October 1929, p. 96.)

1929: Ward Building and Pavilion, State Hospital, Columbia (*MR*, 6 June 1929, p. 107.)

1930: Sunday School, First Baptist Church, Columbia; $84,163 (*MR*, 26 June 1930, p. 79; 3 July 1930, p. 83.)

1930: Dr. H.L. Timmons Eye, Ear, Nose & Throat Hospital, Marion and Taylor streets, Columbia; $35,000 (*MR*, 6 November 1930, p. 84.)

1930: J.W. McCormick Apartment House, Columbia; $18,000 (*MR*, 4 December 1930, p. 68.)

1930: Ben M. Webber Store Building, 1513-1515 Sumter Street, Columbia (*MR*, 12 June 1930, p. 79.)

1930: Residence, Georgetown; $100,000 (*MR*, 17 July 1930, p. 80.)

1930: Barringer Hotel, Sumter and Gervais streets, Columbia; $500,000; H.A. Underwood (q.v.), architect; Lafaye & Lafaye, associated architects (*MR*, 6 March 1930, p. 109; 8 May 1930, p. 97; 5 June 1930, p. 90; 25 September 1930, p. 68.)

1931: Ward Building, State Hospital, Columbia (*MR*, 26 November 1931, p. 41.)

1932-1934: Addition, Federal Land Bank, Hampton Street, Columbia (*MR*, 14 April 1932, p. 37; Withey.)

1935: Hartsville Community Center, Fifth Street, Hartsville (Cornerstone.)

1935: Hospital Building, McLeod Infirmary, Florence; Lafaye & Lafaye, architects; Frank V. Hopkins (q.v.), associate architect (*The Architectural Record*, May 1935, p. 334.)

1939: State Office Building, Columbia (*The State*, 12 May 1939, pp. 1, 8.)

Sources: Columbia city directories; Geddings, *Who's Who in South Carolina*, p. 101; Wyatt Hibbs, Norfolk, Virginia, to John Wells, Columbia, S.C., 2 April 1984; W.S. Kline, *Illustrated 1904 Columbia, South Carolina* (1904: reprint, Columbia: The R.L. Bryan Co., 1962), p. 11; *MR*, various citations; Petty, pp. 133, 143; *The State*, 24 January 1904, p. 16; 12 May 1939, p. 1; Withey, pp. 358-359.

LAFAYE, Robert Stoddard (active 1919-1956) Robert S. Lafaye, brother of George E. Lafaye (q.v.), joined his brother's architectural firm in 1919. The firm of Lafaye & Lafaye was active in South Carolina through the mid-twentieth century. Robert Lafaye directed the office after his brother's death in 1939. Herndon Fair, Walter F. Petty, and George E. Lafaye, Jr., all were members of the firm in later years.

South Carolina projects:

See **Lafaye, George E.** (Lafaye & Lafaye)

Sources: Columbia city directories; Koyl, p. 315.

LAIRD, John M. (1846- ca. 1909) John Laird, a native of Scotland, was a contractor active in the United States from 1870. He was established in Aiken at least by 1879, when he was associated with Siberia Ott (q.v.) as a contractor. In 1891 Laird was connected with a hotel project in that resort community.

Sources: 1900 Federal Census, Aiken County, South Carolina, Reel 1515, Vol. III, p. 29B; *History of Saint Mary Help of Christians Church and Aiken Missions* (Aiken, South Carolina: St. Mary Help of Christians Church, 1942), pp. 38-39; *MR*, 17 January 1891, p. 38.

LAMBLE, Henry S. (active 1898-1904) Henry Lamble advertised as an architect and civil engineer in Charleston from 1898 to 1904. He was employed as an architect with the South Carolina International and West Indian Exposition Company in 1902, under supervision of chief architect Bradford L. Gilbert (q.v.).

Sources: Charleston city directories.

LaMOTTE, Ashbury Gamewell (1868-1929) LaMotte was an architect and civil engineer active in Columbia and central South Carolina. He attended South Carolina College and took an LL.B. degree in 1890. He was associated with Frank M. Niernsee (q.v.) in the 1890s as Niernsee & LaMotte.

LaMotte retired from his architectural and engineering practice by 1915.

South Carolina projects:

1893-1896: See **Niernsee, Frank Machenry** (Niernsee & LaMotte)

1900: A.G. LaMotte Business Building, Gervais Street, Columbia (*The State*, 12 March 1900, p. 8.)

1903-1905: Summerland Hotel, Batesburg (*MR*, 9 April 1903, p. 244; 23 July 1903, p. 15; 2 March 1905, p. 144; 23 March 1905, p. 206.)

Sources: Columbia city directories; *MR*, various citations; Moore, Vol. 4; *The State*, 12 March 1900, p. 8; 30 April 1929, p. 16.

LANKFORD, John Anderson (1874-1946) John A. Lankford was one of the nation's pioneer black architects. He is believed to have been the first professional black architect to practice in the United States. His designs were built in states across the nation in the early twentieth century, and in Central and South America as well.

Lankford was born in Potosi, Missouri, in 1874. He was educated at the Lincoln Institute in Jefferson, Missouri; at Tuskegee Normal and Industrial Institute in Alabama (where he was later employed as an instructor in mechanical engineering); and at the Architectural College at Scranton, Pennsylvania. His degrees included a Bachelor of Science degree from Shaw University in Raleigh, North Carolina, in 1898; a Master of Science degree from Morris Brown College in 1901; a Master of Science degree from Wilberforce University in Ohio in 1902; and a Master of Mechanical Science degree from the State Agricultural College, Normal, Alabama, in 1908. He later won LL.B. and LL.M degrees from Frelinghuysen University in Washington, D.C., and an LL.D. degree from Allen University in Columbia, South Carolina.

Lankford's architectural practice, based in Washington, D.C., included buildings and projects across the nation. While much of his work was for the African Methodist Episcopal Church, Lankford also designed schools, lodges, commercial buildings, apartments, and private residences. Contractor Belton Caughman of Columbia, South Carolina, in a letter of recommendation, wrote of Lankford:

> We have just completed the construction of [Bethel A.M.E. Church in Columbia]. . . . [Lankford, the architect] was careful, conscientious, thoughtful and used good judgement and common sense with the contractors, sub-contractors, and with all the foremen and workmen connected with the job. .

. . We have never met a more capable, competent and honorable Architect.

At the Quadrennial Conference of the A.M.E. Church in 1908, Lankford was elected supervising architect for the Church, and he designed edifices for the denomination in many states. He accepted no compensation for this work. Among Lankford's designs for the Church were Allen Chapel A.M.E. Church, Franktown, Virginia (1921); Allen A.M.E. Church, Staunton, Virginia (1922); Bethel A.M.E. Church, Malvern, Arkansas; Big Bethel A.M.E. Church at 220 Auburn Street, Atlanta, Georgia (1924); St. Philip's A.M.E. Church, Savannah, Georgia; John Wesley A.M.E. Church in Washington, D.C.; and the African Methodist Episcopal Church at Capetown, South Africa.

Palmer Hall at the Agricultural & Mechanical College in Normal, Alabama, and the Masonic Hall in Jacksonville, Florida, built at a cost of $125,000, were also prominent among Lankford's designs. A five-story building designed by Lankford for the People's Federation Bank of Charleston, South Carolina, was evidently never built.

Lankford is also credited with the discovery of a new process for developing blueprints, and with a process for expediting steel welding. He taught mechanical and architectural drawing at Wilberforce University, and he helped promote the expansion of the Harvard University School of Architecture and Engineering as well.

South Carolina projects:

1921-1922: Bethel A.M.E. Church, 1528 Sumter Street, Columbia; $80,000 (Church Records, Bethel A.M.E. Church, Columbia; Cornerstone; *MR*, 25 May 1922, pp. 63, 66; *Lankford's Artistic Churches*, p. 11.)

1922-1925: Chappelle Administration Building, Allen University, Columbia; $125,000 (University Records, Allen University, Columbia; *Lankford's Artistic Churches*, p. 24.)

Ca. 1924: People's Federation Bank Building project, Charleston (*Lankford's Artistic Churches*, p. 23.)

Sources: *The Centenniel Encyclopedia of the African Methodist Episcopal Church* (n.p., n.p., 1916), Vol. 1, pp. 277, 356; Richard K. Dozier, "Caretakers of the Past: Blacks Preserve Their Architectural Heritage," *History News*, Vol. 36, No. 2, February 1981, pp. 15-17; John A. Lankford, *Lankford's Artistic Churches and Other Designs* (Second edition) (Washington, D.C.: Hamilton Printing Co., 1924); *MR*, various citations; *Who's Who in Colored America: A Biographical Dictionary of Notable Living Persons of African Descent in America* (Brooklyn, New York: Thomas Yenser, 1941-1944), p. 311; Frank Lincoln Mather, ed., *Who's Who of the Colored Race: A General Biographical Dictionary of Men and Women of African Descent* (1915: republished, Detroit: Gale Research Company, 1976), Vol. 1, pp. 171-172.

LAPHAM, Samuel Jr. (1892-1972) Lapham, a native of Charleston, was educated at Charleston University School and at the College of Charleston, taking his A.B. degree in 1913. He attended the Massachusetts Institute of Technology in Cambridge, and won a B.S. degree in Architecture in 1916. Lapham worked briefly with Ralph Adams Cram before returning to Charleston and associating with Albert Simons (q.v.) in 1920.

Lapham and Simons, counted among the most prestigious architects in the state, were students of Carolina architectural history. The firm earned a reputation in restoration and creative adaptation of Charleston's historic buildings. Lapham wrote many articles on South Carolina's architectural heritage, including an analysis of Charleston's Rice Mills (1924.)

Lapham was active in the South Carolina Chapter of the American Institute of Architects, serving as president of that body in 1935-1936. In 1937 Lapham was named a Fellow of the A.I.A. His citation read:

Samuel Lapham, of South Carolina: For his charming and studied adaption of the distinctive architecture of his state to the needs of the present day building as well as the preservation of the precious structures of the region of Charleston, Samuel Lapham is advanced to Fellowship in the Institute.

South Carolina projects:

See **Simons, Albert** (Simons & Lapham)

Sources: *American Art Annual*, Vol. 21, p. 426; Charleston city directories; Samuel Lapham, Jr., "The Architectural Significance of the Rice Mills of Charleston, South Carolina," *The Architectural Record*, Vol. 56, No. 2, August 1924, pp. 178-184; *MR*, various citations; Albert Simons and Samuel Lapham, *Charleston, South Carolina* (New York, New York: The Octagon Library of American Architecture, 1927); Samuel Gaillard Stoney, Albert Simons, and Samuel Lapham, Jr., *Plantations of the Carolina Low Country* (Charleston: The Carolina Art Association, 1938); *Who's Who in South Carolina 1934-1935*, p. 267; Charles C. Wilson, Samuel Lapham, and Walter Petty, *Architectural Practice in South Carolina 1913-1963* (Columbia: The State Printing Co., 1963.)

LAURITZEN, Peter J. (active 1870-1899) Peter Lauritzen was working with the United States Department of the Treasury as a draftsman in 1870. He opened an independent architectural office in Washington by 1874, and associated with C.A. Didden by 1877. In 1878 Lauritzen was identified not only as an architect, but also as the Danish Vice-Consul. Lauritzen was active in New York City and Brooklyn from 1887 to 1899. He was associated with Charles L. Perry and Louis H. Voss at various times.

South Carolina project:

1891: Commercial Building, 374-378 King Street, Charleston (*News & Courier*, 21 August 1981.)

Sources: Francis, pp. 49, 92; J.L. Sibley Jennings, Sue A. Kohler, and Jeffrey R. Carson, *Massachusetts Avenue Architecture* (Washington, D.C.: The Commission of Fine Arts, 1975), pp. 40-42; White & Willensky, pp. 370, 453, 464, 465.)

LAWRENCE, James R. (active 1890-1912) James R. Lawrence was an architect, civil engineer, and contractor. He was based in Wilmington, North Carolina, in 1890. Lawrence was working in Charleston in 1897, and moved to Greenville by

1899. He employed his son Joseph T. Lawrence (q.v.) as a draftsman in 1907.

South Carolina projects:

1890: United States Court House and Post Office Building, Main Street, Greenville; $75,430; James H. Windrim (q.v.), architect; James R. Lawrence, contractor (*MR*, 21 June 1890, p. 42; letter, S. Dillon Ripley, Smithsonian Institution, to Henry Bacon McKoy, Greenville, S.C., 17 October 1969; copy in Survey files, S.C. Archives.)

1896-1897: Pythian Temple, Charleston; $16,000 (*MR*, 16 October 1896, p. 199; 1 January 1897, p. 401.)

1904: W.P. Conyers Store Room and Office Building, Greenville; $10,000 (*MR*, 10 March 1904, p. 166.)

1904: Remodeling, Buncombe Street Methodist Church, Greenville (*MR*, 7 April 1904, p. 266.)

1905: Workingmen's Savings & Coal [sic; Loan?] Co. Store Building, Greenville; $4000 (*MR*, 19 October 1905, p. 354.)

1906: H.J. Haynesworth Store Building, Greenville; $10,000 (*MR*, 1 March 1906, p. 183.)

1906: Mrs. Carrie V. Cauble Store and Office Building, Greenville; $30,000 (*MR*, 5 April 1906, p. 331; 7 June 1906, p. 588; 19 June 1906, p. 16.)

1906: Thackerston & Son Office Building, Greenville (*MR*, 26 July 1906, p. 43.)

1907: W.P. Conyers Business Building, Greenville; $12,500 (*MR*, 21 February 1907, p. 168; 28 February 1907, p. 199.)

1912: Dr. G.T. Tyler Hospital, Greenville (*MR*, 19 December 1912, p. 73.)

Sources: Greenville city directories; *MR*, various citations.

LAWRENCE, Joseph T. (active 1909-1918) Joseph Lawrence, son of architect James R. Lawrence (q.v.), worked in his father's office as draftsman in 1907. He opened his own practice by 1908, designing modest residences in the Greenville vicinity. Lawrence appears to have relocated to Augusta, Georgia in 1916.

South Carolina projects:

1908: Perry Hudson Residence, Greenville; $6000 (*MR*, 19 March 1908, p. 59.)

1908: Henry Briggs Residence, Greenville; $6000 (*MR*, 19 March 1908, p. 59.)

1908: L.A. Mills Residence, Greenville; $5000 (*MR*, 19 March 1908, p. 59.)

1911: Two Residences, Christ Church, E. Washington Street, Greenville; $9100 (*MR*, 27 July 1911, p. 71.)

1911: C.F. Haynesworth Residence, Greenville; $3000 (*MR*, 19 October 1911, p. 75.)

1911: S.O. Skelton Residence, Liberty; $10,000 (*MR*, 11 May 1911, p. 72; 18 May 1911, p. 76.)

1912: J. Eugene Carter Residence, Greenville; $3500 (*MR*, 25 January 1912, p. 70.)

1914: J. Robt. Martin Residence, Greenville; $5000 (*MR*, 23 July 1914, p. 57.)

1915: Parsonage, Hampton Avenue M.E. Church, Greenville; $3000 (*MR*, 6 May 1915, p. 69.)

1915: Jail and Jailer's Residence, Greenville; $30,000 (*MR*, 20 May 1915, p. 59; 27 May 1915, p. 51; 15 July 1915, p. 59.)

1915: School, Travelers Rest; $3900 (*MR*, 10 June 1915, p. 52; 1 July 1915, p. 69.)

1915-1916: Davenport Apartments, 400-402 E. Washington Street, Greenville; $57,000 (National Register files, S.C. Archives.)

Sources: Greenville city directories; *MR*, various citations.

LAWTON, St. James Alison (active 1901-1902) Lawton was listed in the Charleston city directories as associate of architect Rutledge Holmes (q.v.) in 1901-1902. He was also described as a planter and as proprietor of the James Island Dairy in these years. In 1903 Lawton was identified as the secretary and treasurer of the St. John Hotel Company, and as a planter.

Sources: Charleston city directories.

LAX, Joe Murry (active 1903) Joe Murry Lax of Barnesville, North Carolina, was identified in the *MR* as the architect for the 1903 Kemper Tobacco Company Warehouse in Kemper, South Carolina.

Sources: *MR*, 20 August 1903, p. 89; 27 August 1903, p. 106.

LEE, Rudolph Edward (1876-1959) Rudolph E. Lee, professor of architecture and drawing at Clemson College from 1898 through 1959, was architect of many of the college's buildings.

Lee was the son of Thomas B. Lee, a civil and mechanical engineer. The younger Lee was associated with Clemson College from its earliest days. He was a member of the first class to graduate from Clemson, taking a degree in mechanical and electrical engineering in 1896. As a student, Lee helped organize his fellows in military companies; he also organized a mischievous campus rabbit hunt in 1893.

Lee took post-graduate courses at the Zanerian Art School in Columbus, Ohio (1899); at Cornell University (1900); and at the University of Pennsylvania (1901.) He earned a Master of Architecture degree from Clemson in 1928.

Lee was retained as a tutor in mathematics by Clemson College in 1896. By 1898 he won an appointment as Instructor in Drawing. He was an Associate Professor of Architecture and Drawing from 1900 to 1914, winning appointment as Professor of Architecture and Drawing, and as College Architect, in 1914. For several years Lee also served as superintendent of construction and repair of the campus facilities.

Professor Lee wrote several articles on South Carolina architecture, including an analysis of the state's rural school design and construction practices in 1910. His own designs included at least eight small schools in rural South Carolina. Lee was also an early student of the state's historic buildings; he worked with Professor R.L. Anderson in the 1930s to document, photograph, and make measured drawings of old houses in Seneca, Pendleton, Anderson, and other Carolina communities.

Lee maintained an office in Charlotte, North Carolina, in 1920-1923; his firm was called Lee, (T. Angus) McEwan & (Arthur R.) Turnbull in 1920; and Lee & Turnbull in 1920-1921.

Governor Richard Ira Manning appointed Lee to the newly created State Board of Architectural Examiners in 1917. Lee served on the Board until 1948; he was the Board's chairman in 1933-1948.

The South Carolina Chapter of the A.I.A. mourned Professor Lee's death in 1959. The chapter records note:

> The committee and Chapter were grateful that the naming of the Rudolph E. Lee Gallery, in the School of Architecture, had been formally approved by the Clemson Trustees prior to this event and in time for Mr. Lee to have knowledge of it. "Pop" Lee will always be remembered for his great contribution, through education, to the advancement of the profession in the state.

South Carolina projects

1908: Clemson College Alumni Association Clubhouse, Clemson; $50,000 (*MR*, 2 July 1908, p. 70.)

1908: Addition, Engineering Building, Clemson College, Clemson; $30,000 (*MR*, 2 July 1908, p. 70; 19 August 1908, p. 62.)

1911: Dairy Buildings, Clemson College, Clemson; $20,000 (*MR*, 23 March 1911, p. 68.)

1911: Three professors' dwellings, Clemson College, Clemson; $6000 (*MR*, 13 April 1911, p. 70; 20 April 1911, p. 74.)

1915: "Model Village Home #2" (*The State*, 21 March 1915, p. 24.)

1915: Y.M.C.A. Building, Clemson College, Clemson; $75,000 (Rudolph E. Lee, *A Young Men's Christian Association Building for Clemson College* (Columbia: The State Company, 1914); *MR*, 4 March 1915, p. 64; 11 March 1915, p. 53; *News & Press*, Darlington, S.C., 10 June 1915, supplement.)

1915: Consolidated School Building, Scotch Cross Roads, Greenwood vicinity; $4000 (*MR*, 1 July 1915, p. 69; 8 July 1915, p. 57.)

1916: School, Pendleton; $4000 (*MR*, 11 May 1916, p. 68.)

1916: School, Arkwright; $8000 (*MR*, 22 June 1916, p. 69.)

1917: Two Schools, Marion; $7000 (*MR*, 10 May 1917, p. 72.)

1917: School, Wilkinsville; $2500 (*MR*, 23 August 1917, p. 70; 27 September 1917, p. 75.)

1918: School, National Highway, Greenville; $5000 (*MR*, 12 December 1918, p. 78.)

1922: West Wing, Administration Building, Epworth Orphanage, Columbia; $50,000 (*MR*, 2 March 1922, p. 109; 9 March 1922, p. 84.)

1922: School, Landrum; $17,000 (*MR*, 16 March 1922, p. 91; 6 April 1922, p. 125.)

1923: Addition, Dormitory and Mess Hall, Clemson College, Clemson; $45,000 (*MR*, 10 May 1923, p. 109.)

1923: Women's Dormitory, University of South Carolina, Columbia (*MR*, 2 August 1923, p. 150; 9 August 1923, p. 111.)

1923: Union Bleachery Community Building, Greenville; $27,000 (*MR*, 12 April 1923, p. 99 h; 19 April 1923, p. 100.)

1924: Enlargement, Auditorium, Clemson College, Clemson; $40,000 (*MR*, 13 March 1924, p. 117.)

1924: Dormitory, Lander College, Greenwood; $61,000 (*MR*, 12 June 1924, p. 114.)

1925: Sloan Brothers Store Building, Calhoun Road and State Highway No. 2, Clemson; $118,000 (*MR*, 19 March 1925, p. 124; 26 March 1925, p. 118.)

1925: Remodeling, Agricultural Building (for use as library), Clemson College, Clemson (*MR*, 30 July 1925, p. 121.)

1927: Riggs Hall of Engineering and Architecture, Clemson College, Clemson; $225,000 (*MR*, 9 June 1927, p. 115; *South Carolina Magazine*, Vol. 13, No. 1, January 1950, p. 58.)

1929: Field House, Clemson College, Clemson (*MR*, 27 June 1929, p. 94.)

Sources: Charlotte, North Carolina city directories; Clemson College Catalogs, 1893-1925; Garlington, pp. 255-256; Rudolph E. Lee, "Rural School Improvement," *The Clemson Agricultural College Extension Bulletins*, Vol. VI, No. 3, July 1910; Petty, p. 90; *MR*, various citations; *Who's Who at Clemson* (n.p., n.p.: October, 1920); Bryan Wright, *Clemson: An Informal History of the University 1889-1979* (Columbia: The R.L. Bryan Co., 1979), pp. 44, 48, 50, 115, 124, 275.

LEGARE, Artemus E. (1875- ca. 1904) Artemus Legare, a South Carolina native, was a draftsman with W.B. Smith Whaley & Co. (q.v.) in Columbia in 1897. Legare associated with Frank C. Walter by 1900 as Walter & Legare, Architects. The firm was dissolved by 1902. Legare was working as superintendent for the Columbia street railway system in 1904.

South Carolina projects:

See **Walter, Frank C.** (Walter & Legare)

Sources: Columbia city directories; *MR*, various citations; *The State*, 5 December 1900, p. 4; 1900 United States Census, Richland County, South Carolina, Enumeration District 84, p. 13A.

LeGRAND, Leon (active 1919-1940) LeGrand graduated from Clemson College with a degree in architecture in 1915. He worked as a draftsman for Joseph E. Sirrine (q.v.) for several years; and from 1919 through 1940 he was associated with fellow Clemson and Sirrine alumnus James D. Beacham (q.v.) in Greenville and in Asheville, North Carolina.

South Carolina projects:

See **Beacham, James D.** (Beacham & LeGrand)

Sources: Greenville city directories; *MR*, various citations.

LEITNER, Joseph F. (1871- ca. 1927) Joseph Leitner helped shape South Carolina's architectural heritage through many associations, partnerships, and offices. His work is evident in Aiken, in Florence, and in Charleston.

Leitner, son of Major H.B. Leitner and Annie E. Leitner, was born in Atlanta in 1871. Records of Leitner's schooling and professional training have not been identified. In 1893, at the age of twenty-two, Leitner was associated with established architect Albert W. Todd (q.v.) in Augusta, Georgia. He opened his own office the next year, and from 1894 through 1900 Leitner pursued a modest career in Augusta and in Aiken. In 1898 Leitner was associated with Heinrich H. Johannsen (q.v.) in Augusta.

Leitner moved to Columbia around 1901 and took a position with architect Charles Coker Wilson (q.v.) He was listed as a draftsman in Wilson's office in 1903, and as a travelling representative for the firm in 1905. In 1906 Leitner and Florence contractor William J. Wilkins (q.v.) collaborated to win the commission for the new Florence Graded School (Poynor School) from Wilson. The firm of

Leitner & Wilkins was active in Florence and in Wilmington, North Carolina, through 1908.

In 1907 Leitner & Wilkins designed a railway station in Florence for the Atlantic Coast Line Railway. Leitner won the appointment as official architect for the A.C.L. Railway in 1909, and he held this position through 1912. His work for the A.C.L. included the 1910 Union Station at Tampa, Florida, for the A.C.L., Seaboard Coast Line, and Tampa Northern Railways; the 1911 A.C.L. YMCA building in Rocky Mount, North Carolina; the 1911 A.C.L. Depot and Office Building, Rocky Mount, North Carolina; and the 1912 A.C.L. Office Building at Wilmington, North Carolina.

Leitner was an inventor as well as an architect. He patented a "fractional adding machine" in 1915, which he claimed was "invaluable" for architects, engineers, contractors, and machinists. Manufacturing rights to the machine were sold to the Fractional Adding Machine Company of Virginia.

Leitner moved to Atlanta in 1917. In 1918 he associated with C.P. Niederhauser in Atlanta. In 1919 Leitner was an associate of William Augustus Edwards (q.v.) and William Sayward (q.v.). Leitner's career in Georgia seems not to have flourished; he was listed as the secretary-treasurer of the Perfect Packing Company in the 1920 Atlanta city directory.

Leitner's whereabouts after 1920 are not known. An architect named Leitner was active in St. Petersburg, Florida, in 1926 and 1927; this may have been Joseph F. Leitner.

South Carolina projects:

1893: See **Todd, Albert Whitner** (Todd & Leitner)

1894: Ten Cottages and Five Buildings, Port Royal (*MR*, 4 May 1894, p. 235.)

1899: Judge Beckwith Residence, Aiken; $35,000 (*MR*, 30 June 1899, p. 390.)

1900: Ed Smith Residence, Aiken; $9000 (*The State*, 29 January 1900, p. 2.)

1900: Sheffield Phelps Residence, Aiken (*The State*, 29 January 1900, p. 2.)

Leitner & Wilkins

1906: Horry County Courthouse, Conway; $40,000 (*The Horry Herald*, Conway, 12 April 1906, p. 1; 22 February 1906, p. 1; *MR*, 19 April 1906, p. 387; 2 August 1906, p. 68; 16 August 1906, p. 118; Plaque, Horry County Courthouse, Conway.)

1906: Poynor School, Florence (Minutes, Board of Trustees, Florence City Schools, Florence, 8 May 1906, p. 94.)

1906: W.R. Barringer Business Building, Florence; $15,000 (*MR*, 19 April 1906, p. 387.)

1906: E.F. Douglas Residence, Florence; $7000 (*MR*, 19 April 1906, p. 387.)

1906: John L. Barringer Residence, Florence; $12,000 (*MR*, 19 April 1906, p. 387.)

1906: S.C. State Industrial School Building, Florence (*MR*, 9 August 1906, p. 94; 25 October 1906, p. 371.)

1906: School, Summerton; $15,000 (*MR*, 10 May 1906, p. 480.)

1906: Randle, DuRant and DuRant Business Building, Sumter (*MR*, 19 April 1906, p. 388.)

1906: M.B. Randle Residence, Sumter; $6000 (*MR*, 19 April 1906, p. 388.)

1906: John E. Whilden Store Building, Sumter; $20,000 (*MR*, 28 June 1906, p. 681.)

1907: Atlantic Coast Line Railway Passenger Station, Florence; $47,000 (*MR*, 7 February 1907, p. 111; 30 May 1907, p. 641; 4 July 1907, p. 804; 11 July 1907, p. 836.)

1908: Julian Mitchell School, Fishburne, Perry and Sheppard streets, Charleston; $34,588 (*MR*, 25 June 1908, p. 58; 2 July 1908, p 70; 20 August 1908, p. 63; 27 August 1908, p. 56; 3 September 1908, pp. 71-72.)

Joseph F. Leitner

1908: Addition, Central Hotel, Florence; $12,000 (*MR*, 5 November 1908, p. 71.)

1909: Methodist Church, Conway; $18,000 (*MR*, 10 June 1909, p. 65; 26 August 1909, p. 55.)

1909-1910: School, Walterboro; $16,000 (*MR*, 24 June 1909, p. 60; 29 July 1909, p. 62; 5 August 1909, p. 72; 19 August 1909, p. 62; 26 August 1909, p. 57; 2 September 1909, p. 73; 30 September 1909, p. 73; 20 January 1910, p. 67; 27 January 1910, p. 65.)

1911: Y.M.C.A., Florence (*MR*, 19 January 1911, p. 71.)

1919: See **Edwards, William Augustus** (Edwards, Sayward & Leitner)

Sources: Atlanta, Georgia, city directories; Columbia city directories; 1900 Federal Census, Aiken County, South Carolina, Vol. III, p. 47A; *MR*, various citations; Wilmington, North Carolina, city directories; Tony P. Wrenn, *Wilmington, North Carolina: An Architectural and Historical Portrait* (Charlottesville, Virginia: The University Press of Virginia, 1984); Tony P. Wrenn, Washington, D.C., unpublished research.

LEO, Gustave E. (active 1890-1891) Gustave E. Leo established an architectural practice in Atlanta, Georgia, around 1870. Little is known of his career. Thomas H. Morgan (q.v.) identified DeGive's Opera House, which stood on the corner of Marietta and Forsyth Streets in Atlanta, as Leo's work.

One building in South Carolina was designed by Leo: the Central Graded School at 309 Academy Street in Union. This brick Richardsonian-Romanesque building was constructed in 1890-1891.

Sources: *Catalogue of Union Graded Schools, Union, S.C. 1902-1903* (Union: Allan Nicholson Press, 1903), p. 5; *MR* 31 May 1890, p. 43; Morgan, pp. 140, 145; *Sholes' Georgia State Gazetteer and Business Directory for 1879 & 1880* (Atlanta, Georgia: A.E. Sholes & Co., 1879); *Architects and Builders in Georgia*.

LETELLIER, Louis S. (active 1908-1962) Louis S. Letellier, a native of Virginia, was trained in drawing at the Miller School in Albemarle County. He worked as an instructor in drawing at Miller School, and in 1908 won a position as professor of drawing at The Citadel in Charleston.

In 1917 Letellier was appointed a member of the newly-created South Carolina Board of Architectural Examiners. He served on the Board until 1921. In later years he served on the State Board of Engineering Examiners.

Sources: Charleston city directories; Petty, pp. 112-116, 133; *The State*, 7 August 1908, p. 10.

LEVY & CLARKE (active 1916-1931) The Savannah, Georgia, firm of Morton H. Levy and Captain William Bordley Clarke (1890-ca. 1944) designed the Ancient Free and Accepted Masons, Lodge No. 98 Temple and Store Building, in Ridgeland, South Carolina. The building was contracted in 1931 at $9996. The firm's work in Savannah included the $100,000 Savannah Savings and Real Estate Corporation Bank and Theater Building, contracted in 1920. Levy & Clarke were associate architects for the Independent Presbyterian Church Sunday School in Savannah, designed in 1928 by the prominent Boston architects Cram & Ferguson.

Sources: *MR*, 9 April 1931, p. 57; 16 April 1931, p. 58; and various other citations; Morgan, p. 105; *Architects and Builders in Georgia*.

LINTHICUM, Hill C. (1860-1919) Hill C. Linthicum was the son of architect William H. Linthicum of Durham, North Carolina. He studied architecture in Baltimore, Maryland, and entered his father's office in 1883. In private practice, Linthicum designed Durham's first skyscraper, the six-story Trust Building, in 1905. He is credited with the design of some forty school buildings.

South Carolina project:

1919: Terrell & Satterfield Tobacco Sales Warehouse, Manning; $17,473 (*MR*, 6 March 1919, p. 127.)

Sources: *MR*, various citations; Claudia P. Roberts et.al., *The Durham Architectural and Historic Inventory* (Durham, North Carolina: City of Durham, 1982), pp. 28, 345; Withey, p. 374.

LIVINGSTON, William T. (active 1907-1921)
William T. Livingston of Newberry was a contractor and builder. He and J.T. Sample operated as Sample & Livingston, Lumber, in 1921. Livingston was identified as architect for one project in Newberry in 1907.

South Carolina projects:

1907: Shelley & Summer Business Building, Newberry; $6000; W.T. Livingston, architect and contractor (*MR*, 16 May 1907, p. 574.)

1913: School, Pomaria; $3800; W.T. Livingston, contractor (*MR*, 13 March 1913, p. 66.)

1921: Negro School, Newberry; $25,000; James C. Hemphill (q.v.), architect; W.T. Livingston, contractor (*MR*, 1 December 1921, p. 105 f; 8 December 1921, p. 84 e.)

Sources: *MR*, various citations; Newberry city directories.

LOCKWOOD, GREENE & Co. (active 1882-present) Lockwood Greene & Co. is a major architectural and engineering firm active in the eastern United States. The company played a major role in the development of South Carolina's cotton processing industry. Between 1873 and 1911 the firm engineered and built over fifty cotton processing mills in the state.

The New England prototype textile mill, owing its configuration as much to the insurance companies as to the engineers, was introduced in South Carolina by Lockwood Greene. Other major mill engineers to work in South Carolina, including Joseph Sirrine (q.v.) and W.B.S. Whaley (q.v.), followed the precedents of Lockwood Greene. The nation's first fully electrical powered textile mill, Columbia Mills, was designed and built by Lockwood Greene in South Carolina in 1893-1894.

Amos D. Lockwood (1811-1884) began work as a mill engineer in Lewiston, Maine, in 1858. He was established as an architect and consulting engineer by 1871. Stephen Greene, a former textile mill supervisor, associated with Lockwood shortly thereafter. The two men, together with John W. Danielson, organized in Providence, Rhode Island as Lockwood, Greene & Co. in 1882, shortly before Lockwood's death. Greene died in 1901, and his eldest son Edwin Farnham Greene became president of the firm. Greene expanded the firm's operations to include ownership and management, as well as engineering, of textile mills and other industries. The firm maintained offices in Boston, Massachusetts; Charlotte, North Carolina; and Atlanta, Georgia, as well as Greenville and Spartanburg.

In 1901 Lockwood, Greene & Co. advertised in the Boston city directory as Mill Architects and Engineers, designing and building textile plants, finishing plants, industrial plants, water power systems, steam power systems, and electric power systems. South Carolina was undergoing an industrial revolution in the late nineteenth century, as northern investors capitalized on the state's plentiful water power, cheap labor, and proximity to the raw materials to build textile processing mills. The firm's standard fee for designing a textile mill in 1898 was $1500, plus 10¢ per spindle.

Lockwood Greene opened a branch office in Greenville, South Carolina in 1898, as a base for the firm's southern operations. Joseph E. Sirrine was appointed regional manager at the Greenville office. Sirrine, a Greenville surveyor and engineer, began work with Lockwood Greene in 1895, preparing surveys for the F.W. Poe Textile Mill in Greenville. As manager at the Greenville office, Sirrine was associated with nearly all of the firm's work in South Carolina and Georgia from 1898 to 1902. In 1903 Sirrine declined an opportunity to become a partner in the firm, choosing instead to open his own architectural and engineering office in Greenville. Albert L. Scott and Roland A. Thayer were managers of Lockwood Greene's Greenville office between 1903 and 1909.

Robert E. Barnwell (q.v.) joined the Boston office of Lockwood Greene in 1907, and worked as architect and industrial engineer for the firm through 1958. He succeeded Thayer as manager of the Greenville office in 1910, and, after that office was closed, served as manager of the Atlanta office from 1912 to 1920. When the firm opened an office in Spartanburg in 1924, Barnwell was named manager, with supervision of the Atlanta and Charlotte regions. Lockwood Greene's Spartanburg offices were located in the Montgomery Building (1923-1924), a landmark skyscraper that still dominates the city's skyline.

Walter W. Cook was appointed head of Lockwood Greene's architectural department in 1919, with George F. Blount as his assistant. Cook was with the firm in 1919-1928, and provided plans for the Henry J. Blackford Residence in Spartanburg, in 1924. He later established an independent office in Dallas, Texas, and worked in collaboration with Lockwood Greene for the Spartanburg Memorial Auditorium.

Adlai Osborne (q.v.) worked with Lockwood Greene's Charlotte office in 1920-1922.

Major Lockwood Greene projects in South Carolina, in addition to the textile mills, included the new campus of The Citadel, the South Carolina Military College, at Hampton Park in Charleston. This work was commissioned in 1919, and the campus was built in phases over the next twenty years.

South Carolina projects:

Amos D. Lockwood

1873: Piedmont Manufacturing Company, Piedmont (Lincoln, p. 95.)

Ca. 1878: Mill Building, Graniteville Mills, Graniteville (Lincoln, p. 97.)

1880: Mill No. 2, Piedmont Manufacturing Company, Piedmont (Lincoln, p. 97.)

1880: Clifton Mills, Glendale (Lincoln, p. 97.)

Ca. 1880: Col. Leroy Springs Mill, Lancaster (Lincoln, p. 97.)

1881: Charleston Mills, Charleston (Lincoln, p. 97.)

1881: Pelzer Mills, Pelzer (Lincoln, p. 101.)

1882: Mill No. 1, Pacolet Manufacturing Company, Pacolet (Lincoln, pp. 101-102, 165, 178.)

Lockwood, Greene & Co.

1883: Newberry Cotton Mills, Newberry (Lincoln, pp. 149, 178.)

1883: Mill No. 2, Pelzer Mills, Pelzer (Lincoln, p. 101.)

1884: Darlington Manufacturing Co. Cotton Mill, Darlington (Lincoln, p. 178.)

1884: Reedy River Manufacturing Company Cotton Mill, Greenville (Lincoln, p. 178.)

1884: Mill No. 3, Pelzer Mills, Pelzer (Lincoln, p. 101.)

1887: Mill No. 2, Pacolet Manufacturing Company, Pacolet (Lincoln, pp. 165, 178.)

1888: Whitney Manufacturing Company Cotton Mill, Whitney (Lincoln, p. 178.)

1889: Spartan Mills Cotton Mill, Spartanburg (Lincoln, pp. 122, 178.)

1891: Camden Cotton Mill, Camden (Lincoln, p. 178.)

1892: Mill No. 3, Pacolet Manufacturing Company, Pacolet (Lincoln, pp. 165, 178.)

1893: Lockhart Mills Cotton Mill, Lockhart (Lincoln, pp. 145, 178.)

1893-1894: Columbia Mills Cotton Mill, Columbia (Lincoln, p. 178; *The State*, 26 April 1894, 3 June 1894, 12 June 1894; Fenelon DeVere Smith, "The Economic Development of the Textile Industry in the Columbia, South Carolina Area From 1790 through 1916" (Ph.D. dissertation, University of Kentucky, 1952), pp. 75-76); "The Story of the First Electrically Operated Textile Mill," (n.p.: General Electric, 1931.)

1894: Mill No. 4, Pelzer Manufacturing Co., Pelzer (Lincoln, p. 178.)

1894: Tucapau Mills Cotton Mill, Tucapau (Lincoln, p. 178.)

1894: American Spinning Company Cotton Mill, Greenville (Lincoln, pp. 155, 178.)

1894: Addition, Newberry Cotton Mills, Newberry (Lincoln, p. 149.)

1895: Greenwood Cotton Mill, Greenwood (Lincoln, p. 178.)

1895: Mill No. 3, Piedmont Manufacturing Company Cotton Mill, Piedmont (Lincoln, p. 178.)

1895: F.W. Poe Manufacturing Company Cotton Mill, Greenville (Lincoln, pp. 155, 178.)

1895: Hydroelectric Plant, Mill No. 4, Pelzer (Lincoln, p. 178.)

1896: Abbeville Cotton Mills, Abbeville (Lincoln, p. 178.)

1896: Grendel Mills Cotton Mill, Greenville (Lincoln, p. 178.)

1896: Mill No. 2, Spartan Mills, Spartanburg (Lincoln, p. 178.)

1896: Mill No. 2, Whitney Manufacturing Co., Whitney (Lincoln, p. 178.)

1897: Addition, Poe Manufacturing Company, Greenville (*Southern Architect and Building News*, October 1897, p. 284.)

1899: Easley Cotton Mill, Easley (Lincoln, p. 179.)

1899: Belton Mills Cotton Mill, Belton (Lincoln, p. 179.)

1899: Mill No. 2, Abbeville Cotton Mills, Abbeville (Lincoln, p. 179.)

1899: Orr Cotton Mill, Anderson (Lincoln, p. 179.)

1900: Mill No. 2, American Spinning Co., Greenville (Lincoln, p. 179.)

1900: Mill No. 2, Darlington Manufacturing Co., Darlington (Lincoln, p. 179.)

1900: Brandon Mills Cotton Mill, Greenville (Lincoln, p.179.)

1900: American Spinning Company Cotton Mill, Greenville (Lincoln, p. 179.)

1900: Hartsville Cotton Mills, Hartsville (Lincoln, p. 179.)

1900: Graniteville Manufacturing Company Cotton Mill, Graniteville (Lincoln, p.179.)

1900: Monoghan Mills Cotton Mill, Greenville (Lincoln, p. 179.)

1900: Monarch Cotton Mill, Union (Lincoln, p. 179.)

1900: F.W. Poe Manufacturing Company Cotton Mill, Greenville (Lincoln, p. 179.)

1900: Mill No. 4, Pacolet Manufacturing Company, Pacolet (Lincoln, pp. 165, 179.)

1900: Saxon Mills Cotton Mill, Spartanburg (Lincoln, pp. 165, 179.)

1901: Mollohon Manufacturing Company Cotton Mill, Newberry (Lincoln, pp. 169, 179.)

1904: Addition, Spartan Mills, Spartanburg (Lincoln, p. 254.)

1904: Addition, Drayton Mills, Spartanburg (Lincoln, p. 254.)

1904: Addition, Brandon Mills, Spartanburg (Lincoln, p. 254.)

1905: Pacolet Mill No. 5, Pacolet (Lincoln, p. 254.)

1905: Glenwood Mill, Easley (Lincoln, p. 254.)

1906: Pickens Mill, Pickens (Lincoln, p. 263.)

1907-1909: Addition, Newberry Cotton Mills, Newberry; $250,000 (Lincoln, p. 265; Stone, p. 139.)

1908-1909: Mill No. 2, Brandon Mills, Greenville; $1,400,000 (Lincoln, p. 265; Stone, p. 138.)

1910: Panola Cotton Mill, Greenwood (Lincoln, p. 272.)

1910: Westervelt (Judson) Mill, Greenville (Lincoln, p. 272.)

1910: Addition, Carolina Mill, Greenville (Lincoln, p. 272.)

1910: Addition, American Spinning Company Building, Greenville (Lincoln, p. 272.)

1910: Oakland Cotton Mills, Newberry (Lincoln, p. 272.)

1911: Glenn-Lowry Manufacturing Company Mill, Whitmire (Lincoln, p. 278.)

1911: Addition, Greer Manufacturing Company, Greer (Lincoln, p. 278.)

1913: General Asbestos & Rubber Company Building, Charleston (Lincoln, p. 287.)

1919-1920: The Citadel, New Campus, including Barracks, Academic Buildings, Mess Hall, Kitchens, etc.; Charleston; $750,000 (MR, 20 November 1919, p. 148 m; 27 November 1919, p. 140; 6 May 1920, p. 201; 17 June 1920, p. 149.)

1922: Infirmary, The Citadel, Charleston; $52,950 (MR, 8 June 1922, p. 80.)

1923: Alumni Building, The Citadel, Charleston; $45,000 (MR, 29 March 1923, p. 102; 5 April 1923, p. 122.)

1923: Twenty-Two Residences, Langley Cotton Mills, Langley (MR, 29 November 1923, p. 100.)

1923: Thirty-Five Operatives' Residences, Winnsboro Mills, Winnsboro (MR, 26 April 1923, p. 110.)

1923: Cotton Mill, 305 Operatives' Residences, and other buildings, Pacific Mills, Lyman (MR, 27 September 1923, p. 87.)

1923: Southern Worsted Corporation Mill, Greenville (Lincoln, pp. 477-478.)

1923-1924: Montgomery Office Building, Elm and N. Church streets, Spartanburg; $850,000 (MR, 18 October 1923, p. 129; 29 November 1923, p. 99; 24 January 1924, p. 105; 21 February 1924, p. 105; 13 March 1924, p. 115; 1 May 1924, p. 152; 8 May 1924, p. 110; 5 June 1924, p. 137.)

1923-1924: First Presbyterian Church, E. Main Street, Spartanburg; $300,000 (MR, 20 December 1923, p. 74; 17 April 1924, p. 117; 4 September 1924, p. 127; 30 October 1924, p. 90.)

1923-1924: Mary Black Clinic, Oakland Avenue and E. Main Street, Spartanburg; $100,000 (MR, 3 April 1924, p. 152; 24 April 1924, p. 111; 26 June 1924, p. 113; Lincoln, p. 482.)

1924: Remodeling, American National Bank Building, 108 Morgan Street, Spartanburg (MR, 17 July 1924, p. 114; 24 July 1924, p. 124.)

1924: Addition, Joanna Mills, Goldville (Lincoln, p. 489.)

1924: Fifty Residences, Banna Cotton Mills, Goldville; $81,000 (MR, 19 June 1924, p. 116.)

1924: Twenty-Seven Residences, Winnsboro Mills, Winnsboro (MR, 28 February 1924, p. 118; 6 March 1924, p. 149; 27 March 1924, p. 120.)

1924: Henry J. Blackford Residence, Connecticut Avenue, Ezell Park, Spartanburg; $10,000 (MR, 24 July 1924, p. 126.)

1924: James Chapman Residence, R.F.H. Chapman Residence, and Dr. L.J. Blake Residence ("group estate"), Plume Street, Converse Heights,

Spartanburg; $100,000 (*MR*, 28 August 1924, p. 113; 4 September 1924, p. 128.)

1924: Ben Hill Brown Residence, Connecticut Avenue, Spartanburg; $30,000 (*MR*, 2 October 1924, p. 141.)

1924: Alteration of Douglas Home for Hotel, S. Congress Street, Winnsboro (*MR*, 2 October 1924, p. 142.)

1924-1925: Addition, Frank Evans High School, Spartanburg; $165,000 (*MR*, 27 November 1924, p. 98; 15 January 1925, p. 110; 3 September 1925, p. 136.)

1925: Summit Realty Co. Apartment Building, W. Henry and Spring streets, Spartanburg; $150,000 (*MR*, 21 May 1925, p. 118.)

1925: H.O. Wallace Warehouse, Ezell Street, Spartanburg; $15,000 (*MR*, 5 February 1925, p. 126.)

1925: Fifty Operatives' Residences, Joanna Mills, Goldville (*MR*, 24 December 1925, p. 96.)

1925: August W. Smith Co. Department Store Building, E. Main Street, Spartanburg; $325,000 (*MR*, 3 December 1925, p. 126.)

1926: Dormitory, The Citadel, Charleston; $275,000 (*MR*, 13 May 1926, p. 107; Lincoln, p. 507.)

1926: Forty-Five Operatives' Residences, Pacific Mills, Lyman; $150,000 (*MR*, 26 August 1926, p. 102; 16 September 1926, p. 119.)

1927: Apartment House and President's Residence, The Citadel, Charleston (*MR*, 10 March 1927, p. 100.)

1927: Two Residences, Kendall Mills, Inc., Newberry; $9500 (*MR*, 27 January 1927, pp. 96-97; 3 February 1927, p. 135.)

1927: Fifty Residences, Oakland Cotton Mills, Newberry; $135,000 (*MR*, 16 June 1927, p. 115.)

1928: Seventy Operatives' Residences, Joanna Mills, Goldville (*MR*, 27 September 1928, p. 84; 4 October 1928, p. 102; Lincoln, p. 514.)

1928: School, Saxon Mills, Spartanburg; $75,000 (*MR*, 12 July 1928, p. 93.)

1928: Addition, Mill Office, Saxon Mills, Spartanburg (*MR*, 22 November 1928, p. 88.)

1928: Cotton Mill, Twenty-Nine Operatives' Residences, and other buildings, Powell Knitting Company, Spartanburg (*MR*, 15 March 1928, p. 99; 29 March 1928, p. 91; *The Architectural Record*, Vol. 65, No. 5, May 1929, p. 72.)

1929: Forty-Nine Residences, Kendall Mills, Edgefield; $160,000 (*MR*, 14 February 1929, p. 106.)

1929: Joanna School, Goldville; $50,000 (*MR*, 27 June 1929, p. 94.)

1929: Warehouse, Oakland Cotton Mills, Newberry (*MR*, 7 February 1929, p. 113.)

1929: Annex, Spartanburg County Courthouse, Spartanburg (*MR*, 15 August 1929, p. 92.)

1929: Finishing Plant and Thirty Employees' Residences, Fairforest Finishing Co., Spartanburg; $55,000 (*MR*, 13 June 1929, pp. 87-88; Lincoln, p. 592.)

1930: Addition, Roper Hospital, Charleston (*MR*, 1 May 1930, p. 91; 3 July 1930, p. 84.)

1930: Administration Building, The Citadel, Charleston; $123,650 (*MR*, 20 November 1930, p. 58; Lincoln, p. 613.)

1930: Clubhouse, Spartanburg Country Club, Spartanburg; $35,000 (*MR*, 24 April 1930, p. 85.)

1930: Community Building, Winnsboro Mills, Winnsboro; $80,000 (*MR*, 18 September 1930, p. 72.)

1931: Duplex Residence, The Citadel, Charleston (*MR*, 24 September 1931, p. 44.)

1931: School, Pacific Mills, Lyman; $55,000 (*MR*, 19 February 1931, p. 67.)

1931: Boilerhouse Building and Additions, The Citadel, Charleston (Lincoln, p. 615.)

1935: Mill Unit Addition, Rock Hill Printing & Finishing Co., Rock Hill (*MR*, November 1935, p. 36; Lincoln, p. 630.)

1937: Barracks, Hospital Addition, Library Addition, Administration Building Addition, and Boilerhouse Addition, The Citadel, Charleston (Lincoln, p. 644.)

1938: Cleveland Junior High School, Spartanburg (Lincoln, p. 650.)

1947: Spartanburg Memorial Auditorium, Spartanburg; Lockwood, Greene & Co., engineers; Hudson & Chapman, supervising architects; Walter W. Cook & Associates, consulting architects (Lincoln, p. 725; *South Carolina Magazine*, Vol. 13, #10, October 1950, p. 22.)

1952: Liberty Life Insurance Company Building, Greenville; Lockwood, Greene & Co., engineers; Carson & Lundin, architects (Lincoln, pp. 742-743; *South Carolina Magazine*, Vol. 20, #4, April 1955, p. 48.)

1955: Amerotron Corporation Factory, Barnwell (Lincoln, p. 754; *South Carolina Magazine*, Vol. 21, #6, June 1956, p. 54.)

1956: Field House (Rex Enright Athletic Center), Rosewood Drive, University of South Carolina, Columbia (*South Carolina Magazine*, Vol. 21, #6, June 1956, p. 25; Russell Maxey, *South Carolina's Historic Columbia* (Columbia: The R.L. Bryan Co., 1980), p. 192.)

Sources: *Directory of Historic American Architectural Firms* (New York: Committee for the Preservation of Architectural Records, 1979), p. 20; Greenville city directories; William J. Heiser, *Lockwood Greene 1958-1968: Another Period in the History of an Engineering Business* (New York, New York: Lockwood Greene Engineers, Inc., 1970); Samuel B. Lincoln, *Lockwood Greene: The History of an Engineering Business 1832-1958*

(Brattleboro, Vermont: The Stephen Greene Press, 1960); *MR*, various citations; *South Carolina Magazine*, various citations; Spartanburg city directories; William H. Stone, "Typical Building in the South in 1909," *MR*, 6 January 1910, pp. 137-140.

LOFTIS, M.T. (active 1921) M.T. Loftis of Greenville was identified as the architect-contractor for the $12,000 J.D. Bridges Residence, built in Greenville in 1921.

Source: *MR*, 7 April 1921, pp. 145-146.

LOUCAS, J. (active 1887) Loucas, of Orangeburg, was listed as an architect in Clark W. Bryan's 1887 *Directory of Architects*.

LOVATT, George Ignatius Sr. (1872-1958) George Lovatt's architectural work was primarily in the service of the Catholic church. He studied at the Philadelphia Museum and School of Industrial Art, and began work as an architect in 1892 in Philadelphia, Pennsylvania. Prominent among his designs were the Church of the Holy Child and the Church of the Most Precious Blood, both in Philadelphia.

South Carolina projects

1901: Rectory, St. Peter's Catholic Church, Columbia (Tatman/Moss, p. 490.)

1902: O'Donnell Residence, Sumter (Tatman/Moss, p. 490.)

Sources: Tatman/Moss, pp. 489-492.

LOWERY, Samuel F. (active 1912-1916) Samuel F. Lowery advertised as a contractor in Greenville in 1912. He was identified as the architect and contractor for the $5000 H.P. Burbage Residence, built in Greenville in 1916.

Sources: Greenville city directories; *MR*, 13 April 1916, p. 70.

LUDLOW & PEABODY (1909-1935) William Orr Ludlow (1871-1954) and Charles S. Peabody (1880-1935) were prominent New York architects in the early twentieth century. Peabody was educated at the Ecole des Beaux Arts in Paris. Their work in the South included several buildings at the University of Georgia, in Athens, and at the George Peabody College for Teachers in Nashville, Tennessee.

South Carolina project:

1918: State Industrial School for Girls, Columbia; Ludlow & Peabody, architects; J. Carroll Johnson (q.v.), associate architect (*MR*, 3 October 1918, p. 107.)

Sources: Herndon, pp. 117-118; Francis, p. 51; Withey, p. 462.

LYNCH, L. Earl Caldwell (active 1896-1908) Lynch was a contractor and builder active in Spartanburg from 1896 to 1908. In 1900 Lynch was a partner of Avery Carter (q.v.) Lynch & Carter advertised as architects and contractors.

Sources: Spartanburg city directories.

MACDONALD, C. Roy (active 1915-1917) C. Roy Macdonald worked for architect C. Gadsden Sayre (q.v.) in Anderson from 1915 through 1917. Macdonald was the architect for a residence in North Anderson for H.R. Fitzgerald. The project was contracted in 1915 for $3000.

Sources: Anderson city directories; *MR*, 5 August 1915, p. 70.

MACMURPHY, Augustus Mitchell (active 1886-1915) Augustus M. Macmurphy practiced architecture in Augusta, Georgia, in association with Joseph B. Story (q.v.) from 1889 through 1912. The firm designed two buildings in South Carolina, including the elegant Gothic-Revival St. Mary Help of Christians Church in Aiken. Prominent among the firm's Georgia projects was an addition to the Bon Air Hotel in Augusta, which was contracted in 1907 at $150,000.

South Carolina projects:

Macmurphy & Story

1905: Saint Mary Help of Christians Church, York Street and Park Avenue, Aiken; $20,000 (*MR*, 14 September 1905, p. 226; *History of Saint Mary Help of Christians Church and Aiken Missions: Compiled for the Seventy-Fifth Anniversary* (Aiken: St. Mary Help of Christians Church, 1942, p. 47.)

1911: Remodeling, Farmers' Bank, Edgefield (*MR*, 6 April 1911, p. 85.)

Sources: Augusta, Georgia, city directories; *MR*, various citations.

MAKIELSKI, Stanislaw John (1893-1969) Stanislaw Makielski was born at South Bend, Indiana, on 6 October 1893. He was educated at Notre Dame University and at the University of Virginia, taking his Bachelor of Science in Architecture degree at U.Va. in 1922. From 1921 to 1964 he was on the faculty of the University of Virginia School of Architecture. He pursued a modest architectural practice over the same period, with most of his work being in Charlottesville and Albemarle County. Representative works include the All Saints Episcopal Church, Stony Point, Virginia, 1926; the Thomas Jefferson Unitarian Church, Charlottesville, 1947; and the Louisa High School, Louisa County, Virginia, 1951.

South Carolina projects:

1931: Classroom Building, Voorhees Normal and Industrial School, Denmark; $80,000 (*MR*, 5 February 1931, p. 68.)

1932: Girls' Trades Building (St. James Building), Voorhees Normal and Industrial School, Denmark; $13,635 (*MR*, 18 February 1932, p. 36; 10 March 1932, p. 41; Cornerstone.)

Sources: Charlottesville, Virginia, city directories; Koyl. p. 361; K. Edward Lay, "Charlottesville's Architectural Legacy," *The Magazine of Albemarle County History*, Vol. 46, May 1988, p. 73; William B. O'Neal, *Architectural Drawing in*

Virginia 1819-1969 (Charlottesville, Virginia: University of Virginia, 1969), pp. v, ix.

MARSH, Marion Rossiter (1893-1977) Marion Marsh, a native of Florida, learned the profession as a draftsman for his brother W.M. Marsh in Jacksonville. He came to Charlotte, North Carolina, in 1915 to work for James M. McMichael (q.v.) After periods working for Charles C. Hook (q.v.) and for engineer Peter S. Gilchrist, Marsh opened his own architectural office in 1922.

Prominent among Marsh's work in North Carolina was the seven-story Builders Building at 314 West Trade Street, Charlotte, built in 1926. The Mutual Savings and Loan Office Building in Charlotte is an International Style highrise building completed in 1962. Marsh worked as district officer for the Historic American Buildings Survey in North Carolina in 1933-1934. Teebe Hawkins, a graduate of Clemson College, associated with Marsh in 1945.

South Carolina projects:

1925: County Office Building and remodeling of County Courthouse, Lancaster; $39,880 (*MR*, 5 March 1925, p. 136; Hanchett.)

1929: Cherokee County Courthouse, Gaffney; $125,000 (*MR*, 14 February 1929, p. 105; Hanchett.)

1930: Victor Cotton Oil Company Warehouse, Gaffney (*MR*, 2 October 1930, p. 73.)

1951: Educational Building, First Baptist Church, Winnsboro (Hanchett.)

n.d.: H.G. Phillips Residence and Barn, Winnsboro (Hanchett.)

n.d.: Dr. S.L. Bryson Residence, Winnsboro (Hanchett.)

n.d.: Everett Enterprises Theater, Union (Hanchett.)

n.d.: Theater, Lake City (Hanchett.)

Sources: *The Charlotte Observer*, Charlotte, North Carolina, 5 September 1977; Thomas Hanchett, Charlotte-Mecklenburg Historic Properties Commission, "The Work of M.R. Marsh and Successor Architects" (unpublished paper, 1983); Koyl, p. 632; *MR*, various citations.

MARTIN, Haskell Hair (1889- ca. 1965) Haskell H. Martin, a native of Anderson County, studied architecture at Alabama Polytechnic Institute and at Clemson College. He established an architectural practice in Greenville in 1912, in association with a man named Andrews. William J. Ward (q.v.) associated with Martin in 1916, a partnership which lasted through 1925.

Martin served with the American Expeditionary Forces in Europe during the First World War.

Martin's work included projects in North Carolina, Florida, Georgia, and Louisiana, but the vast majority of his works were in Greenville. Martin's residential designs were described variously as "colonial," "Spanish type," and "English Colonial type." Apartment buildings for the Southeastern Life Insurance Company (1921) and for A.C. Walker (1925) were his largest commissions.

Martin continued his practice in Greenville through the 1950s.

South Carolina projects:

Martin & Andrews

1914: J.O. Cauble Residence, Greenville; $10,000 (*MR*, 26 February 1914, p. 70.)

1914: St. James Powell Memorial Church, Lloyd and Buncombe streets, Greenville; $10,000 (*MR*, 9 April 1914, p. 70.)

1914: L.A. Mills Store Building, North and Laurens streets, Greenville; $4500 (*MR*, 23 April 1914, p. 71.)

1914: E.C. Pilgrim Residence, Williamston; $4200 (*MR*, 26 February 1914, p. 70.)

1915: L.H. Cary Residence, Greenville; $6000 (*MR*, 8 July 1915, p. 56.)

1915: Reconstruction, Bon Air Hotel, Williamston (*MR*, 18 November 1915, p. 67.)

1916: Methodist Episcopal Church South, Easley; $3000 (*MR*, 16 March 1916, p. 69.)

Martin & Ward

1916: Raven I. McDavid Apartment House, Greenville; $15,000 (*MR*, 8 June 1916, p. 70; 15 June 1916, p. 71; 9 November 1916, p. 68; 16 November 1916, p. 69.)

1916: F.E. Schroeder Residence, Greenville; $6000 (*MR*, 15 June 1916, pp. 71-72.)

1916: Sunday School and Parish House, Christ Church, Greenville; $6000 (*MR*, 16 November 1916, p. 69.)

1916: Mrs. Willie C. Belk Residence, Williamston; $3500 (*MR*, 16 March 1916, p. 69; 23 March 1916, p. 69.)

1917: Vivian Q. Guion Residence, Greenville; $5500 (*MR*, 18 January 1917, p. 72.)

1920: Addition, C.O. Hobbs Building, Greenville; $50,000 (*MR*, 29 January 1920, p. 154.)

1920: L.H. Stringer Residence, Greenville; $20,000 (*MR*, 8 April 1920, p. 147.)

1920: J.C. Redmon Residence, Mills Avenue, Greenville; $20,000 (*MR*, 3 June 1920, p. 182.)

1921: First Baptist Church, Blackville; $50,000 (*MR*, 24 March 1921, p. 112.)

1921: Southeastern Life Insurance Company Apartment House, W. McBee Avenue and Richardson Street, Greenville; $75,000 (*MR*, 21 April 1921, p. 120 b.)

1921: Fire Station, Pendleton and Markley streets, Greenville; $6597 (*MR*, 5 May 1921, p. 155.)

1922: Mrs. H. Cleveland Beattie Store and Apartment Building, E. North and Richardson streets, Greenville; $40,000 (*MR*, 13 April 1922, p. 79; 25 May 1922, p. 90.)

1922: C.J. Morgan Residence and Garage, E. Washington Street, Greenville; $12,000 (*MR*, 3 August 1922, p. 100.)

1923: W.D. Parrish Residence, Crescent Avenue, Greenville; $19,500 (*MR*, 22 February 1923, p. 99.)

1923: Traxler Tire Company Building, College Street, Greenville (*MR*, 16 August 1923, p. 116.)

1923: S.W. Reams Residence, Greenville; $16,400 (*MR*, 6 December 1923, p. 126.)

1923: J.C. Redmon Residence, 100 Crescent Avenue, Greenville (*MR*, 13 December 1923, p. 116.)

1924: W.O. Grace Residence, W. Earle Street, Greenville; $20,000 (*MR*, 17 April 1924, p. 119; 24 April 1924, p. 111.)

1924: Marion Brawley Store Building, College Street, Greenville; $17,000 (*MR*, 3 April 1924, p. 154; 24 April 1924, p. 113.)

1924: Thomas Parker "Welfare Building," E. Broad Street, Greenville; $30,000 (*MR*, 14 August 1924, p. 108.)

1925: Hampton Smith Residence, Greenville (*MR*, 14 May 1925, p. 115.)

1925: A.C. Walker Apartment Building, W. Washington Street, Greenville; $150,000 (*MR*, 6 August 1925, p. 121; 9 July 1925, p. 123.)

1925: R.B.R. Land Development Co., Four Residences, 41 Fairview Avenue, 46-A McIver Street, and 91-95 McIver Street, Greenville; $38,000 (*MR*, 8 October 1925, pp. 107-108.)

1925: Remodeling and enlarging, First Baptist Church, Laurens; $50,000 (*MR*, 30 July 1925, p. 119.)

Haskell H. Martin

1926: J.E. Stuckey Duplex Residence, E. Earle Street, Greenville; $15,000 (*MR*, 12 August 1926, p. 97.)

1926: School, Judson Mills, Greenville; $25,000 (*MR*, 18 February 1926, p. 127.)

1927: Apartment House, E. North Street, Greenville; $10,000 (*MR*, 3 November 1927, p. 123.)

1927: Judson Mills Community Building, Second Avenue, Greenville; $65,000 (*MR*, 31 March 1927, p. 111; 5 May 1927, p. 117.)

1927: Dr. J.G. Buford Residence, North Avenue and Church Street, Greer (*MR*, 13 October 1927, p. 116.)

1928: B.A. Morgan Apartment House, E. Washington and Pettigru streets, Greenville; $17,500 (*MR*, 19 July 1928, p. 93.)

1929: Two Additions and Remodeling of Auditorium, Pendleton Street Baptist Church, Greenville; $50,000 (*MR*, 4 July 1929, p. 96.)

1930: Poinsett School, Hale Street, Greenville; $22,000 (*MR*, 20 November 1930, p. 58.)

Sources: Greenville city directories; *MR*, various citations; Snowden, *History of South Carolina*, Vol. 5, p. 126; Wallace, Vol. IV, p. 56.

MARYE, Philip Thornton (1872-1935) Marye, a native of Alexandria, Virginia, was educated at Randolph-Macon College and at the University of Virginia. He worked in the early 1890s for Glenn Brown, a well-connected society architect of Washington, D.C. Marye began independent architectural practice in 1893 in Newport News, Virginia, and moved to Atlanta around 1904.

Marye attained regional distinction in the early twentieth century, winning major commissions in many southeastern states. His more important designs included the 1905 Terminal Station in Atlanta; the 1905-1909 Terminal Station in Birmingham, Alabama; the 1909 Municipal Building and Auditorium in Raleigh, North Carolina; the 1912 Citizens' National Bank Building in Raleigh; the 1915 Wake County Courthouse in Raleigh; the Florida Supreme Court Building in Tallahassee; and the Civil Court Building at New Orleans. The Fox Theatre (Shrine Mosque) in Atlanta, designed by Marye's firm and built in 1927-1929, is described as "one of the last surviving great movie houses of the era."

Marye served in the United States Army during the Spanish-American War and the First World War. He was a member of the City Planning Commission of Washington, D.C., and of the A.I.A.'s Commission for the Preservation of Historical Buildings of America. Marye was also Georgia's first district officer of the Historic American Buildings Survey. He served as regional director for Georgia of the housing administration under the Civil Works Administration.

South Carolina project:

1916-1917: Greenville County Courthouse, Greenville; $110,000; P. Thornton Marye, architect; H. Olin Jones (q.v.), supervising architect (*MR*, 24 February 1916, p. 66; 23 March 1916, p. 69; 4 May 1916, p. 88; 12 October 1916, p. 65; 9 November 1916, p. 53; 5 April 1917, p. 92; Withey.)

Sources: Keith L. Bryant, Jr., "Cathedrals, Castles, and Roman Baths: Railway Station Architecture in the Urban South," *Journal of Urban History*, February 1976; *MR*, various citations; Kenneth H. Thomas, "Philip Thornton Marye," in *Dictionary of Georgia Biography*, pp. 696-697; "Thornton Marye, Architect, Dies," *Atlanta Constitution*, 2 December 1935, p. 1; *Who's Who in the South*, 1927, p. 472; Withey, pp. 395-396.

MAYFIELD & CO. (active 1886) Mayfield & Co. of Anderson were described as architects in the 1886 South Carolina State Gazetteer.

MAYNARD, R.W. (active 1914) R.W. Maynard of Charlotte, North Carolina, was described as the architect for the $5000 S.F. Maynard Residence in Greenwood, South Carolina. Maynard was not identified in the Charlotte city directories of the period.

Source: *MR*, 5 November 1914, p. 71.

MAYRANT, William R. (active 1898-1902) William R. Mayrant was associated with S. Lewis Simons (q.v.) in Charleston. The firm practiced architecture, engineering, and construction through 1902, after which time they concentrated on construction.

South Carolina projects:

1898-1902: See **Simons, S. Lewis** (Simons & Mayrant)

Sources: Charleston city directories; *MR*, various citations.

McCLARE, C. Herbert (active 1894-1918) C.H. McClare of Cambridge, Massachusetts was the architect for the 1911 Mather Academy School Building in Camden, South Carolina. This project was contracted at $20,000.

Sources: *MR*, 5 October 1911, p. 82; 12 October 1911, p. 63; Robert Bell Rettig, *Guide to Cambridge Architecture: Ten Walking Tours* (Cambridge, Massachusetts: Cambridge Historical Commission, 1969.)

McCOLLOUGH, E.H. (active 1887-1909) E.H. McCollough was active as a surveyor, engineer, and architect in northwestern South Carolina in the late nineteenth century. His office was in Walhalla through 1901, after which he relocated to Greenville.

South Carolina projects:

1901: Oconee County Jail and Sheriff's Residence, Walhalla (*MR*, 18 April 1901, p. 245; 13 June 1901, p. 399; *The Keowee Courier*, 10 April 1901, 17 April 1901, 1 May 1901, 8 May 1901, 12 June 1901, 17 July 1901, 14 August 1901.)

1901: Remodeling, Oconee County Courthouse, Walhalla (*The Keowee Courier*, 17 July 1901, 24 July 1901, 14 August 1901.)

1904: St. Andrew's Church, Greenville (*MR*, 26 May 1904, p. 431.)

1904: Charles McAlister Office Building, Greenville; $10,000 (*MR*, 7 July 1904, p. 570; 21 July 1904, p. 18.)

Sources: *MR*, various citations.

McCRADY BROTHERS & CHEVES (active 1913-1920) The firm of McCrady Brothers, later McCrady Bros. & Cheves, was active in building construction, civil engineering, and surveying in Charleston. In two projects the firm was identified also as architects.

John McCrady was president of the firm, W. Shackelford McCrady was vice-president, and Henry C. Cheves, Jr., was secretary-treasurer.

South Carolina projects:

McCrady Brothers

1916: H.C. Cheves, Two Residences, Charleston (*MR*, 6 April 1916, p. 82.)

McCrady Brothers & Cheves

1918: Remodeling, Exchange Restaurant Company Building, 9-11 Exchange Street, Charleston; $3000 (*MR*, 5 September 1918, p. 99.)

Sources: Charleston city directories; *MR*, various citations.

McCROSSIN, Edward J. (active 1887-1890) Edward J. McCrossin was active in Charleston as partner in the firms of McCrossin, (Edward W.) Burkholder & Co., 1887; and McCrossin Brothers & (John W.) Thomas, 1887. The firm relocated to Birmingham, Alabama, by 1888. Edward McCrossin was active in Lynchburg, Virginia, in the 1880s.

Sources: S. Allen Chambers, *Lynchburg: An Architectural History* (Charlottesville, Virginia: The University Press of Virginia, 1981), pp. 273-274, 286; Charleston city directories.

McCULLOUGH, J.D. (active 1848-1902) Reverend J.D. McCullough was an Episcopal priest who prepared plans for many South Carolina congregations. Albert Sidney Thomas' history of the Church describes thirteen Episcopal churches with which McCullough was connected; he is said to have designed at least eight of these buildings, and to have assisted in the carpentry on several. McCullough was a chaplain in the Holcombe Legion during the Civil War. He served as secretary of the church council from 1864 to 1896.

South Carolina projects:

1854: St. Stephens Church, Ridgeway (Thomas, p. 604.)

Ca. 1855: Christ Church, Greenville (Thomas, p. 562.)

1856: Christ Church, Mars Bluff (Thomas, p. 309.)

1859: Church of the Nativity, Union (*Southern Episcopalean*, October 1859, p. 383.)

1869: Christ Church, Lancaster (Thomas, p. 586.)

1872: Church of Our Savior, Rock Hill (Thomas, p. 607.)

1893: Church of the Resurrection, Greenwood (Thomas, p. 677.)

1899: Holy Trinity P.E. Church, Clemson (Thomas, p. 515.)

n.d.: St. Stephens Church, Willington (Thomas, p. 622.)

Sources: National Register files, S.C. Archives; Albert Sidney Thomas, *A Historical Account of the Protestant Episcopal Church in South Carolina, 1820-1957* (Columbia: The R.L. Bryan Company, 1957.)

McDONALD BROTHERS (active 1878-1904) The Louisville, Kentucky firm of Harry P. McDonald (1848-1904) and Kenneth McDonald, Sr. (1852-1940) prepared designs for many major projects in the eastern and midwestern United States between 1878 and 1904. Their important commissions included the Kansas State Capitol Building in Topeka; the Sevier County Courthouse in Sevierville, Tennessee, 1895-1896; and the courthouses of Gibson and Washington counties, Indiana. McDonald Brothers prepared an unsuccessful proposal for the reconstruction of Thomas Jefferson's Rotunda at the University of Virginia, Charlottesville, in 1895. In South Carolina the firm designed the Spartanburg County Courthouse in 1890-1892. Photographs of the building, which was destroyed in the mid-twentieth century, show a polychrome Romanesque design with a prominent tower.

Sources: Herndon, pp. 126-127; *MR*, 21 June 1890, p. 43; William B. O'Neal, *Architectural Drawing in Virginia 1819-1969* (Charlottesville, Virginia: The University Press of Virginia, 1969), pp. 110-113; *Spartanburg of Today: The Progressive City of the Piedmont* (W.S. Kline; n.p., n.d., ca. 1905); *The Spartanburg Herald-Journal*, 17 September 1939; Withey, pp. 404-405.

McDOWELL, Nonus O. (active 1924) Nonus O. McDowell and his brothers T.R. and C.E. McDowell operated as realtors in Spartanburg in the 1920s. McDowell provided plans for 27 bungalow-type dwellings in Spartanburg in 1924. The buildings, located on Wood, N. Church, Peal, Edgewood, and McDowell streets, were contracted at a total cost of $72,500. McDowell & Hammond were named as owners and builders, and it is likely that N.O. McDowell was a member of this firm.

Source: *MR*, 9 October 1924, p. 118; Spartanburg city directories.

McELFATRICK, John Bailey (1828-1906) In association with his sons John M. and William H. McElfatrick, John B. McElfatrick of New York City pursued a career as a theatre architect. The firm had projects in New York City and in many states. Their work in the Southeast included the 1891 T.F. Johnson Theatre in Savannah; the 1901 Galveston, Texas, Opera House; the 1902 Elks' Home & Auditorium in Winston-Salem, North Carolina; and the 1906 Gaiety Theater in Memphis.

South Carolina projects:

1891: Remodeling, Owens Academy of Music, Charleston; $10,000 (*MR*, 7 March 1891, p. 43.)

1906: Remodeling, Columbia Theatre, Columbia; $11,926 (*The State*, 17 February 1906, p. 8; 21 February 1906, p. 10; 6 March 1906, p. 1; *MR*, 5 April 1906, p. 331; 3 May 1906, p. 446.)

Sources: Francis, p. 53; *MR*, various citations; Withey, p. 406.

McGHEE and McGHEE (active 1912-1929) McGhee & McGhee, also called McGhee Brothers, were contractors in Aiken in the early twentieth century. They were identified as architects, as well as contractors, for George W. Chipchase's $20,000 "Dutch cottage style" residence in Aiken, built in 1924.

Sources: *MR*, 7 August 1924, p. 132, and various other citations.

McGOODWIN & HAWLEY (active 1910-1913) Robert Rodes McGoodwin (1886-1967) and Samuel Davis Hawley II (1885-ca. 1936) of Philadelphia, Pennsylvania, prepared plans for the 1912-1914 Charleston Library Society Building on King Street in Charleston, South Carolina. McGoodwin, a native of Kentucky, received his B.S. and M.S. degrees in architecture from the University of Pennsylvania, and studied further in the atelier Duquesne in Paris. He worked for Horace Trumbauer (q.v.) in Philadelphia before associating with Hawley in 1910. Hawley had been McGoodwin's classmate at Pennsylvania, and he had also worked in Trumbauer's office.

Sources: Hewitt, p. 279; *MR*, 24 April 1913, p. 75; Tatman/Moss, pp. 347-348, 514-517; Koyl, p. 353.

McGRATH, Robert N. (active 1872-1894) Robert N. McGrath, architect of at least two South Carolina county courthouses, practiced in Georgia and Alabama in the late nineteenth century. He was active in Macon, Georgia, in 1872. McGrath moved to Augusta, Georgia, by 1880, and worked there through 1887. He was working in Montgomery, Alabama, in 1887-1894.

McGrath designed the Aiken County Courthouse in Aiken, 1881, and the Beaufort County Courthouse in Beaufort, 1883. Both buildings were Second Empire compositions, with Mansard-roofed entrance pavilions centered on a longitudinal plan. The buildings had county offices on the ground floor and courtrooms on the main floor. Both courthouses were extensively remodeled by architect Willis Irvin (q.v.) in the twentieth century.

County courthouses in Chesterfield and Bennettsville, South Carolina, were built during this period, and these may have been designed by McGrath. Both buildings feature tall entrance towers with Mansard roofs, similar to McGrath's Aiken and Beaufort designs. Documentation on the design of these two buildings has not yet been found.

South Carolina projects:

1881: Aiken County Courthouse, Aiken (Cornerstone; Minutes, County Commissioners, Aiken County, 1881, pp. 420, 427-429, 434, 457; National Register files, S.C. Archives.)

1883: Beaufort County Courthouse, Beaufort (Cornerstone.)

Sources: Augusta, Georgia, city directories; Macon, Georgia, city directories; *MR*, various citations.

McINERNEY, Michael Joseph (1877-1963) Reverend Father Michael, O.S.B., of the Diocese of North Carolina, a Benedictine monk, provided architectural services for many ecclesiastical projects in the Southeast. Prior to entering Belmont Abbey as a student in 1900, McInerney had studied at Duquesne University and worked for Pittsburgh architect W.A. Thomas. He offered his skills to the Abbey when the College Building was ruined by a fire in 1900. From this beginning McInerney pursued a fruitful architectural service, designing most of the buildings at the abbey and at nearby Sacred Heart College in Belmont.

Father Michael's work outside North Carolina included the Sacred Heart Church in Savannah, Georgia, begun in 1902; a college building for the Benedictine Order of Savannah, begun in 1904; and several buildings for the Benedictine High School (Southern Benedictine Society Military College) in Richmond, Virginia, begun in 1911.

South Carolina projects:

1930: St. Patrick's Parochial School, Radcliffe and St. Philip streets, Charleston; $80,000 (*MR*, 6 February 1930, p. 100; 27 February 1930, pp. 86-87.)

1930: Sacred Heart School Building, 5 Benson Street, Charleston; $20,000 (*MR*, 27 February 1930, pp. 86-87.)

1938: Providence Hospital, Columbia (Koyl.)

1946-1949: St. Joseph's Catholic Church, 3600 Devine Street, Columbia; Father Michael McInerny and G. Thomas Harmon, architects (Russell Maxey, *South Carolina's Historic Columbia* (Columbia: The R.L. Bryan Co., 1980), p. 210.)

1952: Rectory, St. Joseph's Catholic Church, Columbia (Koyl.)

Sources: Kim Withers Brengle, *The Architectural Heritage of Gaston County, North Carolina* (Gastonia, North Carolina: Gaston County, 1982);, pp. 238, 266; Koyl, p. 354; *MR*, various citations.

McMICHAEL, James M. (active 1901-1929) James M. McMichael was associated with Oliver Duke Wheeler (q.v.) in Charlotte, North Carolina, in 1901. By 1902, McMichael established an independent office in Charlotte. Leonard L. Hunter (q.v.) was McMichael's partner in 1903-1904.

Some eighteen Baptist churches in North Carolina, and at least four in South Carolina, were designed by McMichael. The "Byzantine Style" First Baptist Church in Charlotte (1907), featured a 44-foot diameter dome and two domed towers. McMichael's North Carolina Baptist churches included buildings in Charlotte, 1903; Waynesville, 1903; High Point, 1903; Pineville, 1904; Statesville, 1906; Charlotte, 1907; Lumberton, 1909; North Wilkesboro, 1909; Rocky Mount, 1911; Kinston, 1914; Asheville, 1914; Forest City, 1914; Edenton, 1916; Washington, 1916; Henderson, 1917-1919; Badin, 1918; Concord, 1922-1923 ("English Gothic Type"); and Charlotte, 1925. McMichael also designed the Anson County Courthouse in Wadesboro, North Carolina, in 1903.

South Carolina projects:

1901: See **Wheeler, Oliver Duke** (Wheeler & McMichael)

McMichael & Hunter

1903-1904: Carroll & Steacy Business Building (National Bank of Gaffney Building), Gaffney; $30,000 (*MR*, 23 July 1903, p. 15; 15 October 1903, p. 251; 24 March 1904, p. 217; 31 March 1904, p. 238.)

J.M. McMichael

1904: A.J. Matheson Hotel and Store Buildings, Bennettsville; $25,000 (*MR*, 16 June 1904, p. 501; 1 December 1904, p. 486.)

1905: Carnegie Library, Winthrop College, Rock Hill (*MR*, 13 April 1905, p. 281; 20 April 1905, p. 309; 11 May 1905, p. 385.)

1905: Leroy Springs Residence, Lancaster (*MR*, 27 April 1905, p. 331.)

1905: Leroy Springs Business Building, Lancaster (*MR*, 27 April 1905, p. 331.)

1905: L.P. Roddy Residence, Lancaster (*MR*, 27 April 1905, pp. 331-332.)

1905: C.J. Henry Residence, Lancaster (*MR*, 27 April 1905, p. 332.)

1905: W.W. Boyce Residence, Rock Hill; $5000 (*MR*, 5 October 1905, p. 301; 12 October 1905, p. 326.)

1905: G.H. O'Leary Business Building, Yorkville (*MR*, 6 April 1905, p. 257.)

1906: Dr. W.G. Stevens Residence, Rock Hill; $10,000 (*MR*, 26 April 1906, p. 419.)

1908: Methodist Episcopal Church, Lancaster; $10,000 (*MR*, 12 March 1908, p. 58; 25 June 1908, p. 57; 2 July 1908, p. 68.)

1911: South Main Street Baptist Church, Greenwood; $25,000 (*MR*, 17 August 1911, p. 68.)

1914: Second Baptist Church, Columbia; $40,000 (*MR*, 28 May 1914, p. 61.)

1916: First Baptist Church, McColl; $20,000 (*MR*, 16 March 1916, p. 69.)

1929: Shandon Baptist Church, Columbia (*MR*, 28 November 1929, p. 75.)

Sources: Charlotte, North Carolina city directories; *MR*, various citations.

McMILLEN, Charles (active 1898-1908) Charles McMillen came to Wilmington, North Carolina, from Duluth, Minnesota, in 1899 to build the Masonic Temple there. McMillen had designed over fourteen Masonic temples before coming to Wilmington. He remained in Wilmington through 1908. His work included the 1904 Masonic Temple in Portsmouth, Virginia.

South Carolina project:

1906: Farmers and Merchants' Bank Building, Lake City (*MR*, 27 December 1906, p. 614.)

Sources: *MR*, various citations; Tony P. Wrenn, *Wilmington, North Carolina: An Architectural and Historical Portrait* (Charlottesville, Virginia:

The University Press of Virginia, 1984), pp. 30, 35, 87, 112, 183.

McNEIL, _____ (active 1904-1905) McNeil (also spelled **McNeal**) was a partner of Luther B. Proffitt (q.v.) in Spartanburg.

South Carolina projects:

See **Proffitt, Luther B.** (Proffitt & McNeil)

MEDARY, Milton Bennett (1874-1929) Milton B. Medary was a prominent Philadelphia architect. He entered the University of Pennsylvania in 1890, but left after one semester to take a position with architect Frank Miles Day. Medary opened his own practice in 1895, in association with Richard L. Field. From 1910 to 1929 Medary was a partner in the firm of Zantzinger, Borie & Medary.

Medary served on many public commissions, including the National Commission on the Fine Arts and the National Capitol Park and Planning Commission. He was president of the American Institute of Architects in 1926-1928.

Medary was consulting architect for the John C. Calhoun State Office Building in Columbia, South Carolina, designed in 1925. Harold Tatum (q.v.), a Columbia architect who had studied at the University of Pennsylvania, was designing architect for this six-story, $608,000 building. Tatum may have known Medary from his years in Philadelphia.

Zantzinger, Borie & Medary designed the Pilot Mutual Life Insurance Company Building in Greensboro, North Carolina, in 1927, in association with Greensboro architect Harry Barton.

Sources: *American Art Annual*, Vol. 21, p. 436; Jeffrey S. Eley, *Milton Bennett Medary* (Master's thesis, University of Virginia, Charlottesville, 1982); *MR*, various citations; Tatman/Moss, pp. 523-524; Withey, pp. 415-416.

MELTON, Allen L. (active 1895-1917) Melton practiced in relative obscurity in Asheville, North Carolina. He provided plans for the 1895 Drhumor

Building in Asheville, described as "an exceptional Romanesque office structure." In 1896 Melton's advertisements claimed "heavy building and fire-proof construction a specialty."

South Carolina projects:

1896: J.L. Carson Store and Merchantile Building, Spartanburg; $7000 (*MR*, 15 May 1896, p. 269.)

1907: J.P. Rickman Residence, Greenville; 410,000 (*MR*, 4 April 1907, p. 356.)

Sources: *MR*, various citations; Douglas Swaim, ed., *Cabins and Castles: The History and Architecture of Buncombe County, North Carolina* (Asheville, North Carolina: Historic Resources Commission of Asheville and Buncombe County, 1981), pp. 83, 172.

MERRY, A. Brian (active 1926-1932) A. Brian Merry worked as a draftsman and designer for Scroggs & Ewing (q.v.) in Augusta, Georgia, for several years. He began independent practice around 1930. A $10,000 addition to the Fred H. Post Residence in Aiken, South Carolina, was among his first commissions.

Sources: Augusta, Georgia, city directories; *MR*, 12 June 1930, p. 77, and other citations; Morgan, p. 112.

MILBURN, Frank Pierce (1868-1926) Frank Pierce Milburn was an enterprising architect who won major commissions in many southern states during the period 1889-1926. Milburn thrived on architectural competitions, and often relocated his main office upon winning a new commission. He was one of the architects of the South Carolina State House in Columbia. Some writers, including Lawrence Wodehouse, place Milburn among the leading architects of the South during the early twentieth century; but several earlier critics cast doubt on his ability. Milburn appears to have been a consummate salesman.

Milburn was born in Bowling Green, Kentucky, son of Thomas Thurmond Milburn, a Scottish immigrant. Thomas Milburn worked as a contractor, builder, and architect in Kentucky. Frank Milburn was educated at Arkansas University and at Arkansas Industrial University, and spent the years 1884-1889 in Louisville, Kentucky, presumably in architectural work and study. Thomas and Frank Milburn collaborated as architects and builders for the Clay County Courthouse in Manchester, Kentucky, in 1889; and in 1890 the younger Milburn established an architectural office in Kenova, West Virginia. The Magoffin County Courthouse in Salversville, Kentucky (1892) was among his earliest projects.

Frank Milburn won the competition for the design of the Forsyth County Courthouse in Winston, North Carolina, ca. 1893, and he promptly relocated to that city. In 1896 Milburn won the competition for the Mecklenburg County Courthouse in Charlotte, North Carolina, against the efforts of twenty-six other architects; again, he relocated his office to the city of the new commission. Milburn's first South Carolina project was the Anderson County Courthouse and Jail, won in a competition in 1897. He reportedly used second-hand plans prepared for the Forsyth County Courthouse to build the Anderson courthouse. Photographs of the two buildings show marked similarities, especially the curvilinear parapets, diapered brickwork, and greater and lesser towers; but since the Forsyth Courthouse is destroyed and the Anderson Courthouse substantially altered, it is difficult to be certain.

Milburn pursued architectural competitions around the Southeast in the last years of the nineteenth century. He counted among his successful entries the Glynn County (Georgia) Courthouse in 1897, where his plans were labeled "Court House No. 43." Milburn was also chosen as architect for the Thomson Auditorium in Charleston (South Carolina) in 1898-1899, the Danville (Virginia) Masonic Temple, and the Columbia (South Carolina) City Hall and Opera House in 1899-1900. Charles C. Wilson (q.v.) decried the widespread practice of unregulated competitions for architectural commisions in the southeast, and it is possible that Wilson had Milburn in mind when he wrote "The chief occupation of architects was the preparation or purchase of gaily colored pictures [for competitions], and the winners were generally those showing in the foreground the finest team of horses and the gayest Gibson girls."

The South Carolina State House had been under construction since 1852, under direction of a number of architects. After the death of Frank Niernsee (q.v.) in 1899, the State Legislature authorized a competition for an architect to complete the building, and budgeted $175,000 for the work. Milburn's plans were chosen (by a vote of 6 to 4 to 4) over those of W.B. Smith Whaley & Co. (q.v.) and Wilson & Edwards. Milburn's design called for a neoclassical dome, in place of the tower planned by John Niernsee. Having already won several other commissions in South Carolina, Milburn moved to Columbia in 1900 to direct this new project.

Milburn's dome was completed in 1902, and the finished work was roundly castigated. State Senator J. Quitman Marshall, a member of the building commission, described the dome as "infamous, no uglier creation could be devised, and it is nothing short of a miserable fraud." Marshall suggested "the architect must be looking forward to having this work done in as shoddy and cheap a manner as possible." Several Columbia architects agreed with Marshall's view; Gustavus Berg (q.v.), Charles Wilson, William Edwards (q.v.), and Frank Walter (q.v.) joined in condemnation of the work. The commission summoned S.S. Hunt, superintendent constructing the United States Capitol Building in Washington, to review the work; and Hunt concluded that the specifications were "indefinite and not specific," their execution crude and cheap, and the whole "a parody upon the science of architecture, an insult to the fame of John R. Niernsee, and a disgrace to the State of South Carolina." Milburn presented a more favorable evaluation of the work from engineer Kort Berle, but to no avail. He was relieved of responsibility for the work, and Charles Wilson was appointed in his stead. A lawsuit was initiated against Milburn, with a mistrial resulting. Although Wilson and other architects advocated demolition of Milburn's dome, funding for this work was never authorized.

Milburn, still asserting his integrity, maintained his practice in Columbia for several years. He was named official architect of the Southern Railway Company in 1902. Milburn had designed a number of railway stations and depots, including the Columbia Union Station in 1899-1902; and he designed many more depots, terminals, and stations in the southeast in the following years. Milburn's nine-story Southern Railway Co. Office Building in Washington, D.C., was contracted at $400,000 in 1916.

The South Carolina State House was not the only Milburn commission to draw fire. Milburn boasted of his 1898-1899 Thomson Auditorium Building in Charleston, describing it as "one of the best-constructed buildings in the South. . . the best known manner of construction. Everything has been carefully figured with a factor of safety of four to one." Yet, when the building was evaluated by the city in 1906, it was determined that the auditorium "appears to have been very hastily constructed and the annual repairs and expenditures for keeping it in presentable condition would be a very serious item." These observations are relevant in light of Milburn's preface to his 1901 book of designs:

> It has been a matter of some wonder to me that while the law is very particular in seeing that the lawyer and doctor are up to a certain standard in their professions, an Architect is allowed to practice with no credentials other than the sketch he carries. An Architect may render a beautiful drawing and still not have sufficient knowledge of construction to use proper material and workmanship to avert a calamity which has frequently happened by the total collapsing of large buildings.

Milburn's 1905-1907 Atlantic Coast Line Station in Charleston was condemned on artistic grounds. It was "an artistic disaster," according to Keith Bryant (1976); the building's facade was "broken by arches, three roof lines and two three-story towers, and balconies, canopies, brick, terra cotta, and tile came together in no apparent pattern." Bryant suggests that the Southern Railway agreed with this evaluation:

> Milburn's capacity for growth had been limited, and he proved unable to enhance the aesthetic qualities of his stations. Indeed, the Southern Railway seems to have realized this, for when its management joined other railroads to erect truly massive stations at Atlanta and Birmingham, the Southern and the other participants abandoned Milburn and turned to P. Thornton Marye.

Michael Heister (q.v.) joined Milburn's staff around 1903. Heister and Milburn became partners in 1906, and the firm became known as Milburn, Heister & Company. The firm relocated to Washington, D.C., in 1907. Although they designed major buildings in North Carolina and other southeastern states in later years, Milburn & Heister did no further work in South Carolina. Milburn's practice was lucrative in these years. He designed many major buildings in Washington, including several government commissions; and in 1921 he was a developer, as well as architect, for a $300,000, eight-story apartment building in Washington. The 1916 United States Department of Labor Building, designed by Milburn, Heister & Co., was commissioned at $420,000. The largest project undertaken by Milburn was the Imperial Chinese Bureau of Engraving and Printing complex in Peking, China.

Milburn's career included work at three other state capitol buildings. In 1902 the Florida State Capitol was enlarged under Milburn's direction; and he prepared plans for the enlargement of the North Carolina Capitol Building in 1905. Milburn also prepared an unsuccessful design for the Kentucky State Capitol at Frankfort in 1903. The Bourbon County Courthouse (1902-1905) in Paris, Kentucky, designed by Milburn as a prototype for the Frankfort State Capitol Building, was characterized by monumental massing and elaborate ornamentation. A cartouche over the main entrance of the Paris Courthouse symbolized three of Kentucky's proudest boasts: faster horses, younger women, and older whiskey.

Lesser buildings designed by Milburn in South Carolina show a variety of stylistic influences. The State Dispensary Office Building in Columbia (1900-1901) features a peculiar curvilinear parapet. The Newberry County Courthouse (1906-1907) has a fussy and heavy Neoclassical composition; while St. Peter's Roman Catholic Church in Columbia (1902-1906) and the 1907 A.R.P. Church in Newberry have competent Gothic Revival designs.

Throughout his career, Milburn advertised his designs in small monographs. Books of Milburn's designs were published in 1899, 1901, 1903, 1905, and 1922.

Milburn died in Asheville, North Carolina on 21 September 1926. His son, Thomas Yancey Milburn, assumed responsibility for the firm.

South Carolina projects:

1897: Anderson County Courthouse and Jail, Anderson; $28,000 (Cornerstone; *MR*, 19 February 1897, p. 70; 16 April 1897, p. 211; 23 April 1897, p. 232; 7 May 1897, p. 266; 14 May 1897, p. 284; 4 June 1897, p. 335; 9 July 1897, p. 412; Frank A. Dickson, *Journeys Into the Past: The Anderson Region's Heritage* (Anderson: Frank A. Dickson, 1975); Milburn, *Designs*, 1903.)

1897: Jail, Greenwood (*MR*, 23 April 1897, p. 232; 30 April 1897, p. 250.)

1898: C.H. Speights Residence, Greenville (*MR*, 24 June 1898, p. 362.)

1898-1899: John Thomson Memorial Auditorium, 121 Rutledge Avenue, Charleston; $34,450 (*MR*, 4 November 1898, p. 261; 11 November 1898, p. 277; 25 November 1898, p. 311; 2 December 1898, p. 327; 30 December 1898, p. 397; 6 January 1899, p. 412; Robert P. Stockton, "Old Museum Site Built As Memorial," *News and Courier*, Charleston, 22 June 1981; Milburn, *Designs*, 1903.)

1899: Nicholson Hotel, Union; $15,000 (*MR*, 13 January 1899, p. 429; *The Bricklayer and Mason*, Vol. I, No. 8, 20 February 1899, p. 19.)

1899: Southern Railway Co. Passenger Station, Blackville (*MR*, 23 November 1899, p. 308; 7 December 1899, p. 341.)

1899: Wylie Home, Erskine College, Due West (*MR*, 10 February 1899, p. 48; 16 June 1899, p. 356.)

1899: School, Due West; $2800 (*MR*, 18 August 1899, p. 68.)

1899-1900: Remodeling, J.L. Mimnaugh Grand Central Hotel and Department Store, Columbia (*MR*, 28 December 1899, p. 385; 29 March 1900, p. 170; *The State*, 3 January 1900.)

1899-1900: City Hall and Opera House, Main and Gervais streets, Columbia; $50,000 (*MR*, 9 June 1899, p. 340; 28 July 1899, p. 15; 9 November 1899, p. 274; 14 December 1899, p. 354; 11 January 1900, p. 415; *The State*, 3 December 1899, 6 December 1899, 6 January 1900, 10 January 1900; *The Bricklayer and Mason*, Vol. II, No. 7, 1 January 1900, p. 20; Kline; Milburn, *Designs*, 1903.)

1899-1902: Union Passenger Station, 401 S. Main Street, Columbia (*MR*, 11 August 1899, p. 52; 28 December 1899, p. 385; 24 May 1900, p. 309; 4 October 1900, p. 182; 11 October 1900, p. 199; 25 July 1901, p. 10; *The State*, 29 December 1899, 12 January 1902; Kline; Milburn, *Designs*, 1903.)

1900: Completion, South Carolina State House, Columbia (*MR*, 29 March 1900, p. 170; 19 April 1900, p. 223; 5 July 1900, p. 410; 2 August 1900, p. 28; *The State*, 14 January 1900; Kline.)

1900: J.M. Jackson Residence, Bennettsville (*MR*, 5 July 1900, p. 409.)

1900: D.K. Morris Residence, Cateechee; $4500 (*MR*, 27 December 1900, p. 384.)

1900: S.M. Jones & Co. Store and Office Building, Chester (*MR*, 15 February 1900, p. 65.)

1900: Building, South Carolina Deaf, Dumb & Blind Institute, Cedar Springs; $10,000 (*MR*, 14 June 1900, p. 359.)

1900: Courthouse, Greenville; $50,000 (*MR*, 20 December 1900, p. 364.)

1900: Keystone Granite Company Hotel, Pacolet (*MR*, 18 October 1900, p. 216.)

1900: East Dormitory, Winthrop Normal College, Rock Hill; $40,000 (*MR*, 8 March 1900, p. 117; 25 October 1900, p. 236; Milburn, *Designs*, 1903.)

1900: Southern Railway Company Passenger Station, Summerville (*MR*, 11 October 1900, p. 200; Milburn, *Designs*, 1903.)

1900-1901: South Carolina Dispensary Building, 1205 Pulaski Street, Columbia; $7000 (*MR*, 27 December 1900, p. 384; *The State*, 18 December 1977.)

1901: Mrs. Owen Daly Residence, Columbia; $6000 (*MR*, 7 March 1901, p. 132; Milburn, *Designs*, 1903.)

1901: Chas. Narey Store and Flats Building, Columbia (*MR*, 7 March 1901, p. 132; Milburn, *Designs*, 1903.)

1901: Remodeling and addition, South Carolina Dispensary System Warehouse, Pulaski and Gervais streets, Columbia; $18,000 (*MR*, 14 March 1901, p. 152; 30 May 1901, p. 356.)

1901: Bank of Jonesville Office Building, Jonesville (*MR*, 29 August 1901, p. 97; 5 September 1901, p. 114.)

1901: W. Boyd Evans Residence, Columbia; $6000 (*MR*, 17 October 1901, p. 217; Milburn, *Designs*, 1903.)

1901: City Hall and Opera House, Darlington; $21,000 (*MR*, 21 February 1901, p. 96; 14 March 1901, p. 152; 18 April 1901, p. 245; 16 May 1901, p. 318; Milburn, *Designs*, 1903.)

1901: Chapel, Newberry College, Newberry (*MR*, 6 June 1901, p. 377.)

1901: Alumni Hall, Wofford College, Spartanburg; $15,000 (*MR*, 7 February 1901, p. 53; 7 March 1901, p. 133; 30 May 1901, p. 356.)

1901: Atlantic Coast Line Railway Passenger Depot, Sumter; $8000 (*MR*, 22 August 1901, p. 76.)

1901: People's Bank of Union Bank Building, Union; $8000 (*MR*, 20 June 1901, p. 418; 4 July 1901, p. 457; Milburn, *Designs*, 1903.)

1901: T.C. Duncan Store and Office Building, Union; $18,000 (*MR*, 4 July 1901, p. 457.)

1901: A.H. Foster Store Building, Union (*MR*, 15 August 1901, p. 64.)

1901: Twelve storehouses, McCreery Land & Investment Co., Columbia (*MR*, 14 November 1901, p. 291.)

1902: Henry Horne Trousers Factory and Carriage Repository, Columbia (*MR*, 3 July 1902, p. 444.)

1902: McCreery Land & Investment Co. Store and Office Building, Columbia (*MR*, 21 August 1902, p. 89; Kline.)

1902: F.D. Kendall Flats Building, Columbia (*MR*, 13 November 1902, p. 318.)

1902-1906: St. Peter's Roman Catholic Church, 1529 Assembly Street, Columbia (*MR*, 30 October 1902, p. 278; 14 May 1903, p. 351; 1 October 1903, p. 219; 8 October 1903, p. 235; 22 February 1906, p. 155; 1 March 1906, p. 183; Kline, pp. 4, 23; Milburn, *Designs*, 1903.)

1903: Holland Hall, Newberry College, Newberry; $18,953 (*MR*, 15 January 1903, p. 513; 12 March 1903, p. 164; 19 March 1903, p. 182; 25 June 1903, p. 470; Milburn, *Designs*, 1903.)

1903: James S. Gibbes Art Gallery, Meeting Street, Charleston; $100,000 (*MR*, 28 May 1903, p. 386; 30 July 1903, p. 52; 6 August 1903, p. 52; 24 September 1903, p. 190; Kline, p. 4.)

1903: Remodeling, Masonic Temple, Columbia; $12,000 (*MR*, 30 April 1903, p. 310.)

1903: Hospital, Roman Catholic Church, Columbia; $7000 (*MR*, 19 November 1903, p. 352; 26 November 1903, p. 369.)

1903: A.J.C. Cottingham Residence, Dillon (*MR*, 27 August 1903, p. 106.)

1903: Masonic Temple, Union (*MR*, 26 November 1903, p. 370.)

1903-1904: Southern Railway Depot, Spartanburg; $75,000 (*MR*, 9 July 1903, p. 511; 24 September 1903, p. 190; 3 December 1903, p. 393; 31 March 1904, p. 239; 16 June 1904, p. 502; *Southern Architect and Building News*, 5 February 1904, p. 10; Kline, p. 4.)

1904: Catholic Home, Columbia; $10,000 (*MR*, 31 March 1904, p. 238.)

1904: Howard Caldwell Residence, Senate Street, Columbia (*Southern Architect and Building News*, 15 July 1904, p. 8; *MR*, 21 July 1904, p. 18.)

1904: Carolina National Bank Building, Columbia (*MR*, 22 December 1904, p. 567.)

1904: Three store buildings, Columbia (*MR*, 22 December 1904, p. 567.)

1904: Southern Railway Passenger Depot, Greenville; $30,000 (*MR*, 23 June 1904, p. 523; 4 August 1904, p. 62; 1 December 1904, p. 486; *Southern Architect and Building News*, 15 July 1904, p. 8; Kline, p. 4.)

1905-1907: Atlantic Coast Line and Southern Railway Union Station, Charleston; $152,000 (*MR*, 1 June 1905, p. 461; 13 July 1905, p. 611; 16 November 1905, p. 467; 30 November 1905, p. 525; Bryant.)

1905: Clarence Richards Residence, Columbia (*MR*, 8 June 1905, p. 486.)

1905: Remodeling, Neill O'Donnell Residence, Sumter; $10,000 (*MR*, 5 October 190, p. 301.)

1905: Seaboard Air Line Depot, Union (*MR*, 27 April 1905, p. 332.)

1906: Catholic Chapel, Walhalla (*MR*, 21 June 1906, p. 649.)

1906: Improvement, Palmetto National Bank Building, Columbia; $80,000 (*MR*, 21 June 1906, p. 648.)

1906: Robert W. Parsons Residence, 828 W. Richardson Avenue, Summerville (*MR*, 12 April 1906, p. 363; 21 June 1906, p. 649; *News and Courier*, Charleston, 17 December 1985, p. 17.)

1906-1907: Newberry County Courthouse, Newberry; $39,472 (*MR*, 8 March 1906, p. 211;; 30 August 1906, p. 169; 13 December 1906, p. 562; 3 January 1907, p. 668; 7 February 1907, p. 111.)

1907: A.R.P. Church, Newberry; $13,200 (*MR*, 14 February 1907, p. 137; 18 April 1907, p. 424.)

Sources: W. Ted Alexander, "Frank Milburn: His New South Courthouses in General and the Buncombe County Courthouse in Specific," unpublished paper, Cornell University, 1983; Keith L. Bryant, Jr., "Cathedrals, Castles, and Roman Baths: Railway Station Architecture in the Urban South," *Journal of Urban History*, February 1976; Charlotte, North Carolina, city directories; Columbia city directories; Christie Zimmerman Fant, *The State House of South Carolina: An Illustrated Historic Guide* (Columbia: The R.L. Bryan Co., 1970); Mary Kathryn Frye, "Frank Pierce Milburn, Architect 1868-1926," master's thesis, University of South Carolina, Columbia, 1978; W.S. Kline, *Illustrated 1904 Columbia, South Carolina* (1904: Reprint edition, Columbia: The R.L. Bryan Co., 1962), p. 4; *MR*, various citations; Frank Pierce Milburn, *Designs From The Work of Frank P. Milburn, Architect, Columbia, S.C.* (Columbia: The State Company, 1903); Frank Pierce Milburn, *Designs From The Work of Frank P. Milburn, Architect, Columbia, S.C.* (Columbia: The State Company, 1905); Milburn, Heister & Co., *Selections From The Latest Works of Milburn, Heister & Co., Architects, Washington, D.C. 1922* (Washington, D.C.: National Publishing Company, 1922); Petty; *Reports and Resolutions*, 1903 (Columbia: The State Co., 1903); *Reports and Resolutions*, 1904 (Columbia: The State Co., 1904); *Southern Architect and Building News*, 8 July 1904, p. 9; Lawrence Wodehouse, "Frank Pierce Milburn (1868-1926), a Major Southern Architect," *The North Carolina Historical Review*, Summer 1973, pp. 289-303.

MILLER, Robert (active 1891-1892) Miller worked as an architect, builder, and supplier of builders' supplies in Spartanburg. His advertisement in the *MR* in 1892 claimed "private residences a specialty."

South Carolina projects:

1891: Alterations, Baptist Church, Spartanburg; $10,000 (*MR*, 7 March 1891, p. 43; 14 March 1891, p. 42.)

1891: Store Block, Spartanburg; $10,000 (*MR*, 14 March 1891, p. 42.)

1891: Addition, Converse College, Spartanburg; $14,000 (*MR*, 14 March 1891, p. 42.)

Sources: *MR*, 23 January 1892, p. 39, and various other citations; Spartanburg city directories.

MIMS, _____ (active 1892) Mims was described as the architect for the $40,000 W.N. Burnett Hotel in Edgefield in 1892.

Source: *MR*, 18 November 1892, p. 329.

MITCHAM, Robert W. (ca. 1862-1940) Robert Mitcham, a native of North Carolina, worked as an architect, in association with John F. Beach (q.v.), in Camden in 1905-1909. He described himself as a contractor in the 1910 Census, and several Camden area projects built by Mitcham have been identified.

In 1916-1917, Mitcham practiced as Mitcham & Mitcham. The second Mitcham has not been identified; it may have been Robert K. Mitcham, son of Robert W., who would have been seventeen years old in 1916. Robert W. Mitcham was listed as an architect in South Carolina as late as 1940, when he appeared on the listing of registered architects in the state.

In 1891, an "Architect Mitchem" of Pickens, South Carolina, prepared plans for the Sharp County (Arkansas) Courthouse, a $50,000 project. This may have been Robert W. Mitcham.

South Carolina projects:

1914: E.J. McLeod Residence, Camden; R.W. Mitcham, contractor (*MR*, 15 January 1914, p. 70; 29 January 1914, p. 69.)

1914: Camden Cotton Storage Company Warehouse, Camden; R.W. Mitcham, architect; Mitcham & Stokes, contractors (*MR*, 1 October 1914, p. 71.)

1915: School, Bethune; $8500 (*MR*, 9 September 1915, p. 59.)

1915: School, Blenheim; $7500 (*MR*, 9 September 1915, p. 59.)

1915: Henry Savage Bank and Apartment Building, DeKalb Street, Camden; $25,000 (*MR*, 9 December 1915, p. 68.)

Mitcham & Mitcham

1916: Stable, Kirkwood Hotel Company, Camden; $4000 (*MR*, 12 October 1916, p. 65.)

1917: T. Edmond Krumholtze Residence, Camden; $8000 (*MR*, 5 July 1917, p. 93.)

R.W. Mitcham

1922: B.G. Sanders Business Building, Camden; $10,000 (*MR*, 18 May 1922, p. 91.)

1924: School, Bethune; $17,000 (*MR*, 4 September 1924, p. 129; 11 September 1924, p. 107.)

1924: Mt. Pisgah High School, Kershaw County (*MR*, 17 January 1924, p. 108.)

Sources: 1910 Census, Kershaw County, South Carolina; *MR*, various citations.

MITCHELL, R. Elliott (active 1929) Mitchell, of Orangeburg, was included among registered South Carolina architects in 1929.

MORGAN, Thomas Henry (1857-1940) Thomas H. Morgan, a native of New York, began study of architecture in Knoxville, Tennessee, in the office of Alexander C. Bruce (q.v.) When Bruce went to Atlanta, Georgia, in 1879, Morgan joined him as a draftsman. Morgan became a full partner in the firm in 1882; and Bruce & Morgan became the dominant architectural firm in Atlanta and the Southeast. The firm's work in South Carolina included the main buildings at Clemson College, Winthrop College, Converse College, and the Graham Male and Female College.

John Robert Dillon joined Morgan in 1904, and the firm practiced as Morgan & Dillon. Mor-gan's 1940 account of the Georgia chapter of the A.I.A., drawing on his memories of sixty years of architectural practice in Atlanta, is a valuable source for study of the profession.

Morgan was a socially prominent architect, widely respected among his peers. He founded a regional architectural journal, *Southern Architect* (later called *Southern Architect and Building News*) published 1889-1932. Morgan was charter president of the Georgia chapter of the A.I.A. in 1906, and later the first president of the state's board of architectural registration.

South Carolina projects:

1890-1894: See **Bruce, Alexander Campbell** (Bruce & Morgan)

Sources: Elizabeth A. Lyon, "Thomas Henry Morgan," in *Dictionary of Georgia Biography*, pp. 726-728; *MR*, various citations; Thomas Henry Morgan, "The Georgia Chapter of the American Institute of Architects," in *The Atlanta Historic Bulletin*, Vol. VII, No. 28, September 1943; *Who's Who in the South*, 1927, pp. 529-530; Withey, pp. 426-427.

MORRISON, R.V. (active 1886) Morrison, of McClellanville, was identified as an architect in the 1886 *Charleston Directory and Gazetteer of Berkeley and Charleston Counties*.

MOSES & JACKSON (active 1890) Moses & Jackson were active in Anderson in 1890. No projects (or first names) for the firm have been identified to date.

Source: 1890 Bryan *Directory of Architects*.

MOWBRAY & UFFINGER (active 1896-1924) The New York City firm of Louis M. Mowbray and Justin M. Uffinger designed many major buildings across the Southeast. They were architects for the seventeen-story Woodside Building in Greenville; this landmark, contracted at $1,500,000 in 1920, was South Carolina's tallest building for many years. Mowbray & Uffinger also designed the twelve-story

Commercial National Bank Building in Charlotte, North Carolina (1911); the twenty-story American Trust Co. Building in Birmingham, Alabama (1911); and the seven-story Guarantee Trust & Banking Company Building in Atlanta, Georgia (1909).

The firm's 1903 People's Trust Company building in Brooklyn has been described as "a D.W. Griffith version of a Roman Temple."

Justin M. Uffinger was registered as an architect in South Carolina as late as 1929.

South Carolina projects:

1903: Bank of Greenwood Building, Greenwood; $10,000 (*MR*, 11 June 1903, p. 429.)

1920: Woodside Securities Company Bank and Office Building, Greenville; $1,500,000 (*MR*, 27 May 1920, p. 125; 25 November 1920, p. 128 c.)

Sources: Francis, pp. 56-57; *MR*, various citations; White & Willensky, pp. 188, 379.

MULLINAX, R.D. (active 1925) R.D. Mullinax of Greenville designed a $10,000 bank building for the Savings Bank of Fort Mill in 1925. The project was described in the *MR* on 3 September 1925, p. 134. Mullinax is not listed in Greenville city directories of the period.

MURPHY, E.A. (active 1923) E.A. Murphy, superintendent of buildings with the American Railway Express Company in Atlanta, Georgia, provided plans for the company's $22,000 office building in Florence, South Carolina.

Sources: *MR*, 13 September 1923, p. 108; 8 November 1923, p. 111.

NASH, Paul H. (active 1911) Paul Nash is identified as an architect and civil engineer in the 1911 Spartanburg city directory.

NEVES, William D. (active 1917-1930) Neves was an architect and civil engineer in Greenville for many years. He was associated with engineer R.E. Dalton in 1928-1930. Neves was the city engineer of Greenville from 1921 through 1924. In 1921 Neves, in association with Martin & Ward (q.v.), planned the city's fire station at Pendleton and Markley streets. The building was contracted at $6597.

Sources: Greenville city directories; *MR*, 5 May 1921, p. 155.

NEWCOMER, John D. (1867-1931) John Newcomer was born at Shippensburg, Pennsylvania. He was educated at Cornell University and at an architectural school in Kansas City, Missouri. He worked for the federal government for fourteen years as a superintendent of building construction. Newcomer came to Charleston around 1895 to work at Fort Moultrie, and he remained in Charleston as an architect.

Newcomer's projects included the remodeling of several of the city's historic buildings. He was called "the dean of Charleston architects" in his obituary notice.

South Carolina projects:

1907: Episcopal Chapel of the Holy Cross, Sullivan's Island; $10,000 (*MR*, 11 April 1907, p. 389.)

1907: Alterations, Thomson Auditorium (Charleston Museum), 121 Rutledge Avenue, Charleston (*MR*, 24 October 1907, p. 60.)

1908: C.D. Franke Co. Warehouse, Meeting Street, Charleston; $41,000 (*MR*, 9 April 1908, p. 59; 16 April 1908, p. 64.)

1908: Apartment House, Charleston (*MR*, 4 June 1908, p. 69.)

1908: Improvements, Sidney S. Riggs Commercial Building, 11 Broad Street, Charleston (*MR*, 6 August 1908, p. 66.)

1909: Remodeling, Wm. Minnis Co. Store Building, Charleston; $15,000 (*MR*, 12 August 1909, p. 58.)

1911: R.H. Wichman Hotel, Store, and Bank Building, Walterboro; $20,000 (*MR*, 16 November 1911, p. 75; 14 December 1911, p. 67.)

1911: Farmers and Merchants' Bank Building, Main and Bridge streets, Walterboro (*MR*, 14 December 1911, p. 66.)

1912: Baker-Craig Sanatorium, 55 Ashley Avenue, Charleston; $55,000; J.D. Newcomer and Ernest V. Richards (q.v.), architects (*MR*, 29 February 1912, p. 69; *American Art Annual*; "John D. Newcomer Found Dead.")

1912: G.G. Creighton Residence, Charleston; $8000 (*MR*, 25 April 1912, p. 70.)

1912: Sunday School building, Bethel Methodist Episcopal Church, Pitt and Calhoun streets, Charleston; $22,250 (*MR*, 22 August 1912, p. 67; "John D. Newcomer Found Dead.")

1912: Fourteen operatives' residences, Charleston Bagging Manufacturing Company, Charleston; $30,000 (*MR*, 5 December 1912, p. 83.)

1913: Remodeling, Bluestein Brothers Store Building, Charleston (*MR*, 27 March 1913, p. 71.)

1913: James W. Frazier Flats Building, 139-141 Tradd Street, Charleston (*MR*, 15 May 1913, p. 71.)

1913: B.H. Rutledge Residence, Charleston; $12,500 (*MR*, 22 May 1913, p. 69.)

1913: Remodeling, Estate of Henry Seigling Building, Charleston (*MR*, 7 August 1913, p. 85.)

1913: Remodeling, Commercial Savings Bank, Charleston (*MR*, 6 November 1913, p. 75.)

1913: Evening Post Building, Charleston (*American Art Annual*; Withey; "John D. Newcomer Found Dead.")

1914: Alterations, Citizen's Bank, Charleston; $12,000 (*MR*, 4 June 1914, p. 79.)

1914: Remodeling, Courtenay School, Charleston; $26,344 (*MR*, 4 June 1914, p. 80.)

1914: West Shore Development Company Store Buildings, 200 Meeting Street and 213 Meeting Street, Charleston (*MR*, 11 June 1914, p. 63.)

1914: C.B. Huiel Store and Warehouse Building, Charleston; $12,000 (*MR*, 9 July 1914, p. 60.)

1915: Charleston Building & Investment Company Bank Building, 302 King Street, Charleston; $13,000 (*MR*, 12 August 1915, p. 59.)

1915: Dr. John T. Townsend Residence, Rutledge Avenue and South Bay Street, Charleston; $7600 (*MR*, 25 November 1915, p. 60.)

1916: St. Margaret's Home, Charleston; $12,000 (*MR*, 3 August 1916, p. 81; "John D. Newcomer Found Dead.")

1917: C.D. Franke Co. Office and Warehouse, Charleston (*American Art Annual*; "John D. Newcomer Found Dead.")

1919: Thompson-Miller Hardware Company Building, Charleston (*MR*, 25 September 1919, p. 143.)

Ca. 1920: Alterations, 10 Meeting Street, Charleston (National Register files, S.C. Archives.)

1921: Catholic Diocese School, Charleston; $12,000 (*MR*, 21 July 1921, p. 85.)

1921: Addition and remodeling, Roper Hospital Building, Calhoun and Lucas streets, Charleston; $30,000 (*MR*, 1 December 1921, p. 105 f.)

1922: J.A. Waddell Residence, Georgetown (*American Art Annual*.)

1923: Simonton Public School, Charleston (*American Art Annual*.)

1923: Remodeling and addition, Star Gospel Mission, Meeting Street, Charleston; $14,000 (*MR*, 2 August 1923, p. 149.)

1924: Florence Crittenden Home, Charleston; $50,000 (*MR*, 3 January 1924, p. 109; *American Art Annual*; "John D. Newcomer Found Dead.")

1925: St. Francis Xavier Infirmary and Sanitarium Hospital Building, Calhoun Street and Ashley Avenue, Charleston; $175,000; Ferdinand Durang (q.v.), architect, and J.D. Newcomer, associate architect (*MR*, 8 January 1925, p. 116; 2 July 1925, p. 130; 9 July 1925, p. 122.)

1925: Summerville Club Clubhouse, Charleston; $15,000 (*MR*, 31 December 1925, p. 90.)

1925: Improvements, Haverty Building, King and Society streets, Charleston; $15,000 (*MR*, 16 July 1925, p. 116.)

1925: Auditorium, Berkeley High School, Moncks Corner; $19,919 (*MR*, 27 August 1925, p. 105.)

1926: School, Rosemont, North Charleston; $34,952 (*MR*, 22 April 1926, p. 130; 29 April 1926, p. 109.)

1926: Gloria Theater, King Street, Charleston; Claude K. Howell (q.v.), architect; John D. Newcomer, associated architect (*MR*, 20 May 1926, p. 124.)

1926: School, Meggetts; $83,700 (*MR*, 26 August 1926, p. 104; "John D. Newcomer Found Dead.")

1926: School, Ridgeland; $36,837 (*MR*, 3 June 1926, p. 135.)

1926: School, Tillman; $13,843 (*MR*, 3 June 1926, p. 135.)

1926: Carolina Inn, Summerville; $21,333 (*MR*, 19 August 1926, p. 109.)

1928: Hotel, Summerville; $75,000 (*MR*, 23 August 1928, p. 84.)

1929: Addition, South Atlantic Mortgage Company Building, Charleston (*MR*, 10 January 1929, p. 114.)

1930: Parish House and Rectory, St. Peter's Protestant Episcopal Church, Charleston; $38,088 (*MR*, 11 September 1930, p. 89; "John D. Newcomer Found Dead.")

1931: Dr. J. Sumter Rhame Residence, South Battery, Charleston; $22,705 (*MR*, 19 February 1931, p. 66; "John D. Newcomer Found Dead.")

n.d.: Atlantic National Bank Building, Charleston ("Newcomer Found Dead"; Withey.)

n.d.: J.M. Connelly Memorial Chapel, Charleston ("Newcomer Found Dead.")

n.d.: Citizens Bank Building, King Street, Charleston (Withey.)

n.d.: High School, St. Paul's Parish, Charleston (Withey.)

Sources: *American Art Annual*, Vol. 21, p. 441; Charleston city directories; "John D. Newcomer Found Dead at 64," *News & Courier*, 31 December 1931, p. 1; *MR*, various citations; "Services Held for Architect," *News & Courier*, 1 January 1932, p. 2; Withey, p. 439.

NIERNSEE, Frank MacHenry (1849-1899) Frank Niernsee was the son of the Austrian architect John Rudolph Niernsee, who began construction of the South Carolina State House in Columbia in 1853. The younger Niernsee was born in Baltimore, where his father had worked for several years before accepting the South Carolina commission.

Frank Niernsee was a courier for the Confederate cavalry in the Civil War. After the war he studied engineering at the University of Virginia, and by 1878 he was associated with his father in Baltimore. Niernsee & Son designed the 1878-1879 Opera House in Lynchburg, Virginia.

In 1882 John and Frank Niernsee returned to South Carolina to continue work on the State House in Columbia. The elder Niernsee died in 1885, and his former Baltimore associate John Crawford Neilson was appointed State House architect. Neilson returned to Maryland after two years, and in 1888 Frank Niernsee and Edwin I. White of Charleston (q.v.) assumed direction of the project. Niernsee's daughter, Virginia Niernsee Floyd, described her father's work at the building:

> . . . my father was called to come and complete the Major's work on the State House. Papa's work was mostly in the interior of the building, including finishing the Major's design and installing a beautiful library ceiling, which became known everywhere for its beauty.

Niernsee pursued a private architectural and engineering practice in these years as well. From 1893 to 1896 he was associated with A. Gamewell LaMotte (q.v.) in Columbia. Their practice included schools, dwellings, and public buildings across the state, as well as many civil engineering projects. He advertised in 1898 as "Frank Niernsee & Co., Sanitary Engineers & Architects." Prominent among Niernsee's surviving designs are the Matthews Residence (Oakhurst) in Newberry, a competent Queen Anne composition; and the Ladson Presbyterian Church in Columbia, a severe Romanesque Revival building with twin battlemented towers.

Niernsee died on 28 May 1899. His obituary in *The State* stated:

> He was the architect in charge of the roof and interior furnishings of the State Capital done about 10 years ago. Mr. Niernsee was for a number of years the city engineer here and supervised the construction of the present city waterworks plant. Mr. Niernsee was a talented man and as an architect was considered among the best.

South Carolina projects:

1888: St. Paul's Lutheran Church and Chapel, Columbia; $40,000 (*MR*, 14 January 1888, pp. 1027, 1031.)

1888: Completion, South Carolina State House, Columbia (*MR*, 18 February 1888, p. 23.)

1891: School, Sumter; $10,900 (*MR*, 14 February 1891, p. 44; 14 March 1891, p. 42; 21 March 1891, p. 41; 11 April 1891, p. 43.)

1892: Jail and Sheriff's Residence, Sumter (*MR*, 1 April 1892, p. 49; 6 May 1892, p. 44.)

Niernsee & LaMotte

1893: School, Camden; $10,000 (*MR*, 24 March 1893, p. 155; 16 June 1893, p. 370.)

1893: Memorial Building, Connie Maxwell Orphanage, Greenwood (*MR*, 31 March 1893, p. 173.)

1893: R.P. Monaghan Residence, Sumter; $9000 (*MR*, 31 March 1893, p. 173.)

1893: York County Courthouse, Yorkville; $25,000 (*MR*, 17 March 1893, p. 137; 24 March 1893, p. 155; 31 March 1893, p. 173; 26 May 1893, p. 317.)

1894: F.H. Hayett Residence, Columbia; $6000 (*MR*, 13 April 1894, p. 175.)

1894: Casino Building, Columbia (*MR*, 16 March 1894, p. 108; 13 April 1894, p. 175.)

1894: Improvements, Sunday School Building, Columbia (*MR*, 25 May 1894, p. 285.)

1894: Maxwell Asylum, Greenwood; $5000 (*MR*, 13 April 1894, p. 175.)

1894: Bud Cate Matthews Residence, Newberry; $8000 (*MR*, 25 May 1894, p. 285; National Register files, S.C. Archives.)

1894-1895: Ladson Presbyterian Church, 1720 Sumter Street, Columbia; $8000 (*MR*, 25 May 1894, p. 285; 22 March 1895, p. 123.)

1896: Columbia Electric Railway Company Casino Building, Columbia; $6000 (*MR*, 5 June 1896, p. 319; 19 June 1896, p. 353.)

1896: Infirmary Building, Winthrop Normal College, Rock Hill (*MR*, 3 July 1896, p. 386.)

Frank M. Niernsee

1898: Alterations, South Carolina Dispensary Warehouse, Gervais and Pulaski streets, Columbia (*The State*, 18 December 1977, p. 14-E.)

Sources: S. Allen Chambers, *Lynchburg: An Architectural History* (Charlottesville, Virginia: The University Press of Virginia, 1981), pp. 223-225; Columbia city directories; Christie Z. Fant, *The State House of South Carolina: An Illustrated Historic Guide* (Columbia: The R.L. Bryan Co., 1970); *MR*, various citations; "Architect Niernsee Dead," *The State*, 29 May 1899, p. 8.

NORRMAN, Gottfried L. (1846-1909) Gottfried L. Norrman, a native of Sweden, was educated at Copenhagen University and at a technical school in Germany. He emigrated to the United States and eventually settled in Spartanburg, South Carolina, where he designed a number of buildings in the early 1880s. An 1880 directory stated that Norrman, "by his skillful drawings, has very much improved the appearance of our rapidly growing town." Norrman moved to Atlanta, Georgia, around 1883, where he was associated with G.P. Humphries.

Norrman left Atlanta in 1887, owing, it has been suggested, to the passage of a local prohibition law. He worked briefly in Greenville, South Carolina, before returning to Atlanta. In 1896 Norrman provided gratis plans for a children's ward at Grady Hospital in Atlanta.

Prominent among Norrman's designs in Georgia were the nine-story John Silvey & Co. Building in Atlanta, designed in 1893; the Venable Bros. Office Building in Atlanta, contracted in 1896 at $400,000; the $225,000 Edward A. Horne Hotel in Macon, contracted in 1902; and the five-story Citizens' Bank Building in Savannah, commissioned that same year. Norrman's 1893 Georgia State Building at the World's Columbian Exposition in Chicago was described by critic Montgomery Schuyler as "the most literal reproduction of a classic temple among the designs for State buildings."

Norrman's buildings in South Carolina, including the Newberry City Hall and the Bowden Building in Spartanburg, were of the more eccentric Victorian Gothic Revival modes, with extravagant brickwork, picturesque towers, and tall gables prominent.

Thomas Morgan, describing Norrman as a wit, quoted from the architect's 1895 "autobiography":

I was born in Sweden in about the same manner as all other Swedes -- nothing of any note happened at the event. . . The only sensation that my coming into this world created was a little stir among some old aunts and other lady friends, who found it difficult to decide whom I looked like, but they finally came to the conclusion that I resembled my great-grandmother. I suppose they came to this decision on account of my being bald-headed, wrinkled in the face, and of a very unsettled disposition.

Norrman was associated with John Falkner in Atlanta from 1906 to 1909. In 1909 he re-organized his firm, with Hal Hentz (q.v.) and Neel Reid (q.v.) becoming partners. Hentz and Reid continued the office after Norrman's death later that year.

South Carolina projects:

1880: Opera House, Spartanburg (Emerson, p. 22.)

Ca. 1880: R.L. Bowden & Co. Business Building (Spartan Inn), Morgan Square, Spartanburg (Emerson, opp. p. 112; *Spartanburg, S.C. City and Suburban Directory 1910* (Asheville, North Carolina: Piedmont Directory Co., 1910, opp. p. 355.)

Ca. 1882: City Hall and Opera House, Newberry (National Register files, S.C. Archives; Lyon, "Gottfried L. Norrman.")

1896: W.H. Clark Residence, Spartanburg; $4000 (*Southern Architect and Building News*, November 1896, p. 23.)

1898: Oregon Hotel, Main and Maxwell streets, Greenwood (*MR*, 21 January 1898, p. 409; *Greenwood Index*, 3 February 1898.)

1909: Improvements, Central Methodist Church, Spartanburg; $10,000 (*MR*, 11 February 1909, p. 65.)

Norrman, Hentz & Reid

1909: C.C. Tweety Casino, Hartsville (Grady, p. 199.)

1909: W.S. Manning Residence, Spartanburg (Grady, p. 199.)

1909-1910: Recreation Building, Hartsville Cotton Mills, Hartsville; $10,000 (*MR*, 12 May 1910, p. 81.)

Sources: "Architect G.L. Norrman Speeds A Fatal Bullet Through Right Temple," *The Atlanta Constitution*, 17 November 1909, p. 1; Atlanta, Georgia, city directories; *Chas. Emerson & Co.'s Spartanburg & Greenville Directories, 1880-1881* (Atlanta, Georgia: H.H. Dickson, 1880), pp. 22, 50, 63, 112; James Grady, *Architecture of Neel Reid in Georgia* (Athens, Georgia: University of Georgia Press, 1973); Greenville city directories; Elizabeth Lyon, "Gottfried L. Norrman," in *Dictionary of Georgia Biography*, pp. 750-751; *MR*, various citations; Morgan; Montgomery Schuyler, "State Buildings At The World's Fair," *The Architectural Record*, July-September 1893, pp. 66, 69; Withey, p. 444.

O'CONNOR, James W. (1875-1952) James W. O'Connor, a native of New York, studied architecture at Columbia University and at the Ecole des Beaux-Arts in Paris. He worked with McKim, Mead & White prior to establishing his own practice in New York City. He designed the W.R. Grace "Winter Residence," complete with stables, garage, and servants' quarters, in the popular "winter colony" of Aiken, South Carolina. The Grace complex was contracted in 1929. O'Connor also designed a house for W.R. Grace in The Plains, Virginia, in 1931.

Sources: *Architectural Record*, January 1953; *MR*, 20 June 1929, p. 91; 27 June 1929, p. 93; Moore, *McKim*, p. 335; Noffsinger, pp. 108, 115.

OKEL & COOPER (active 1908-1929) Edward Okel, Jr., and Carl B. Cooper of Montgomery, Alabama, designed buildings in several southeastern states, including Tennessee, Georgia, and South Carolina, as well as Alabama. The four-story, $120,000 Knighten Furniture Company Building at 105-107 Commerce Street, Montgomery, contracted in 1929, was among their largest commissions.

South Carolina project:

1910: Bank of Dillon Office Building, Dillon; $20,000 (*MR*, 28 April 1910, p. 68.)

Sources: *MR*, various citations.

OLIVER, Henry (active 1892-1909) Henry Oliver worked as a contractor in Charleston in the 1890s; he rebuilt the main building of the old Citadel Academy after a fire in 1892. He worked under Bradford L. Gilbert (q.v.) to build several buildings at the 1901 South Carolina Interstate and West Indian Exposition. In 1902 Oliver was described as "superintendent architect" for the Roman Catholic Cathedral of St. John the Baptist, a building designed by Patrick C. Keely (q.v.)

Sources: Charleston city directories; *MR*, 1 April 1892, p. 48; 25 April 1901, p. 262; 8 May 1902, p. 286; 12 August 1909, p. 58.

OLNEY, A.C. (active 1898-1899) Olney was a partner of W.B.W. Howe (q.v.) in Spartanburg.

South Carolina projects:

1898: See **Howe, W.B.W.** (Howe & Olney)

Sources: *MR*, various citations; Spartanburg city directories.

ORR, Fred J. (active 1896-1930s) Fred J. Orr of Athens, Georgia, designed several small buildings in Georgia and South Carolina in the years preceding the First World War. He was working as a landscape architect in the 1930s. Orr wrote a description of "Classic Architecture in Athens" for the *Southern Architect and Building News* in December 1896.

South Carolina projects:

1914: North Chester Development Company School, Charleston (*MR*, 1 October 1914, p. 71.)

1915: Store Building, North Charleston (*MR*, 15 April 1915, p. 58.)

Sources: *MR*, various citations; *Architects and Builders in Georgia*.

OSBORNE, Adlai (active 1909-1928) Adlai Osborne pursued an undistinguished practice as an architect and civil engineer in Charlotte, North Carolina, for several years. He worked for Lockwood, Greene & Co. (q.v.) in 1920-1922. Osborne was no longer listed in the city directories by 1930.

South Carolina project:

1915: Addition, High School, Blacksburg; $8441 (*MR*, 13 May 1915, p. 62.)

Sources: Charlotte, North Carolina city directories; *MR*, various citations.

OTT, Siberia (active 1873-1895) Siberia Ott was a contractor, builder, and architect active in Aiken in the later nineteenth century. He was associated with John Laird (q.v.) in Aiken for several years. Ott's most noted work is the Gothic-Revival Chapel St. Claire in Aiken. Some sources suggest that James Renwick was the architect for the building, and Ott the contractor; other sources suggest that Ott prepared the plans.

South Carolina projects:

1879: St. Claire's Chapel, Aiken (S. Ott to Rev. D.J. Quigley, 14 August 1879 and 27 December 1879, in Archives, Roman Catholic Diocese, Charleston; *History of Saint Mary Help of Christians Church and Aiken Missions: Compiled for the Seventy-Fifth Anniversary* (Aiken: St. Mary Help of Christians Church, 1942); National Register files, S.C. Archives.)

1890: School, Aiken; $10,000 (*MR*, 16 August 1890, p. 42.)

1893: Friendship Baptist Church, 505 Richland Avenue, Aiken (*MR*, 1 September 1893, p. 89; "Friendship Baptist Church, 100th anniversary, a brief sketch of Friendship Baptist Church, Aiken, SC 1866-1965," National Register files, S.C. Archives.)

OTTO, Olaf (1881- ca. 1930) Otto was born in Norway and educated at technical schools in Norway and Germany. He worked as a draftsman and industrial engineer in England before emigrating to the United States around 1903. He worked in New York and in Alabama before setting up practice in Savannah, Georgia, around 1912.

Otto worked as an engineer, builder, and contractor in Savannah; he was sometimes described as an architect. A 1925 bridge over the Savannah River was attributed to Otto. Some twenty-four houses in Savannah's Ardsley Park/Chatham Crescent district were also designed by Otto. He was identified as engineer and contractor for two bank buildings in Charleston, South Carolina, in 1928.

South Carolina projects:

1928: Atlantic Savings Bank Building, Charleston; $100,000 (*MR*, 10 May 1928, p. 91; 17 May 1928, p. 93.)

1928: Citizens & Southern Bank Building, Broad and Church streets, Charleston; $100,000 (*MR*, 9 August 1928, p. 85.)

1929: H.K. Hudson Residence, Beaufort; Henry Corse (q.v.), architect; Olaf Otto, contractor (*MR*, 28 March 1929, p. 88.)

Sources: *MR*, various citations; *Architects and Builders in Georgia*; *Who's Who in the South*, 1927, p. 558.

PARKER, Charles Edward (active 1876-1889) Charles Edward Parker of Boston, Massachusetts prepared plans for reconstruction of the ruined Old Circular Church in Charleston, South Carolina, in

1876. Parker's plans were not carried out, however, and the church was not rebuilt until 1890-1892.

Sources: *American Architect and Building News*, 12 August 1876, pp. 260-261; Withey, p. 454.

PARKINS, William H. (1836-1894) William H. Parkins, a native of New York, was working in Columbia, South Carolina, in 1860 as a carpenter. He established an architectural office in Atlanta, Georgia, shortly after the Civil War. Several of Atlanta's leading architects of the late nineteenth and early twentieth centuries, including Thomas H. Morgan (q.v.) and Alexander C. Bruce (q.v.), worked with Parkins in Atlanta. As a member of the firm Kimball, Parkins & Wheeler, Parkins prepared plans for the 1885 Bendella Hotel in Laurens, South Carolina.

Sources: 1860 Federal Census, Richland County, South Carolina, p. 80; S.F. Garlington, "Historical Sketch of the Town of Laurens, S.C.," (typescript), 1888; copy in National Register files, S.C. Archives; Morgan, pp. 139, 140, 142; *Architects and Builders in Georgia*; Withey, p. 426.

PARNHAM, _____ (active 1908) Parnham (also spelled **Parham**) was associated with William A. Edwards (q.v.) and Frank C. Walter (q.v.) when they established their Atlanta, Georgia, office in 1908. It is not clear who Parnham was; both Charles D. Parnham, manager of the Art Metal Construction Company, and Ralph E. Parnham, district manager for the Pauly Jail Building Company, were listed in the 1909 Atlanta city directory.

South Carolina projects:

1908: See **Edwards, William Augustus** (Edwards, Walter & Parnham)

Sources: Atlanta, Georgia city directories; *MR*, various citations.

PARSONS, Ernst May (d. 1967) E.M. Parsons of Boston, Massachusetts, prepared plans for the Wappoo Country Club clubhouse in Charleston, South Carolina, in 1924. The $69,170 project was designed in association with Olmstead Brothers, landscape architects, and with Seth Raynor of Southampton, New York, a "golf architect."

Parsons graduated from the Lawrence Scientific School at Harvard University in 1903. He was a partner in the Boston architectural firm of (John) Somes & Parsons in 1906-1919. Parsons practiced independently until 1927, when he became a partner in Parsons & Wait. Parsons worked as an architect until the 1960s. He died in Santa Barbara, California, on 6 January 1967.

Sources: *MR*, 24 July 1924, p. 127; Susan Moon, Boston Public Library, to Robert E. Dalton, 21 January 1988.

PEABODY, Julian (1881-1935) Julian Peabody, senior partner of the New York City architectural firm Peabody, Wilson & Brown, was trained in architecture at Harvard University and the Ecole des Beaux-Arts in Paris. After an apprenticeship in New York, he organized his firm in 1924. Peabody's work included four projects in Aiken, South Carolina, a winter resort community popular among wealthy northerners.

South Carolina projects:

Peabody, Wilson & Brown

1925: Thos. Hitchcock Residence, Aiken; $50,000 (*MR*, 16 April 1925, p. 114; 23 April 1925, p. 115.)

1928: Winthrop Rutherford Residence, Aiken; $100,000; Scroggs & Ewing (q.v.), architects; Peabody, Wilson & Brown, associated architects (*MR*, 17 May 1928, p. 93.)

1928: Seymour Knox Stables, Aiken; $25,000; Peabody, Wilson & Brown, architects; Scroggs & Ewing (q.v.), associated architects (*MR*, 25 October 1928, p. 102.)

1930: Bayard Warren Residence, Aiken; $40,000 (*MR*, 10 July 1930, p. 76.)

1931: Devereaux Milburn Residence, Aiken (*MR*, 30 April 1931, p. 62.)

Sources: *American Art Annual*, Vol. 21, p. 445; Hewitt, p. 280; *MR*, various citations; Noffsinger, pp. 108, 116; Withey, p. 462.

PEEPS, William H. (active 1915-1940) William H. Peeps of Charlotte, North Carolina, was the architect for a number of modest buildings in Charlotte and neighboring communities in the period 1915-1940. He designed several buildings for the Charlotte Consolidated Construction Company in 1918. The $440,000 J.B. Ivey & Co. Department Store Building in Charlotte, contracted in 1923, was among Peeps's largest projects.

South Carolina projects:

1919: Charles D. Jones Residence, Lancaster; $20,000 (*MR*, 8 May 1919, p. 120.)

1930: E.T. Cannon Residence, Ocean Drive and Beach Place, Myrtle Beach; $30,000 (*MR*, 20 March 1930, p. 81; 24 April 1930, p. 85; 1 May 1930, p. 91.)

Sources: Bisher, *North Carolina Architecture*, p. 401; Charlotte, North Carolina, city directories; *MR*, various citations.

PELZ, Paul J. (1841-1918) Pelz, a native of Silesia in eastern Europe, emigrated to the United States around 1859 and took a position with architect Detlef Lienau in New York. Pelz went to Washington, D.C., around 1866 to work for the United States Lighthouse Board, where he became chief draftsman.

Pelz associated with John L. Smithmeyer in Washington in 1873. Smithmeyer & Pelz won the 1873 commission for the Library of Congress, in a competition with twenty-seven other firms. Nothing was done with the plans until 1886, when Pelz was appointed official architect of the building. Further bureaucratic disputes led to other architects completing the design of the Library.

Pelz designed a number of buildings in the Southeast, including the U.S. Armory and Naval Hospital at Hot Springs, Arkansas, the Chamberlin Hotel at Hampton, Virginia, and several buildings at the University of Virginia. Pelz was associated with Fred W. Carlyle in 1893.

South Carolina projects:

Pelz & Carlyle

1893: W.B. Whaley Residence, Charleston (*MR*, 3 November 1893, p. 242.)

1893: W.B. Whaley Stable Building, Charleston (*MR*, 3 November 1893, p. 242.)

Paul J. Pelz

1897: Benjamin H. Rutledge Residence, Charleston; $20,000 (*MR*, 5 February 1897, p. 32.)

Sources: Jeffrey Carson et.al., *Massachusetts Avenue Architecture*, Vol. 1 (Washington, D.C.: The Commission of Fine Arts, 1973), p. 265; *MR*, various citations; Herbert Small, *The Library of Congress: Its Architecture and Decoration* (New York: W.W. Norton & Co., 1982); Withey, p. 466.

PERKINS, Frank Edson (active 1899-1912) Frank E. Perkins of New York City was the architect for two buildings at Furman University in Greenville, South Carolina. He prepared plans for a library building at Furman, contracted at $20,000 in 1905. The $75,000 James C. Furman Hall of Science Building (1910-1912) was also designed by Perkins, with Joseph E. Sirrine (q.v.) as superintendent of construction.

Sources: Francis, pp. 60-61; *MR*, 19 October 1905, p. 354; *The State*, 19 January 1912, p. 2; 22 January 1912, p. 2.

PINCKNEY, Thomas M. (active 1887-1915) Thomas Pinckney of Charleston, a black carpenter, was described as the architect for the E.G. Haselton Undertaking Establishment and Residence in Charleston. The building was contracted at $7000 in 1914.

Camilla Pinckney, widow of Thomas Pinckney, was listed in the 1917 Charleston city directory.

Sources: Charleston city directories; *MR*, 6 August 1914, p. 75.

POLEY, G.M. (active 1911-1931) G.M. Poley was employed as an architect and engineer by the Atlantic Coast Line Railway in Wilmington, North Carolina in 1916-1917. He designed passenger and freight stations for the A.C.L. in Georgia, Virginia, and the Carolinas. Poley had worked earlier for the Central of Georgia Railway in Savannah.

South Carolina projects:

1916: Atlantic Coast Line Railway Passenger and Freight Station, Clio (*MR*, 27 July 1916, p. 65; 3 August 1916, p. 81.)

1916: Improvements, Atlantic Coast Line Railway Passenger Station, Sumter (*MR*, 12 October 1916, p. 65.)

Sources: *MR*, various citations.

PORTER, A.H. (active 1906-1916) A.H. Porter, an architect and engineer, worked for the Charleston & Western Carolina Railway Company in Augusta, Georgia ca. 1906-1916.

South Carolina projects:

1906: Charleston & Western Carolina Railway Depot, Anderson; $4000 (*MR*, 20 September 1906, p. 243.)

1916: Charleston & Western Carolina Railway Freight Depot, Anderson; $40,000 (*MR*, 8 June 1916, p. 80; 15 June 1916, p. 72.)

Sources: *MR*, various citations.

POWELL, S.L. (active 1905-1906) S.L. Powell prepared plans for two buildings in Newberry. Powell, described in one reference as a professor at Newberry College, planned a technological building for the college in 1906.

South Carolina projects:

1905: James M. McCaughrin, Five Store Buildings, Newberry; $12,000 (*MR*, 13 July 1905, p. 611; 20 July 1905, p. 25; 17 August 1905, p. 122; 24 August 1905, p. 149.)

1906: Technological Building, Newberry College, Newberry; $15,000 (*MR* 19 July 1906, p. 16.)

PREACHER, Geoffrey Lloyd (1882-1972) G. Lloyd Preacher was born in Fairfax, South Carolina, in 1882. He attended Clemson College, graduating in 1904 with a degree in mechanical and electrical engineering. Preacher was a draftsman for the Lombard Iron Works in Augusta, Georgia, by 1905, and he worked with Lombard through 1908. In 1909 he established an architectural office in Augusta, and in association with Arthur E. Holman (q.v.), Preacher prepared plans for twelve buildings in west central South Carolina.

Holman left the firm late in 1909, leaving Preacher to continue the practice. Philander P. Scroggs (q.v.) and Whitley Ewing (q.v.) entered the office as draftsmen around 1915. Preacher won many important commissions in Augusta during the war years, including the 1916 Modjeska Theater, the 1916 Houghton Elementary School, the 1917 Tubman High School for Girls, and the 1917 Masonic Temple. He incorporated in 1918 as G. Lloyd Preacher & Co., Inc., Architects and Engineers.

Preacher moved his office from Augusta to Atlanta in 1921, and he pursued a profitable career in the 1920s. George Harwell Bond, J.F. Wilhoit, and Nicholas Mitchell worked for Preacher in the early 1920s. The firm's major commissions in these years included the eleven-story American National Insurance Company Building in Atlanta (1922), a ten-story hotel in Asheville, North Carolina (1922), and the twelve-story Medical Arts Building in Atlanta (1926.) Preacher also worked in Florida, designing large hotels in West Palm Beach, Lake Worth, St. Petersburg, Cocoa, and elsewhere.

Preacher's more important designs in South Carolina include the McCormick County Courthouse, a competent though uninspired Georgian Revival composition; the Allendale County Courthouse; the Spartanburg High School; and the Fort Sumter Hotel,

Charleston, and Community Hotel, Orangeburg, each a modest high-rise with Spanish Colonial Revival detailing.

A contemporary biographical sketch of Preacher observed:

> His greatest hobby is his business and he possesses a remarkable personal knowledge of the details of his extensive undertakings. Extraordinary executive capacity is combined with a pleasing personality, and he is a representative of that type of man to whom success in any field of endeavor is assured.

Preacher was president of the Georgia state board for the examination and registration of architects in 1926. He maintained a full slate of society connections; his memberships included York and Scottish Rite Masons, the Mystic Shrine, the B.P.O.E., the Atlanta Chamber of Commerce, and several athletic clubs.

South Carolina projects:

Preacher & Holman

1909: Jas. M. Patterson Residence, Allendale (*MR*, 22 April 1909, p. 60.)

1909: Barnwell County Jail and Jailer's Residence, Barnwell; George G. Smith (q.v.), architect; Preacher & Holman, supervising architects (*MR*, 27 May 1909, p. 68; 17 June 1909, p. 67.)

1909: Christian Congregation Edifice, Brunson; $5000 (*MR*, 16 September 1909, p. 62.)

1909: John T. Compton Store and Office Building, Fairfax; $15,000 (*MR*, 18 February 1909, pp. 67, 69.)

1909: J.B. Brunson Residence, Fairfax (*MR*, 11 March 1909, p. 59.)

1909: Mrs M.E. Terry Store Building, Fairfax (*MR*, 22 April 1909, p. 62.)

1909: J.H. Adams Residence, Furman (*MR*, 28 January 1909, p. 59.)

1909: W.C. Mauldin Residence, Hampton; $6500 (*MR*, 24 June 1909, p. 58.)

1909: High School, Varnville and Hampton; $20,000 (*MR*, 26 August 1909, p. 57; 2 September 1909, p. 73; 9 September 1909, p. 59.)

1909: J.R. Hoover Residence, Hampton; $8000 (*MR*, 16 December 1909, p. 62.)

1909: Jno. M. Clark Residence, Summerville; $5000 (*MR*, 24 June 1909, p. 58.)

1909: J. Frank Clark Residence, Summerville; $5000 (*MR*, 24 June 1909, p. 58.)

G. Lloyd Preacher

1909: Mrs. M.B. McSweeney Store and Office Building, Hampton (*MR*, 16 December 1909, p. 68; 23 December 1909, p. 65.)

1909: J.S. Williams Store Building, Hampton (*MR*, 16 December 1909, p. 69.)

1909: Mrs. M.B. McSweeney, Two Residences, Hampton (*MR*, 23 December 1909, p. 64.)

1911: Aiken Theater Company Theater, Aiken (*MR*, 9 November 1911, p. 75.)

1911: School, Hampton; $10,000 (*MR*, 6 July 1911, p. 83.)

1911-1912: School, Lexington; $3525 (*MR*, 5 October 1911, p. 82; Cornerstone.)

1912: B.W. Crouch, four store buildings, Saluda; $13,000 (*MR*, 9 May 1912, p. 73; 16 May 1912, p. 75.)

1913: Aiken Institute Building, Aiken; $20,000 (*MR*, 29 May 1913, p. 71.)

1913: School, Blackville; $18,258 (*MR*, 20 March 1913, p. 70.)

1914: High School, Johnston; $25,000 (*MR*, 28 May 1914, p. 62; 25 June 1914, p. 59.)

1914: Bank of Ward Bank and Office Building, Ward; $5000 (*MR*, 24 September 1914, p. 62.)

1916: High School, Ridge Springs; $15,000 (*MR*, 2 March 1916, p. 77; 16 March 1916, p. 69.)

1917: School, Pelion; $7500 (*MR*, 12 July 1917, p. 72.)

1917: School, Trenton; $12,000 (*MR*, 12 July 1917, p. 72.)

1918: Wittenburg Lutheran Church and Sunday School Building, Leesville; $20,000 (*MR*, 9 May 1918, p. 78.)

G. Lloyd Preacher & Co.

1921: High School, Spartanburg; $213,125 (*MR*, 24 March 1921, p. 113.)

1921-1922: Allendale County Courthouse and Jail, Allendale; $100,000 (Plaque in building; *MR*, 11 August 1921, p. 91.)

1921-1922: Completion of Center Portion and Two Additions, Administration Building, De La Howe School, Willington (*MR*, 1 September 1921, p. 118; 18 May 1922, p. 90.)

1921-1922: High School, Abbeville; $75,000 (*MR*, 28 July 1921, p. 90; 25 August 1921, p. 87; 18 May 1922, p. 90.)

1922: Carteret Street Methodist Church and Sunday School Building, Beaufort; $48,000 (*MR*, 16 March 1922, p. 90.)

1922: Edward J. Murphy Apartment House, Rutledge Avenue and Beaufain Street, Charleston; $300,000 (*MR*, 27 April 1922, p. 84; 4 May 1922, p. 104.)

1922: City Hotel Company Hotel, Laurens and Washington streets, Greenville; $500,000 (*MR*, 17 August 1922, p. 86.)

1922-1923: McCormick County Courthouse and Jail, McCormick; $61,400 (Plaque on building;

MR, 13 July 1922, p. 89; 20 July 1922, p. 83; 19 April 1923, p. 99.)

1923: Fort Sumter Hotel, King Street and South Battery, Charleston; $405,000 (*MR*, 8 March 1923, p. 100; 15 March 1923, p. 100.)

1925: Industrial School Building, De La Howe School, Willington (*MR*, 4 June 1925, p. 140; 19 November 1925, p. 99.)

1926: City Hall and Jail, Orangeburg; $150,000 (*MR*, 9 December 1926, p. 117.)

1926: Community Hotel Building, Russell Street, Orangeburg; $173,800 (*MR*, 21 October 1926, p. 102.)

1927: Municipal Theater, Spartanburg (*MR*, 28 July 1927, p. 103.)

Sources: *Atlanta Constitution*, 19 June 1972, p. 4-C; Atlanta, Georgia, city directories; Augusta, Georgia, city directories; *History of Georgia*, Vol. IV (Chicago and Atlanta: The S.J. Clarke Publishing Co., 1926), pp. 22-26; Charles Lowe, "Changing the Face of Augusta," *Augusta Magazine*, Augusta, Georgia, Fall 1981, pp. 14-21; *MR*, various citations; *Who's Who in the South*, 1927, p. 591.

PRINGLE, Robert Smith (1883-1937) Pringle, a native of Summerville, studied at the Verners Academy in Columbia. He worked as a draftsman for James H. Sams (q.v.) in 1903-1904. In 1905 Pringle formed a partnership in Columbia with Avery Carter (q.v.), a former partner of Sams, and the firm Carter & Pringle designed several buildings in central South Carolina. In 1906 Pringle was identified as a contractor and builder in the city directory.

Around 1907 Pringle moved to Atlanta, Georgia. He worked with Walter T. Downing (q.v.) in Atlanta and Chattanooga, Tennessee, for several years. Pringle was associated with Francis P. Smith in Atlanta as Pringle & Smith in 1922-1934. One of the firm's largest projects was the seventeen-story Rhodes-Haverty Building, at 134 Peachtree Street in Atlanta, contracted at $750,000 and built in 1928-1929.

South Carolina projects:

1905-1906: See **Carter, Avery** (Carter & Pringle)

1907: Remodeling, Thomson Auditorium, Charleston (*MR*, 6 June 1907, p. 672.)

Sources: Columbia city directories; Herndon, p. 151; *MR*, various citations; Morgan, pp. 102, 105, 106, 162; *The State*, 7 March 1905, p. 8; *Architects and Builders in Georgia*; *Who's Who in South Carolina 1934-1935*, p. 380; Withey, p. 491.

PROFFITT, Luther B. (active 1899-1936) Luther D. Proffitt was listed as a carpenter in the 1899-1900 Spartanburg city directory. He began practice as an architect by 1904, in association with a man named McNeal (or McNeil.) Thomas Keating (q.v.) joined Proffitt in 1905, and the firm designed a number of buildings in Spartanburg. Proffitt was associated with S.P. Tinsley (q.v.) in 1908; and with Martin Luther Hampton (q.v.) in 1910-1911.

Anthony Ten Eyck Brown (q.v.) of Atlanta worked with Proffitt on two major projects: the 1911 enlargement and remodeling of the Laurens County Courthouse, and the 1913 Oregon Hotel in Greenwood.

Proffitt was described as "a prominent and promising young architect" when his Gastonia, North Carolina, Central School Building was completed in 1914.

Proffitt pursued other vocations as well as architecture. He was identified as proprietor of "Proffitt Flats" apartments in Spartanburg in 1916; and as president-treasurer of the Spartanburg Lumber Manufacturing Company in 1918-1928. In 1934 he worked as an architect with the Spartanburg County Emergency Relief Administration.

South Carolina projects:

Proffitt & McNeal

1904: Improvements, J.F. Cleveland and J.B. Cleveland Store Building, Spartanburg; $6000 (*MR*, 4 August 1904, p. 63.)

1905-1906: See **Keating, Thomas** (Keating & Proffitt)

Luther D. Proffitt

1907: Presbyterian Church, Gaffney; $4000 (*MR*, 31 October 1907, p. 62.)

1907: School, Simpsonville; $5000 (*MR*, 25 July 1907, p. 54.)

1907: City Hall, Spartanburg; $30,000; Luther D. Proffitt and W.B.W. Howe (q.v.), architects (*MR*, 7 February 1907, p. 112.)

1907: Church, Whitney Mills, Spartanburg; $5000 (*MR*, 11 July 1907, p. 837; 25 July 1907, p. 54.)

1907: Second Presbyterian Church, Spartanburg; $5000 (*MR*, 19 September 1907, p. 258.)

Proffitt & Tinsley

1908: Thomas A. Fairey Residence, Spartanburg; $4000 (*MR*, 2 July 1908, p. 69; 9 July 1908, p. 56.)

Luther D. Proffitt

1909: John B. and Jesse Cleveland Store Building, Spartanburg (*MR*, 25 March 1909, p. 58; 10 June 1909, p. 67.)

1909: J. Walter Allen Residence, Spartanburg; $12,000 (*MR*, 7 October 1909, p. 79.)

1909: Firehouse, Union; $4000 (*MR*, 11 March 1909, p. 60; 25 March 1909, p. 60; 1 April 1909, p. 71.)

1910: Remodeling, A.M. Alexander Apartment House, Spartanburg; $20,000 (*MR*, 10 February 1910, p. 62.)

1910: Luther D. Proffitt Apartment House, Spartanburg (*MR*, 24 February 1910, p. 68.)

1910: Realty Corporation Clubhouse, Spartanburg; $10,000 (*MR*, 31 March 1910, p. 71.)

Proffitt & Hampton

1911: Remodeling and Enlarging, Laurens County Courthouse, Laurens; $40,951; Proffitt & Hampton, architects; A. Ten Eyck Brown (q.v.), associated architect (*MR*, 10 August 1911, p. 69.)

Luther D. Proffitt

1911: Woodruff Presbyterian Church, Woodruff; $6000 (*MR*, 25 May 1911, p. 73.)

1913: Bowman Methodist Church, Bowman; $7400 (*MR*, 1 May 1913, p. 83; 14 August 1913, p. 67.)

1913: J.D. Goudelock Residence, Gaffney; $6000 (*MR*, 10 July 1913, p. 70.)

1913: Oregon Hotel, Greenwood; $93,900; Luther D. Proffitt and A. Ten Eyck Brown (q.v.), architects (*MR*, 30 January 1913, p. 68; 6 February 1913, pp. 79, 80.)

1913: First Baptist Church, Simpsonville; $16,000 (*MR*, 1 May 1913, p. 70.)

1913: Spartanburg Land & Improvement Company Building, Magnolia Street, Spartanburg; $15,000 (*MR*, 13 February 1913, p. 69.)

1914: Miss Gwynn's Boarding School for Girls Building, Spartanburg; $11,000 (*MR*, 23 July 1914, p. 58.)

1914: Girls' Dormitory Building, Spartanburg Academy, Groce's Station, Spartanburg; $12,000 (*MR*, 10 September 1914, p. 59; 17 September 1914, p. 59.)

1915: School, Spartanburg; $30,186 (*MR*, 1 April 1915, p. 64.)

1916: Steedly Hospital Building, Spartanburg; $34,793 (*MR*, 24 February 1916, p. 66.)

1917: B'Nai Israel Congregation Synagogue, Spartanburg; $10,000 (*MR*, 22 February 1917, p. 118.)

1922: Prospect Baptist Church, Spartanburg; $20,000 (*MR*, 25 March 1922, p. 90.)

1929: High School, Pacolet; $35,000 (*MR*, 28 February 1929, p. 91.)

Sources: Kim Withers Brengle, *The Architectural Heritage of Gaston County, North Carolina* (Gastonia, North Carolina: Gaston County, 1982), p. 157; *MR*, various citations; Spartanburg city directories.

RANKIN, KELLOGG & CRANE (active 1903-1925) The Philadelphia, Pennsylvania, firm of John Hall Rankin (1868-1952), Thomas Kellogg (1862-1935), and Edward A. Crane (1867-1935), described as "one of the most successful Beaux-Arts firms in Philadelphia," was active from 1903 to 1925. Penn School in Beaufort County, where Rankin, Kellogg & Crane designed a dormitory in 1905, was founded by northern philanthropists after the Civil War to aid the freedmen of South Carolina.

South Carolina project:

1905: Dormitory, Penn Normal Industrial and Agricultural School, St. Helena Island (Tatman/-Moss, p. 645.)

Sources: Tatman/Moss, pp. 171-172, 437, 643-647; Withey, pp. 147, 336.

RAYFIELD, Wallace A. (active 1909-1929) Wallace A. Rayfield of Birmingham, Alabama, a black architect, was active in church design in the Southeast from 1909 through 1929. Rayfield studied at the Pratt Institute and at the Columbia School of Architecture. He was later associated with Tuskegee. He designed many buildings for the African Methodist Episcopal Church in the southeastern states.

South Carolina project:

1922: Trinity A.M.E. Church, Spartanburg; $51,000 (*MR*, 19 January 1922, p. 76 g; 25 May 1922, p. 66.)

Sources: *MR*, various citations; Marjorie Longenecker White et.al., *Downtown Birmingham*

Architectural and Historical Walking Tour Guide, 2nd edition (Birmingham, Alabama: Birmingham Historical Society and The First National Bank of Birmingham, 1980.)

REID, Joseph Neel (1885-1926) Reid was a native of Jacksonville, Florida. He obtained his first architectural training from Curran R. Ellis of Macon, Georgia, whom he met in 1903 when Ellis was commissioned to remodel a house for Reid's mother. Reid subsequently worked for Willis F. Denny in Atlanta, Georgia. He met Hal F. Hentz (q.v.) in Denny's office; and Hentz accompanied Reid in schooling at Columbia University in New York, and at the Ecole des Beaux-Arts in Paris, France.

After brief periods of work in New York and in Macon, Reid and Hentz joined the office of Gottfried Norrman (q.v.) in Atlanta, and they became junior partners in the firm by 1909. Hentz assumed management of the firm upon Norrman's death, and the firm of Hentz & Reid (later Hentz, Reid & Adler) enjoyed professional and social prominence in the Southeast.

Reid's work with the firm was concentrated on residential design. The sources describe Reid's attention to detail, his concern for design within the landscape, and his ability to inspire a sense of pride in the craftsmen carrying out his designs. Thomas H. Morgan (q.v.) described Reid's work in Georgia:

> His work, both public and private, was almost always designed in the Classic or Italian Renaissance style of architecture, never following precedent too closely, but giving to each design a sure touch of individuality.

Reid's obituary described him as:

> . . . an architect of extraordinary insight, vision, and practical ability; a friend and leader in all things tending towards the beautiful, a diplomat who won his points, kept his friends — a simple, genial gentleman, Neel Reid.

South Carolina projects:

1909: See **Norrman, Gottfried** (Norrman, Hentz & Reid)

1912-1926: See **Hentz, Hal F.** (Hentz & Reid; Hentz, Reid & Adler)

Sources: James Grady, *Architecture of Neel Reid in Georgia* (Athens, Georgia: University of Georgia Press, 1973); Hewitt, p. 281; *The Journal of the American Institute of Architects*, April 1926, p. 190; Morgan, p. 110; Eugenia Coleman Payne, "Joseph Neel Reid," in *Dictionary of Georgia Biography*, 1983, pp. 834-835; Withey, pp. 500-501.

REID, Thomas G. (active 1919-1953) Thomas G. Reid, son of Rev. T.W. and Annie M. Reid, was a draftsman, clerk, and city official in Greenville. He was working as a grocery clerk in 1919. From 1921 through 1924 Reid was not listed in the Greenville directories. He was described as the architect for two Greenville projects in 1927-1928: a Sunday-School building for the Central Baptist Church in 1927, and, after the church auditorium was damaged by fire, the remodeling of the damaged building in 1928. In later years Reid worked variously as a draftsman and city building inspector; he was a draftsman for Leon LeGrand (q.v.) in 1953. Reid lived with his widowed mother and his sister in Greenville for most of his life.

South Carolina projects:

1927: Sunday School, Central Baptist Church, Lloyd and Pinckney streets, Greenville; $39,640 (*MR*, 17 March 1927, p. 121; 24 March 1927, p. 99; 31 March 1927, p. 109.)

1928: Remodeling, Central Baptist Church, Greenville; $31,500 (*MR*, 22 March 1928, p. 85.)

Sources: Greenville city directories; *MR*, various citations.

REISE, J.T. (active 1886) J.T. Reise (or **Ruse**) of Modoc was identified as an architect in the 1886 State Gazetteer.

RICE, James Henry III (active 1917) James Henry Rice Jr., editor, teacher, and author of *Glories of the South Carolina Coast* (1925), commissioned a $15,000 residence at Chee-Ha, South Carolina, in 1917. The architect for the project was identified as James Henry Rice III, presumably the son of James Henry Rice Jr.

Sources: *MR*, 18 January 1917, p. 72; Moore, Vol. 6.

RICHARDS, Ernest Vincent (1859-1915) Ernest V. Richards practiced architecture in eastern South Carolina in the early years of the twentieth century. Richards, a native of Oxford, England, was trained in wood engraving and related arts in England. He emigrated to the United States in 1877. By 1889 Richards was established as a stained glass designer, fresco painter, and wood sculptor in Wilmington, North Carolina.

Richards moved to Bennettsville, South Carolina, around 1907, and he opened an architectural office in that city. While his practice focused on large residences in the state's eastern towns, several schools and commercial buildings designed by Richards have also been identified. When the South Carolina chapter of the American Institute of Architects was formed in 1913, Richards was elected vice-president of the chapter.

The houses designed by Richards were generally of the Colonial Revival mode, frequently featuring two-story entrance porticos. Most of these buildings have elegant interior detailing in wood and stained glass, reflecting Richards's background in these associated arts.

Richards removed to Galveston, Texas, in 1915, where he worked as a theatrical designer. He died suddenly after two months in Texas.

South Carolina projects:

Ca. 1906: Roper Residence, 405 W. Main Street, Bennettsville (National Register files, S.C. Archives.)

1907: School, Kingstree; $12,000 (*MR*, 4 July 1907, p. 805; 11 July 1907, p. 837; 10 October 1907, p. 66; 17 October 1907, p. 69.)

1907: School, Latta; $14,000 (*MR*, 18 April 1907, p. 423; 5 September 1907, p. 205; 12 September 1907, p. 229.)

1908: C.E. Exum Store Building, Bennettsville; $4000 (*MR*, 6 February 1908, p. 68; 19 March 1908, p. 60.)

1908: C.B. Crosland Store, Office & Lodge Building, Bennettsville; $10,000 (*MR*, 12 March 1908, p. 57; 19 March 1908, p. 59.)

1908: S.J. Pearson/A.J. Matheson Store and Office Building, Bennettsville (*MR*, 12 March 1908, p. 57; 19 March 1908, p. 59.)

1908: S. Brown Store Building, Bennettsville; $4000 (*MR*, 19 March 1908, p. 60.)

1908: Rectory, St. David's Episcopal Church, Cheraw; $10,000 (*MR*, 28 May 1908, p. 65.)

1908: J.W. Covington Store and Clubroom Building, Cheraw; $10,000 (*MR*, 28 May 1908, p. 66.)

1908: School, Chesterfield; $10,000 (*MR*, 19 March 1908, p. 60; 7 May 1908, p. 70.)

1908: Latta Methodist Church, Latta; $15,000 (*MR*, 16 January 1908, p. 61; 19 March 1908, p. 59; 23 April 1908, p. 59; 21 May 1908, p. 60.)

1909: Cotton Warehouse Association Cotton Storage Warehouse, Bennettsville; $10,000 (*MR*, 15 July 1909, p. 67; 22 July 1909, p. 62; 9 September 1909, p. 59.)

1909: Marlboro Medical Association Hospital and Nurses' Training School Building, Bennettsville; $20,000 (*MR*, 9 September 1909, p. 58.)

1909: Marvin Adams Office Building, Bennettsville; $5500 (*MR*, 16 December 1909, p. 68.)

1909: J.W. Covington Hotel, Cheraw; $45,000 (*MR*, 16 December 1909, p. 69; 23 December 1909, p. 64.)

1909: J.H. Melton Hotel, Chesterfield; $5000 (*MR*, 16 December 1909, p. 69.)

1909: Jefferson Bank Building, Jefferson; $7000 (*MR*, 9 September 1909, p. 57.)

1909: Pine Grove Methodist Episcopal Church, Pine Grove; $6000 (*MR*, 16 December 1909, p. 68.)

1910: W.S. Mowrey Residence, Bennettsville (*MR*, 24 February 1910, p. 69.)

1910: Remodeling, Farmers and Merchants Bank Building, McColl (*MR*, 27 January 1910, p. 63.)

Ca. 1910: Fred Goforth Hollis Residence, 725 W. Main Street, Bennettsville (National Register files, S.C. Archives.)

1912: Baker-Craig Sanatorium, Charleston; E.V. Richards and John D. Newcomer (q.v.), associated architects; $55,000 (*The State*, 20 January 1912, p. 3; *MR*, 29 February 1912, p. 69.)

1913: Hartsville Arcade Co. Hotel, Hartsville; $35,000 (*MR*, 9 January 1913, p. 64.)

1914: A.F.A.M. Lodge/Theatorium, Hartsville; $8000 (*MR*, 15 January 1914, p. 70; 22 January 1914, p. 65; 29 January 1914, p. 68.)

n.d.: A.P. Breeden Residence, 404 W. Main Street, Bennettsville (National Register files, S.C. Archives.)

n.d.: Matheson Residence, Fayetteville Avenue, Bennettsville (National Register files, S.C. Archives.)

n.d.: Walter S. Rowe Residence, 122 Parsonage Street, Bennettsville (National Register files, S.C. Archives.)

n.d.: Mrs. Grady A. Vickers Residence, Society Street, Clio (National Register files, S.C. Archives.)

Sources: *A.I.A. Journal*, July 1915, p. 305; *MR*, various citations; Petty, pp. 134, 144; Withey, p. 507; Tony P. Wrenn, Washington, D.C., unpublished research.

RISER, Albert F. (active 1916) Albert Riser was named architect and superintendent of construction for an addition to the Westminster High School, contracted in 1916.

Source: *MR*, 4 May 1916, p. 89.

RITCHER, Abner A. (1872- ca. 1929) Abner A. Ritcher had a thriving architectural practice in Reading, Pennsylvania, from 1900 until his death ca. 1929. From 1922 he was associated with H.T. Eiler in Reading. Ritcher was a high-school graduate with no formal architectural training; his knowledge was derived from twelve years work in the offices of H.T. Hauer and H.A. Roby in Lebanon, Pennsylvania. Ritcher's professional work included church designs in many parts of the nation.

South Carolina project:

1913: St. Paul's Lutheran Church, Columbia; James B. Urquhart (q.v.), architect; Abner A. Ritcher, consulting architect (*MR*, 24 July 1913, p. 69; 31 July 1913, p. 68.)

Sources: Sandra Tatman and Roger Moss, The Athenaeum, Philadelphia, Pennsylvania, unpublished research; Withey, p. 511.

ROBINSON, Charles M. (1867-1932) Robinson was the son of architect James T. Robinson of Virginia. The younger Robinson studied architecture under D.S. Hopkins of Grand Rapids, Michigan, and under John K. Peebles of Virginia. After a period of practice in Pittsburgh, Pennsylvania, Robinson established an office in Richmond, Virginia, in 1906.

Robinson was noted as a school architect. He designed many school buildings in Richmond, including the Binford School (1914-1915), the Bainbridge School (1915), the Robert E. Lee School (1917), the Forest Hill Grade School (1921), the William Fox School, the Albert Hill School, and the Thomas Jefferson High School. He also designed buildings for the Roanoke Women's College, for the College of William and Mary, and for Mary Washington College.

In 1912 Robinson was commissioned by Lee Paschall and Jonathan R. Paschall of Richmond to design a hotel in Sumter, South Carolina. Robinson was also the architect for a $100,000 seven-story hotel project for the Paschalls in Durham, North Carolina, commissioned in 1912.

Robinson was a member of the Virginia State Board for Examination and Certification of Architects.

South Carolina projects:

1910-1911: Beam Dormitory, Lutheran Theological Seminary, Columbia; $40,157 (*MR*, 10 November 1910, p. 67; *Lutheran Church Visitor*, 19 October 1911, p. 4.)

1912: Paschall & Paschall Hotel, Main and Bartlett streets, Sumter; $75,000 (*MR*, 4 April 1912, p. 83; 11 April 1912, p. 70.)

1915: Nurses' Home, Tuomey Hospital, Calhoun Street, Sumter; $11,000 (*MR*, 15 July 1915, p. 60.)

1915-1917: Cleveland Hotel, 178 W. Main Street, Spartanburg; $184,000 (*MR*, 1 July 1915, p. 68; 2 December 1915, p. 74; 20 January 1916, p. 66; 3 February 1916, p. 80; 10 February 1916, p. 63; 9 March 1916, p. 55.)

1916: Dr. S.W. Pryor Hospital, Chester; $60,000 (*MR*, 8 June 1916, p. 70.)

1917: Mrs. S. McNeel Store and Office Building, York; $17,522 (*MR*, 22 March 1917, p. 72.)

Sources: *American Art Annual*, Vol. 21, p. 452; *MR*, various citations; Richmond, Virginia city directories; Robert Winthrop, *Architecture in*

Downtown Richmond (Richmond, Virginia: Historic Richmond Foundation, 1982), p. 242; Withey, pp. 516-517.

ROGERS, Fred G. (active 1903-1919) Fred G. Rogers was an architect and civil engineer in Greenville. Three buildings in the Greenville area are attributed to Rogers.

South Carolina projects:

1909-1910: Remodeling, City Hall, Greenville; $5000 (*MR*, 23 December 1909, p. 65; 30 December 1909, p. 64; 13 January 1910, p. 60; 27 January 1910, p. 65; 3 February 1910, p. 82.)

1916: Community Building and School, Judson Mills, Judson; $10,000 (*MR*, 14 September 1916, p.155; 21 September 1916, p. 67.)

1919: Professional Building Co. Office Building, Greenville; $20,000; Fred G. Rogers, architect; H. Olin Jones (q.v.), supervising architect (*MR*, 26 June 1919, p. 129; 3 July 1919, p. 156.)

Sources: Greenville city directories; *MR*, various citations.

ROGERS, James Gamble (1867-1947) James G. Rogers was a prominent New York City architect whose practice included buildings in seventeen states. He was a graduate of Yale University, and he worked as a draftsman for Chicago architect William LeBaron Jenney before attending the Ecole des Beaux-Arts in Paris. Rogers opened an architectural office in Chicago in 1897. He moved his main office to New York City in 1906. For several years Rogers was associated with Herbert D. Hale.

Rogers's major works included the Harkness Memorial Quad at Yale, the Butler Library Building (South Hall) at Columbia University, and the Columbia-Presbyterian Medical Center in New York. Hale & Rogers were the architects for the Federal Post Office in New Orleans and for the Shelby County Courthouse in Memphis, Tennessee, 1905-1908. Major southeastern buildings designed by Rogers included the 19-story Central Bank & Trust Company Office Building in Memphis, 1909; the Samuel

Hamilton Brooks Memorial Art Museum, Memphis, 1914; Norton Hall at the Southern Baptist Theological Seminary, Louisville, Kentucky, 1924; the Methodist Episcopal Church South, Chapel Hill, North Carolina, 1925; and the Administration Building at Atlanta University, 1932.

South Carolina project:

1927: Yeaman's Hall Clubhouse, Charleston; $120,000; James Gamble Rogers, architect; Simons & Lapham (q.v.), associated architects (*MR*, 9 June 1927, p. 114; 30 June 1927, p. 105; 15 September 1927, p. 121; *The New York Times*, 2 October 1947, p. 27.)

Sources: *Architectural Record*, November 1947, p. 14; Carl W. Condit, "James Gamble Rogers," *Dictionary of American Biography*, Supplement 4, 1946-1950 (New York: Charles Scribner's Sons, n.d., ca. 1974), pp. 697-698; Herndon, p. 156; Hewitt, p. 281; *Macmillan Encyclopedia of Architects*, Vol. III, p. 602; *MR*, various citations; *The New York Times*, 2 October 1947, p. 27; Noffsinger, pp. 109, 116; White & Willensky, pp. 232, 257, 294, 387; Withey, pp. 522-523.

ROGERS, Willard G. (active 1905-1940) Willard G. Rogers was associated with Charles C. Hook (q.v.) in Charlotte, North Carolina, from 1905 to 1915. He practiced independently from 1916. His work in North Carolina included the 1921 First Baptist Church in Gastonia, described as "a substantial Romanesque pile"; the eight-story, $325,000 Community Hotel in Fayetteville (1921); and the ten-story, $650,000 Wilder Building in Charlotte (1925).

South Carolina projects:

1905-1913: See **Hook, Charles C.** (Hook & Rogers)

1917: Remodeling, A.N. Wood, Two Store Buildings, Gaffney; $7500 (*MR*, 16 August 1917, p. 73.)

1918-1919: First Baptist Church, Rock Hill (Cornerstone; *MR*, 25 July 1918, p. 75; 19 September 1918, p. 94; 10 October 1918, p. 90.)

Sources: Kim Withers Brengle, *The Architectural Heritage of Gaston County, North Carolina* (Gastonia, North Carolina: Gaston County, 1982), p. 160; Charlotte, North Carolina, city directories; *MR*, various citations.

RORKE, Edwyn Grant (1890- ca. 1955) Edwyn G. Rorke, a native of Pennsylvania, received professional training as a draftsman for Philadelphia architects Lawrence Boyd and Horace Trumbauer. Around 1912 Rorke came to Columbia, South Carolina, entering a partnership with Arthur Williams Hamby (q.v.). Hamby & Rorke won several important commissions in Columbia in 1913, including the St. Timothy Protestant Episcopal Church and the Richland County Jail. Hamby & Rorke also designed a Carnegie Library in Gaffney.

Rorke returned to Philadelphia around 1914. He opened his own office in Norristown, Pennsylvania in 1924, and he practiced in the mid-Atlantic states through 1955. The Alden Park Apartments in Philadelphia, built in 1928, was among his more important commissions.

South Carolina projects:

See **Hamby, Arthur Williams** (Hamby & Rorke)

Sources: Columbia city directories; Koyl, p. 471; *MR*, various citations.

RUNGE, Neil (active 1902-1912) Neil Runge was an associate of Oliver Duke Wheeler (q.v.) in Charlotte, North Carolina, from 1902 through 1907. The firm of Wheeler, Runge and (D. Anderson) Dickey opened an office in Nashville, Tennessee, by 1907; and in 1908 Runge and Dickey separated from Wheeler and established their own practice in Nashville.

South Carolina projects:

1902-1907: See **Wheeler, Oliver Duke** (Wheeler & Runge; Wheeler, Runge & Dickey)

148

Sources: Charlotte, North Carolina, city directories; Herndon, pp. 157-158; *MR*, various citations; Nashville, Tennessee, city directories.

RUSSELL, William P. (active 1876-1895) William P. Russell is listed as an architect in the Charleston city directories from 1880 to 1895. He is identified as the architect of the baronial Calhoun Mansion at 16 Meeting Street, built in 1876-1878.

South Carolina project:

1876-1878: George W. Williams Residence (Calhoun Mansion), 16 Meeting Street, Charleston; $200,000 (*News and Courier*, 25 April 1932; 26 June 1977, p. 13-E.)

RUTLEDGE, E.B. (active 1883-1894) E.B. Rutledge of Greenville prepared plans for enlarging and repairing the Pickens County Courthouse in Pickens, South Carolina, in 1890. Comstock's 1894 *Architects' Directory* located Rutledge in Atlanta, Georgia. An E.B. Rutledge, perhaps the same man, worked in the New York offices of McKim, Mead & White from August 1891 to November 1892.

Sources: Greenville city directories; *MR*, 29 March 1890, p. 43; Moore, *McKim*, p. 330.

RYNO & BRACKNEY (active 1920-1940) John H. Ryno (1873- ca. 1941) of Knoxville, Tennessee worked for George F. Barber (q.v.) from 1894 through 1908. He entered independent practice in 1913. Claude C. Brackney (1879- ca. 1963) of Indiana, who had also worked for Barber, associated with Ryno in 1920, and the firm practiced in Knoxville until the Second World War. Their work included the Magnolia Avenue Methodist Episcopal Church in Knoxville, designed in 1925.

South Carolina project:

1921: Mrs. A.C. Ferguson Store and Apartment Building, Greenville; $12,500 (*MR*, 28 April 1921, p. 117; 21 May 1921, p. 156.)

Sources: Herndon, pp. 25-26, 159; *MR*, various citations.

SALTER, James A. (1874-1939) Salter, a native of Wisconsin, studied at the Rochester, New York, Athenaeum and Mechanical Institute. He came to Raleigh, North Carolina, in 1912. Salter was named North Carolina's "State Architect" by Governor Bickett, and he handled many state commissions, including buildings for the Caswell Training School, East Carolina Teachers' Training School, North Carolina College for Women, the University of North Carolina, the State School for the Blind, and the North Carolina State College of Agriculture and Engineering.

South Carolina project:

1922: Dormitory, Women's College, Due West; $75,000 (*MR*, 23 February 1922, p. 74 b.)

Sources: *MR*, various citations; Obituary, *Raleigh Times*, Raleigh, North Carolina, 19 December 1939, p. 1; 20 December 1939, p. 2.

SAMS, James Hagood (1872-1935) Sams, a native of Beaufort, attended the Porter Military Academy in Charleston. He came to Columbia in 1895, where he took a position as draftsman for architect Charles C. Wilson (q.v.) He opened his own office in Columbia in 1898. Paul Youmans (q.v.), who had also worked in Wilson's office, joined Sams in 1899; and in 1900 Sams & Youmans won the commission for the Columbia Police Station in direct competition with Wilson & Edwards.

Avery Carter (q.v.) associated with Sams in 1903, and the firm was active until 1905. Sams pursued independent practice in Columbia from then until his death in 1935.

The architect's surviving work includes several competent commercial designs, including the adjacent Boyne and Brown buildings in Columbia. Sams designed a number of churches in a fundamentally correct late Gothic Revival style, including the Good Shepherd Episcopal and Arsenal Hill Presbyterian churches in Columbia and the Zion Protestant Episcopal Church in Eastover. Sams also designed many school buildings in the state's rural communities.

Sams was secretary-treasurer of the State Board of Architectural Examiners for many years. He worked as an architect for C.W.A. projects in the 1930s.

South Carolina projects:

Sams & Youmans

1900: Columbia Police Station, Columbia (*The State*, 11 July 1900, p. 8; 25 July 1900, p. 8.)

1900: Thos. A. Boyne Commercial Building, Main Street, Columbia (*MR*, 13 September 1900, p. 128; Kline.)

James H. Sams

1901: Good Shepherd Episcopal Church, Columbia (*The State*, 11 March 1901, p. 8; Kline; Withey.)

1901: DesPortes Business Building, 1434-1438 Assembly Street, Columbia (Cornerstone.)

1902: Second Presbyterian Church, Columbia (*MR*, 5 June 1902, p. 365; Kline.)

Sams & Carter

1903: Tree of Life Synagogue, 1320 Lady Street, Columbia; $5000 (*MR*, 10 December 1903, p. 412; Kline.)

1903: Episcopal Church, Darlington; $6000 (*MR*, 10 December 1903, p. 412.)

1903-1904: Jno. McSween Co. Store Building, 165 W. Main Street, Timmonsville; $15,000 (*MR*, 10 December 1903, p. 413; 9 June 1904, p. 480; *The State*, 1 June 1904, p. 2; Withey.)

1904: Arsenal Hill Presbyterian Church, 1103 Laurel Street, Columbia (Cornerstone; Withey.)

1904: Recitation Hall, Benedict College, Columbia; $20,000 (*MR*, 7 January 1904, p. 495; 7 July 1904, pp. 569-570.)

1904: Carnegie Library, Benedict College, Columbia; $5000 (*MR*, 4 August 1904, p. 62.)

1904: School, Jonesville (*MR*, 28 April 1904, p. 335; 12 May 1904, p. 384; 19 May 1904, p. 410.)

Ca. 1904: James H. Sams Residence, Columbia (Kline.)

Ca. 1904: C.O. Brown & Bros. Store Building, Main Street, Columbia (Kline.)

Ca. 1904: Dr. Gilmore Residence, Columbia (Kline.)

Ca. 1904: Dr. Augustus B. Knowlton Infirmary, Marion Street, Columbia (Kline.)

James H. Sams

1905: School, Clio; $8500 (*MR*, 13 April 1905, p. 281; 20 April 1905, p. 308; 4 May 1905, p. 354; 7 September 1905, p. 200; 12 October 1905, p. 326.)

1905: Presbyterian Church, Manning (*MR*, 20 April 1905, p. 309.)

1906: L.B. Dozier Plumbing & Supply Company Building, Columbia; $30,000 (*MR*, 15 March 1906, p. 237; 22 March 1906, p. 262.)

1907: School, Allendale; $10,000 (*MR*, 22 August 1907, p. 158; 29 August 1907, p. 181.)

1907: Methodist Church, Timmonsville; $8000 (*MR*, 29 August 1907, p. 183; 5 September 1907, p. 206.)

Ca. 1907: Bundy-Vickers Residence, Society Street, Clio (National Register files, S.C. Archives.)

1909: Citizens' Bank Building, Allendale (*MR*, 23 September 1909, p. 59.)

1909: Dr. L.B. Owens Store Building, Columbia; $5000 (*MR*, 13 May 1909, p. 62.)

1909: School, Mayesville; $7000 (*MR*, 18 March 1909, p. 65; 13 May 1909, p. 63; 20 May 1909, p. 64.)

1909: School, Olanta; $4000 (*MR*, 8 April 1909, p. 62; 13 May 1909, p. 63; 20 May 1909, p. 64.)

1911: Zion Protestant Episcopal Church, County Road 263, Eastover (National Register files, S.C. Archives.)

1912: B.R. Myrick Store Building, Allendale; $7000 (*MR*, 6 June 1912, p. 90.)

1912: Addition, Knowlton Infirmary, Columbia; $26,000 (*The State*, 8 January 1912, p. 7; 31 January 1912; 2 February 1912, p. 8; *MR*, 8 February 1912, p. 68.)

1914: Varnville Hardware & Supply Company Warehouse and Store Buildings, Varnville; $7500 and $8500 (*MR*, 2 July 1914, p. 80.)

1915: Waverly Methodist Church, Columbia; $4500 (*MR*, 3 June 1915, p. 68.)

1915: Simpson & Taylor Store and Residence Building, Columbia (*MR*, 24 June 1915, p. 54.)

1915: M.H. Bowen Store and Residence Building, Columbia; $6000 (*MR*, 24 June 1915, p. 54; 1 July 1915, p. 69.)

1916: Blossom Street School, Columbia; $13,567 (*MR*, 10 February 1916, p. 63; Withey.)

1916: Farmers' Bank & Trust Company Bank Building, Lancaster; $12,000 (*MR*, 15 June 1916, p. 71.)

1916: School, Swansea; $9000 (*MR*, 24 August 1916, p. 69.)

1917: Beaufort Public Library (Municipal Court Building), Beaufort; $7000 (Cornerstone; *MR*, 12 April 1917, p. 69.)

1921: School, Neeses; $15,000 (*MR*, 14 April 1921, p. 116.)

1922: Presbyterian Church, Winnsboro (*MR*, 27 July 1922, p. 77.)

Ca. 1922: DeSoto Hotel, 1108 Lady Street, Columbia (Withey.)

1923: Addition, Barnwell County Courthouse, Barnwell; $8000 (*MR*, 4 October 1923, p. 124.)

1924: Sunday School Building, Second Baptist Church, Columbia (*MR*, 10 January 1924, p. 118.)

1924: J.E. Leitsey Residence, Columbia (*MR*, 4 September 1924, p. 128.)

1924: Inman Mills Baptist Church, Inman; $20,000 (*MR*, 10 July 1924, p. 103.)

1925: Industrial School Building, Booker Washington School, Columbia; $34,682 (*MR*, 26 February 1925, p. 120; 5 March 1925, p. 138; 19 March 1925, p. 124.)

1925: Presbyterian Church, Main and Singletary streets, Lake City (*MR*, 29 January 1925, p. 99.)

1925: School, Lynchburg; $31,064 (*MR*, 23 April 1925, p. 117.)

1925: Ameen Brothers Stores, Winnsboro (*MR*, 12 March 1925, p. 120; 7 May 1925, p. 141.)

1926: Remodeling, Park Street Baptist Church, Columbia (*MR*, 6 May 1926, p. 131.)

1926: A.F.A.M. Temple Building, Eau Claire; $10,000 (*MR*, 16 September 1926, p. 118.)

1926: School, Fairfax; $42,989 (*MR*, 2 September 1926, p. 138.)

1926: Baptist Church, Heath Springs; $25,000 (*MR*, 28 January 1926, p. 100.)

1926: Sunday School, First Baptist Church, Lancaster; $36,000 (*MR*, 8 April 1926, p. 114.)

1927: School, Garnett; $23,000 (*MR*, 10 March 1927, p. 100.)

1928: School, Hardeeville; $26,562 (*MR*, 21 June 1928, p. 97.)

1928: Addition, School, Pelion (*MR*, 2 August 1928, p. 103.)

1928: Two Schools, Ridgeland (*MR*, 3 May 1928, pp. 119-120.)

1928: School, Yemassee; $20,492 (*MR*, 21 June 1928, p. 97.)

1929: Sunday School, First Baptist Church, Sumter; $39,000 (*MR*, 16 May 1929, p. 85.)

1931: School, Grays; $14,000 (*MR*, 16 April 1931, p. 59.)

Sources: *American Art Annual*, Vol. 21, p. 455; Columbia city directories; Kline, *Illustrated 1904 Columbia*, p. 11; *MR*, various citations; "J.H. Sams Dies Here Suddenly," *The Columbia Record*, 12 February 1935, p. 1; "Sams Funeral This Morning," *The State*, 13 February 1935, p. 1; Withey, pp. 534-535.

SAWNER, John W. (active 1872-1890) Sawner was listed in Charleston city directories as a carpenter and contractor in 1872 through 1890. From 1886 to 1888 Sawner was listed as an architect and builder. He died on 7 May 1890.

Sources: Charleston city directories.

SAWYER, Frank McMaster (active 1898-1903) Sawyer was a draftsman for architect Frank P. Milburn (q.v.) in Charlotte, North Carolina, in 1897. He worked independently in Anderson before joining Charles C. Hook (q.v.) in Charlotte in 1898.

An F.M. Sawyer, perhaps the same man, was practicing architecture in Miami Beach, Florida, in 1924.

South Carolina projects:

1898: F.E. Watkins Residence, Anderson; $3000 (*MR*, 29 April 1898, p. 243.)

1898: Alterations and additions, Parsonage, First Baptist Church, Anderson; $2000 (*MR*, 27 May 1898, p. 303.)

1898: H.S. Dowling Residence, Bamberg (*MR*, 27 May 1898, p. 303.)

1898: Dr. Holcombe Residence, Belton (*MR*, 29 April 1898, p. 243.)

1898: D.L. Barnes Residence, Lowndesville (*MR*, 16 September 1898, p. 131.)

1898: Dr. D.B. Darby Hotel and Store Building, Walhalla (*MR*, 16 September 1898, p. 131.)

1898-1903: See **Hook, Charles C.** (Hook & Sawyer)

Sources: Charlotte, North Carolina, city directories; *MR*, various citations.

SAYRE, Christopher Gadsden (1876- ca. 1935) Christopher Gadsden Sayre, a native of Mt. Pleasant, was educated at Porter Military Academy in Charleston and at the South Carolina College, where he took a degree in civil, electrical, and mechanical engineering in 1897. He was engaged in surveying and civil engineering for several years, working in Rock Hill, Abbeville, and Anderson. Sayre was resident engineer for the Ware Shoals Manufacturing Company, in connection with W.B. Smith Whaley & Co. (q.v.) from 1902.

From 1908 to 1914, Sayre was associated with James J. Baldwin (q.v.) in Anderson. Sayre & Baldwin opened an office in Raleigh, North Carolina, in 1914, as their practice expanded. Baldwin left to open his own office in 1915, and Sayre pursued work in Georgia and the Carolinas. He had branch offices in Greensboro, North Carolina, in 1924-1927; in Winston-Salem, North Carolina, 1925; and in Asheville, North Carolina, 1926. His practice was concentrated in North Carolina after 1918.

Sayre was connected with the Anderson Hosiery Mills in Anderson for several years. He was identified as president-treasurer of the company in the Anderson city directories from 1925 to 1931.

Sayre was prominent as a designer of school buildings in South and North Carolina. The Shandon Graded School Building in Columbia (1909) was described by Rudolph E. Lee (q.v.) as one of a type, "a number of which type have been erected by the architects, Messrs. Sayre & Baldwin." A rendering of the building by Sayre & Baldwin was labeled "School Building # 32." Some twenty school buildings designed by Sayre or by Sayre & Baldwin have been identified in South Carolina, while thirty-six school projects by Sayre have been identified in North Carolina. Sayre also designed at least seven school buildings in Georgia.

Several county courthouses were designed by Sayre. His work in Georgia included the 1913 Bleckley County Courthouse in Baldwin, contracted at $35,000. The $123,500 Moore County Courthouse in Carthage, North Carolina, was designed by Sayre and contracted in 1922. In South Carolina, Sayre was the architect for the 1917 Saluda County Courthouse, contracted at $49,000. The Saluda Courthouse is a competent Neoclassical design in limestone and buff brick, dominating the county seat.

In 1927 Sayre was the architect for a proposed $1,250,000, twelve-story hotel in Columbia. This would have been among the largest construction projects in the state at the time; it appears, though, that construction was never begun.

South Carolina projects:

1906: Farmers' Union Warehouse Company Cotton Warehouse, Anderson; $17,800 (*MR*, 3 May 1906, p. 446; 14 June 1906, p. 616; 26 July 1906, p. 42.)

1907: J.M. Payne Business Building, Anderson; $16,000 (*MR*, 18 April 1907, p. 422; 20 June 1907, p. 736.)

1907: J.J. Fretwell Residence, Anderson (*MR*, 18 April 1907, p. 422.)

1907: J.T. McCown Residence, Anderson; $6000 (*MR*, 18 April 1907, p. 422.)

1907: G.W. Chambers Residence, Anderson (*MR*, 20 June 1907, p. 736.)

1907: Bleckley Office Building, Anderson; $50,000 (*MR*, 20 June 1907, p. 736.)

1907: J. Reed Watson Residence, Anderson (*MR*, 20 June 1907, p. 736.)

1907: Mrs. O.M. Chenault Residence, Anderson (*MR*, 20 June 1907, p. 736.)

1907: A.M. McFall Residence, Anderson (*MR*, 20 June 1907, p. 736.)

1907: W.A. Watson Business Building, Anderson (*MR*, 20 June 1907, p. 736.)

1907: Martin Seligman Residence, Anderson (*MR*, 20 June 1907, p. 736.)

1907: Trowbridge Residence, Anderson (*MR*, 20 June 1907, p. 736; 1 August 1907, p. 81.)

1907: J.J. Fretwell Tenement House, Anderson (*MR*, 10 October 1907, p. 64.)

1907: F.S. Baldwin Residence, Shandon (Columbia) (*MR*, 10 October 1907, p. 64.)

1907: J.J. McSwain Residence, Greenville (*MR*, 3 October 1907, p. 71.)

1907: S.R. Parker Residence, Greenwood; $4000 (*MR*, 20 June 1907, p. 737; 27 June 1907, p. 771.)

1907: Mrs. E.P. Harrison Residence, Greenwood (*MR*, 20 June 1907, p. 737.)

1907: J. Pyle Residence, Greenwood; $2800 (*MR*, 20 June 1907, p. 737; 27 June 1907, p. 771.)

1907: Copeland Brothers, three store buildings, Newberry (*MR*, 20 June 1907, p. 738.)

1907: School, St. George; $15,000 (*MR*, 11 April 1907, p. 390; 16 May 1907, p. 575;

23 May 1907, p. 606; 1 August 1907, p. 83; 8 August 1907, p. 112; 3 October 1907, p. 73.)

1907: T.L. Clinkscales Business Building, Seneca; $12,000 (*MR*, 18 April 1907, p. 424.)

1907: J.J. Smith Residence, Starr; $5000 (*MR*, 18 April 1907, p. 424.)

1907: H. Little John Business Building, Starr (*MR*, 20 June 1907, p. 738.)

1907: Howard Little John Residence, Starr (*MR*, 20 June 1907, p. 738.)

1907: Mrs. Bessie Allen Residence, Starr (*MR*, 1 August 1907, p. 83.)

1907-1908: School, North; $6000 (*MR*, 29 August 1907, p. 183; 3 October 1907, p. 73; 11 June 1908, p. 58; 18 June 1908, p. 64.)

1908: G. Walter Chambers Residence, Anderson; $3000 (*MR*, 26 March 1908, p. 59.)

1908: Bleckley Estate Store and Office Building, Anderson (*MR*, 30 April 1908, p. 60; 21 May 1908, p. 60.)

1908: Dr. J.B. Johnson Residence, St. George; $10,000 (*MR*, 14 May 1908, p. 58.)

1908: Methodist Church, Leesville; $8000 (*MR*, 18 June 1908, p. 62.)

1908: Masonic Building, St. George (*MR*, 14 May 1908, p. 59.)

1908: School, St. George; $20,000 (*MR*, 11 June 1908, p. 58.)

1908: C.E. von Lehe Store, Residence, and Office Building, St. George; $4500 (*MR*, 29 October 1908, p. 65; 5 November 1908, pp. 70, 71.)

1908: School, Woodruff; $15,000 (*MR*, 14 May 1908, p. 60; 21 May 1908, p. 63.)

1908: School, Holly Hill; $8000 (*MR*, 4 June 1908, p. 71; 1 June 1908, p. 58.)

1908: Presbyterian Church, Iva; $8000 (*MR*, 29 October 1908, p. 65; 5 November 1908, p. 69.)

1908-1909: City Hall, Bamberg; $10,000 (*MR*, 22 October 1908, p. 59; 3 December 1908, p. 77; 10 December 1908, p. 68; 14 January 1909, p. 58.)

1908-1909: School, Central; $10,000 (*MR*, 2 July 1908, p. 70; 19 November 1908, p. 75; 28 January 1909, p. 60.)

Sayre & Baldwin

1909: W.P. Wright Residence, Anderson; $2500 (*MR*, 22 February 1909, p. 66.)

1909: Shandon School, Columbia; $9675 (*MR*, 14 January 1909, p. 59; 4 March 1909, p. 80; 18 March 1909, p. 65; 1 April 1909, p. 72; 8 April 1909, p. 62; 15 April 1909, p. 66; 6 May 1909, p. 77; Lee, "Rural School Improvement.")

1909: School, Starr; $6000 (*MR*, 10 June 1909, p. 68; 1 July 1909, p. 72; 8 July 1909, p. 64; 12 August 1909, p. 60; 7 October 1909, p. 81.)

1909: Miss Ida Clement Residence, Union; $3000 (*MR*, 12 August 1909, p. 59.)

1910: W.K. Hudgens Post Office Building, Williamston (*MR*, 6 January 1910, p. 166.)

1910: S.H. Byron Residence, Anderson; $2300 (*MR*, 29 September 1910, p. 69.)

1910: School, Bennettsville; $18,500 (*MR*, 1 December 1910, pp. 86-87.)

1910: School, Chester; $15,000 (*MR*, 30 June 1910, p. 64; 7 July 1910, p. 82.)

1911: First Baptist Church, Abbeville; $25,000 (*MR*, 16 March 1911, p. 74.)

1911: J. Walter Dickson Residence, Anderson; $4000 (*MR*, 20 April 1911, p. 73.)

1911: Hospital, Greenwood; $40,000 (*MR*, 18 May 1911, p. 76.)

1911: Methodist Episcopal Church, Greer; $16,000 (*MR*, 14 September 1911, p. 63; 28 September 1911, p. 66.)

1911: Enlargement, School, Honea Path; $7000 (*MR*, 28 September 1911, p. 67.)

1911: Orphanage, York; $8000 (*MR*, 24 August 1911, p. 67.)

1912: Dormitory, Presbyterian College, Clinton; $25,000 (*MR*, 13 June 1912, p. 72.)

1912: School, Dillon; $30,000 (*MR*, 25 April 1912, p. 71.)

1913: Two School Buildings, Anderson; $7711 and $9813 (*MR*, 25 September 1913, p. 66.)

1913: School, McBee; $10,000 (*MR*, 22 May 1913, p. 70.)

1913: Washington Street Baptist Church, Sumter; $20,000 (*MR*, 18 September 1913, p. 72; 2 October 1913, p. 76.)

1913: Addition, Graded School, Walhalla; $9830 (*MR*, 19 June 1913, p. 75.)

1914: Science Hall, Presbyterian College, Clinton; $25,000 (*MR*, 28 May 1914, p. 62.)

1914: Baptist Church, Edgefield; $15,000 (*MR*, 19 February 1914, p. 69.)

1914: High School, Latta; $12,500 (*MR*, 2 July 1914, p. 79.)

1914: Completion, First Baptist Church, Orangeburg; $20,000 (*MR*, 26 March 1914, p. 68.)

C. Gadsden Sayre

1915: Storefront, Dr. A.P. Johnstone Building, Anderson (*MR*, 16 September 1915, p. 67.)

1916: Palmer Memorial Presbyterian Church Building, Greenville; $15,000 (*MR*, 15 June 1916, p. 71.)

1917: Mrs. A.G. Fretwell Residence, Anderson; $3500 (*MR*, 7 June 1917, p. 95.)

1917: Wm. Gelder Residence, Laurens; $15,000 (*MR*, 21 June 1917, p. 79.)

1917: High School, McColl (*MR*, 30 August 1917, p. 74.)

1917: Saluda County Courthouse, S. Main and E. Church streets, Saluda; $49,000 (Plaque on building; *MR*, 26 July 1917, p. 74.)

1922: Addition, N. Fant Street School, Anderson; $16,700 (*MR*, 2 November 1922, p. 118 i; 9 November 1922, p. 87.)

1927: Caldwell and Company Hotel, Columbia; $1,250,000 (*MR*, 31 March 1927, p. 111; 7 April 1927, p. 120.)

Sources: *American Art Annual*, Vol. 21, p. 456; Anderson city directories; Rudolph E. Lee, "Rural School Improvement," *The Clemson Agricultural College Extension Work Bulletins*, Vol. VI, No. 3, July 1910, n.p.; *MR*, various citations; Moore, Vol. 6; "The Work at Ware's Shoals," *The State*, 24 January 1904, p. 20.

SAYWARD, William J. (1875-1945) Sayward, a native of Vermont, studied at the University of Vermont and at the Massachusetts Institute of Technology. After a period working for New York architects McKim, Mead & White, he associated with William A. Edwards (q.v.) in Atlanta, Georgia. Edwards & Sayward maintained a profitable practice, focusing on university buildings in the Southeast, from 1914 until the death of Edwards in 1939. Sayward continued practice in Atlanta until his own death in 1945.

South Carolina projects:

1915-1930: See **Edwards, William Augustus** (Edwards & Sayward)

Sources: *American Art Annual*, Vol. 21, p. 456; *MR*, various citations; Withey, pp. 190-191, 537-538.

SCROGGS, Philander Pearsall (1888- ca. 1960)
Scroggs, a native of North Carolina, studied architecture at Alabama Polytechnic Institute. He worked as a draftsman for G. Lloyd Preacher (q.v.) in Augusta, Georgia, for many years, and spent 1915-1916 in the office of New York architect W.L. Stoddart (q.v.). He established his own office in Augusta in 1917. Whitley Lay Ewing (q.v.), who had also worked in Preacher's office, associated with Scroggs in 1919; this partnership was maintained into the 1950s.

Scroggs & Ewing designed many buildings in Augusta, including the $220,000 Central YMCA Building in 1921. A $500,000, seventeen-story hotel project in Augusta, reported in 1931, was among the firm's largest projects. Scroggs & Ewing also designed many large residences in the popular winter resort town of Aiken, South Carolina. The 1928-1929 Kenneth Schley residence was representative of their work. Many of the Aiken residences were described as "colonial."

Scroggs served on the Georgia State Board of Architectural Examiners. He was president of this body from 1928 through 1936.

South Carolina projects:

Scroggs & Ewing

1920: Batesburg-Leesville Consolidated High School, Batesburg-Leesville (Plaque on building.)

1921: Dormitory, Summerland College, Summerland; $68,840 (*MR*, 1 September 1921, p. 118; 8 September 1921, p. 90.)

1924-1925: School, Estill; $41,400 (*MR*, 4 September 1924, p. 129; 6 August 1925, p. 124; 13 August 1925, p. 117.)

1925: School, McCormick; $35,000 (*MR*, 12 February 1925, p. 121.)

1925: School, Plum Branch (*MR*, 22 January 1925, p. 110.)

1926: Remodeling, John W. Converse Residence, S. Boundary Street and Whiskey Road, Aiken; $7,000 (*MR*, 22 July 1926, p. 111.)

1928: Allen Pinkerton Residence, Aiken; $25,000 (*MR*, 3 May 1928, p. 118.)

1928: Winthrop Rutherford Residence, Aiken; Scroggs & Ewing, architects; Peabody, Wilson & Brown (q.v.), associated architects; $100,000 (*MR*, 17 May 1928, p. 93; 9 August 1928, p. 86.)

1928: W.C. Pittfield Residence, S. Boundary Street, Aiken; $32,391 (*MR*, 31 May 1928, p. 79; 28 June 1928, p. 87.)

1928: John M. Dwyer Residence, Aiken; $50,000 (*MR*, 7 June 1928, p. 118.)

1928: Jerome E.J. Keane Residence, Aiken; $50,000 (*MR*, 7 June 1928, pp. 118-119.)

1928: Improvements and additions, Willcox Hotel, Aiken; $75,000 (*MR*, 7 June 1928, p. 119.)

1928: Additions and remodeling, W.E. Duncan Residence, Aiken; $15,000 (*MR*, 6 September 1928, p. 90.)

1928: Wilbur J. Driver Residence, Aiken; $17,800 (*MR*, 6 September 1928, p. 90; 13 September 1928, p. 94.)

1928: S.A. Warner Baltazzo Residence, Aiken; $25,000 (*MR*, 4 October 1928, p. 102; 1 November 1928, p. 99.)

1928: Allen Case Residence, Aiken; $20,000 (*MR*, 11 October 1928, p. 106.)

1928: Seymour Knox Stable Building, Aiken; Peabody, Wilson & Brown (q.v.), architects; Scroggs & Ewing, associated architects; $25,000 (*MR*, 25 October 1928, p.102.)

1928-1929: Kenneth B. Schley Residence, Aiken; $100,000 (*MR*, 18 April 1929, p. 105; Koyl; *Southern Architect and Building News*, January 1931, pp. 22-31.)

1929: Eugene G. Grace Guest House, Aiken (*MR*, 13 June 1929, p. 87.)

1929: W.H. Pardue Residence, Aiken; $18,975 (*MR*, 20 June 1929, p. 91.)

1929: Mrs. W.C. Clark Residence, Aiken; $42,000 (*MR*, 8 August 1929, pp. 82-83.)

1929: Remodeling, Mrs. Nelson Johnson Residence, Aiken; $15,000 (*MR*, 17 October 1929, p. 96.)

1929: Alterations and additions, Mrs. Henry W. Bull Residence, Aiken; $40,000 (*MR*, 17 October 1929, p. 96.)

1929: Remodeling, Hotel Aiken (Commercial Hotel), Aiken (*MR*, 11 April 1929, p. 90.)

1929: Geraldyn L. Redmond Residence, Hunting Lodge, Stables, etc., Yemassee vicinity; $100,000 (*MR*, 2 May 1929, p. 100.)

Ca. 1929: Lanier Branson Residence, Aiken (*Southern Architect and Building News*, April 1930, pp. 53-55.)

Sources: Augusta city directories; Koyl, p. 495; *MR*, various citations.

SEYLE, John H. (active 1840-1890) John H. Seyle of Charleston was an architect and builder in antebellum South Carolina. He was associated with architect Louis J. Barbot in Charleston from 1853 to 1859. The 1856-1857 Carpenter-Gothic style Church of the Holy Apostles in Barnwell was among their designs; so was the 1856 Roman Revival style Spring Street Methodist Church in Charleston.

Seyle was identified as a builder in the 1867-1868 Charleston directory. From 1875 to 1890 he was associated with Theodore Abrahams (q.v.) as Abrahams & Seyle. The 1890 Charleston directory noted that Seyle had removed to Savannah, Georgia.

South Carolina projects:

1874-1890: See **Abrahams, Theodore** (Abrahams & Seyle)

Sources: Charleston city directories; Ravenel, pp. 231-236.

SHAND, Gadsden Edwards (1868- ca. 1948) Gadsden E. Shand, a native of Columbia, studied engineering at South Carolina College, graduating in 1888. He pursued further studies at the school of Mines, Columbia University, New York. Shand worked as superintendent of construction at the South Carolina State House from 1888 to 1890, under direction of architect Frank Niernsee (q.v.) He practiced architecture and engineering in Columbia from 1891 to 1895. Among his surviving designs is the Richardsonian-Romanesque Canal Dime Savings Bank Building (1893) in Columbia.

In 1895 Shand associated with William Burroughs Smith Whaley (q.v.) The firm, called W.B. Smith Whaley & Co., pursued an active practice in South Carolina through 1903, focusing on textile mill engineering and development. Shand and George E. Lafaye (q.v.) provided most of the company's architectural services. The firm submitted an unsuccessful proposal in the 1900 competition for the completion of the State House, a competition won by Frank Milburn (q.v.)

Whaley left Columbia in 1903, and Shand and Lafaye reorganized as Shand & Lafaye, Architects and Engineers. An article in *The State* described the firm:

Mr. Gadsden E. Shand and Mr. George LaFaye have entered into partnership, and will continue to do business at the offices formerly occupied by the firm of W.B.S. Whaley & Co. The new firm will do architectural and engineering work of all kinds. Formerly more attention was paid to engineering construction than to any other branch, but hereafter architecture will be given equal attention.

Shand & Lafaye won commissions for many important buildings in the state, including banks, hotels, and schools. The 1908 Clarendon County Courthouse, in Manning, was among their prominent designs. The five-story, reinforced-concrete Ottaray Hotel in Greenville was another design by Shand & Lafaye. The Ottaray, contracted at $100,000 and built in 1907-1908, was among the state's earliest high-rise buildings. When the Eau Claire campus of Columbia College was destroyed by fire in 1909,

Shand & Lafaye prepared plans for its reconstruction. The new campus, an elegant Georgian Revival composition, was contracted at $100,000, and work was completed in 1910. In 1964 this new campus, too, was destroyed by fire.

The firm was active in North Carolina and Georgia as well. The seven-story Fulton Bag and Cotton Mills Warehouse in Atlanta was designed by Shand & Lafaye and contracted in 1909.

Shand left architectural practice in 1912 and formed the Shand Engineering Company. This firm was active in development of industrial plants, water power projects, and municipal works. The company also provided structural steel and iron for many buildings in the state in the 1920s.

South Carolina projects:

1893: Columbia Hospital Association Building, Columbia; $5000 (*MR*, 3 March 1893, p. 99.)

1893: Canal Dime Savings Bank, Main Street, Columbia (*MR*, 24 March 1893, p. 155.)

1895-1903: See **Whaley, William Burroughs Smith** (W.B. Smith Whaley & Co.)

Shand & Lafaye

1904: Church Home, Protestant Episcopal Church, Charleston (*MR*, 12 May 1904, p. 383.)

1904: Office Building, Lancaster Cotton Mills, Lancaster (*MR*, 24 March 1904, p. 217.)

1904: State Fair Buildings, State Fair Grounds, Columbia (*The State*, 26 February 1904, p. 5.)

1905: Columbia Hospital Building, Columbia; $20,000 (*MR*, 9 March 1905, p. 164.)

1906: Building, Bamberg; $10,000 (*MR*, 15 February 1906, p. 130.)

1906: Carolina National Bank Building, Columbia; $80,000 (*MR*, 5 April 1906, p. 331;

12 April 1906, p. 362; 21 June 1906, p. 648; 30 August 1906, p. 168.)

1906: Richland Investment Company Tourist Hotel, Columbia; $100,000 (*MR*, 3 May 1906, p. 446; 10 May 1906, p. 479.)

1906: Richland County Courthouse, Columbia; $100,000 (*MR*, 22 March 1906, p. 262; 11 October 1906, p. 317; 18 October 1906, p. 348.)

1907: School, Bamberg; $15,000 (*MR*, 28 November 1907, p. 58; 5 December 1907, p. 74; 26 December 1907, p. 59.)

1907: Farmers' Union Cotton Warehouse, Bishopville; $15,000 (*MR*, 5 December 1907, p. 74.)

1907: Columbia Savings Bank and Trust Company Building, Columbia (*MR*, 31 January 1907, p. 78.)

1907: E.A. Jenkins Automobile Garage, Columbia (*MR*, 17 October 1907, p. 68.)

1907: Surgical and Medical Building, Columbia Hospital, Columbia; $30,000 (*MR*, 28 November 1907, p. 57; 5 December 1907, p. 74.)

1907: Farmers' Warehouse Company Cotton Warehouse, Gaffney; $7000 (*MR*, 14 November 1907, p. 66.)

1907-1908: Wallace Thompson Memorial Infirmary, University of South Carolina, Columbia; $15,000 (*MR*, 3 October 1907, p. 73; 7 November 1907, p. 79; 5 December 1907, p. 74; *The State*, 8 August 1908, p. 10.)

1907-1908: Greenville Hotel Company Hotel (Ottaray Hotel), N. Main Street, Greenville; $100,000 (*MR*, 7 March 1907, p. 227; 14 March 1907, p. 261; 25 April 1907, p. 457; 30 May 1907, p. 642; 2 April 1908, p. 70; 18 June 1908, p. 63; 30 July 1908, p. 56.)

1908: High School, Brunson; $10,000 (*MR*, 16 April 1908, p. 64; 23 April 1908, p. 60; 13 August 1908, p. 59.)

1908: Washington Clark Office Building, Columbia; $7500 (*MR*, 29 October 1908, p. 65; 5 November 1908, p. 69.)

1908: Addition, J.L. Mimnaugh Store Building, Columbia (*MR*, 12 November 1908, p. 62.)

1908: Shandon Baptist Church, Columbia; $6000 (*MR*, 17 December 1908, p. 67; 24 December 1908, p. 66.)

1908: Farmers' Warehouse Co. Warehouse, Gaffney; $40,000 (*MR*, 20 August 1908, p. 64.)

1908: Greeleyville School, Greeleyville (*MR*, 18 June 1908, p. 64; 20 August 1908, p. 63; 27 August 1908, p. 56; Rudolph E. Lee, "Rural School Improvement," *The Clemson Agricultural College Extension Work Bulletins*, Vol. VI, #3, July 1910.)

1908: Clarendon County Courthouse, Manning (*MR*, 27 February 1908, p. 57; 2 July 1908, p. 68; *The State*, 2 July 1908, p. 3.)

1908: School, Ninety Six (*MR*, 28 May 1908, p. 67; 30 July 1908, p. 57; 17 September 1908, p. 69.)

1908: School, Pinewood (*MR*, 26 March 1908, p. 60; 28 May 1908, p. 67; 18 June 1908, p. 64; 13 August 1908, p. 59.)

1909: N. Christensen & Sons Store Building, Beaufort (*MR*, 25 November 1909, p. 66.)

1909: Olympia Mills School, Columbia; $9000 (*MR*, 6 May 1909, p. 77.)

1909: Columbia College, Columbia; $100,000 (*MR*, 16 September 1909, p. 64; 14 October 1909, p. 62.)

1909: School, Newberry (*MR*, 25 March 1909, p. 60; 8 April 1909, p. 62; 13 May 1909, p. 63; 19 August 1909, p. 62.)

1909: People's National Bank, Rock Hill; $40,000 (*MR*, 27 May 1909, p. 66; 17 June 1909, p. 65; 29 July 1909, p. 59; 30 September 1909, p. 65.)

1910: Waverly School, Columbia; $11,983 (*MR*, 20 January 1910, p. 67; 3 February 1910, p. 83; 8 September 1910, p. 62.)

1910: School, Hopkins; $7000 (*MR*, 7 July 1910, p. 82.)

1911: Adminstration Building and Two Dormitories, Anderson College, Anderson; $74,600; Shand & Lafaye and Joseph H. Casey (q.v.), architects (*MR*, 31 August 1911, p. 66.)

1911: Annex, Carolina Inn, Chester (*MR*, 22 June 1911, p. 70.)

1911: Commercial Bank Building, Chester; $20,000 (*MR*, 3 August 1911, p. 82.)

1911: Y.M.C.A. Building, 1420 Sumter Street, Columbia; $98,000 (*MR*, 26 January 1911, p. 59; 6 April 1911, p. 85; Cornerstone.)

1911: Edgewood School, Columbia; $10,000 (*MR*, 18 May 1911, p. 77.)

1911: Elmwood Park Baptist Church, Columbia; $12,000 (*MR*, 14 September 1911, p. 63.)

1911-1912: School, Batesburg; $13,250 (*MR*, 17 August 1911, p. 69; 2 May 1912, p. 83.)

1912: Remodeling, Bank of Western Carolina Building, Barnwell (*MR*, 6 June 1912, p. 89.)

1912: City Jail, Columbia; $40,000 (*MR*, 26 December 1912, p. 66.)

1912: School, Eau Claire; $21,271 (*MR*, 4 April 1912, p. 83.)

Shand Engineering Company

1915: Capital City Garage, 1218 Lady Street, Columbia (*The State*, 31 March 1915, p. 8.)

1915: W.G. Mullins Residence, Saluda Avenue, Columbia; $10,000 (*MR*, 25 November 1915, p. 60.)

Sources: Columbia city directories; Garlington, *Men of the Time*, p. 376; Leonard, *Who's Who in Engineering*, p. 1132; *MR* various citations; Moore, Vol. 6; "Shand & Lafaye," *The State*, 24 January 1904, p. 16.

SHARKEY, E.D. (active 1886) Sharkey was identified as an architect in Union in 1886. No further identification on Sharkey has been found.

SHATTUCK & HUSSEY (active 1909-1918) Chicago architects Walter F. Shattuck and _____ Hussey provided plans for Y.M.C.A. buildings across the nation. A history of the Young Men's Christian Association notes:

In the years just before the First World War more than one Association executive became dissatisfied with the inability of local architectural firms to design adequately functional Y.M.C.A. buildings. Architectural services were therefore added to the financial agencies of the Bureau . . . Buildings almost at once showed improved architectural character as well as improved function; better materials were used and problems of maintenance, operation, and management were reduced.

The 1913-1914 Y.M.C.A. building in Spartanburg, South Carolina, was one of many designed by Shattuck & Hussey in the Southeast. Architect J. Frank Collins (q.v.) of Spartanburg was associated with Shattuck & Hussey on this project, which was contracted at $70,000. The firm also designed Y.M.C.A. buildings in Greensboro, Raleigh, Wilmington, Winston-Salem and Durham (remodeling) in North Carolina; in Atlanta and Athens, in Georgia; in Nashville, Tennessee; and in Charlottesville, Petersburg, Staunton, and Danville, in Virginia. The 1917 Central Y.M.C.A. building in Minneapolis, Minnesota, designed by Shattuck & Hussey, in association with Long, Lamoreaux & Long, was an elegant thirteen-story edifice with terra-cotta ornamentation.

In 1924, Shattuck and his new partner Robert W. Layer advertised a specialty in club and community buildings, and cited several Y.M.C.A. buildings among their representative works.

Sources: C. Howard Hopkins, *History of the Y.M.C.A. in North America* (New York, New York: Association Press, 1951), p. 576; *Key to the Architects of Chicago* (New York: Charles Scribner's Sons, 1924), p. 50; Robert C. Mack, "The Manufacture and Use of Architectural Terra-Cotta in the United States," in H. Ward Jandl, ed., *The Technology of Historic American Buildings* (Washington, D.C.: The Foundation for Preservation Technology, 1983); *MR*, 6 November 1913, p. 75, 2 April 1914, p. 76, and various other citations.

SHAW, Fred Gordon (active 1902-1903) Shaw, of Augusta, Georgia, was the architect for the 1902 Sanitarium contracted for Drs. Thomas Coleman and W.H. Doughty in North Augusta, South Carolina.

Sources: Augusta, Georgia, city directories; *MR*, 4 September 1902, p. 120; 11 September 1902, p. 139.

SHORT, Richard Thomas (active 1894-1906) Short was active in New York City in the late nineteenth century. He was associated with James E. Ware for several years. He provided plans for the 1906-1907 Charleston, South Carolina, Police Station, which was contracted at $56,858.

Sources: Francis, pp. 69, 95; *MR*, 12 July 1906, p. 732; 8 November 1906, p. 432; 22 November 1906, p. 479; 7 February 1907, p. 110; 21 March 1907, p. 292.

SIBBERT, Edward Frederick (1899- ca. 1960) Sibbert was company architect for the S.H. Kress Company in New York City from 1929-1954. He had been trained at Cornell University, and worked in private practice before joining the Kress Company. Sibbert's designs for S.H. Kress & Co. Department Stores, which survive in many cities across the nation, are elegant essays in Art-Deco design, with polychromatic terra-cotta and brick.

South Carolina projects:

1930: S.H. Kress & Co. Store Building, King and Wentworth streets, Charleston (*MR*, 9 October 1930, p. 69.)

Ca. 1938: S.H. Kress & Co. Store Building, 1508 Main Street, Columbia (National Register files, S.C. Archives.)

Source: Koyl, p. 505.

SILBER, Norman (active 1917-1925) Norman Silber, son of grocer/preacher Jacob Silber, worked as a clerk in Columbia for many years. Norman Silber was associated with the Socialist Party in America in 1918. In 1919 he advertised in the city directory as a surveyor and civil engineer, boasting of government experience and promising speed, accuracy, and reliability. Silber was identified as the architect for the Jacob Orenstein brick store building at 1229 Huger Street, Columbia, contracted at $6000 in 1921.

Silber's architectural career did not last. He had returned to clerking for the M. Citron dry goods company by 1922.

Sources: Columbia city directories; *MR*, 17 February 1921, p. 130 c.

SIMMONS, William Walter (active 1925-1951) Simmons was an obscure architect working in Augusta, Georgia, in the 1920s. His firm was called W.W. Simmons & Son in 1925. Simmons provided plans for seven school buildings in Aiken County, South Carolina, in 1925-1926. His work in Georgia included the $80,000 Adminstration Building at the Agricultural & Mechanical Institute in Cochran (1926).

South Carolina projects:

1925: High School, Langley; $25,487 (*MR*, 11 July 1925, p. 119.)

1925: Addition, North Augusta School, North Augusta; $16,090 (*MR*, 11 July 1925, p. 119.)

1925: School, Windsor; $28,017 (*MR*, 11 July 1925, p. 119.)

1925: School, Warrenville; $28,276 (*MR*, 6 August 1925, p. 124.)

1925: School, Montmorenci; $4227 (*MR*, 6 August 1925, p. 124.)

1925: School, Talatha; $17,447 (*MR*, 17 September 1925, p. 116.)

1926: High School, Dunbarton; $21,000 (*MR*, 3 June 1926, p. 135.)

Sources: Augusta, Georgia, city directories; *MR*, various citations; *Architects and Builders in Georgia*.

SIMON, Louis Adolphe (active 1894-1958) Louis Simon, an 1891 graduate of M.I.T., established an office in Baltimore in 1894. He took a position with the office of the supervising architect of the United States Treasury Department in 1896, and remained with that office through 1944. From 1905 to 1933 Simon was chief of the architectural division; and in 1933 he was appointed supervising architect. In this capacity Simon directed designs for post offices, courthouses, customs houses, mints, assay offices, hospitals, and federal office buildings across the nation.

Most of Simon's designs are severe, conservative Colonial Revival style buildings; they have been called "starved classical." A noteworthy exception is the Art Deco-style Rockingham, North Carolina, post office. Many of the smaller Simon post offices feature murals executed by WPA artists.

South Carolina projects:

1931: Post Office, Dillon (Cornerstone; *MR*, 12 February 1931, p. 58.)

1934-1935: Post Office, Ware Shoals (Cornerstone.)

1935: Post Office, York (Cornerstone.)

1936: Post Office, Walterboro (Cornerstone.)

1936: Post Office, Winnsboro (Cornerstone.)

1936: Federal Building and Courthouse, Greenville; Louis A. Simon and Eric Kebbon (q.v.), architects (Cornerstone.)

1937: Post Office, Bamberg (Cornerstone.)

1937: Post Office, Kingstree (Cornerstone.)

1937: Post Office, Chesterfield (Cornerstone.)

1937: Post Office, Summerville (Cornerstone.)

1937: Post Office and Federal Courthouse, Anderson; Louis A. Simon and Thomas Harlan Ellett, architects (Cornerstone.)

1937: Post Office, Batesburg (Cornerstone.)

1939: Post Office, Woodruff (Cornerstone.)

1939: Post Office, Bishopville (Cornerstone.)

Sources: *American Art Annual*, Vol. 21, p. 461; *A.I.A. Journal*, July 1958, p. 70; Lois Craig, *The Federal Presence: Architecture, Politics, and Symbols in United States Government Buildings* (Cambridge: The M.I.T. Press, 1972-1977), p. 328; Koyl, p. 507; Smith, *The Office of the Supervising Architect.*

SIMONS, Albert (1890-1980) Albert Simons, a native of Charleston, was acknowledged as a pioneer in the renovation and adaptation of the state's historic buildings. He was educated at the College of Charleston and at the University of Pennsylvania, and studied architecture under Paul Cret and Ernest Hebrard. Simons worked as a draftsman for Baltimore architect Lawrence Hall Fowler in 1914. After

a period as an instructor in architecture at Clemson College in 1916-1917, Simons took a position with Charleston architect Albert W. Todd (q.v.) He opened independent practice in Charleston in 1920, and in that same year associated with Samual Lapham Jr. (q.v.)

Simons & Lapham were among the first architects to study Carolina's architectural history, and their drawings and publications are valuable for any modern study of the subject. They were the architects of choice for renovations of historic buildings in the state's coastal region for many years. The firm planned additions, alterations, restorations, and rehabilitations for a great many older buildings. These restorations often involved considerable license; Simons & Lapham used salvaged materials, they discarded features they considered inappropriate, and they designed new features to enhance a building's historic appearance. In the 1928 Simons & Lapham remodeling of Wappaoola House, Stoney noted that the building's "very plain interiors were decorated with old mantels from Charleston and with cornices of conforming design."

South Carolina projects:

1920: Thompson Memorial Infirmary Building, Charleston (*MR*, 3 June 1920, p. 182.)

Simons & Lapham

1920: Julius M. Visanska Residence, Charleston (*American Art Annual*, Vol. 21; Kimball, pp. 218-219.)

1920-1921: Choir and Chancel Addition, St. Philip's Episcopal Church, Church Street, Charleston; $15,180 (*MR*, 12 August 1920, p. 144; 2 September 1920, p. 165; *American Art Annual*, Vol. 21; Kimball, p. 255.)

1921-1922: Alterations and additions, Masonic Temple, King and Wentworth streets, Charleston; $70,000 (*MR*, 27 October 1921, p. 77; *American Art Annual*, Vol. 21.)

1922: Theodore Simons Jr. Residence, Charleston (*American Art Annual*, Vol. 21.)

162

Ca. 1922: Joseph E. Jenkins Residence, Charleston (Kimball, p. 217.)

1923: Annex, Burke Industrial School, Charleston; $13,685 (*MR*, 19 April 1923, p. 100; 5 July 1923, p. 119.)

1924: Parish House addition and remodeling of existing building, St. Michael's Church, Meeting and Broad streets, Charleston; $25,000 (*MR*, 3 July 1924, p. 136; 10 July 1924, p. 103.)

1925: Extension and remodeling, Omar Temple Lodge, 40 East Bay Street, Charleston; $40,000 (*MR*, 30 July 1925, p. 118.)

1926: Alterations and addition, St. Thaddeus Protestant Episcopal Church, Aiken; $30,000 (*MR*, 27 May 1926, p. 111; 3 June 1926, p. 132; 10 June 1926, p. 108.)

1926: Remodeling and addition, Sumter Guards Building, 80 Society Street, Charleston; $14,500 (*MR*, 21 October 1926, p. 102; 28 October 1926, p. 82.)

1927: Westminster Presbyterian Church Building, Rutledge Avenue and McCormick Street, Charleston; $41,000 (*MR*, 24 March 1927, p. 99.)

1927: Remodeling and addition to Sunday School, St. Johannes Lutheran Church, Charleston; $19,000 (*MR*, 1 September 1927, p. 115.)

1927: Parish House, St. Philip's Episcopal Church, Charleston; $20,000 (*MR*, 15 September 1927, p. 121.)

1927: W.S. Griswold Residence, Yeoman's Hall Club, Goose Creek, Charleston (*MR*, 15 September 1927, p. 121.)

1927-1930: Yeoman's (Yeaman's) Hall Building, Charleston; $120,000; James G. Rogers (q.v.), architect; Simons & Lapham, associated architects (*MR*, 9 June 1927, p. 114; 30 June 1927, p. 105; 15 September 1927, p. 121; Koyl.)

1927: Heating Plant, College of Charleston, Charleston; $8967 (*MR*, 13 January 1927, p. 105.)

1927: Repairs to Dormitories, Porter Military Academy, Charleston (*MR*, 18 August 1927, p. 125.)

1928: Marshall Crane Residence, Hope Plantation, Jacksonboro; $40,000 (*MR*, 31 May 1928, p. 79.)

1928: Alterations and additions, Wappaoola House, Berkeley County (Stoney, p. 76.)

1928: Alterations and additions, Gippy Plantation House, Berkeley County (Stoney, p. 236.)

1928: Alterations and additions, William Seabrook House, Edisto Island, Charleston County (Stoney, pp. 78-79, 215.)

1929: Restoration, The Grove, Charleston County (Stoney, p. 83.)

1929: Alterations and additions, The Wedge, Charleston County (Stoney, pp. 81-82, 225.)

1930: Additions and improvements, College of Charleston, Charleston; $37,000 (*MR*, 13 March 1930, p. 95.)

1930: Library and Department of Pathology Building, Medical College of South Carolina, Charleston; $44,500 (*MR*, 7 August 1930, p. 82.)

1931: Parish House, St. Matthew's Lutheran Church, Charleston; $21,916 (*MR*, 3 December 1931, p. 42.)

1934: Restoration, Fenwick Hall, Johns Island, Charleston County (Stoney, p. 125.)

1937: Chelsea Plantation (Marshall Field III Residence), Ridgeland (Koyl.)

1937: Windsor Plantation (Paul D. Mills Residence), Georgetown (Koyl.)

1938: Alterations and additions, Lowndes' Grove, Charleston County (Stoney, p. 202.)

Ca. 1938: Restoration, Planters Hotel, Church Street, Charleston (*Architectural Record*, January 1938, pp. 20-25.)

1940: Charles W. Coker Residence, Hartsville (Koyl.)

Sources: *American Art Annual*, Vol. 21, p. 460; Charleston city directories; Fiske Kimball, "Recent Architecture in the South," *Architectural Record*, March 1924, pp. 209-271; Koyl, p. 508; *MR*, various citations; Albert Simons and Samuel Lapham, Jr., *The Early Architecture of Charleston* (Columbia: University of South Carolina Press, 1927); Samuel Gaillard Stoney, Albert Simons, and Samuel Lapham, Jr., *Plantations of the Carolina Low Country* (Charleston: The Carolina Art Association, 1938; revised editions, 1955, 1964.)

SIMONS, S. Lewis (active 1886-1932) S. Lewis Simons was active as a civil engineer and architect in Charleston during the later nineteenth century. He was associated with Gadsden E. Howe (q.v.) in 1880-1882; with Frank P. Huger (q.v.) in 1889-1891; and with Rutledge Holmes (q.v.) in 1895. William R. Mayrant joined Simons in 1898, and the firm of Simons & Mayrant practiced as engineers and building contractors into the mid-twentieth century. They were listed as architects in a 1900 state business directory, but their work was focused on construction. Simons & Mayrant were the contractors for Charleston's first skyscraper, the eight-story, $239,000 People's Bank Building on Broad Street, designed by Thomson & Frohling (q.v.) and begun in 1909.

South Carolina projects:

Simons & Huger

1889: Summerville Hotel, Summerville (*MR*, 26 January 1889, p. 24; 16 February 1889, p. 28.)

1889: Carolina Rifles Armory, Charleston (*MR*, 9 March 1889, p. 27.)

1890: S.W. Simons Residence, Charleston; $5000 (*MR*, 29 November 1890, p. 40.)

1890: Y.M.C.A. Building, Walterboro (*MR*, 3 May 1890, p. 46.)

1890: W.H. Richardson Hall Building, Summerville (*MR*, 29 November 1890, p. 40.)

S.L. Simons

1892: St. Helena by the Sea Hotel, St. Helena Island, Beaufort County; $15,000 (*MR*, 9 January 1892, p. 37; 16 January 1892, p. 35.)

Simons & Mayrant

1920: Middleton Compress & Warehouse Company Cotton Warehouse, Charleston; $48,000 (*MR*, 17 June 1920, p. 149.)

Sources: Charleston city directories; *MR*, various citations.

SIMPSON, Joseph B. (active 1915-1930) Joseph Simpson was a minor architect who practiced in Spartanburg for several years. He was associated with his brother William D. Simpson (q.v.) in 1915, and in 1923-1926 he was a partner of J. Frank Collins (q.v.)

South Carolina projects:

1915: J.H. Anderson Store Building, Anderson; $6500; Casey & Fant (q.v.) and J.B. and W.D. Simpson, architects (*MR*, 17 June 1915, p. 60.)

1923-1926: See **Collins, J. Frank** (Collins & Simpson)

1927: G.J. Tezza Residence, High Point Road, Park Hills, Spartanburg (*MR*, 25 August 1927, p. 98.)

Sources: *MR*, various citations; Petty, p. 145; Spartanburg city directories.

SIMPSON, William David (active 1913-1930) William D. Simpson worked as a draftsman for Anderson architect Joseph H. Casey (q.v.) in 1913. He was associated with his brother Joseph B. Simpson (q.v.) in Spartanburg in 1915, and had returned to Anderson by 1917, where he worked for architect James J. Baldwin (q.v.) Simpson maintained membership in the South Carolina chapter of the A.I.A. through 1930.

South Carolina projects:

1915: See **Simpson, Joseph B.**

Sources: Anderson city directories; Petty, p. 145.

SIRRINE, Joseph Emory (1872-1947) Joseph Emory Sirrine was the most important industrial architect and engineer to practice in South Carolina. The emerging industrial complexes of South Carolina's Appalachian corridor, including mills, warehouses, worker housing, schools, commercial buildings, and related structures, owed their shaping and structure more to Sirrine than to any other architect. Sirrine's work spanned five decades and included projects as far away as Texas and Maine.

Sirrine, son of George William and Sarah Rylander Sirrine, was born in 1872 at Americus, Georgia. He was educated at the Greenville Military Institute and at Furman University, where he received a B.S. degree in 1890.

Sirrine commenced professional practice as a civil engineer in Greenville ca. 1890. He was identified as an architect in city directories as early as 1899. In 1895 Sirrine took a position with Lockwood, Greene & Co. (q.v.), in Greenville, as surveyor for the new F.W. Poe Textile Mill. When Lockwood Greene's southern regional office was opened in Greenville in 1898, Sirrine was named manager, with authority over projects in Georgia and the Carolinas. Lockwood Greene designed some twenty-two cotton mills in South Carolina between 1895 and 1903, as well as many mills in other states.

Lockwood Greene historian Samuel Lincoln suggests that Sirrine was in position at this time to become an equal partner in the firm; but Sirrine left the firm and opened his own office in Greenville in 1903, to practice architecture and civil engineering. In 1921 Sirrine formed a partnership with eight of his associates, called J.E. Sirrine & Co., Engineers, based in Greenville.

Among the South Carolina architects who worked in Sirrine's office were Joseph G. Cunningham (q.v.), H. Olin Jones (q.v.), James D. Beacham (q.v.), Leon LeGrand (q.v.), and Hugh Chapman (q.v.)

The Southern Textile Association Exposition and Auditorium Building (Textile Hall) in Greenville, a temple to the textile industry, was among Sirrine's most important buildings. The structure was contracted at $90,000 in 1917, and expanded in several later campaigns.

Construction notices in the *MR* describe over 1600 textile mill village houses built in South Carolina to Sirrine designs.

In 1919 Sirrine prepared plans for the "Model Cotton Mill" complex of the Southern Textile Institute, at Spartanburg. The complex was described in contemporary accounts:

> A permanent exhibit of the best machinery produced in America, not jumbled up in any old way, but efficiently organized into the most perfect cotton mill in the world, running on a production basis; a model mill from the standpoint of construction, equipment and organization, to which the mill men will look for the latest in these lines; the latest in engineering, to which the engineers will look for ideas; an educational center, to which the operatives of the whole South will look for their education, ideas, ideals, inspiration and leadership.

Sirrine was a leading industrialist in Greenville and piedmont South Carolina; he had connections with most major enterprises. His authority, outlined in the *Transactions of the American Society of Civil Engineers*, included:

> Chairman of the Board of the Brandon Corporation, vice president of four South Carolina textile concerns, and a director of nineteen other textile companies throughout the southeast. He was also a director of the First National Bank of Greenville, the Liberty Life Insurance Company, and the *Greenville News-Piedmont* (morning and afternoon newspapers in Greenville.)

South Carolina projects:

1903: Piedmont Warehouse Company Cotton Warehouse, Greenville (*MR*, 9 July 1903, p. 511; 6 August 1903, p. 53.)

1905: City Hall, Greenville; $35,000 (*MR*, 12 January 1905, p. 642.)

1905: Union Bleaching and Finishing Company Warehouse, Greenville (*MR*, 24 August 1905, p. 149; 31 August 1905, pp. 177-178.)

1906: Electric Elevator addition, Standard Warehouse Cotton Warehouse, Columbia; $40,000 (*MR*, 26 July 1906, p. 43.)

1906: Masonic Temple Building, Greenville (*MR*, 26 April 1906, p. 419; 3 May 1906, p. 447.)

1906: Markley Hardware and Carriage Manufacturing Company Warehouse, Greenville; $7000 (*MR*, 4 October 1906, p. 294.)

1906: City Hospital, Greenville; $15,000 (*MR*, 18 October 1906, p. 348.)

1907: Bamberg Cotton Mills Co. Warehouse, Bamberg; $8000 (*MR*, 10 October 1907, p. 66.)

1909: Mill Building, Cotton Storehouse, Church, Mechanical Building, and Seventy-Five Residences, Woodside Cotton Mills, Greenville; $500,000 (Stone, p. 138.)

1909: Mill Building, Arcadia Mills, Arcadia (Stone, p. 139.)

1909: Republic Cotton Mills, Great Falls; $600,000 (Stone, p. 139.)

1909-1910: Masonic Temple, Greenville; $125,000 (*MR*, 9 September 1909, p. 57; 21 October 1909, p. 65; 28 October 1909, pp. 125, 126; 28 April 1910, p. 68; 13 October 1910, p. 67.)

1910: Two Buildings, County Poorhouse, Greenville; $7258 (*MR*, 23 June 1910, p. 70.)

1910-1911: Alice Textile Mills, Easley; $500,000 (*MR*, 20 April 1911, p. 56.)

1910-1912: James C. Furman Hall of Science, Furman University, Greenville; $75,000; F.E. Perkins (q.v.), architect; J.E. Sirrine, superintendent of construction (*The State*, 19 January 1912, p. 2; 22 January 1912, p. 2.)

1912: Gower & Houston Store and Office Building, Greenville; $11,000 (*MR*, 11 April 1912, p. 70.)

1912: W.A. Wallace Building, Washington Street, Greenville; $27,000 (*MR*, 25 April 1912, p. 70; 9 May 1912, p. 72; 25 July 1912, p. 72.)

1912: Dormitory, Greenville Female College, Greenville; $33,000 (*MR*, 9 May 1912, p. 72.)

1913: Fourth Presbyterian Church, Washington Street and Broadus Avenue, Greenville; $17,000 (*MR*, 27 February 1913, p. 70; 6 March 1913, p. 76.)

1913: Greenville, Spartanburg & Anderson Railway Warehouse, Greenville; $30,000 (*MR*, 9 October 1913, p. 66; 16 October 1913, p. 68 c.)

1913: Greenville, Spartanburg & Anderson Railway Company Store Buildings, Greenville; $45,000 (*MR*, 9 October 1913, p. 66; 16 October 1913, p. 68 c.)

1913: Carolina Supply Company Building, Court and Jackson streets, Greenville; $37,000 (*MR*, 13 November 1913, p. 70.)

1914: J. Thomas Arnold Tourist Hotel and Summer Resort, Chick Springs; $75,000 (*MR*, 1 January 1914, p. 82.)

1914: Drs. Jordan and Jervey Office Building, Greenville; $16,000 (*MR*, 16 July 1914, p. 69.)

1914: Southeastern Life Insurance Company Bank and Office Building, Greenville; $40,000 (*MR*, 19 November 1914, p. 64.)

1914: Piedmont & Northern Railway Depot and Warehouse, Spartanburg; $40,000 (*MR*, 23 July 1914, p. 57; 16 July 1914, p. 70.)

1915: Warehouse and Twenty-Five Residences, Equinox Mills, Anderson (*MR*, 1 July 1915, p. 68; 12 August 19115, p. 60.)

1915: Forty Operatives' Residences, Dunean Mills, Greenville (*MR*, 4 March 1915, p. 63.)

1915: A.L. Mills Store Building, Main Street, Greenville (*MR*, 4 March 1915, p. 64.)

1915: Addition, Southeastern Life Insurance Company Building, Main and Broad streets, Greenville; $10,000 (*MR*, 8 July 1915, p. 56.)

1916: One Hundred Residences, Republic Cotton Mills, Great Falls; $750,000 (*MR*, 19 October 1916, p. 71; 9 November 1916, p. 69.)

1916: School, Greenville; $28,000 (*MR*, 30 March 1916, p. 67.)

1916: School, N. Main Street, Greenville; $7000 (*MR*, 10 August 1916, p. 67.)

1916: Thirty-One Residences, Watts Mills, Laurens (*MR*, 17 February 1916, p. 66.)

1917: One Hundred Operatives' Residences, Baldwin Cotton Mills, Chester (*MR*, 22 February 1917, p. 119.)

1917: Republic Cotton Mills Bank and Store Building, Great Falls; $35,000 (*MR*, 19 April 1917, p. 74 m.)

1917: Southern Textile Association Exposition and Auditorium Building, Greenville; $90,000 (*MR*, 3 May 1917, p. 93.)

1917: School, Stone Avenue, Greenville (*MR*, 7 June 1917, p. 96.)

1917: Twenty-Five Residences, Watts Cotton Mills, Laurens (*MR*, 4 January 1917, p. 80.)

1917: Four Warehouses, Sewerage and Water Plant, Camp Sevier, Greenville (*MR*, 16 May 1918, p. 84.)

1919: Warehouse and Opener-Room Building, Clinton Cotton Mills, Clinton (*MR*, 13 November 1919, p. 134 c.)

1919: Hayne Grammar School, Toy Street, Greenville; $40,000 (*MR*, 29 May 1919, p. 129; 5 June 1919, p. 150.)

1919: High School, Greenville; $150,000 (*MR*, 2 October 1919, p. 168 n; 9 October 1919, p. 134 m.)

1919: One Hundred Residences, Blue Buckle Cotton Mills, Rock Hill (*MR*, 27 November 1919, p. 140.)

1919: Store and Office Building, Drayton Mills, Spartanburg (*MR*, 17 April 1919, p. 131; 24 April 1919, p. 136.)

1919-1920: Storage Warehouse, Southern Textile Machinery Company, Greenville; $25,000 (*MR*, 18 December 1919, p. 150 l; 1 January 1920, p. 173.)

1920: Warehouse, School, and Y.M.C.A. Building, Norris Cotton Mills, Cateechee; $30,000 (*MR*, 19 August 1920, p. 139; 9 September 1920, p. 137.)

1920: Dormitory and Dining Room, Furman University, Greenville; $250,000 (*MR*, 8 January 1920, p. 130 m; 20 May 1920, p. 142.)

1920: Twenty Operatives' Residences, Judson Mills, Greenville; $60,000 (*MR*, 15 January 1920, p. 152 i.)

1920: Oscar Hodges Department Store Building, Greenville (*MR*, 25 March 1920, p. 150 b.)

1920: Warehouse, Spindle Duck Mill, and Steam Power Plant, Brandon Mills, Greenville (*MR*, 13 May 1920, p. 127.)

1920: Sunday School Addition, Christ Church, Greenville; $30,000 (*MR*, 15 July 1920, p. 6 c; 22 July 1920, p. 126.)

1920: Clubhouse, Bois-Terre Country Club, Laurens; $11,000 (*MR*, 16 December 1920, p. 139; 23 December 1920, p. 126.)

1920: Twelve Operatives' Residences, Piedmont Manufacturing Company, Piedmont (*MR*, 1 January 1920, p. 172.)

1920: Salvation Army Hospital, Greenville; J.E. Sirrine and Beacham & Legrand (q.v.), architects; $200,000 (*MR*, 8 January 1920, p. 130 m; 15 January 1920, p. 152 j.)

1921: Passenger Station, Piedmont & Northern Railway, Belton (*MR*, 22 December 1921, p. 87; 29 December 1921, p. 79.)

1921: Refectory and Kitchen, Furman University, Greenville; $80,000 (*MR*, 16 June 1921, p. 110; 30 June 1921, p. 104.)

1921: Republic Cotton Mills High School, Great Falls (*MR*, 21 July 1921, p. 85.)

1921: Republic Cotton Mills Picture Theater, Great Falls (*MR*, 21 July 1921, p. 85.)

1921: Twenty-Four Store Buildings, Republic Cotton Mills, Great Falls (*MR*, 3 November 1921, p. 113.)

1921: Twenty-Five Residences, Republic Cotton Mills, Great Falls (*MR*, 3 November 1921, p. 113.)

1921: School, John Street, Greenville; $17,500 (*MR*, 2 June 1921, p. 143.)

1922: Passenger Station, Piedmont & Northern Railway, Anderson; $50,000 (*MR*, 9 November 1922, p. 87.)

1922: Storage Building, Dunean Mills, Greenville; $12,500 (*MR*, 1 June 1922, p. 119.)

1922: Warehouse, Union Bleaching and Finishing Company, Greenville; $30,000 (*MR*, 20 April 1922, p. 92.)

1922: Nineteen Operatives' Residences, Dunean Mills, Greenville; $22,000 (*MR*, 16 November 1922, p. 93.)

1922: One Hundred Thirty-Two Operatives' Residences, Chiquola Manufacturing Company, Honea Path (*MR*, 13 July 1922, p. 89.)

1922: Warehouse, Victor-Monaghan Company, Seneca (*MR*, 27 July 1922, p. 79.)

1922: Fifty Bungalow Apartment Houses, Ware Shoals Manufacturing Company, Ware Shoals (*MR*, 18 May 1922, pp. 88, 89.)

1922: Warehouse Addition, Ware Shoals Manufacturing Company, Ware Shoals (*MR*, 15 June 1922, p. 77.)

1923: Sixty Residences, Dunean Mills, Greenville; $100,000 (*MR*, 18 January 1923, p. 82.)

1923: One Hundred Ninety Residences, Dunean Mills, Greenville; $250,000 (*MR*, 26 April 1923, p. 110.)

1923: Clubhouse, Country Club, Greenville; $20,000 (*MR*, 8 March 1923, p. 100.)

1923: C.O. Allen Commercial Building, E. Washington and Brown streets, Greenville (*MR*, 7 June 1923, pp. 130 l, 130 m.)

1923: Baptist Church, Brandon Mills, Greenville; $35,000 (*MR*, 15 November 1923, p. 114.)

1923: Hotel and Twelve Residences, Watts Cotton Mills, Laurens (*MR*, 18 January 1923, p. 82; 25 January 1923, pp. 93, 94.)

1923: Grammar School and Moving-Picture Theater, Pelzer Manufacturing Company, Pelzer (*MR*, 8 March 1923, p. 110.)

1924: Reconstruction, Twenty Residences, Riverside Manufacturing Company, Anderson (*MR*, 22 May 1924, p. 112.)

1924: Addition, Textile Hall, Greenville; $12,000 (*MR*, 24 April 1924, p. 112.)

1924: High School, Greenville; $76,000 (*MR*, 3 January 1924, p. 109; 10 January 1924, p. 120.)

1924: Parker High School, Greenville; $114,000 (*MR*, 24 January 1924, p. 107; 27 March 1924, p. 122.)

1924: Eighty-Five Residences, Lonsdale Mills, Seneca; $135,000 (*MR*, 27 March 1924, p. 120.)

1924: Poinsett Hotel, Main and Court streets, Greenville; $1,000,000; W.L. Stoddart (q.v.), architect; Joseph E. Sirrine & Co., engineers (*MR*, 1 May 1924, p. 154.)

1924: Webb Memorial Infirmary, Furman University, Greenville; $35,000 (*MR*, 21 August 1924, p. 120.)

1924-1925: Chamber of Commerce Building, Greenville; $257,418; Beacham & LeGrand (q.v.), architects; J.E. Sirrine & Co., associated architects & engineers (*MR*, 28 August 1924, p. 111; 25 September 1924, p. 114; 6 November 1924, p. 127; 4 June 1925, p. 137.)

1925: Gymnasium, High School, Greenville; $45,000 (*MR*, 19 February 1925, p. 121.)

1925: D.D. Little Residence, Connecticut Avenue, Spartanburg (*MR*, 19 March 1925, p. 122.)

1925: Fifty Residences, Aragon-Baldwin Mills, Whitmire; $79,000 (*MR*, 12 March 1925, p. 118; 19 March 1925, p. 122.)

1925: Six Residences, Riverside Manufacturing Company, Pendleton; $12,000 (*MR*, 24 December 1925, p. 96.)

1926: James F. Mackey & Son Mortuary, N. Main and Elfird streets, Greenville; $40,000 (*MR*, 5 August 1926, p. 125.)

1926: High School, Ware Shoals; $100,000 (*MR*, 20 May 1926, p. 123.)

1926: One Hundred Seventy-Five Residences, Lonsdale Company, Seneca; $300,000 (*MR*, 13 July 1926, p. 101.)

1927: Twenty-Five Residences, Appleton Manufacturing Company, Anderson; $40,000 (*MR*, 24 March 1927, p. 100.)

1927: Office Building, Appleton Manufacturing Company, Anderson; $10,000 (*MR*, 17 November 1927, p. 107.)

1927: One Hundred Operatives' Residences, Appleton Manufacturing Company, Anderson; $135,000 (*MR*, 1 December 1927, p. 109.)

1927: Conversion of Building Basement for Warehouse, Appleton Manufacturing Company, Anderson; $10,000 (*MR*, 19 May 1927, p. 113.)

1927: Y.M.C.A. Building, Victor-Monaghan Company, Greenville; $50,000 (*MR*, 25 August 1927, p. 96; 1 September 1927, p. 114.)

1927: Vocational Building, Parker High School, Greenville; $50,000 (*MR*, 7 July 1927, p. 114; 14 July 1927, p. 112.)

1927: One Hundred Residences, S. Slater & Son, Inc., Marietta; $160,000 (*MR*, 1 September 1927, p. 116; 8 September 1927, p. 108; 15 September 1927, p. 121.)

1927: Twenty-Five Residences, Aragon-Baldwin Mills, Whitmire; $40,000 (*MR*, 1 September 1927, p. 116; 13 October 1927, p. 116.)

1928: Temporary Addition, Textile Hall, Greenville (*MR*, 28 June 1928, p. 88.)

1928: Two Grammar Schools, Greenville County; $50,000 (*MR*, 9 August 1928, p. 88.)

1928: Addition, Parish House, Christ Church, Greenville; $12,000 (*MR*, 11 October 1928, p. 105.)

1928: School, Marietta; $15,000 (*MR*, 9 August 1928, p. 88.)

1928: Sixty Residences, Slater Manufacturing Company, Marietta; $90,000 (*MR*, 11 October 1928, p. 106.)

1928: Sixty Residences, Piedmont Print Works, Inc., Taylors; $105,000 (*MR*, 8 March 1928, p. 97.)

1928: Twenty-Five Operatives' Residences, Aragon-Baldwin Mills, Whitmire; $40,000 (*MR*, 19 April 1928, p. 85.)

1928: School, Whitmire (*MR*, 11 October 1928, p. 108.)

1929: Grammar School, John Street, Greenville; $47,000 (*MR*, 29 August 1929, p. 80.)

1929: Elementary School, Oscar Street, Greenville; $12,000 (*MR*, 19 September 1929, p. 98.)

1929: Victor-Monaghan Co. Gymnasium, Greer (*MR*, 3 October 1929, p. 97.)

1929: Ten Residences, Draper Corp., Spartanburg (*MR*, 28 February 1929, p. 90.)

1929: Draper Corp. Warehouse, Spartanburg (*MR*, 28 February 1929, p. 91; 14 March 1929, p. 99.)

1932: Miss Nancy P. Bowie Residence, McDaniel Avenue, Greenville; $10,000 (*MR*, 4 February 1932, p. 42.)

Sources: *Construction*, September 1947, p. 60; Greenville city directories; Samuel B. Lincoln, *Lockwood Greene: The History of an Engineering Business 1832-1958* (Brattleboro, Vermont: The Stephen Greene Press, 1960); *MR*, various citations; J. Louis Spencer, "The Republic Cotton Mills, A Textile Community Established Upon Modern Lines," *MR*, 25 May 1911, pp. 49-50; William H. Stone,

"Typical Building in the South in 1909," *MR*, 6 January 1910, pp. 137-140; *Transactions of the American Society of Civil Engineers*, Vol. 113, 1948, pp. 1546-1547; Wallace, Vol. 4, p. 38; *Who's Who in Commerce and Industry*, 4th edition (Chicago: The A.N. Marquis Co., 1944), Vol. IV, p. 920.)

SMITH, Bartholomew F. (active 1897-1912) B.F. Smith, president of the B.F. Smith Fireproof Construction Company in Washington, D.C., specialized in design and construction of fireproof public records buildings, jails, and courthouses between 1897 and 1912. The firm's work included remodeling of existing buildings, construction of "fireproof" additions, especially records rooms, and other improvements. Smith was the architect for most of the firm's work. County courthouses in Jackson, Sparta, and Taylorsville, North Carolina, and in Accomac, Eastville, King George, and Wytheville, Virginia, were designed and built by Smith.

South Carolina projects:

1899: Fireproof Record Building, Marion (*MR*, 7 July 1899, p. 407.)

1902: Fireproof Clerks' Office Building, Aiken; $7850 (*MR*, 17 July 1902, p. 476.)

1902: Two Fireproof Record Rooms, Orangeburg (*MR*, 22 May 1902, p. 326.)

Sources: *MR*, 10 September 1897, p. 102, and various other citations; Washington, D.C., city directories.

SMITH, Elroy G. (active 1928-1930) Smith, of Augusta, Georgia, was the architect and supervisor of construction for the 1928-1930 remodeling and additions to the Edgefield County Courthouse in Edgefield, South Carolina.

Sources: *MR*, 18 October 1928, p. 98; 22 May 1930, p. 81.

SMITH, Frederick J. (active 1880-1895) Smith was identified as an architect, civil engineer, and surveyor in Charleston directories from 1880 through 1895.

SMITH, George G. (active 1906-1911) Smith worked as agent of the Pauly Jail Building Company of St. Louis, Missouri, in 1906. He was practicing as an architect in Asheville, North Carolina, by 1909. Jail buildings in Conway and Barnwell, South Carolina, and in Erwin, Tennessee, are attributed to Smith.

South Carolina projects:

1906: Jail, Conway; $9400; Pauly Jail Building Company, St. Louis (George G. Smith, Asheville, agent), contractor (*MR*, 16 August 1906, p. 118.)

1909: County Jail, Barnwell; George G. Smith, architect; Preacher & Holman (q.v.), supervising architects (*MR*, 27 May 1909, p. 68; 17 June 1909, p. 68.)

Sources: *MR*, various citations.

SMITH, Jesse M. (active 1900) Smith worked as an architect in Anderson in 1900. He was born in South Carolina in 1848.

Source: 1900 Federal Census, Anderson County, South Carolina, Vol. 5, p. 10A.

SMITH, J.W. (active 1894) J.W. Smith of Edgefield was listed as an architect in William T. Comstock's *The Architects' Directory for 1894*.

SMITH, Walter H. (active 1912-1918) Smith worked as a draftsman for Todd & Benson (q.v.) and for John D. Newcomer (q.v.) in Charleston from 1912 to 1916. He was listed as an architect in the Charleston city directories in 1917-1918. He prepared plans for the $4000 Joseph E. Jenkins Residence in Charleston in 1917.

Sources: Charleston city directories; *MR*, 8 February 1917, p. 69.

SMITH, William W. (1862-1937) Smith was a black brickmason, contractor, and architect active in Charlotte, North Carolina. He designed several buildings for black clients in Charlotte and in neighboring communities. Smith's designs were distinguished by their masonry:

His skillful and highly imaginative brickwork is a characteristic of all his designs. Structures feature robust corbelling and polychromy. Smith especially liked mixing red and yellow brick, and plain and textured brick, to produce ornamental effects.

Goler Hall at Livingstone College, Salisbury, North Carolina (1917) is among his larger projects. This building features "strikingly colorful decorative brickwork of geometric design."

South Carolina project:

Ca. 1915: Afro American Mutual Insurance Building, Hampton Street and Dave Lyle Boulevard, Rock Hill (Hanchett.)

Sources: Thomas Hanchett, Charlotte, North Carolina, unpublished research; Davyd Foard Hood, *The Architecture of Rowan County* (Salisbury, North Carolina: Rowan County Historic Properties Commission, 1983), pp. 322-323; Richard Mascal, "Dreams of an Architect," *The Charlotte Observer*, 11 October 1984, p. 6-C.

SNOOK, John Butler (1815-1901) Snook, a native of London, England, was a leading architect of cast-iron buildings in New York City in the middle and late nineteenth century. Snook and his sons James H., Samuel Booth, and Thomas Edward Snook practiced as John B. Snook & Sons from 1887 to 1901. The firm's work in New York is described by White & Willensky, variously, as "elegant, ornate Victoriana," "vigorous Corinthian cast iron," and (of the original, 1871-1872 Grand Central Station on 42nd Street) "a cupolaed confection with a vast iron and glass train shed."

South Carolina project:

J.B. Snook and Sons

1893: Waring History Library, Porter Military Academy, 167 Ashley Avenue, Charleston (Cornerstone.)

Sources: *American Architect and Building News*, 9 November 1901, p. 41; Francis, p. 71; *Macmillan Encyclopedia*, Vol. IV, p. 95; White & Willensky, pp. 15, 45, 46, 49, 79, 94, 147; Withey, p. 563; Wodehouse, pp. 181-182.

SNYDER, Jacob (1823-1890) Jacob Snyder, a native of Pennsylvania, studied architecture at Dickinson College. He was active as a contractor in Akron, Ohio by 1855. In 1864 he associated with Simon B. Weary, engineer and industrialist, and directed his efforts to architectural design. He was identified in the 1881 Akron directory as architect, heating and ventilating engineer, and president of the Weary, Snyder, Wilcox Manufacturing Company.

Snyder made a specialty of church design, and his buildings were erected in many states. He was the architect for the Abbeville Presbyterian Church in Abbeville, South Carolina, built in 1887.

Sources: Abbeville *Press & Banner*, 10 August 1887; Herndon, p. 172; Samuel A. Lane, *Fifty Years and Over of Akron and Summit County* (Akron, Ohio: Beacon Job Department, 1892), pp. 146, 193, 201, 287, 486, 487, 1090, 1092; *Nineteenth Century Churches of Downtown Memphis* (Memphis, Tennessee: Memphis Chapter, Association for the Preservation of Tennessee Antiquities, 1974), n.p.)

SOMPAYRAC, Edwin Douglas (1868-1935) Sompayrac, a native of Society Hill, studied at South Carolina College in 1889-1890. He entered the United States Military Academy at West Point in 1890, and was at Cornell University in 1892-1894. He received a B.S. degree from Cornell in 1894. From 1894 to 1897 Sompayrac worked in architectural offices in Buffalo, New York; and he was a chief insurance inspector for the Southern Railway in Washington, D.C., in 1897-1907.

In 1907 Sompayrac returned to South Carolina and associated with Charles C. Wilson (q.v.) The firm, called Wilson, Sompayrac & Urquhart through 1910, and afterwards Wilson & Sompayrac, was the state's most prominent and successful firm during the pre-war years. They were architects for the expansion of the University of South Carolina, for several of the state's larger school buildings, and many important commercial buildings. Wilson & Sompayrac expanded their operations into North Carolina in 1916-1917.

When the World War interrupted this prosperity, Sompayrac took a position with the United States Shipping Board in New York in 1918. He was working with the General Chemical Company in New York in 1924.

South Carolina projects:

1907-1918: See **Wilson, Charles Coker** (Wilson, Sompayrac & Urquhart; Wilson & Sompayrac)

Sources: *A.I.A. Annuary*, 1919-1920, p. 25; 1924-1925, p. 73; Columbia city directories; *MR*, various citations; Moore, Vol. 7; Petty, p. 145.

SOUTHARD, R.P. (active 1880) Southard was listed as a Charleston architect in the 1880 *South Carolina State Gazetteer and Business Directory*.

STARR, Julian Stewart (active 1902-1931) Starr worked in Rock Hill in the early twentieth century at several jobs. When the Eagle Manufacturing Company was chartered in Rock Hill in 1901, J.S. Starr was listed as the company's secretary. A 1905 reference noted that "Contractor J.S. Starr is now at work on an eight-room dwelling on Wilson Street for his sister, Mrs. Lillian Adams." Starr was later the contractor for buildings designed by architects Hook & Rogers (q.v.), Carter & Pringle (q.v.), and J.M. McMichael (q.v.)

The contracting business led to an architectural career. Starr began calling himself architect in 1908, and he designed houses, churches, and commercial buildings in north central South Carolina in the 1920s. Starr's buildings tended towards the Colonial and Georgian Revival styles. The 1909 Union High School is among his finer designs.

In 1925 Starr relocated to Sarasota, Florida. He had returned to Rock Hill by 1928.

South Carolina projects:

1908: C.L. Dunlap Residence, Fort Lawn (*MR*, 19 November 1908, p. 74.)

1908: Sunday School Addition, Second Baptist Church, Lancaster (*MR*, 19 November 1908, p. 74.)

Ca. 1908: Stokes Residence, Oakland Avenue, Rock Hill (National Register files, S.C. Archives.)

1909: Arnold Freidheim Residence, Rock Hill (*MR*, 8 April 1909, p. 60.)

1909: S.J. Kimball, Two Residences, Rock Hill (*MR*, 7 October 1909, p. 79.)

1909: E.B. Cook Residence, Rock Hill (*MR*, 28 October 1909, p. 125.)

1909: Union High School, Union; $24,000 (Cornerstone; *MR*, 15 July 1909, p. 67; 19 August 1909, p. 62; 7 October 1909, p. 81; 28 October 1909, p. 127.)

1909-1910: School, Carlisle; $5000 (*MR*, 7 October 1909, p. 81; 11 November 1909, p. 66; 20 January 1910, p. 67.)

1910: High School, Lowryville; $4000 (*MR*, 7 July 1910, p. 82.)

1910: A.T. Quantz Residence, Rock Hill (*MR*, 20 January 1910, p. 66.)

1910: John Williams Residence, Rock Hill (*MR*, 20 January 1910, p. 66.)

1910: S.M. McNeel Store and Office Building, Yorkville (*MR*, 20 January 1910, p. 67; 28 April 1910, p. 69.)

1911: R.S. Hannah Residence, Rock Hill; $4000 (*MR*, 4 May 1911, p. 85.)

1911: Albert Whitesides Residence, Rock Hill; $5000 (*MR*, 4 May 1911, p. 85.)

1911: Improvements, Associate Reformed Church, Rock Hill; $6000 (*MR*, 13 July 1911, p. 71.)

1911: J. Barron Steele Residence, Rock Hill (*MR*, 16 November 1911, p. 75.)

1911: School, Sharon (*MR*, 24 August 1911, p. 67.)

1911: D.E. Finley Residence, Yorkville; $7000 (*MR*, 16 February 1911, p. 74; 23 February 1911, p. 67.)

1912: Pride Raterree Store Building, Rock Hill; $20,000 (*MR*, 22 February 1912, p. 66; 18 April 1912, p. 72.)

1912: Miss Julia Campbell Residence, Rock Hill (*MR*, 30 May 1912, p. 72.)

1912: Mrs. D. Hutchison Store and Office Building, Rock Hill (*MR*, 13 June 1912, p. 72.)

1914: Remodeling and addition, People's Bank, Chester; $10,000 (*MR*, 23 April 1914, p. 70; 30 April 1914, p. 65.)

1914: T.E. Whitesides Hotel and Store Building, Chester; $10,000 (*MR*, 30 April 1914, p. 66.)

1915: Hospital, Chester; $5000 (*MR*, 28 January 1915, p. 52.)

1915: N.S. Witherspoon Residence, Lancaster; $10,000 (*MR*, 19 August 1915, p. 63.)

1915: J. Sidney Adams Residence, Oakland Avenue, Rock Hill; $4000 (*MR*, 11 February 1915, p. 53; 18 February 1915, p. 58.)

1916: J.L. Douglas Store Building, Chester; $7000 (*MR*, 12 October 1916, p. 66.)

1916: Associate Reformed Presbyterian Church, Edgemoor; $7000 (*MR*, 2 November 1916, p. 84.)

1916: Foreman's Residence, Great Falls Farming Company, Great Falls; $6500 (*MR*, 18 May 1916, p. 73.)

1917: Dr. J.L. Hamilton Residence, Chester; $6000 (*MR*, 14 June 1917, p. 73.)

1918: J.T. Collins Residence, Chester (*MR*, 17 January 1918, p. 78.)

1924: School, Richburg; $12,000 (*MR*, 27 November 1924, p. 98; 4 December 1924, p. 123.)

1924: School, Leeds (*MR*, 24 July 1924, p. 128.)

1924: J.D. Leseman Residence, Park Avenue, Rock Hill; $10,000 (*MR*, 10 April 1924, p. 110.)

1924: High School, Rossville; $10,000 (*MR*, 7 August 1924, p. 133.)

1925: Mrs. J.M. Williams, Sr., Residence, McConnellsville; $20,000 (*MR*, 8 October 1925, p. 108.)

1928: J.A. Greene Residence, Fort Mill; $12,000 (*MR*, 19 April 1928, p. 85.)

1929: W.G. Reid & Son Store Building, E. Main Street, Rock Hill; $20,000 (*MR*, 21 March 1929, p. 92.)

1930: School, Kershaw; $22,700 (*MR*, 19 June 1930, p. 82.)

Sources: *Acts and Joint Resolutions of the General Assembly of the State of South Carolina, 1902* (Columbia: n.p., 1902), p. 1325; *MR*, various citations; Rock Hill city directories; *The State,* 3 March 1905.

STEPHENSON, Robert S. (1858-1929) Robert S. Stephenson of New York City was noted as a designer of churches. He studied architecture at Cornell and worked as a draftsman with McKim, Mead & White. Stephenson associated with Ernest S. Greene (1864-1936) in New York from 1890 to 1898. Stephenson & Greene are believed to have been the architects for the Romanesque-Revival Circular Congregational Church in Charleston (1890.)

South Carolina projects:

1890: Independent Circular Church (Circular Congregational Church), 150 Meeting Street, Charleston (Cornerstone; *MR*, 29 March 1890, p. 43; Harlan McClure and Vernon Hodges, *South Carolina Architecture 1670-1970* (Columbia: South Carolina Tricentennial Commission, 1970), p. 96.

1899: Hotel, Aiken; "Mr. Stevenson" of New York, architect (*MR*, 7 April 1899, p. 184.)

Sources: Francis, pp. 35, 72; *MR*, various citations; Withey, pp. 249, 570-571.

STEWART, George Wilson (1862-1937) George W. Stewart was associated with James W. Golucke (q.v.) in Atlanta, Georgia from 1893 through 1900, when he began independent practice. He collaborated with George E. Murphy to design Atlanta's magnificent terra-cotta Candler Building in 1906. Stewart had relocated to St. Petersburg, Florida, by 1918, where he was still active in 1924.

South Carolina projects:

1894-1899: See **Golucke, James Wingfield** (Golucke & Stewart)

1905: School, Orangeburg; $15,000 (*MR*, 19 January 1905, p. 17.)

Sources: *MR*, various citations; Morgan, p. 146; *Architects and Builders in Georgia.*

STODDART, William Lee (1861-1940) William L. Stoddart was one of the nation's premier designers of hotel buildings in the early twentieth century. A native of New Jersey, Stoddart studied architecture at Columbia University. He worked with George B. Post for ten years, and he opened his own office in New York City in 1905.

Stoddart designed two major hotels in South Carolina, the Francis Marion in Charleston and the Poinsett in Greenville. Other works by Stoddart in the Southeast included the 10-story Joseph F. Gatlins Apartment Hotel in Atlanta, Georgia, 1910; the 10-story, $334,800 Greater Savannah (Georgia) Hotel in 1911; the $1,000,000 Hotel Farragut in Knoxville, Tennessee, 1917-1919; the O. Henry Hotel in

Greensboro, North Carolina, 1919; the Lord Baltimore Hotel in Baltimore; and the 14-story, $713,480 Citizens Hotel, Charlotte, North Carolina, 1922.

South Carolina projects:

1920-1922: Francis Marion Hotel, King and Calhoun streets, Charleston; $1,250,000 (*MR*, 10 June 1920, p. 127; 4 May 1922, p. 106; 26 October 1922, p. 59.)

1923-1924: Poinsett Hotel, Main and Court streets, Greenville; $1,000,000; W.L. Stoddart, architect; J.E. Sirrine & Co. (q.v.), engineers (*MR*, 13 December 1923, p. 71; 1 May 1924, p. 154; 19 June 1924, p. 117; 3 July 1924, p. 137; 7 August 1924, p. 132; 4 September 1924, p. 128.)

Sources: *MR*, various citations; "William L. Stoddart, A Hotel Architect," *The New York Times*, 3 October 1940, p. 25; Withey, p. 575.

STONE, Joseph (active 1895-1900) Stone was born in Tennessee in 1872. He came to Columbia around 1895 and sought to establish himself as an architect. In 1900 he shared a house with two other prospective architects, Fred Dennis (q.v.) and George E. Lafaye (q.v.)

Sources: Columbia city directories; 1900 Census, Richland County, South Carolina, Enumeration District 84, p. 12B.

STORK, Robert Caughman (1898- ca. 1948) Robert C. Stork, a native of Columbia, studied architecture at Clemson College. He worked as a draftsman for Charles C. Wilson (q.v.) and for Harold Tatum (q.v.) in Columbia in 1923-1928. He joined Jesse W. Wessinger (q.v.) in 1929, and the firm Wessinger & Stork was active in central South Carolina for ten years. During the Depression, Stork worked with the Historic American Buildings Survey, recording the Ainsley Hall House in Columbia.

Stork was associated with William G. Lyles in Columbia from 1938 to 1948.

South Carolina projects:

1929-1938: See **Wessinger, Jesse W.** (Wessinger & Stork)

Sources: Columbia city directories; Koyl, p. 346; Wallace, pp. 708-709.

STORY, Joseph B. (active 1886-1932) Joseph Story was a draftsman working for Augustus M. MacMurphy (q.v.) in 1886. Story became an associate by 1889. The firm was active in Augusta, Georgia, through 1911. Story associated with Cortez Clark (Story & Clark) by 1919, and the firm was active through 1932.

South Carolina projects:

1905-1911: See **MacMurphy, Augustus Mitchell** (MacMurphy & Story)

Sources: Augusta, Georgia city directories; *MR*, various citations.

SUMMER, J. Ernest (active 1909-1927) Summer began his professional practice in Florida. He was present at a statewide architects' convention in Jacksonville, Florida, in 1912. Architect W.B. Talley (q.v.), who had been active in Jacksonville since 1908, was associated with Summer by 1913; Talley & Summer were listed in the Jacksonville city directories through 1917. The Palm Beach County Courthouse in West Palm Beach ($183,700) was designed by Talley, Summer & Hamilton, Architects, of Jacksonville in 1913.

Summer had established an office in Greenwood, South Carolina, by 1915. Talley worked with Summer on at least one South Carolina project, the 1915 Bank of Saluda Building in Saluda. Summer was associated with James C. Hemphill (q.v.) in 1916-1917. His largest project in the state was the 1917 Exchange Bank of Newberry Building in Newberry. This five-story structure was contracted at $75,000, and it is still the tallest building in Newberry.

Hemphill was working independently in Greenwood by 1919. Summer's activities after 1917 are not clear. The 1920 remodeling of Carnegie Hall at Newberry College is attributed to Summer. His membership in the South Carolina chapter of the A.I.A. lapsed in 1927.

South Carolina projects:

1915: Dr. R.M. Stevenson Residence, Due West; $3175 (*MR*, 22 July 1915, p. 60.)

1915: Dr. G.W. Connor Residence, Greenwood; $2500 (*MR*, 25 March 1915, p. 54.)

1915: Remodeling, B.T. Seago Residence, Greenwood; $2000 (*MR*, 17 June 1915, p. 58.)

1915: J.B. Walton Store Building, Greenwood; $6227 (*MR*, 15 July 1915, p. 61.)

1915: T.M. Miller Residence, Greenwood; $4000 (*MR*, 9 December 1915, p. 68.)

1915: See **Talley, W.B.** (Talley & Summer)

J. Ernest Summer

1916: John Rennie Blake School, Greenwood; $23,500 (*MR*, 30 March 1916, p. 67.)

1916: Girls' Dormitory, Connie Maxwell Orphanage, Greenwood (*MR*, 4 May 1916, p. 88.)

1916: Grendel Mill No. 1 School, Greenwood; $7500 (*MR*, 28 September 1916, p. 65; 5 October 1916, p. 87.)

1916: A.R.P. Church Residence, Greenwood (*MR*, 30 November 1916, p. 66.)

Summer & Hemphill

1916: Alterations, E.S.F. Giles Building, Main Street, Greenwood; $3800 (*MR*, 3 August 1916, p. 82; 10 August 1916, p. 67.)

1916: J.C. Harper Residence, Greenwood; $6000 (*MR*, 3 August 1916, p. 81; 24 August 1916, p. 69.)

1916-1917: Carnegie Library, Greenwood; $12,500 (*MR*, 19 July 1917, p. 78; George S. Bobinski, *Carnegie Libraries: Their History and*

Impact on American Public Library Development (Chicago: American Library Association, 1969), p. 220.)

1917: Enoree Manufacturing Company School, Enoree; $16,000 (*MR*, 14 June 1917, p. 73.)

1917: Main Street Methodist Church, Greenwood; $45,000; Summer & Hemphill and H.D. Harrall (q.v.), architects (*MR*, 5 April 1917, p. 92.)

1917: W.C. Strawhorn Residence, 311 E. Cambridge Avenue, Greenwood (*MR*, 3 May 1917, p. 93; Survey files, S.C. Archives.)

1917: William Lomax Residence, Greenwood (*MR*, 3 May 1917, p. 93.)

1917: E.W. Stalnaker Residence, Greenwood (*MR*, 17 May 1917, p. 76.)

1917: Exchange Bank of Newberry Building, Newberry; $75,000 (*MR*, 9 August 1917, p. 72; 30 August 1917, p. 73.)

1917: National Bank Building, Newberry; $50,000 (*MR*, 4 October 1917, p. 94.)

1917: County Jail, Newberry; $60,000 (*MR*, 8 November 1917, p. 78.)

Sources: Jacksonville, Florida, city directories; Greenwood city directories; *MR*, various citations; Petty, p. 145; George L. Pfeiffer, "History of Organization of the Florida Association of Architects, Now A Chartered Body," *Yearbook of Current Architecture in Florida* (n.p.: The Florida Association of Architects, 1933.)

SWAN, Charles D. (active 1909) Charles Swan, of Darlington, was listed as an architect in the 1909 Comstock *Architects' Directory*.

SWEENY, Frank R. (active 1912-1929) Sweeny, called "Professor," designed the Clemson College Methodist Episcopal Church in 1912 and supervised its construction, working without compensation. Sweeny was an engineer for the Anderson County Highway Commission in 1920-1922; he later had private practice as an engineer. In 1927 Sweeny worked with J. Frank Collins (q.v.) on construction of the Masonic Temple Building in Spartanburg. He was city engineer of Anderson in 1929.

Sources: Anderson city directories; *MR*, 21 April 1927, p. 100; *The State*, 26 February 1912, p. 10.

TALLEY, Wilbur B. (active 1902-1928) Wilbur B. Talley was working as an architect in Savannah, Georgia in 1902. He relocated to Jacksonville, Florida, by 1907. Talley was associated with J. Ernest Summer (q.v.) in Jacksonville from 1913 through 1917. The Palm Beach County Courthouse in Palm Beach, Florida, contracted in 1913 at $183,700, was prominent among Talley's work. Summer was designing buildings in Greenwood, South Carolina by 1915; and Talley was occasionally identified as Summer's partner in the Greenwood projects.

South Carolina project:

Talley & Summer

1915: Bank of Saluda Building, Main and Church streets, Saluda (*MR*, 2 September 1915, p. 66.)

Sources: Jacksonville, Florida, city directories; *MR*, various citations; Wayne W. Wood, *Jacksonville's Architectural Heritage: Landmarks for the Future* (Jacksonville: University of North Florida Press, n.d., ca. 1985), p. 13.

TATUM, Harold (1887-1958) Tatum was a native of Woodbury, New Jersey. He studied architecture at the University of Pennsylvania, and took a position with John T. Windrim in 1911. He worked later with Rankin, Kellogg & Crane (q.v.), and with Day & Klauder.

Tatum opened an architectural office in Columbia in 1920. James E. Hunter, Jr. (q.v.) was a draftsman and architect with Tatum in 1922-1929. From 1929 to 1932 Tatum was associated with Charles C. Wilson (q.v.) in Columbia. After Wilson's death in 1933, Tatum continued his practice in

Columbia for a few years. He then relocated to Charleston in 1934, where he was associated with R.L. Boinest. Tatum died at his home in Mount Pleasant in 1958.

Two of Columbia's major government buildings were designed by Tatum: the John C. Calhoun State Office Building (1925-1926) and the United States Courthouse (1935-1936.) These are formidable Neoclassical designs, architectural expressions of the state and federal presences in Columbia.

South Carolina projects:

1921: Julius H. Walker Residence, Columbia; $15,000 (*MR*, 29 September 1921, p. 88; 6 October 1921, p. 115.)

1921: Dr. P.V. Mikell Residence, Columbia; $24,000 (*MR*, 29 September 1921, p. 88; 6 October 1921, p. 115.)

1921: Shepard Pender Residence, Columbia; $6000 (*MR*, 6 October 1921, p. 115.)

1921: John Crews Residence, Columbia; $9000 (*MR*, 6 October 1921, p. 115.)

1921: Anthony Craig Residence, Columbia; $7000 (*MR*, 6 October 1921, p. 115.)

1923: Henry L. Forbes Residence, Park Place, Columbia (*MR*, 10 May 1923, p. 108.)

1923: Dr. Ralph K. Foster Residence, College Street, Columbia; $13,000 (*MR*, 2 August 1923, p. 150.)

1923: School, Monarch Mills, Union (*MR*, 17 May 1923, p. 110.)

1923: Remodeling and Additions, J. Ross Cannon Residence, York; $45,000 (*MR*, 31 May 1923, p. 95.)

1924: Methodist Church, Lockhart; $48,000 (*MR*, 31 July 1924, p. 114; 14 August 1924, p. 106.)

1925: Auditorium, Gymnasium, and Classroom Addition, Grammar School, Union; $48,000 (*MR*, 16 July 1925, p. 116; 23 July 1925, p. 105.)

1925-1926: John C. Calhoun State Office Building, 1025 Sumter Street, Columbia; $608,000; Harold Tatum, architect; Milton B. Medary (q.v.), consulting architect (*MR*, 1 January 1925, p. 131 g; 6 August 1925, p. 121; Plaque in building.)

1927: Sumter County Jail, Sumter; $32,895 (*MR*, 20 January 1927, p. 120; 27 January 1927, p. 95.)

1927: Industrial School (Colored), Council Street, Sumter; $7044 (*MR*, 3 November 1927, p. 123.)

1929-1932: See **Wilson, Charles Coker** (Wilson & Tatum)

1932: Hagood Bostic Residence, Columbia; $18,000 (*MR*, 4 February 1932, p. 42; 24 March 1932, p. 39.)

1932: Calder Seibels Residence, Columbia (*MR*, 21 June 1932, p. 27.)

1935-1936: Federal Courthouse, 1100 Laurel Street, Columbia; $253,920 (*MR*, June 1935, p. 32; National Register files, S.C. Archives.)

n.d.: Restoration, First Scots Presbyterian Church, Meeting Street, Charleston (Tatman.)

n.d.: Restoration, Greek Orthodox Church, Charleston (Tatman.)

Sources: *American Art Annual*, Vol. 21, p. 469; Charleston city directories; Columbia city directories; *MR*, various citations; Sandra Tatman, The Athenaeum, Philadelphia, Pennsylvania, unpublished research.

TAYLOR, James Knox (1857-1929) James Knox Taylor was supervising architect of the United States Department of the Treasury from 1897 to 1912. In this capacity, he directed the design of federal projects, especially courthouses and post offices, across the nation.

Taylor studied architecture at the Massachusetts Institute of Technology, and worked as a draftsman in New York before commencing independent practice. After working for several years in St. Paul and in Philadelphia, Taylor entered the Supervising Architect's office in Washington, D.C., in 1895. He was appointed supervising architect in 1897.

Taylor practiced independently in Boston for several years after leaving Washington. He served as director of the Department of Architecture at M.I.T. in 1912. Around 1920, Taylor retired to Florida, where he died in 1929.

As supervising architect, Taylor dictated in 1901 that federal designs would return to the "classic style of architecture"; and his buildings interpreted this policy in lucid interpretations of the prevailing Georgian Revival and neoclassical styles. Federal architecture under Taylor was presented as an expression of Classical and democratic ideals. *The Brickbuilder* in 1907 described Taylor's work as "a splendid success in keeping abreast with the spirit of the times." Taylor's buildings in South Carolina are characterized by sophisticated architectural elements and compositions, including classical porticos and arcades; Spanish pantile roofs, with deep eaves and modillions; Georgian Revival Flemish-bond brickwork; and, at the 1910 Aiken Post Office, a domed Ionic rotunda, Jeffersonian in character.

South Carolina projects:

1904: Post Office and Federal Courthouse, Florence; $100,000 (*MR*, 20 October 1904, p. 337; 27 October 1904, p. 367.)

1904: Post Office and Customs House, Georgetown (*MR*, 27 October 1904, p. 367.)

1905: Post Office, Rock Hill; $32,500 (Cornerstone; *MR*, 22 June 1905, p. 536.)

1905: Post Office, Spartanburg; $44,989 (*MR*, 29 June 1905, p. 560; 17 August 1905, p. 122.)

1908: Addition, Post Office, Greenville; $53,000 (*MR*, 6 February 1908, p. 67; 19 March 1908, p. 60.)

1908: Post Office, Greenwood; $45,000 (*MR*, 20 August 1908, p. 62; 1 October 1908, p. 69; 15 October 1908, p. 73; 22 October 1908, p. 59.)

1908-1909: Post Office and Federal Courthouse, Anderson; $52,500 (*MR*, 9 July 1908, p. 56; 20 August 1908, p. 62; 24 December 1908, p. 67; 4 February 1909, p. 77; 18 February 1909, p. 67.)

1908-1909: Post Office and Federal Building, Chester; $31,000 (Cornerstone; *MR*, 16 April 1908, p. 63; 4 June 1908, p. 70; 11 June 1908, p. 57.)

1908-1910: Post Office and Federal Building, 53 S. Main Street, Sumter; $54,000 (*MR*, 28 May 1908, p. 66; 9 July 1908, p. 56; 18 March 1909, p. 64; 29 April 1909, p. 70; *The State*, 13 July 1908, p. 6.)

1910: Post Office, 203 Laurens Street, Aiken; $45,618 (Cornerstone; *MR*, 7 July 1910, p. 82.)

1911: Immigration Station, Charleston; $60,000; Taylor, supervising architect; Walker & Burden (q.v.), architects (*MR*, 7 September 1911, p. 77.)

1911: Post Office, Newberry; $49,700 (*MR*, 7 December 1911, p. 86.)

1912: Post Office, Abbeville; $39,460 (*MR*, 16 May 1912, p. 74.)

1912: Post Office, Gaffney; $49,495 (*MR*, 8 February 1912, p. 68; 9 May 1912, p. 72.)

1912: Post Office, Laurens; $45,354 (*MR*, 16 May 1912, p. 74.)

1912: Post Office, Orangeburg; $45,250 (*MR*, 2 May 1912, p. 83.)

1912: Post Office, Union; $48,975 (*The State*, 26 January 1912, p. 1; *MR*, 18 July 1912, p. 78.)

1912: Post Office, Darlington; $43,302 (*MR*, 18 April 1912, p. 72.)

Sources: *American Art Annual*, Vol. 21, p. 469; "Government Building in the South," *MR*, 23 March 1911, p. 51; Herndon, p. 180; *History of Post Office Construction 1900-1940* (Washington, D.C.: United States Postal Service, 1982); Antoinette J. Lee and William Seale, *History of the Office of the Supervising Architect of the Treasury, Washington, D.C.* (publication anticipated 1990); *MR*, various citations; Smith, *The Office of the Supervising Architect*; *Who Was Who in America*, Vol. IV (Chicago, Illinois: Marquis Who's Who, Inc., n.d., ca. 1968), p. 930; Tatman/Moss, pp. 780-781; Withey, p. 592.

THOMAS, Stephen (active 1929-1942) Stephen Thomas of Charleston was registered as an architect by 1929. He was employed with Simons & Lapham (q.v.) through 1932.

Sources: Charleston city directories; Petty, p. 145.

THOMAS, MARTIN & KIRKPATRICK (active 1919-1931) The Philadelphia firm of Walter Horstman Thomas (1876-1948), Sydney Errington Martin (1883-1970), and Donald Morris Kirkpatrick (1887-1966) was active in ecclesiastical and residential design from 1919 to 1931. Thomas was educated at the University of Pennsylvania and at the Ecole des Beaux-Arts in Paris. He was an authority on church design, and served as advisory architect for the Methodist Church in the United States from 1925 to 1933. Martin and Kirkpatrick were also students at the University of Pennsylvania, and Kirkpatrick attended the Ecole des Beaux-Arts as well.

In addition to the Ebenezer Lutheran Church in Columbia, South Carolina, the firm's southern work included the $2,300,000 All-States Society Club Hotel in Miami, Florida. This 14-story building was begun in 1925.

South Carolina project:

1929-1931: Ebenezer Lutheran Church, 1301 Richland Street, Columbia; $120,000; Thomas, Martin & Kirkpatrick, architects; James B. Urquhart (q.v.), associated architect (*MR*, 10 October 1929, p. 93; 17 October 1929, p. 95; *The State*, 4 October 1931.)

Sources: Koyl, p. 466; Tatman/Moss, pp. 448-449, 508-509, 783-786.

THOMSON, John R. (active 1922) John R. Thomson, of Union, was identified as an architect in the 1922 F.W. Dodge directory, *Architects of the Middle Atlantic States*.

THOMSON & FROHLING (active 1909-1914) Theo E. Thomson and N. Victor Frohling of New York City were architects for the eight-story People's Bank Building in Charleston, the second skyscraper to be built in South Carolina.

South Carolina project:

1909: People's Building and Investment Co. Bank and Office Building, Broad and State streets, Charleston; $239,000 (*MR*, 18 March 1909, p. 62; 5 August 1909, p. 71; 30 September 1909, p. 65; 25 November 1909, p. 64; 2 December 1909, p. 62.)

Sources: *MR*, various citations; Withey, p. 598.

THROWER, James R. (active 1922-1926) Thrower was listed as an architect in Cheraw in the 1922 F.W. Dodge directory, *Architects of the Middle Atlantic States*. In the 1926 Charlotte, North Carolina, city directory, James R. Thrower was identified as a partner in the architectural firm Thrower & (Victor W.) Breeze.

TILTON, Edward Lippencott (1861-1933) Tilton was a distinguished Beaux-Arts trained architect active in New York City and the eastern United States from 1890 through the 1920s. Tilton was born in New York on 19 May 1861, and obtained practical architectural education in the office of McKim, Mead & White. He attended the Ecole des Beaux-Arts in Paris, graduating in 1888. Tilton began architectural practice in New York in 1890 as a partner of William A. Boring.

Tilton won note as a designer of libraries. He was architect for the 1920-1921 Durham (North Carolina) Public Library, a building constructed with assistance of Carnegie Foundation funding. Tilton also designed the Pack Memorial Library in Asheville, North Carolina; the library at Peabody College

in Nashville, Tennessee; and the library at Emory University in Decatur, Georgia. He also designed over sixty libraries and thirty theatres at various United States Army camps during the First World War. The 1917 American Library Association Building at Camp Sevier, Greenville, South Carolina, was among Tilton's designs.

Sources: Herndon, p. 184; *MR*, 6 December 1917, p. 92; Noffsinger, pp. 105, 106, 117; Withey, p. 601.

TIMMONS, _____ (active 1907) Timmons was associated with James Herbert Johnson (q.v.) in Sumter. The firm designed the Farmers' Bank and Trust Company Building in Sumter in 1907. No further information on Timmons has been found.

Source: *MR*, 27 June 1907, p. 773.

TINSLEY, Staten Peyton (active 1905-1924) Staten P. Tinsley worked as a draftsman for Keating & Proffitt (q.v.) in Spartanburg in 1905. In 1908 he was associated with Luther D. Proffitt as Proffitt & Tinsley; and by 1910 Tinsley had established an independent practice in Spartanburg.

The six-story Finch Hotel, the third skyscraper to be built in Spartanburg, was Tinsley's most prominent building in the state. He had earlier designed a residence for W.T. Finch in Spartanburg. Tinsley was also the architect for the ten-story, $200,000 Hotel Wilmington in Wilmington, North Carolina, in 1914.

South Carolina projects:

1907: School, Cross Anchor; $5000 (*MR*, 25 July 1907, p. 52; 10 October 1907, p. 65; 31 October 1907, p. 63.)

1908: See **Proffitt, Luther B.** (Proffitt & Tinsley)

1910: T.R. Hagood Residence, Spartanburg; $4000 (*MR*, 14 April 1910, p. 67.)

1911: Isaac Turner Residence, S. Church Street, Spartanburg; $11,000 (*MR*, 13 April 1911, p. 70.)

1912: Gramling School, Gramling; $6000 (*MR*, 18 July 1912, p. 78.)

1913: J.D. Burnett et.al. Store Building, S. Liberty Street, Spartanburg; $6000 (*MR*, 24 July 1913, p. 70.)

1915: T.E. Smith Store Building, Trade Street, Greer; $10,000 (*MR*, 8 July 1915, p. 57; 22 July 1915, p. 61.)

1915: W.T. Finch Residence, Advent Street, Spartanburg; $7000 (*MR*, 28 October 1915, p. 58.)

1916: J.M. Jackson Residence, Campobello; $12,000 (*MR*, 15 June 1916, p. 71.)

1916: Presbyterian Church, Spartanburg; $6377 (*MR*, 20 April 1916, p. 69; 27 April 1916, p. 65.)

1917: Baptist Parsonage, Greer; $3000 (*MR*, 26 April 1917, p. 70; 10 May 1917, p. 72.)

1918-1920: W.T. Finch Hotel, 185 E. Main Street, Spartanburg; $150,000 (*MR*, 9 May 1918, p. 79; 16 May 1918, p. 84.)

1921: Salvation Army Building, Spartanburg; $32,000 (*MR*, 24 March 1921, p. 112.)

1922: School, Fairforest; $33,455 (*MR*, 17 August 1922, p. 87.)

1922: J.W. Bell Residence, E. Main Street, Spartanburg (*MR*, 4 May 1922, pp. 105-106.)

1923: First Baptist Church, Greer; $50,000 (*MR*, 15 February 1923, p. 109.)

1923: R. Skalowski Residence, Spartanburg; $22,000 (*MR*, 10 May 1923, p. 108.)

Sources: *MR*, various citations; Spartanburg city directories.

TINSLEY, Walter P. (active 1880-1913) Walter P. Tinsley was a practicing architect in Knoxville, Tennessee, as early as 1882. He established his office in Lynchburg, Virginia, around 1887. In an 1893 application to the American Institute of Architects, Tinsley noted that he had been in practice for thirteen years.

Tinsley associated with Charles Coker Wilson (q.v.) in Lynchburg in 1895, and the firm designed one building in South Carolina. Wilson left Lynchburg that same year. In November 1896 Tinsley, who had just been ordained a Baptist minister, left Lynchburg for Charlotte, North Carolina, where he was active as an architect in 1897. He relocated to Jackson, Mississippi, by 1905, where he was still practicing in 1913.

South Carolina project:

Tinsley & Wilson

1895: Anderson Graded School, W. Market Street, Anderson (*MR*, 26 April 1895, p. 205; 31 May 1895, p. 282.)

Sources: S. Allen Chambers, *Lynchburg: An Architectural History* (Charlottesville, Virginia: The University Press of Virginia, 1981), pp. 286, 345, 540-541; Charlotte, North Carolina, city directories; Herndon, pp. 184-185; *MR*, various citations.

TIPPETT, Robert L. (active 1903-1905) Tippett was listed as an architect in the 1903 and 1905 Spartanburg city directories.

TODD, Albert Whitner (1856-1924) Albert W. Todd of Charleston had parallel careers as an architect and legislator. He was born in Anderson on 20 April 1856, son of Archibald and Jane Todd. As a young man Todd worked in the Anderson area as a contractor and builder, and pursued an architectural education through correspondence courses. By 1877 Todd was advertising as an architect in Anderson; in 1879 he was working in association with F.W. Hahn. Two early designs by Todd, the Bank of Anderson Building and an opera house in Anderson, won a measure of local acclaim.

Todd moved to Augusta, Georgia around 1889 to continue his architectural practice. He worked in Augusta until the late 1890s. He was associated briefly with Daniel G. Zeigler (q.v.) in 1890, and with Joseph F. Leitner (q.v.) in 1893. Todd relocated to Charleston around 1899, and maintained his office in that city until his death.

Todd's practice was centered in Charleston, and included the remodeling of many of the city's historic structures. He also designed several buildings in the Columbia area, including projects for the South Carolina State Penitentiary in 1900 and 1904. Todd's associates in Charleston included his son Robert C. Todd, from 1916 until 1922; James D. Benson (q.v.) from 1908 until 1915; Albert Simons (q.v.) from 1917 to 1919; and James Fogarty (q.v.) in 1920.

Todd & Benson prepared plans for an extensive remodeling of the South Carolina State House in 1911. Their plans called for the removal of the existing dome, the construction of a new dome, and the construction of two large office wings on the east and west sides of the building. The work, estimated to cost $1,000,000, was never begun; the State Legislature withheld funding.

Todd became a member of this legislature himself in 1910, when he won election to the State House of Representatives. He introduced the bill to define and regulate the practice of architecture in 1917. Todd was elected to the State Senate in 1917, and served until his death in 1924. David Duncan Wallace characterized Todd's work in the Senate:

> Brilliant and forceful, keen of mind and of speech, he immediately won recognition for leadership and, during his terms in office served on many of the most important committees, and was foremost in some of the most constructive legislation introduced at the capital.

Todd was a charter member of the South Carolina chapter of the American Institute of Architects, and served as president of the chapter in 1915-1916.

South Carolina projects:

Ca. 1888: Bank of Anderson Building, Anderson (Wallace.)

Ca. 1888: Opera House, Anderson (Wallace.)

Todd & Zeigler

1890: John W. Fairey Hotel, Orangeburg; $15,000 (*MR*, 23 August 1890, p. 41.)

1890: H. Harley Residence, Sumter; $10,000 (*MR*, 23 August 1890, p. 41.)

1890: D.W. Mason Residence, Sumter; $7000 (*MR*, 23 August 1890, p. 41.)

Albert W. Todd

1891: Western Carolina Land & Improvement Co. Hotel, Calhoun Falls (*MR*, 2 May 1891, p. 44.)

1891: Masonic Temple, Sumter (*MR*, 18 April 1891, p. 45; 25 April 1891, p. 47; 1 August 1891, pp. 46-47.)

Todd & Leitner

1893: Academy Building, Seneca (*MR*, 1 September 1893, p. 89.)

Albert W. Todd

1899: Seashore Improvement Co. Hotel, Isle of Palms (*MR*, 27 January 1899, p. 12; 7 April 1899, p. 184.)

1899: Town Hall and Municipal Building, Moultrieville (*MR*, 3 November 1899, p. 258.)

1900: Remodeling, St. Charles Hotel, Charleston (*MR*, 3 May 1900, p. 257; 10 May 1900, p. 273; 24 May 1900, p. 309; *The State*, 17 May 1900, p. 8.)

1900: Remodeling and enlarging, South Carolina State Penitentiary, Columbia; $13,000 (*MR*, 14 June 1900, p. 359; 19 July 1900, p. 443; 16 August 1900, p. 68.)

182

1902-1903: Commercial Club Clubhouse, Charleston; $60,000 (*MR*, 9 October 1902, p. 216; 25 December 1902, p. 450; 12 March 1903, p. 159.)

1903: Christian Congregation Edifice, Charleston (*MR*, 2 July 1903, p. 490.)

1904: Hospital Building and Officers' and Guards' Quarters, South Carolina State Penitentiary, Columbia (*MR*, 3 March 1904, p. 143.)

1904: Administration Building, Dormitory, and Other Buildings, Columbia Female College, Columbia; $100,000 (*MR*, 31 March 1904, p. 238; 29 September 1904, p. 265; 3 November 1904, p. 393; *Southern Architect and Building News*, 8 April 1904, p. 10.)

1906: School, Charleston (*MR*, 5 July 1906, p. 706; 19 July 1906, p. 15; 15 November 1906, p. 456.)

1907: High School, Sumter; $23,595 (*MR*, 11 April 1907, p. 390; 16 May 1907, p. 575; 11 July 1907, p. 838; 25 July 1907, p. 54.)

1907: First Methodist Church, Sumter; $35,000 (*MR*, 7 November 1907, p. 77.)

Todd & Benson

1908: Remodeling, Police Barracks, South Carolina Military Academy, Charleston; $13,678 (*MR*, 30 April 1908, p. 60; 14 May 1908, p. 59.)

1908: Remodeling, Men's Hall and Officers' Quarters Building, South Carolina Military Academy, Charleston; $20,000 (*MR*, 14 May 1908, p. 59.)

1908: Domestic Science Building, Memminger Normal School, Charleston; $10,000 (*MR*, 25 June 1908, p. 58.)

1908-1909: Academy of Our Lady of Mercy Convent Building, Charleston; $42,700 (*MR*, 17 December 1908, p. 68; 4 February 1909, p. 78; 11 February 1909, p. 67.)

1909: School, Charleston (*MR*, 19 August 1909, p. 62.)

1909: Citizens' Exchange Bank Building, Denmark; $4000 (*MR*, 10 June 1909, p. 65; 12 August 1909, p. 58.)

1910: Addition, The Citadel (South Carolina Military Academy), Charleston; $26,800 (*MR*, 21 April 1910, p. 71.)

1911: Armory and Quarters Building, The Citadel, Charleston; $40,000 (*MR*, 19 January 1911, p. 72.)

1911-1912: Remodeling, South Carolina State House, Columbia (*The State*, 5 February 1912, p. 10.)

1913: Medical College of South Carolina Building, Charleston; $53,000 (*MR*, 4 December 1913, p. 79.)

1914: City Hall, Andrews; $8305 (*MR*, 23 April 1914, p. 70.)

1914: School, Andrews; $7500 (*MR*, 23 July 1914, p. 58.)

Todd, Simons & Todd

1916: Dr. Joseph Maybank Residence, Charleston; $11,000 (*MR*, 7 December 1916, p. 84.)

Todd & Fogarty

1920: Victory Housing Corporation, Three Apartment Buildings, Charleston; $250,000 (*MR*, 1 July 1920, p. 172; 14 October 1920, p. 154 m; 21 October 1920, p. 136 l.)

Albert W. Todd

1924: School, Ladson; $10,000 (*MR*, 28 August 1924, pp. 114-115.)

n.d.: Timrod Inn Building, Charleston (*News & Courier*, 31 December 1924.)

n.d.: Thompson Memorial Annex, Riverside Infirmary, Charleston (*News & Courier*, 31 December 1924.)

n.d.: T.T. Hyde Residence, Murray Boulevard, Charleston (*News & Courier*, 31 December 1924; Wallace.)

n.d.: Remodeling, 41 Church Street, Charleston (Wallace.)

n.d.: Albert W. Todd Residence, Queen Street and Rutledge Avenue, Charleston (Wallace.)

Sources: Augusta, Georgia, city directories; Charleston city directories; *MR*, various citations; *News & Courier*, 31 December 1924; Zach Watson Rice, Brooklyn, New York, unpublished research; Wallace, Vol. IV, pp. 520-521.

TOMLINSON, William Sidney (ca. 1885-1961) Tomlinson, a native of North Carolina, worked as city engineer of Columbia for forty years, retiring in 1950. He prepared plans for the $31,000 City Market buildings on Assembly Street in 1924; and for a $13,300 addition to the Central Fire Station on Sumter Street in 1925.

Sources: *MR*, 5 June 1924, p. 138; 30 April 1925, p. 123; 14 May 1925, p. 115; *The State*, 3 June 1951, p. 5-A.

TOMPKINS, Daniel Augustus (1851-1914) D.A. Tompkins was a mill architect, engineer, machinist, journalist, and industrial apostle in Charlotte, North Carolina. A native of Edgefield, South Carolina, he studied engineering at South Carolina College before entering Rensselaer Polytechnic Institute in Troy, New York. He established his engineering practice in Charlotte in 1882 after work in New York with the Bethlehem Iron Works and the John A. Griswold & Co. Steel Works.

Tompkins's work included industrial plants in South and North Carolina. Textile training schools at Clemson College (1898) and North Carolina Agricultural and Mechanical College (1901) were among his designs.

Tompkins wrote and published many textbooks and pamphlets on the cotton industry, including a treatise on mill planning, financing, development, construction, and operation called *Cotton Mills,*

Commercial Features. Here Tompkins described the basic design parameters of cotton processing mills, especially "slow-burning construction," as developed in the Northeast and codified by the insurance companies. Tompkins also provided plans, elevations, and specifications for model "operatives' homes" for the developing textile communities. These buildings, simple frame dwellings without amenities, ranged in size from two to six rooms, with estimated construction costs of $250 - $600. It is likely that many of the rental dwellings built in South Carolina by the textile barons were based on the Tompkins models.

A contemporary account described him thus:

Mr. Tompkins is not only one of the best-known engineers in the South, but is one of the best-equipped millmen in the entire country, North or South. The mills which he has built rank among the finest in existence.

Tompkins was also active in management of the textile industry. He was a founder of the High Shoals Textile Company in Gaston County, North Carolina in 1893. The mill building and operatives' houses at High Shoals were probably designed by Tompkins. Tompkins was appointed to the Board of Trustees of North Carolina College of Agriculture and Mechanic Arts in 1893. Tompkins was identified as president of the Charlotte Sanatorium Company in 1907.

South Carolina projects:

Ca. 1895: Edgefield Manufacturing Company, Edgefield (*Cotton Mills, Commercial Features*, Fig. 19, opposite p. 34.)

Ca. 1895: Fairfield Cotton Mills, Winnsboro (*Cotton Mills, Commercial Features*, Fig. 22, opposite p. 40.)

Ca. 1895: Norris Cotton Mills, Norris (*Cotton Mills, Commercial Features*, Fig. 24, opposite p. 44.)

1897-1898: Textile School Building, Clemson College, Clemson; $8000 (Winston, pp. 187-195; *MR*, 1 April 1898, p. 176; 16 September 1898, p. 124; *The Southern Architect*, May 1898, p. 453.)

1901-1902: Mill Building, Engine House, Boiler Room, and Annex, Royal Bag and Yarn Manufacturing Company, Charleston (*MR*, 7 February 1901, p. 53.)

Sources: Kim Withers Brengle, *The Architectural Heritage of Gaston County, North Carolina* (Gastonia: Gaston County, 1982), pp. 16, 20-21, 37, 132; Charlotte, North Carolina, city directories; *MR*, various citations; Daniel A. Tompkins, *Cotton Mills, Commercial Features. A Text-Book for the Use of Textile Schools and Investors* (Charlotte, North Carolina: Observer Printing House, 1899); George Tayloe Winston, *A Builder of The New South: Being the Story of the Life Work of Daniel Augustus Tompkins* (Garden City and New York: Doubleday, Page & Co., 1920.)

TROTT, Henry R. (active 1921-1937) Henry R. Trott, an associate of H. Olin Jones (q.v.) in Greenville from 1921 through 1926, opened his own office by 1929. He was appointed to the South Carolina State Board of Architectural Examiners in 1936, but died shortly thereafter.

South Carolina projects:

1921-1926: See **Jones, H. Olin** (Jones & Trott)

1929: W.S. Griffin Jr. Residence, Greenville (*MR*, 12 December 1929, p. 87.)

Sources: Greenville city directories; *MR*, various citations; Petty, pp. 119, 133.

TROWBRIDGE, Silas Duncan (1885- ca. 1940) Trowbridge was born in Greenville and educated at Furman University. He took a "special course in architecture" at Columbia University in New York, and began architectural practice in Atlanta, Georgia in 1909. In 1927 he was described as a specialist in the construction of apartments and hotels. A $140,000 dormitory at the Georgia Institute of Technology (1920) was among Trowbridge's largest projects in Georgia.

Trowbridge lived in Piedmont, South Carolina, in 1940, when he was still registered for practice in the state.

South Carolina projects:

1915: G.H. and W.A. Williams Store Building, Greenville (*MR*, 25 November 1915, p. 60.)

1917: First National Bank and Piedmont Savings & Trust Company Bank Building, Greenville; $35,000 (*MR*, 15 March 1917, p. 74.)

1917: N.C. Poe Store Building, Greenville (*MR*, 27 September 1917, p. 75.)

1918: Thos. G. Crymes Residence, Greenville (*MR*, 23 May 1918, pp. 77-78.)

1924: Clinton C. Jones Apartment House, Manly Street, Greenville; $85,000 (*MR*, 3 April 1924, p. 153; 1 May 1924, p. 154.)

Ca. 1930: William K. Charles Residence, Calhoun Avenue, Greenwood vicinity (Survey files, S.C. Archives.)

1931: C. Grantville Wyche Residence, Greenville (*MR*, 14 May 1931, p. 60.)

Sources: *MR*, various citations; *Who's Who in the South*, 1927, p. 730.

TRUMBAUER, Horace D. (1868-1938) Horace Trumbauer was among the most prolific and prominent architects practicing in Philadelphia in the early twentieth century. He attained an international repututation. Among his most noted work was the new Duke University campus in Durham, North Carolina, 1924-1938. Trumbauer designed many large country houses in the eastern United States. His 1929 hunting lodge project for Franklin L. Hatta in South Carolina was part of the regional pattern of wealthy northern patrons establishing estates in the southern tidewater.

South Carolina project:

1929: Franklin L. Hatta Hunting Lodge, Charleston County (Tatman/Moss, p. 807.)

Sources: Hewitt, p. 283; *Macmillan Encyclopedia*, Vol. IV, p. 230; Tatman/Moss, pp. 799-807; Withey, pp. 607-608; Wodehouse, p. 203.

TURNER, Joseph C. (active 1892-1902) Joseph C. Turner of Augusta, Georgia was the architect of the magnificent Sumter City Hall and Opera House, built in 1892-1893. The building is a monumental stone and brick structure in the Richardsonian Romanesque style, with a prominent tower dominating Sumter's Main Street. Turner was active in Augusta through 1902, after which time he appears to have relocated to Birmingham, Alabama. In Augusta, the five-story Leonard Phinizy Office Building, contracted at $29,000 in 1899, was designed by Turner.

South Carolina projects:

1892-1893: City Hall and Opera House, Sumter; $26,000 (*MR*, 30 December 1892, p. 450; 24 March 1893, p. 155; 11 August 1893, p. 35; 6 October 1893, p. 173.)

1898: School, Beech Island (*The Southern Architect*, July 1898, p. 501.)

Sources: Augusta, Georgia city directories; *MR*, various citations, *Architects and Builders in Georgia*.

UNDERWOOD, H.A. (active 1922-1940) H.A. Underwood of Raleigh, North Carolina, architect and engineer, provided plans for Columbia's twelve-story Barringer Hotel in 1929-1930. Lafaye & Lafaye of Columbia (q.v.) were associated architects for this $500,000 project. Underwood's work in North Carolina included the ten-story Carolina Hotel in Raleigh (1926-1928.) He was also architect for several buildings at state colleges and training schools in North Carolina.

Sources: *MR*, 12 December 1929, p. 87; 6 March 1930, p. 109; 5 June 1930, p. 90; 25 September 1930, p. 68.

UPJOHN, Hobart Brown (1876-1949) Hobart Upjohn was the son of architect Richard Michell Upjohn, and grandson of architect Richard Upjohn. He studied architecture at Stevens Institute of Technology, and worked in his father's office for several years before opening his own practice in New York City.

Upjohn's work included several buildings at North Carolina State University in Raleigh and Salem Academy in Winston-Salem, as well as many churches in North Carolina.

Upjohn was a prominent society figure in New York. He worked for several years as assistant principal of architectural engineering with the International Correspondence Schools in Scranton, Pennsylvania, and he wrote textbooks on architecture for the ICS.

South Carolina project:

1924: Parish House, Trinity Protestant Episcopal Church, Sumter and Senate streets, Columbia; $103,045 (Cornerstone; *MR*, 9 October 1924, p. 117; *Southern Architect and Building News*, February 1928, pp. 41, 43, 45.)

Sources: *American Art Annual*, Vol. 21, p. 472; *The Architectural Record*, May 1933, p. 322; *The National Cyclopaedia of American Biography*, Volume C (New York: James T. White & Co., 1930), p. 400; *Who Was Who in America*, Vol. 2 (Chicago: The A.N. Marquis Co., 1950), p. 543; Wodehouse, p. 273.

URQUHART, James Burwell (1876-1961) James B. Urquhart, a native of Southampton County, Virginia, was educated in civil engineering at Virginia Polytechnic Institute, receiving his degree in 1897. He was employed in railroad work for several years before coming to Columbia, South Carolina, around 1901, where he took a position as draftsman with Charles C. Wilson (q.v.)

Urquhart and Edwin Sompayrac (q.v.) became associates in Wilson's firm in 1907. Wilson, Sompayrac & Urquhart had a thriving practice for four years. John Carroll Johnson (q.v.), a designer who would later associate with Urquhart, joined the office in 1910. Urquhart left the firm later that same year to establish his own architectural and engineering practice in Columbia.

Among Urquhart's early designs, the (destroyed) Laurens Union Depot, built ca. 1912, was unique. Insurance maps show the building as a triangular structure at the junction of two rail lines, with two-story polygonal towers at all three corners.

J. Carroll Johnson left Wilson's office in 1912 to associate with Urquhart. The firm of Urquhart & Johnson had a thriving practice in the years prior to the World War. Their most important commission was the 1915 Columbia High School Building. Johnson left the firm in 1917, and Urquhart maintained independent practice in Columbia.

Architect Wyatt Hibbs, who was chief designing architect in Urquhart's office from 1935 to 1941, described the senior architect:

> Mr. Urquhart was not trained in architectural design. I am not aware of any distinctive architectural design created by his hand. Mr. Urquhart was an engineer by education and his early experience, I believe, was in railroad engineering. He was a southern gentleman and well known in the right places. He was slender and had a well groomed, youthful appearance.

Hibbs also described Urquhart's role in the design process:

> Mr. Urquhart's participation in the design process in the period 1935-1941 was nil. Mr. Urquhart wrote the specifications. He travelled around the State with Jim Urquhart as chauffeur in their always new, current year, model, Chrysler, making inspections of buildings under construction. Mr. Urquhart did not criticize my design solutions. I do not recall receiving any compliments. Mr. Urquhart did not provide any sketch instructions, except those in the form of field sketches of floor plan arrangements of existing buildings. These records of field measurements were exceptionally good.

Urquhart worked with the Columbia housing authority during the depression. Alex H. Dickson was associated with Urquhart during the 1940s and 1950s.

Prominent among Urquhart's projects were his school buildings. Some twenty-eight graded school, high school, and college buildings designed by Urquhart's firm between 1910 and 1932 have been identified.

South Carolina projects:

1907-1910: See **Wilson, Charles C.** (Wilson, Sompayrac & Urquhart)

1910-1911: Building, Columbia Hospital Association, Columbia; $45,000 (*MR*, 1 September 1910, p. 83; 2 March 1911, p. 81; "Well Known Architects.")

1911: New Marlboro Apartment House, Columbia; $15,000 (*MR*, 26 January 1911, p. 59; 9 February 1911, p. 66.)

1911: New Southern Apartment House, Columbia; $16,000 (*MR*, 9 February 1911, p. 66.)

1911: C.H. Mason Estate Business Building, Columbia; $32,450 (*MR*, 23 March 1911, p. 69.)

1911-1913: Sunday School Building, Ebenezer Lutheran Church, Columbia; $12,000 (*MR*, 30 March 1911, p. 68; *The State*, 15 June 1913, p. 16.)

Ca. 1911-1912: Laurens Union Depot, Laurens ("Well Known Architects.")

Ca. 1911-1912: Lutheran Church of the Ascension, 827 Wildwood Avenue, Eau Claire ("Well Known Architects.")

Ca. 1911-1912: Manson Building, 1207 Taylor Street, Columbia ("Well Known Architects.")

1912: Richard C. Keenan Apartment House and Store Building, Main Street and Elmwood Avenue, Columbia; $50,000 (*MR*, 27 June 1912, p. 70.)

1912-1914: Lutheran Publication Building (Eau Claire Town Hall), 3904 Monticello Road, Eau Claire ("Well Known Architects"; National Register files, S.C. Archives.)

Ca. 1912-1913: Walton H. Greever Residence, 4007 Ensor Street, Eau Claire ("Well Known Architects.")

Urquhart & Johnson

1913: Lutheran Survey Publishing Company Building, Eau Claire ("Well Known Architects"; National Register files, S.C. Archives.)

1913: Camden Hospital, Camden; $30,000 (*MR*, 10 April 1913, p. 74; 1 May 1913, p. 83; "Well Known Architects.")

1913: St. Paul's Lutheran Church, Columbia; $30,000; Abner A. Ritcher (q.v.), architect; J.B. Urquhart, associated architect (*MR*, 24 July 1913, p. 69; 31 July 1913, p. 68.)

1913: Consolidated Holding Company Store and Office Building, Columbia; $24,000 (*MR*, 24 July 1913, p. 70.)

1913: C.J. Cates Residence, Columbia; $4500 (*MR*, 27 November 1913, p. 64.)

1913: Thirty Dwellings, Columbia Building Company, Columbia; $4500-$5500 each (*MR*, 27 November 1913, p. 64.)

Ca. 1913: P.C. Price Residence, 1007 Hillcrest Street, Eau Claire ("Well Known Architects.")

Ca. 1913: Gibbes Machinery Company Factory, 1209 Wheat Street, Columbia; $75,000 ("Well Known Architects.")

1914: St. Timothy's Lutheran Church, Elloree; $12,000 (*MR*, 5 March 1914, p. 74.)

1914: Lorick & Lowrance Merchantile Building, Main Street, Columbia; $30,000 (*MR*, 12 March 1914, p. 73.)

1914: Bank of Elloree Building, Elloree; $4000 (*MR*, 30 July 1914, p. 65.)

1914: Elloree Warehouse Co. Cotton Warehouse, Elloree; $2000 (*MR*, 24 September 1914, p. 63.)

1915: Pastime Theater, Columbia (*The State*, 30 May 1915, p. 23.)

1915: Columbia High School, 1323 Washington Street, Columbia; $97,979 (*MR*, 16 September 1915, p. 67; 25 November 1915, p. 61.)

1915: A.F.A.M. Temple Building, Columbia; $34,000 (*MR*, 18 November 1915, p. 66.)

1915: Alan Johnstone Jr. Residence, Columbia; $4000 (*MR*, 25 November 1915, p. 60.)

1916: Manual Arts School Building, Chester; $10,000 (*MR*, 6 July 1916, p. 84.)

1916: Ridgewood Country Club Clubhouse, Columbia; $15,000 (*MR*, 20 January 1916, p. 66; 27 January 1916, p. 62.)

1916: B.F. Dent Residence, Columbia; $5000 (*MR*, 21 September 1916, p. 66 l.)

1916: Methodist Church, Elloree; $85,000 (*MR*, 13 April 1916, p. 69.)

James B. Urquhart

1919: School, Beaufort; $19,980 (*MR*, 24 July 1919, p. 130 h; 7 August 1919, p. 160; 14 August 1919, p. 125.)

1920: Rose Hill Presbyterian Church and Sunday School Building, Columbia; $16,000 (*MR*, 11 November 1920, p. 129.)

1921: Masonic Temple, 1230 Sumter Street, Columbia; $250,000 (Cornerstone; *MR*, 14 April 1921, p. 114.)

1921: School, Ridgeway; $27,000 (*MR*, 17 July 1921, p. 14.)

1922: Addition, South Carolina Baptist Hospital, Columbia; $50,000 (*MR*, 27 April 1922, p. 85; 17 August 1922, p. 86.)

1922: Addition, Columbia High School, Columbia; $78,000 (*MR*, 3 August 1922, p. 101.)

1923: J.W. McCormick Apartment House, Marion and Senate streets, Columbia; $65,000 (*MR*, 7 June 1923, p. 130 l.)

1923: Addition, School, Eastover (*MR*, 21 June 1923, p. 123.)

1924: High School, Beaufort (*MR*, 25 September 1924, p. 117; 2 October 1924, p. 143.)

1924: Negro School, Beaufort (*MR*, 25 September 1924, p. 117; 2 October 1924, p. 143.)

1924: School, Garner's Ferry Road, Columbia; $22,800 (*MR*, 5 June 1924, p. 140.)

1924: Science Building, Benedict College, Columbia; Hentz, Reid & Adler (q.v.), architects; J.B. Urquhart, associated architect (*MR*, 13 November 1924, p. 111.)

1924: W.H. Greever Building, Sumter Street, Columbia (*MR*, 9 October 1924, p. 121.)

1924: R.J. Byrum Store Building, Oak and Laurel streets, Columbia (*MR*, 11 December 1924, p. 99.)

1924: School, Horrell Hill; $11,250 (*MR*, 17 July 1924, p. 117.)

1924: High School, Lykesland (*MR*, 12 June 1924, p. 114.)

1924: A.F.A.M. Temple, Orangeburg; $41,000 (*MR*, 10 July 1924, p. 103.)

1924: Remodeling, Bank of Ridgeway Building, Ridgeway (*MR*, 17 April 1924, p. 117.)

1924: Lutheran Church Building, Saluda (*MR*, 11 September 1924, p. 105.)

1924: High School and repairs to Graded School, Walterboro; $50,300 (*MR*, 17 January 1924, p. 108.)

1925: Lutheran Church, Clinton (*MR*, 5 November 1925, p. 129.)

1925: Dr. S.B. Fishburne Residence, Terrace Way, Columbia (*MR*, 12 February 1925, p. 120.)

1925: Ashley C. Tobias Jr. Apartment Building, Gervais and Henderson streets, Columbia; $41,000 (*MR*, 17 September 1925, p. 115.)

1925: Forest Lake Country Club Clubhouse, Columbia; $25,112 (*MR*, 4 June 1925, p. 139.)

1925: Bellwood District School, Richland County; $12,000 (*MR*, 30 July 1925, p. 121.)

1926: Infirmary and Dining Hall, Richland County Almshouse, Columbia; $14,997 (*MR*, 6 May 1926, p. 132; 20 May 1926, p. 121.)

1926: Administration Building, Summerland College, Columbia; $39,364 (*MR*, 30 September 1926, p. 114.)

1926: High School, St. George (*MR*, 4 November 1926, p. 132.)

1926: Main Building and Dormitory, Home for Aged and Helpless, White Rock (*MR*, 20 May 1926, p. 123.)

1927: Wardlaw Junior High School, Elmwood Street, Columbia; $209,519 (*MR*, 20 January 1927, p. 121.)

1927: Orangeburg County Courthouse, Orangeburg; $135,000 (*MR*, 28 April 1927, p. 111.)

Ca. 1928: Mobley Residence, 1719 Heyward Street, Columbia (Weston Adams, Columbia.)

1929-1931: Ebenezer Lutheran Church, 1301 Richland Street, Columbia; $150,000; Thomas, Martin & Kirkpatrick (q.v.), architects; J.B. Urquhart, associated architect (Cornerstone; *MR*,

10 October 1929, p. 93; 17 October 1929, p. 95; *The State*, 4 October 1930.)

1929: Addition, High School, Columbia; $83,766 (*MR*, 7 November 1929, p. 101.)

1929: Addition, High School, Walterboro; $15,000 (*MR*, 19 December 1929, p. 90.)

1930: Shandon Junior High School (Hand School), Wheat and Woodrow streets, Columbia; $138,200 (*MR*, 2 January 1930, p. 86.)

1930: Addition, Hyatt Park School, Columbia; $42,573 (*MR*, 20 March 1930, p. 82.)

1930: Addition, Logan School, Elmwood Avenue, Columbia; $30,400 (*MR*, 10 April 1930, p. 87.)

1930: Wayne Street School, Columbia; $37,400 (*MR*, 22 May 1930, p. 83.)

1930: School, Columbia; $27,000 (*MR*, 24 July 1930, p. 79.)

1930: Methodist Church, Holly Hill; $25,000 (*MR*, 1 May 1930, p. 90.)

1930: Howell & Fishburne Office Building, Walterboro (*MR*, 23 October 1930, p. 58.)

1930-1931: Ellis Avenue School, Orangeburg; $59,229 (*MR*, 4 September 1930, p. 74; 27 November 1930, p. 58; Plaque on building.)

1931: Grammar School, Beaufort; $21,730 (*MR*, 24 December 1931, p. 35.)

1931: Sunday School, St. Paul's Lutheran Church, Columbia (*MR*, 12 February 1931, p. 57.)

1931: School, Columbia; $19,700 (*MR*, 16 July 1931, p. 52.)

1931: Cell Block, South Carolina State Penitentiary, Columbia; $41,472 (*MR*, 10 September 1931, p. 47.)

1931: Administration Building, Richland County School District No. 1, Columbia; $10,438 (*MR*, 24 December 1931, p. 35.)

1931: Gymnasium, Orangeburg; $24,600 (*MR*, 10 September 1931, p. 48; 7 September 1931, p. 46.)

1932: Manufacturing Building, South Carolina State Penitentiary, Columbia; $65,450 (*MR*, 19 May 1932, p. 35.)

1932-1933: Addition, Richland County Hospital (Columbia Hospital), Columbia; $62,108 (*MR*, 10 March 1932, p. 40; Cornerstone.)

Ca. 1935-1940: Byrnes Auditorium and School of Music, Winthrop College, Rock Hill ("Urquhart, Architect, Dies"; Hibbs.)

Ca. 1935-1940: Richland County Courthouse, 1237 Washington Street, Columbia ("Urquhart, Architect, Dies"; Hibbs.)

Ca. 1935-1940: Gymnasium and North Class Room Wing, Dreher High School, Columbia (Hibbs.)

Ca. 1935-1940: Gonzales Gardens Housing, Columbia (Hibbs.)

Ca. 1935-1940: Allen-Benedict Court Housing, Columbia (Hibbs.)

Ca. 1935-1940: Library, Benedict College, Columbia (Hibbs.)

Ca. 1935-1940: Drake Edwards Residence, Columbia (Hibbs.)

Ca. 1935-1940: Haltiwanger Residence, Columbia (Hibbs.)

Ca. 1939: University Terrace, Columbia (*The Architectural Record*, March 1939, p. 3.)

n.d.: Married Students' Building, University of South Carolina, Columbia ("Urquhart, Architect, Dies.")

n.d.: St. Andrews School, Columbia ("Urquhart, Architect, Dies.")

n.d.: Booker T. Washington High School, Columbia ("Urquhart, Architect, Dies.")

n.d.: Creighton School, Columbia ("Urquhart, Architect, Dies.")

n.d.: Kilbourne Road Elementary School, Columbia ("Urquhart, Architect, Dies.")

Sources: Columbia city directories; Dorothy Johnson, Columbia, unpublished research; Wyatt Hibbs, Norfolk, Virginia, to John Wells, 10 September 1983, 19 October 1983, 2 April 1984; *MR*, various citations; "Urquhart, Architect, Dies at 84," *The State*, 12 February 1961, p. 1; "Well Known Architects in New Building," *The Columbia Record*, 21 December 1913, p. 6.

VANCE, S.N. (active 1911-1913) S.N. Vance was active in Greenwood on a number of small projects in the period 1911-1913. In December of 1911 he wrote to Columbia architect J. Carroll Johnson (q.v.) that "we have enough work to keep me going in a rush." In 1913 Vance was associated with prominent Anderson architect Joseph H. Casey (q.v.) on three projects in Greenwood.

South Carolina projects:

1913: George W. Rush Residence, 123 Bailey Circle, Greenwood; J.H. Casey and S.N. Vance, associated architects; $6000 (*MR*, 3 April 1913, p. 82.)

1913: Bailey Military Academy Building, Greenwood; J.H. Casey and S.N. Vance, associated architects; $30,000 (*MR*, 10 April 1913, p. 74; 1 May 1913, p. 84.)

1913: D.A.G. Ouzts Residence, Greenwood; J.H. Casey and S.N. Vance, associated architects; $10,000 (*MR*, 24 April 1913, p. 74.)

Sources: Postcard, S.N. Vance to J. Carroll Johnson, 28 December 1911, in possession of Dorothy Johnson, Columbia, South Carolina; *MR*, various citations.

VATET, Oscar V. (1882? -1953) Oscar Vatet was working in the New York City offices of McKim, Mead & White from 1905 to 1906. He established his own architectural office at 15 E. 40th Street in New York shortly thereafter. Vatet was a partner in Vatet & Tissington in 1921. He worked later in Michigan.

South Carolina projects:

1913: First National Bank Building, Sumter; $40,000 (*MR*, 20 November 1913, p. 68; 27 November 1913, p. 64.)

1914-1915: First National Bank Building, Spartanburg; $27,500 (*MR*, 16 July 1914, p. 69; 17 December 1914, p. 56; 31 December 1914, p. 66; 14 January 1915, p. 57.)

Sources: *MR*, various citations; *Michigan Society of Architects Bulletin*, July 1953, p. 29; Moore, *McKim*, p. 335.

VIETT, Emile T. (active 1887-1912) Emile T. Viett was manager of the Viett Marble & Granite Works in Charleston, supplying tombstones and building materials. He was also listed as an architect in the Charleston city directories in 1898-1908. Samuel Lapham (q.v.) of Charleston, decrying the unrestricted use of the title "architect" in the early twentieth century, noted that "a tombstone cutter" and various other tradesmen "classified themselves as architects, along with their main activity" in city directories. Viett is presumed to have been the object of Lapham's scorn.

Sources: Charleston city directories; Petty, p. 6.

WALKER, Henry F. (active 1910-1923) Henry F. Walker was a professor at the College of Charleston and at the Porter Military Academy in 1905-1909. He began architectural practice in Charleston in 1909, and associated with Henry S. Burden (q.v.) by 1910. Walker & Burden were active through 1919. Walker worked in Charleston until 1923, after which time his name disappeared from the city directories.

South Carolina projects:

    1909: Thirty Houses, Navy-Yard Building and Investment Co., Chicora Place, Charleston; $50,000 (*MR*, 14 January 1909, p. 56; 21 January 1909, p. 60.)

    1909: Remodeling, South Carolina Medical College buildings, Charleston (*MR*, 8 July 1909, p. 63.)

    1909: Engine House, Board of Fire Masters, Charleston; $6970 (*MR*, 29 July 1909, p. 61.)

Walker & Burden

    1911: Improvements, Villa Margharita, Charleston; $6900 (*MR*, 27 July 1911, p. 72.)

    1911: Federal Imigration Station, Cooper River, Charleston; $60,000; James Knox Taylor (q.v.), supervising architect; Walker & Burden, architects (*MR*, 7 September 1911, p. 77.)

    1913: Williamsburg Presbyterian Church, Kingstree; $12,000 (*MR*, 22 May 1913, p. 69.)

    1915: National Bank of South Carolina, Sumter; $17,000 (*The State*, 28 January 1915, p. 3.)

    1915: E.A. Williams Residence, Charleston; $8000 (*MR*, 15 April 1915, p. 57.)

    1915: Church of the Redeemer and Harriet Pinckney Home for Seamen, N. Market Street, Charleston; $28,733 (*MR*, 10 June 1915, p. 50; 15 July 1915, p. 59.)

    1917: J.M. Truluck Hotel, Lake City; $18,000 (*MR*, 20 September 1917, p. 86.)

    1917: School, Charleston County; $3500 (*MR*, 6 September 1917, p. 95.)

    Sources: Charleston city directories; *MR*, various citations.

WALKER, Nat Gaillard (active 1909-1946) Nat Gaillard Walker began architectural and engineering practice in Rock Hill ca. 1909. He designed residences, schools, churches, and other small buildings in north central South Carolina through 1925. Walker's largest projects included schools in Barnwell (1914) and Clover (1921), and the 1924 Orangeburg Hospital Administration Building. He served as president of the South Carolina chapter of the A.I.A. in 1921-1922.

In 1910 Walker worked with a partner named Jones. Walker was associated with J. Herbert Johnson of Sumter (q.v.) for the 1915 Girls' High School, the 1916 Carnegie Library, and two store buildings for Neill O'Donnell, all in Sumter. In 1925-1926 Walker was associated with Charlotte, North Carolina architect Leonard L. Hunter; the firm Walker & Hunter had offices in Charlotte and in Fort Myers, Florida. Walker's address was listed as Fort Myers.

Walker transferred his A.I.A. membership to Florida in 1928. He was president of the Florida Association of Architects from 1929 to 1930. He was named a Fellow of the A.I.A. in 1934.

During the Depression Walker sought alternative work with the United States Postal Service. He was postmaster in Fort Myers, Florida, in 1933-1934. Walker was the architect for the new post office building that was dedicated in Fort Myers in 1933.

South Carolina projects:

    1909: R.L. Sturgis Residence, Rock Hill (*MR*, 8 July 1909, p. 64.)

    1909: School, Carhartt Cotton Mills, Rock Hill (*MR*, 30 September 1909, p. 68.)

    1909: Charles S. Cobb Business Building, Rock Hill (*MR*, 28 October 1909, p. 126; 25 November 1909, p. 66.)

    1909: R.M. London Business Building, Rock Hill; $12,000 (*MR*, 25 November 1909, p. 66; 2 December 1909, p. 83.)

    1909: First National Bank Building, Sharon; $10,000 (*MR*, 20 May 1909, p. 61; 27 May 1909, p. 66; 24 June 1909, p. 57.)

1909: Masonic Hall, Winnsboro; $3650 (*MR*, 19 November 1909, p. 69; 25 November 1909, p. 66.)

1909: Remodeling, York County Jail, Yorkville; $4100 (*MR*, 14 January 1909, p. 58; 24 June 1909, p. 59.)

1910: Rock Hill Water & Electric Company Office Building, Rock Hill; Jones & Walker (q.v.), Rock Hill, architects (*MR*, 21 April 1910, p. 70.)

1911: L.A. Niven Residence, Rock Hill (*MR*, 9 March 1911, p. 66.)

1914: School, Barnwell; $23,000 (*MR*, 6 August 1914, p. 75.)

1914: Limestone Baptist Church Building, Gaffney; $8000 (*MR*, 18 June 1914, p. 70.)

1915: Remodeling, City Hall, Rock Hill (*MR*, 17 April 1917, p. 57.)

1915: Girls' High School, Sumter; $23,750; Nat Gaillard Walker and J. Herbert Johnson (q.v.), architects (*MR*, 16 September 1915, p. 67; 30 September 1915, p. 59.)

1916: Two Store Buildings, Neill O'Donnell, Sumter; $25,175; Nat Gaillard Walker and Johnson & Deal (q.v.), architects (*MR*, 30 March 1916, p. 67; 6 April 1916, p. 83.)

1916: Sumter Carnegie Library, Sumter; $7500; Nat Gaillard Walker and J. Herbert Johnson (q.v.), architects (*MR*, 22 June 1916, p. 68; 13 July 1916, p. 65; George S. Bobinski, *Carnegie Libraries: Their History and Impact on American Public Library Development* (Chicago: American Library Association, 1969), p. 237.)

1921: School, Clover; $30,000 (*MR*, 7 July 1921, p. 114; 14 July 1921, p. 107.)

1924: W.L. Craig Residence, Chester (*MR*, 22 May 1924, p. 112.)

1924: Administration Building, Orangeburg Hospital, Orangeburg; $35,000 (*MR*, 26 June 1924, pp. 112-113.)

1924: A.W. Huckle Residence, Rock Hill (*MR*, 10 April 1924, p. 110.)

1925: Parish House/Assembly Hall, Church of the Holy Comforter, Sumter; $11,999 (*MR*, 26 February 1925, p. 117.)

Walker & Hunter

1925: Methodist Church, Mount Holly (*MR*, 17 September 1925, p. 113.)

1925: Grace Lutheran Church, Rock Hill; $30,000 (*MR*, 27 August 1925, p. 102.)

Sources: Charlotte, North Carolina, city directories; Karl H. Grismer, *The Story of Fort Myers* (St. Petersburg, Florida: St. Petersburg Printing Co., Inc., 1949), pp. 241-242, 262; *MR*, various citations; Petty, pp. 135, 146; George L. Pfeiffer, "History of Organization of the Florida Association of Architects, Now a Chartered Body," in *Yearbook of Current Architecture in Florida* (n.p.: Florida Association of Architects, 1933), p. 2; Rock Hill city directories.

WALLIN, Henrik (1873-1936) Henrik Wallin, a native of Sweden, was educated in France and Italy before coming to the United States. Wallin worked in New York for several years, and went to Savannah to work with Hyman Witcover (q.v.) He pursued a career in Savannah from ca. 1906 through the 1930s. Wallin was associated with Warren Young in 1906-1913; with E. Lynn Drummond (q.v.) in 1919-1920, and with Arthur Comer in 1923-1928. The $500,000, Spanish-Renaissance style Hotel Georgia (1912-1913) and the ten-story, $500,000 Realty Building (1924) were among Wallin's major projects in Savannah.

South Carolina projects:

1930: Remodeling, Harrietta House (Shonnard Residence), Charleston County (Stoney, *Plantations of the Carolina Low Country*, p. 72.)

Sources: *MR*, various citations; Morgan, pp. 102, 105; Samuel Gaillard Stoney, Albert Simons, and Samuel Lapham, Jr., *Plantations of the Carolina Low Country* (Charleston: The Carolina

Art Association, 1938: rev. ed., 1955, 1964), p. 72; *Architects and Builders in Georgia.*

WALTER, Frank C. (1869- ca. 1955) Frank C. Walter, a native of Missouri, was active in South Carolina, Florida, Georgia, and Oklahoma in the early twentieth century. He was associated with Artemus E. Legare (q.v.) in Columbia as Walter & Legare, Architects, in 1900-1901. The firm prepared plans for a number of small buildings in various South Carolina communities, and designed several buildings in Florida as well. Prominent among their Florida designs was the $25,000 First Christian Church at Hogan and Monroe streets, in Jacksonville, built 1901-1903.

In March 1901 Walter & Legare were chosen as architects for a mess hall at the South Carolina College in Columbia, and the more established architects Wilson & Edwards (q.v.) were named supervising architects for the project. Shortly thereafter, William Augustus Edwards (q.v.) of Wilson & Edwards allied himself with Walter, and the firm Edwards & Walter practiced in Columbia from 1902 to 1908. In 1908 the firm moved to Atlanta, Georgia, taking as third partner a man named Parnham (q.v.) Parnham left within the same year, and Edwards & Walter maintained the Atlanta office through 1910.

Walter practiced independently in Atlanta in 1911-1912. His whereabouts in the years 1913-1924 are uncertain. He was working as an architect in Tulsa, Oklahoma from 1924 through 1931. Among his work in Oklahoma was the eight-story, $500,000 L.E. Abbott & Co. Department Store in Tulsa, 1929. Walter was employed as building commissioner and plumbing inspector in Augusta, Georgia, from 1947 through 1951.

South Carolina projects:

Walter & Legare

1901: Bank of Brunson Building, Brunson (*MR*, 2 May 1901, p. 280; 9 May 1901, p. 300; 16 May 1901, p. 318.)

1901: Robert Moorman Residence, Columbia; $5000 (*MR*, 7 February 1901, p. 53.)

1901: Col. John D. Frost Residence, Columbia; $5000 (*MR*, 7 February 1901, p. 53.)

1901: Steward's Hall Building, South Carolina College, Columbia; $9000 (*The State*, 16 March 1901, p. 8; *MR*, 21 March 1901, p. 174.)

1901: Rev. S.C. Byrd Residence, Columbia; $3000 (*MR*, 3 October 1901, p. 184.)

1901: Mrs. A.S. Robertson, three dwellings, Columbia; $3000 (*MR*, 3 October 1901, p. 184.)

1901: Remodeling, F.H. Hyatt Residence, Columbia; $4000 (*MR*, 3 October 1901, p. 184.)

1901: Mrs. A.I. Robertson Store Building, Columbia; $4500 (*MR*, 3 October 1901, p. 184.)

1901: P.H. Edwards Hotel, Florence; $20,000 (*MR*, 4 July 1901, p. 456; 18 July 1901, p. 491.)

1901: Remodeling, Central Hotel, Florence (*MR*, 18 July 1901, p. 491.)

1901: Jas. McPherson Office and Store Building, Greenville (*MR*, 11 July 1901, p. 473.)

1901: J.F. Alman Store and Office Building, Jonesville; $5000 (*MR*, 3 October 1901, p. 184.)

1901: Col. George Johnstone Residence, Newberry; $3500 (*MR*, 16 May 1901, p. 318.)

1901: Remodeling, Carolina Hotel, Rock Hill (*MR*, 25 July 1901, p. 16.)

1902-1910: See **Edwards, William A.** (Edwards & Walter; Edwards, Walter & Parnham)

Sources: Atlanta, Georgia, city directories; Augusta, Georgia city directories; 1900 Federal Census, Richland County, South Carolina; Columbia city directories; Patricia Golgart, Augusta-Richmond County Public Library, Augusta, Georgia, to Robert E. Dalton, 1983; Sally Hanford, American Institute of Architects, to Robert E. Dalton, 5 March 1981; Lexie Hopkins, Board of Governors of Licensed

Architects of Oklahoma, Oklahoma City, to Robert E. Dalton, 12 May 1983; Jacksonville, Florida, *Times-Union & Citizen*, 11 August 1901, p. 11, and 8 September 1901, p. 3; *MR*, various citations; *Reports and Resolutions of the General Assembly of the State of South Carolina 1906* (Columbia: Gonzales and Bryan, 1906), pp. 273-338; Tulsa, Oklahoma, city directories; Frank C. Walter, Commissioner of Building, Augusta, Georgia, to Leonard H. Bailey, Oklahoma City, Oklahoma, 15 September 1949.

WARD, William Riddle (1890-1984) William R. Ward, a native of Eutaw, Alabama, was educated at Auburn University. He worked as a draftsman for the New York firm of Hill & Stouth. Haskell H. Martin (q.v.) met Ward in New York and persuaded him to come to Greenville, South Carolina, where they were associated from 1916 to 1925. From 1925 until his retirement in 1957, Ward pursued independent practice in Greenville and surrounding communities. His prominent commissions included the "Mediterranean type" Tyler Hospital of 1926, and the 1929 Laurens City Hall. He was remembered for his Colonial Revival and Georgian Revival residences in Greenville. Over a dozen residences in Greenville's fashionable Crescent Avenue neighborhood, and some 133 residences statewide, are attributed to Ward.

Ward was described by an employee, Robert Farmer, as "a typical, meticulous old bachelor" who maintained strict standards in the drafting room. "He was looking over your shoulder the whole time." W.E. Freeman, another Ward draftsman, recalled that "He [Ward] thought the profile of a moulding was terribly important. I would draw it, and he would come in and erase the whole thing and do it over again for me."

South Carolina work:

1916-1925: See **Martin, Haskell Hair** (Martin & Ward)

1926: Z.T. Cody Residence, Earle Street, Greenville; $15,000 (*MR*, 9 September 1926, p. 110.)

1926: Reconstruction, Tyler Hospital, E. North Street, Greenville (*MR*, 15 July 1926, p. 101.)

1927: Parsonage, First Baptist Church, N. Main Street, Greenville; $22,500 (*MR*, 10 February 1927, p. 107; 17 February 1927, p. 117.)

1927: W.D. Parrish Residence, McDaniel Avenue, Greenville; $15,000 (*MR*, 24 November 1927, p. 108; 1 December 1927, p. 109.)

1927: A.L. Strauss Residence, Greenville; $22,000 (*MR*, 1 December 1927, p. 109.)

1927: Nurses' Home, City Hospital, Greenville; $24,000 (*MR*, 10 November 1927, p. 115; 17 November 1927, p. 108.)

1927: Addition, Brandon Grammar School, Greenville; $50,000 (*MR*, 16 June 1927, p. 116.)

1928: W.E. Greer Residence, Belton; $11,500 (*MR*, 29 March 1928, p. 91.)

1929: Laurens City Hall, Laurens (*MR*, 29 August 1929, p. 78.)

1931: Waddy Thompson Residence, Greenville; $12,000 (*MR*, 2 April 1931, p. 58.)

1931: A.L. Lewis Residence, Ridgeland Avenue, Cleveland Terrace, Greenville; $16,000 (*MR*, 3 September 1931, p. 48.)

1931: J.H. Johnson Residence, 18 Atwood Street, Greenville; $10,000 (*MR*, 24 September 1931, p. 43.)

Ca. 1950: Fidelity Federal Savings & Loan Building, Greenville (*South Carolina Magazine*, October 1950, p. 21.)

Ca. 1950: Hugh Aiken Residence, Greenville (*South Carolina Magazine*, January 1952, p. 28.)

Ca. 1950: James A. Mattison Residence, Belton (*South Carolina Magazine*, January 1952, p. 35.)

Ca. 1950: Elks Club, Greenville (*South Carolina Magazine*, January 1952, p. 42.)

Sources: Alyce Atkinson, "Willie Ward: Architect left a legacy of style and quality in Greenville," *The Greenville News and Greenville Piedmont*, 8 April 1984, p. 1-F; Greenville city directories; Koyl, p. 586; *MR*, various citations; Petty, p. 146.

WARING, George Walker (1864-1943) George Waring, son of contractor and brickmason Clark Waring, was active as a contractor and builder in Columbia for many years. George Waring attended Columbia Male Academy and entered South Carolina College in 1880. He later studied architecture at the Cooper Institute in New York City. Waring was contractor for many buildings across South Carolina from 1890 to 1942. He was also listed as an architect in the city directories from 1891-1893, and for several years thereafter as a supplier of lumber and building supplies. As contractor, Waring worked with most of Columbia's leading architects. He built the 1904 Taylor School in Columbia (Edwards & Walter, architects), the 1907 Newberry County Courthouse (Frank P. Milburn, architect), and the 1915 Columbia High School (Urquhart & Johnson, architects.)

Sources: Columbia city directories; *MR*, various citations; Moore, Vol. 7.

WAYNE, Daniel G. (active 1880-1895) Daniel G. Wayne was active as a carpenter, builder, and architect in Charleston in the late nineteenth century. He is credited with the design of three fire stations in the city. The stations, all of which survive, are substantial brick buildings with bold semicircular-arched engine ports.

South Carolina projects:

Ca. 1887: Fire Station, Meeting Street at Wentworth Street, Charleston (*News & Courier*, 7 September 1981.)

Ca. 1887: Fire Station, Cannon Street, Charleston (*News & Courier*, 7 September 1981.)

Ca. 1887: Fire Station, 116 Meeting Street, Charleston (*News & Courier*, 7 September 1981.)

Sources: Charleston city directories; *News & Courier*, 7 September 1981.

WENDELL, Henry Ten Eyck (active 1880-1917) Henry Ten Eyck Wendell was a much-traveled architect who worked in cities across the nation in the late 19th and early 20th centuries. He was educated at Cornell University and in Europe. Wendell worked in Denver, Colorado, in the 1880s and 1890s. He had offices in Washington, D.C., in 1887, and in New York in 1883-1884 and in 1900.

Wendell came to Columbia, South Carolina, in 1905, where he associated with Charles C. Wilson (q.v.). Wilson & Wendell prepared plans for several public buildings in South Carolina. Wendell moved to Augusta, Georgia, ca. 1908, and worked there until his death in 1917.

South Carolina projects:

See **Wilson, Charles C.** (Wilson & Wendell)

Sources: Augusta, Georgia, city directories; Richard R. Bretel, *Historic Denver: The Architects and The Architecture 1858-1893* (Denver, Colorado: Historic Denver, Inc., 1973), pp. 158; Columbia city directories; James M. Goode, *Capital Losses: A Cultural History of Washington's Destroyed Buildings* (Washington, D.C.: Smithsonian Institution Press, 1979), p. 182; Morgan, pp. 92, 98, 100; Langdon E. Morris, Jr., *Denver Landmarks* (Denver, Colorado: Charles W. Cleworth, 1979), pp. 64-67, 242-243, 242-243, 276-277; Withey, pp. 643-644.

WENDEROTH, Oscar (1871-1938) Oscar Wenderoth was supervising architect of the United States Department of the Treasury in Washington, D.C. from 1912 to 1915. In this capacity, Wenderoth supervised the design and construction of federal buildings, including courthouses and post offices, across the nation. Buildings designed under his supervision included twelve post office projects in North Carolina, eleven in Tennessee, and thirteen in Georgia.

196

Wenderoth was born in Philadelphia. He was employed by the federal government in 1897 as a draftsman for the supervising architect's office. An 1899 drawing by Wenderoth for the Paterson, New Jersey Post Office shows a building with a splendidly ornamented tower and tall stepped gables, vaguely Dutch in inspiration. From 1909 to 1912 he worked for architects John Carrere and Thomas Hastings (q.v.) in New York. Wenderoth was appointed supervising architect by President Taft in 1912. He retired in 1915 owing to failing eyesight.

South Carolina projects:

1913-1914: Post Office, DeKalb Street, Camden (Cornerstone; *MR*, 21 May 1914, p. 72.)

1914: Post Office, Bennettsville (*MR*, 25 June 1914, p. 58.)

Sources: Lois Craig, *The Federal Presence: Architecture, Politics, and Symbols in United States Government Buildings* (Cambridge: The M.I.T. Press, 1972-1977), p. 200; Herndon, p. 195; *MR*, various citations; *New York Times*, 16 April 1938, p. 13; Smith, *The Office of the Supervising Architect*, p. 44.

WESSINGER, Jesse Walter (1895-1970) Jesse Wessinger was the son of Lexington County contractor Paul Jesse Wessinger. He was educated at Newberry College, graduating with a degree in engineering in 1916. Wessinger served with the American Expeditionary Forces, U.S. Army, in the First World War. He secured a position with Charles C. Wilson (q.v.) in 1919, and worked with Wilson through 1928.

Wessinger opened his own office in Columbia in 1929, in partnership with Robert C. Stork (q.v.), another former employee of Wilson. This partnership lasted through 1938. From 1938 to 1942 Wessinger was associated with J. Carroll Johnson (q.v.)

South Carolina projects:

Wessinger & Stork

1930: Smeltzer Hall, Newberry College, Newberry (*MR*, 15 May 1930, p. 81; Wallace, pp. 680, 708.)

1931: High School, New Brookland; $83,000 (*MR*, 18 June 1931, p. 53.)

1935: Lexington County Jail, Lexington (Cornerstone.)

1937: Educational Building, First United Methodist Church, Lancaster (Cornerstone.)

1938: Union High School, Union (Cornerstone.)

n.d.: G. Flavie Cooper Apartment Building, Columbia (Wallace, pp. 680, 708.)

n.d.: Dr. Ernest Cooper Apartment Building, Columbia (Wallace, pp. 680, 708.)

n.d.: Cayce Grammar School, Cayce (Wallace, pp. 680, 708.)

n.d.: Brookland Ice Plant, New Brookland (Wallace, pp. 680, 708.)

n.d.: P.C. Price Store, Columbia (Wallace, p. 708.)

n.d.: May C. Price Residence, Columbia (Wallace, pp. 708-709.)

n.d.: E.M. Ardworth Residence, Columbia (Wallace, p. 709.)

n.d.: O.G. Domy Apartment Building, Columbia (Wallace, pp. 680, 709.)

Wessinger & Johnson

1938: Sims College, University of South Carolina, Columbia (Dorothy C. Johnson, Columbia, South Carolina, unpublished research.)

1939: Lexington County Courthouse, Lexington (Cornerstone.)

Jesse W. Wessinger

1947: Mount Tabor Lutheran Church, West Columbia; $125,000 (*Construction*, December 1947, p. 52.)

1950: Brookland-Cayce Junior High School, Cayce (Koyl.)

1952: Library, Newberry College, Newberry (Koyl.)

1954: George Washington Carver School, Cordova (Koyl.)

1955: Lutheran Church of the Redeemer, Charleston (Koyl.)

1955: Cowpens High School, Cowpens (Koyl.)

1955: Shandon Church of Christ, Columbia (Koyl.)

1970: Addition, Lexington County Courthouse, Lexington (Plaque, Lexington County Courthouse.)

Sources: Columbia city directories; Koyl, p. 595; Wallace, *History of South Carolina*, Vol. 4, pp. 680, 708-709.

WESTON, F.A. (active 1904-1922) Weston pursued a modest architectural career in Greensboro, North Carolina, in the early twentieth century. He was, at various times, a partner in Weston & Hopkins, Rose & Weston, and Weston & Barton. Prominent among his Greensboro work were the six-story City National Bank Building, 1904; a six-story, $60,000 office building for Dr. C.W. Banner in 1911; and the 1922-1923 Carnegie Negro Library.

South Carolina projects:

1904: J.M. Jackson Store Building, Bennettsville; $10,000 (*Southern Architect and Building News*, 9 September 1904, p. 8.)

1904: E. Steinberger & Co. Department Store Building, Clio; $15,000 (*Southern Architect and Building News*, 9 September 1904, p. 8.)

1904: Bank of Clio, Clio; $3000 (*Southern Architect and Building News*, 9 September 1904, p. 8.)

1904: J.C. Carrington Residence, Clio; $4000 (*Southern Architect and Building News*, 9 September 1904, p. 8.)

1904: Charles Manning Residence, Clio; $2500 (*Southern Architect and Building News*, 9 September 1904, p. 8.)

1904: G.A. Lemmeon Residence, Sumter; $3500 (*Southern Architect and Building News*, 9 September 1904, p. 8.)

Sources: *MR*, various citations; *Southern Architect and Building News*, various citations.

WETMORE, James Alphonso (1863-1940) James A. Wetmore, a native of Bath, New York, entered the United States Department of the Treasury in Washington, D.C. in 1885 as a stenographer. In 1908 Wetmore was identified as chief of the Law and Records Division. He acquired power steadily in the Department, and in 1912-1913 and 1915-1932 he served as acting supervising architect of the Treasury Department. In this capacity Wetmore was responsible for the design of federal buildings, including courthouses and post offices, across the nation.

South Carolina post office buildings designed under Wetmore's supervision are competent but uninspired Georgian Revival compositions, usually red brick with concrete trim. The 1930 Spartanburg Federal Building is the largest and most distinguished of the lot. The design of these buildings is attributed to the department's qualified architects, especially Louis Simon (q.v.)

South Carolina projects:

1917: Post Office, Beaufort (*MR*, 19 July 1917, p. 78.)

1917-1920: Post Office, Gervais and Sumter streets, Columbia; James A. Wetmore, Supervising Architect; Hugh E. White (q.v.), architect; $265,000 (*MR*, 9 August 1917, p. 73; 8 November 1917, p. 79; 16 September 1920, p. 139.)

1917: Repairs, Post Office, Greenville (*MR*, 4 October 1917, p. 94.)

1917: Post Office, Marion (*MR*, 8 February 1917, p. 69.)

1922: Addition, Post Office, Charleston; $15,000 (*MR*, 24 August 1922, p. 84.)

1923: Addition, Post Office, Spartanburg; $10,850 (*MR*, 23 August 1923, p. 107; 29 November 1923, p. 100.)

1923-1924: Alterations, Courthouse and Post Office, Greenville; $42,485 (*MR*, 20 December 1923, p. 102; 10 January 1924, p. 119.)

1924: Post Office, Clinton; $43,000 (*MR*, 24 January 1924, p. 106.)

1925: Alterations, Post Office, Anderson; $11,500 (*MR*, 29 January 1925, p. 100.)

1927: Post Office, Lancaster; $75,000 (*MR*, 12 May 1927, pp. 103-104; 26 May 1927, p. 108; 28 July 1927, p. 104; 4 August 1927, p. 117.)

1929: Alterations, Courthouse and Post Office, Greenville (*MR*, 19 September 1929, p. 97.)

1930: Post Office, Hartsville (Cornerstone; *MR*, 23 January 1930, p. 79.)

1930-1931: United States Courthouse and Post Office, Spartanburg; $350,000 (Cornerstone; *MR*, 18 December 1930, p. 54; 15 January 1931, p. 63.)

1931: United States Courthouse and Post Office, Rock Hill; $275,000 (Cornerstone; *MR*, 11 June 1931, p. 61; 25 June 1931, p. 51; 16 July 1931, p. 51; 6 August 1931, p. 54; 17 September 1931, p. 45.)

1932: Post Office, Cheraw; James A. Wetmore, supervising architect; Wilson & Tatum (q.v.), architects (Cornerstone.)

Sources: *American Architect*, Vol. XCIV, No. 1722, 1908, p. 214; *MR*, various citations; *The*

New York Times, New York, 15 March 1940, p. 23; Smith, *The Office of the Supervising Architect*, p. 44; *Who Was Who In America* (Chicago, Illinois: Marquis Who's Who. n.d.), Vol. 1, pp. 1325-1326.

WHALEY, Christopher L. (active 1908-1922) Christopher Whaley had a modest architectural practice in Augusta, Georgia from 1908 to 1922. He designed a number of smaller residences in these years. In 1913 Whaley was associated with Leonard L. Bellonby (q.v.) as Bellonby & Whaley; and this firm prepared plans for a 10-story, $250,000 hotel in Augusta.

South Carolina project:

1922: Catholic Church building, Shepard Street, Charleston; $17,250 (*MR*, 3 August 1922, p. 99; 10 August 1922, p. 87.)

Sources: Augusta, Georgia, city directories; *MR*, various citations.

WHALEY, William Burroughs Smith (1866-1929) W.B. Smith Whaley was an industrial developer, entrepenuer, inventor, engineer, and architect. He was described as "a pioneer in modern industrial methods, having to his credit the erection and outfitting of nearly all chief mill units in North Carolina and South Carolina." Whaley was born in Charleston and studied engineering at Bingham College in Stevens, New York, and at Cornell, where he received a degree in mechanical engineering in 1888. He worked in the office of D.N. Thompson, Architect, in Providence, Rhode Island, after graduating.

Whaley returned to South Carolina in 1892 and formed a partnership in Columbia with architect Gadsden E. Shand (q.v.) The firm, called W.B. Smith Whaley & Co., Architects and Engineers, was active in cotton mill design and construction, hydroelectric developments, water works, and general architectural practice in South Carolina and the southeast over the next ten years. Whaley's greatest mill was the 1899-1900 Olympia Mill outside of Columbia. Olympia was described in a contemporary account: "With its 100,000 spindles and 2400 looms, this will be the largest single mill in the United States."

Though this grand pile of brick and mortar is not equipped with marble floors -- as some who do not know have written -- yet the mill itself and its complement of machinery and of electrical apparatus has been a marvel to the practical mill men of the country.

The Olympia Mill factory boasts two great Romanesque stair towers offseting the enormous mass of the mill proper. Other exemplary textile mill buildings designed by Whaley were the Kendall Mill building in Camden, the Richland Mills building in Columbia, and the Avondale Mills building in Birmingham, Alabama.

Whaley's mill buildings followed the construction and compositional precepts developed in New England for textile mills. Fire prevention and control were the primary concerns; so the mills were built with solid masonry walls, with stair and elevator towers isolated from the body of the building. Interior framing was of "slow-burning construction," heavy timber posts and beams and thick hardwood floors, more resistent to fire than ordinary construction with its multitude of smaller beams and joists. Roofs were flat or shallow-pitched, without the firetrap potential of taller forms. The stairtowers of the Whaley mills were often delineated with Romanesque motifs, including Syrian arches, blind arcades, and Richardsonian terra-cotta ornamentation.

Whaley's firm favored Romanesque compositions and motifs for other buildings as well, especially The State building, a formidable structure with a quarry-faced granite facade commissioned in 1897. Gadsden Shand, who had designed the Richardsonian Canal Dime Savings Bank prior to joining Whaley, was probably responsible for the design of the State Building.

Whaley's own Columbia residence, built on Gervais Street in 1899, is a proud and dominant Queen Anne residence. The three-story building features a cylindrical turret with a conical roof. The 1899 John C. Moore residence in Columbia is a smaller but equally fascinating Queen Anne composition.

The State Legislature sought plans for the completion of the South Carolina State House in 1900. Whaley & Co. submitted a proposal which was defeated in favor of the plan of Frank Milburn (q.v.) Whaley's proposal would have built a tall central tower, similar to that proposed by the first architect of the State House, John R. Niernsee.

George E. Lafaye (q.v.), who later won prominence in independent practice in Columbia, worked with the Whaley firm as architectural designer from 1900 through 1903. Many of the firm's Columbia area projects were designed by Lafaye. When Whaley left Columbia in 1903, Lafaye and Shand formed a partnership to practice architecture and engineering.

In 1902 Whaley & Co. prepared plans for a twelve-story office building for the Carolina National Bank in Columbia. This project was never carried out. It would have been among the state's first skyscrapers; the first such project carried to completion was Edward Brite's 1900-1903 National Loan & Exchange Bank Building in Columbia.

Whaley pursued other vocations in addition to his engineering and architectural practice. He was president of the Columbia textile mills; for the Olympia Mills, Whaley developed a steam-powered electrical plant. Whaley was also an entrepenuer with the Columbia street railway system. A consortium headed by Whaley purchased the Columbia Electric Street Railway, Light & Power Company in 1899, and the system was rapidly expanded under the new directorship.

A branch office of W.B. Smith Whaley & Co. was opened in Boston, Massachusetts, in 1900, and in 1903 Whaley moved to Boston. He pursued a career in textile mill development and engineering in New England, New York, and Oklahoma in the following years. Around 1916 Whaley went to China, where he was connected with the Chinese-American Company. Whaley was later involved with the development of the diesel engine in New York, working under the company name Whaley Engine Patents Corporation. The Baldwin Motor Company, the Sun Ship Company, and the Ford Motor Company collaborated with Whaley's firm in this work.

Whaley was a frequent contributor of commentary and papers in technical journals, including the *Transactions of the American Society of Mechanical Engineers* and the *MR*, on such topics as electric power in cotton mills, the proposed Panama Canal, and sea-island cotton.

South Carolina projects:

1893-1894: Union Cotton Mill, Union ("Whaley and His Works.")

1893-1894: Courtney Cotton Mill, Newry ("Whaley and His Works.")

1894-1895: Richland Cotton Mill, Columbia ("Whaley and His Works.")

1896: Granby Cotton Mill, Columbia ("Whaley and His Works.")

1896: Enterprise Cotton Mill, Orangeburg (*MR*, 25 December 1896, p. 361; "Whaley and His Works.")

1897: Warren Cotton Mill, Warrenville (*Southern Architect and Building News*, February 1897, p. 80; "Whaley and His Works.")

1897: "The State" Building, Columbia (*The State*, 23 December 1897, Part II, p. 9.)

1898-1899: Y.M.C.A. Building, 1246 Main Street, Columbia (*MR*, 26 August 1898, p. 72; 13 January 1899, p. 429; *The State*, 24 February 1900, p. 12.)

1899: John C. Moore Residence, 1611 Hampton Street, Columbia; $5000 (*MR*, 28 April 1899, p. 234.)

1899: Capital City Cotton Mill, Columbia ("Whaley and His Works.")

1899: Buffalo Cotton Mill, Union County ("Whaley and His Works.")

1899-1900: William Burroughs Smith Whaley Residence, 1527 Gervais Street, Columbia (National Register files, S.C. Archives.)

1899-1900: Olympia Cotton Mill, Columbia (*The Bricklayer and Mason*, Vo. II, No. 3, 20 September 1899, p. 20; *MR*, 31 May 1900, p. 321; 17 January 1901, p. 427; "Whaley and His Works.")

1900: Lancaster Cotton Mills, Lancaster ("Whaley and His Works.")

1900: DeKalb Cotton Mill, Camden ("Whaley and His Works.")

1900: Seneca Cotton Mill, Seneca ("Whaley and His Works.")

1900: Williamston Cotton Mill, Williamston ("Whaley and His Works.")

1900: Inman Cotton Mill, Inman ("Whaley and His Works.")

1900: Glenn-Lowry Cotton Mill, Whitmire ("Whaley and His Works.")

1900: South Carolina State House Completion Project, Columbia (*The State*, 13 April 1900, p. 8.)

1900: Carolina National Bank Building, Columbia (*The State*, 7 June 1900, p. 5.)

1900: Columbia Electric Street Railway, Light & Power Company Assembly Street Substation, 1335 Assembly Street, Columbia (Pogue, *South Carolina Electric & Gas Co.*, pp. 51-52; Sloan, interview; *The State*, 16 April 1900, p. 8.)

1901: Farmers and Mechanics' Bank, Columbia; $30,000 (*MR*, 1 August 1901, p. 31.)

1901: Wm. H. Lyles Store Building, Assembly Street, Columbia (*The State*, 16 March 1901, p. 8.)

1901: Southside Baptist Church, Columbia; $5000 (*The State*, 20 October 1901, p. 5.)

1902: Carolina National Bank Building, Columbia (*MR*, 5 June 1902, p. 365.)

1903-1904: Wares Shoals Cotton Mill and Hydroelectric Plant, Ware Shoals ("Mr. Whaley's Work As A Cotton Mill Engineer"; "The Work at Ware's Shoals," *The State*, 24 January 1904, p. 20.)

n.d.: Palmetto Bank & Trust Company Building, Columbia (*The State*, 24 January 1904, p. 16.)

n.d.: F.H. Weston Residence, Columbia (*The State*, 24 January 1904, p. 16.)

n.d.: G.E. Shand Residence, Columbia (*The State*, 24 January 1904, p. 16.)

n.d.: Jno. P. Thomas, Jr., Residence, Columbia (*The State*, 24 January 1904, p. 16.)

n.d.: J.E. Lowry Residence, 1824 Senate Street, Columbia (*The State*, 12 March 1978.)

n.d.: Carolina Glass Factory ("Mr. Whaley's Work As A Mill Engineer.")

Sources: *American Biography: A New Cyclopedia* (New York, New York: The American Historical Society, Inc., 1930), Vol. XLII, pp. 367-368; Boston, Massachusetts, city directories; Columbia city directories; *Handbook of South Carolina* (Columbia: The State Company, 1907); *MR*, various citations; *New York Herald*, New York, N.Y., 28 February 1928, p. 1; "Mr. Whaley's Work as a Mill Engineer," *The State*, 23 November 1903, p. 5; Nell C. Pogue, *South Carolina Electric & Gas Company 1846-1964* (Columbia: The State Printing Co., 1964), pp. 51-52; Interview, Isabell Whaley Sloan (daughter of W.B.S. Whaley), Forest Acres, South Carolina, 14 August 1983; W.B.S. Whaley & Co., *Modern Cotton Mill Engineering* (Columbia, South Carolina: n.p., 1903); "Whaley and His Works," *The State*, 10 December 1900, p. 4; "What One Man Has Done," *The State*, 14 December 1897, p. 4.

WHEATON, Francis B. (active 1891-1918) Lieutenant Colonel Francis B. Wheaton of Washington, D.C. was first chief of the Engineering Division of the U.S. Quartermaster Corps' Construction Service. In this capacity he supervised preparation of plans for many buildings at military camps in the Southeast during the World War.

Wheaton had worked in the office of McKim, Mead & White before joining the Quartermaster Corps.

South Carolina projects:

1918: One Hundred Forty Barracks Buildings, 60 Kitchens, 60 Bathhouses, and other buildings, Camp Sevier, Greenville; $2,225,000; *MR*, 3 October 1918, p. 107; 10 October 1918, p. 90; 31 October 1918, p. 90.

Sources: Bethanie C. Grashof, *A Study of United States Army Family Housing Standardized Plans*, 5 volumes (Atlanta: Center for Architectural Conservation, 1986); *MR*, various citations; Moore, *McKim*, p. 330.

WHEELER, Oliver Duke (1864-1942) Wheeler was born in Freedom, New York, in 1864. He moved to Atlanta, Georgia, as a young man, and was active as a builder there for many years. He entered architectural practice as a partner of Luke Hayden ca. 1892. L.E. Schwend joined the firm in 1899.

Hayden, Wheeler & Schwend moved their primary offices to Charlotte, North Carolina, in 1899. The Presbyterian College Building at Charlotte, built in 1900-1901, was prominent among the firm's works. They maintained branch offices in Greensboro, North Carolina, and in Columbia, South Carolina, in 1901. Wheeler opened independent practice shortly thereafter, and took James M. McMichael (q.v.) as partner in 1901.

When McMichael opened his own architectural office, Wheeler formed a partnership with Neil Runge in Charlotte. Wheeler & Runge were joined by D. Anderson Dickey ca. 1905. Wheeler, Runge & Dickey had offices in Nashville, Tennessee, in 1907-1908, in addition to their primary Charlotte office.

The 1904-1905 Carnegie Library in Union was a small and elegant design by Wheeler & Runge. The building features a central octagonal dome over an Ionic portico *in antis*, with flanking pedimented pavilions. The building is ornamented with polychrome brickwork and terra-cotta.

The firm was reconfigured in 1909. Runge and Dickey opted for practice in Nashville, while C.F. Galliher and Eugene John Stern joined Wheeler's office in Charlotte. Galliher left to join Runge

& Dickey later that same year, and Wheeler & Stern pursued a profitable trade in Charlotte until the First World War. Stern, a native of Austria-Hungary, had studied architecture in New York City; and he practiced in Arkansas and Mexico after leaving Wheeler's office.

Wheeler was a member of the North Carolina State Board of Architectural Examination and Registration for a number of years. He died in 1942.

South Carolina projects:

1897-1901: See **Hayden, Luke** (Hayden & Wheeler; Hayden, Wheeler & Schwend)

Wheeler, McMichael & Co.

1901: School Building, Institution for Deaf & Blind, Cedar Springs; $20,000 (*MR*, 28 February 1901, p. 114; 9 May 1901, p. 300; 16 May 1901, p. 318; 27 June 1901, p. 437; 24 October 1901, p. 234.)

Wheeler & Runge

1902: City Hall, Gaffney (*MR*, 5 June 1902, p. 365.)

1903: Presbyterian Church, South Street, Union (*MR*, 12 February 1903, p. 79.)

1904: Library, Converse College, Spartanburg; $10,000 (*MR*, 24 March 1904, p. 217; 23 June 1904, p. 523.)

1904: Nicholson Bank Building, Union; $20,000 (*MR*, 7 April 1904, p. 267.)

1904: Carnegie Library, South Street, Union; $9980 (*MR*, 12 May 1904, p. 384; 19 May 1904, p. 411; 2 June 1904, p. 455; 30 June 1904, p. 547; George S. Bobinski, *Carnegie Libraries: Their History and Impact on American Public Library Development* (Chicago: American Library Association, 1969), p. 239.)

Wheeler, Runge & Dickey

1905: Chapel, Thornwell Orphanage, Clinton; $8000 (*MR*, 16 March 1905, p. 184.)

1905: G.P. Sloan Residence, Greenwood (*MR*, 23 March 1905, p. 206.)

1905: L.S. Townsend Residence, Union (*MR*, 23 March 1905, p. 207.)

1905: People's Supply Co. Building, Union (*MR*, 27 April 1905, p. 332.)

1905: W.H. Sartor Residence, Union (*MR*, 18 May 1905, p. 416.)

1907: Cherokee Avenue School, Gaffney; $11,500 (*MR*, 11 April 1907, p. 389; 18 April 1907, p. 423; 1 August 1907, p. 82; 29 August 1907, p. 182.)

1907: Remodeling, Central School, Gaffney; $5000 (*MR*, 11 April 1907, p. 389; 18 April 1907, p. 423; 1 August 1907, p. 82; 29 August 1907, p. 182.)

1907: Bethel M.E. Church South, Spartanburg; $15,600 (*MR*, 11 April 1907, p. 390; 2 May 1907, p. 489.)

Wheeler & Stern

1909: Cherokee Avenue Baptist Church, Gaffney; $25,000 (*MR*, 14 October 1909, p. 63; 11 November 1911, p. 64.)

1910: South Side Baptist Church, Spartanburg; $15,000 (*MR*, 3 February 1910, p. 80; 10 February 1910, p. 62.)

1911: Annex Building, Limestone College, Gaffney; $20,000 (*MR*, 28 September 1911, p. 67.)

1911: First Methodist Episcopal Church South, Sumter; $40,000 (*MR*, 3 August 1911, p. 82.)

1912: City National Bank Building, Main and Liberty streets, Sumter; $50,000 (*The State*, 3 February 1912, p. 2; *MR*, 8 February 1912, p. 67; 11 April 1912, p. 70.)

1912: Bank of Sumter, Sumter; $17,348 (*MR*, 25 April 1912, p. 70.)

1913: Methodist Episcopal Church, Bishop-ville; $40,000 (*MR*, 10 April 1913, p. 73.)

1914-1916: St. Paul's Methodist Episcopal Church, St. Matthews; $20,350 (Cornerstone; *MR*, 16 July 1914, p. 69.)

1915: Dr. J.N. Nesbitt Store, Limestone Street, Gaffney; $4000 (*MR*, 20 May 1915, p. 60; 3 June 1915, p. 70.)

Sources: "Death Takes O.D. Wheeler," *Charlotte News*, Charlotte, North Carolina, 28 October 1942, Section 2, p. 1; Herndon, p. 196; Koyl, p. 535; *MR*, 24 January 1901, p. 6, and various other citations.

WHITE, Columbus Bob (1857-1912) Columbus White was a black carpenter and contractor active in Laurens in the late 19th and early 20th centuries. He was born in slavery, and worked as a farmer, laborer and carpenter in his youth. He established a profitable professional career in Laurens as a contractor in the late 19th century. White is credited with the design of several buildings in Laurens.

South Carolina projects:

Ca. 1896: Mary Whitner Residence, 225 Caroline Street, Laurens (National Register files.)

Ca. 1910: St. Paul First Baptist Church, Laurens (National Register files.)

Ca. 1912: Bethel A.M.E. Church, Laurens (National Register files.)

Sources: A.B. Caldwell, ed., *History of the American Negro* (South Carolina Edition) (Atlanta, Georgia: A.B. Caldwell Publishing Company, 1919), pp. 610-612; National Register files, S.C. Archives.

WHITE, Edwin (active 1843-1890) Edwin I. (or J., or R.) White of Charleston was active as a surveyor and architect prior to the Civil War. He was managing a marble & granite works in Charleston in 1887-1888. In 1888, in association with Frank M. Niernsee (q.v.), White was appointed architect of the State House in Columbia. White died on 16 March 1890.

South Carolina projects:

1887: Charleston County Jail, Charleston (*MR*, 3 December 1887, p. 734.)

1888: Completion, South Carolina State House, Columbia; Edwin I. White and Frank M. Niernsee (q.v.), architects (*MR*, 18 February 1888, p. 23.)

Sources: Charleston city directories; *MR*, various citations; Ravenel, *Architects of Charleston*, p. 263.

WHITE, Hugh Edward (1869-1939) Hugh Edward White was born in Fort Mill in 1869. He began his career as an architect in Rock Hill around 1898. White took a position with the United States Department of the Treasury in 1903, keeping this position through 1918. He worked with James A. Wetmore (q.v.) in the design of the Federal Courthouse and Post Office at Gervais Street, Columbia, built in 1917-1921.

White worked in Gastonia, North Carolina, from 1919 to 1939. From 1922 to 1926 he was a partner in White, Streeter & Chamberlain. The 1922 Gastonia High School and the 1926 Gastonia City Hall were among his work in that city.

South Carolina projects:

1898: A. Friedheim Bros. Store Building, Rock Hill; $15,000 (*MR*, 22 April 1898, p. 228.)

1899: Eureka Cotton Mills Store, Chester; $3000 (*MR*, 14 July 1899, p. 424.)

1899: Baptist Church, Lancaster; $5000 (*MR*, 21 April 1899, p. 217; 14 July 1899, p. 425.)

1899: Dr. T.A. Crawford Residence, Rock Hill; $3000 (*MR*, 14 July 1899, p. 425.)

1900: Office Building and Store, Rock Hill (*MR*, 8 February 1900, p. 49.)

1901: Annex, Chester County Courthouse, Chester (*The State*, 8 March 1901.)

1902: School, Yorkville (*MR*, 19 June 1902, p. 409.)

1903: Dr. S.W. Pryor Hospital, Chester (*MR*, 12 March 1903, p. 163.)

1903: School, Chester; $8000 (*MR*, 20 August 1903, p. 89.)

1903: Springs Banking & Merchantile Co. Store and Warehouse, Heath Springs; $5000 (*MR*, 20 August 1903, p. 89.)

1907: C.M. Kuykendall Residence, Rock Hill (*MR*, 22 August 1907, p. 160.)

1907: R.A. Beall Residence, Rock Hill (*MR*, 22 August 1907, p. 160.)

1907: C.E. Coker Residence, Rock Hill (*MR*, 22 August 1907, p. 160.)

1917-1920: United States Post Office, Gervais Street, Columbia (*MR*, 9 August 1917, p. 73; 8 November 1917, p. 79; 16 September 1920, p. 139.)

1926: High School, Pageland; $50,000 (*MR*, 23 September 1926, p. 110.)

1929: High School, Clover; $50,000 (*MR*, 1 August 1929, p. 98.)

Sources: *American Art Annual*, Vol. 21, p. 479; Kim W. Brengle, *The Architectural Heritage of Gaston County, North Carolina* (Gastonia: Gaston County, 1982), pp. 30, 151, 171; *MR*, various citations; Petty, p. 146.

WHITTAKER, Miller Fulton (1892-1949) Miller F. Whittaker was one of South Carolina's first black architects. He had a long career as architect, engineer, and educator, in connection with the South Carolina Agricultural and Mechanical College in Orangeburg (later called South Carolina State College.)

Whittaker was born in Sumter, son of Johnson Chesnutt Whittaker and Page Harrison Whittaker. Johnson C. Whittaker, a prominent lawyer, had won national attention as a black cadet at the United States Military Academy at West Point. Miller F. Whittaker was educated at the South Carolina A and M College, and he received a bachelor of science in architecture degree at Kansas State College in 1913. In 1928 Whittaker won a master of science in architecture degree from Kansas State.

Whittaker was appointed to the faculty of South Carolina A & M College in 1913. He served as instructor in the Drawing and Physics Departments. From 1925 to 1932 Whittaker was dean of the Mechanical Arts Department; and in May of 1932 he became the third president of the institution, serving until his death in 1949. Under Whittaker's leadership the college established a Department of Law, a Reserve Officer's Training Corps, and other new disciplines. Whittaker also served as president of the National Conference of Land Grant Colleges in 1936-1937.

At various times Whittaker was referred to as the college architect for South Carolina A & M. He is credited with the design and supervision of construction for all buildings at the college built between 1916 and 1949. Whittaker's 1928 design for Hodge Hall was said to have been prepared as a master's thesis at Kansas State College.

Whittaker was one of the first professionally-trained black architects to practice in South Carolina. He was registered to practice in the state in 1918. He was also registered as an architect in Georgia in 1928, and during his career he is said to have designed buildings in Georgia and in North Carolina.

South Carolina projects:

1916: Morrill Hall, South Carolina State A & M College, Orangeburg (*MR*, 9 November 1916, p. 68; Potts, *South Carolina State College*, p. 60.)

1916: Bradham Hall, South Carolina State A & M College, Orangeburg (*MR*, 9 November 1916, p. 68; Potts, p. 60.)

1916: Manning Hall, South Carolina State A & M College, Orangeburg (*MR*, 9 November 1916, p. 68; Potts, p. 60.)

1917: Lowman Hall, South Carolina State A & M College, Orangeburg (Potts, p. 60.)

1918-1923: St. Michael's United Methodist Church, 116 Cheraw Street, Bennettsville (National Register files.)

1919: Williams Chapel A.M.E. Church, Glover Street, Orangeburg (Cornerstone.)

1920: White Hall, South Carolina State A & M College, Orangeburg (Potts, p. 61.)

1920: Jacob W. Lowman Hospital, South Carolina State A & M College, Orangeburg (Potts, p. 61.)

1924: Felton Training School and Teacherage, South Carolina State A & M College, Orangeburg (Potts, p. 61.)

1925: Marion Birnie Wilkinson Y.W.C.A. Hut, South Carolina State A & M College, Orangeburg (Potts, p. 61.)

1928: Home Economics Practice Home Building, South Carolina State A & M College, Orangeburg (Potts, p. 61.)

1928: Hodge Hall, South Carolina State A & M College, Orangeburg (Potts, p. 61.)

Ca. 1928: Trinity United Methodist Church, 185 Boulevard, Orangeburg (National Register files.)

1929: Creamery Building, South Carolina State A & M College, Orangeburg (Potts, p. 61.)

1929-1931: Dukes Gymnasium, South Carolina State A & M College, Orangeburg; John H. Blanche (q.v.), designer; Miller F. Whittaker, Architect (Cornerstone, Dukes Gymnasium; National Register files.)

Ca. 1929: House, 540 Amelia Street, Orangeburg (National Register files.)

1930: Garage and Poultry Plant Building, South Carolina State A & M College, Orangeburg (Potts, p. 61.)

Ca. 1930: Frank Limehouse Residence, 921 Russell Street, Orangeburg (National Register files.)

Ca. 1930: Wilkinson Residence, 1308 Russell Street, Orangeburg (National Register files.)

1932: Cafeteria, South Carolina State A & M College, Orangeburg (Potts, p. 61.)

Ca. 1948: East End Motors Building, Orangeburg (National Register files.)

1949: Orangeburg Lutheran Church, 610 Ellis Avenue, Orangeburg (National Register files.)

n.d.: Harry Daniels Residence, 1220 Russell Street, Orangeburg (National Register files.)

n.d.: Clinkscales Residence, 1226 Russell Street, Orangeburg (National Register files.)

n.d.: Staley Residence, 121 Wilkinson Avenue, Orangeburg (National Register files.)

n.d.: Dukes-Harley Funeral Home, Orangeburg (National Register files.)

Sources: *Catalog*, South Carolina State College, Orangeburg, Vol. LXVII, No. 3, June 1980, p. 1; National Register files, S.C. Archives; *MR*, various citations; John F. Potts, Sr., *A History of South Carolina State College 1896-1978* (Columbia: The R.L. Bryan Co., and Orangeburg: S.C. State College, 1978), pp. 60-61, 67; John F. Marszalek, "Whittaker, Johnson Chesnutt" and "Whittaker, Miller Fulton," in *Dictionary of American Negro Biography*, Rayford W. Logan and Michael R. Winston, editors (New York: W.W. Norton & Co., 1982), pp. 651-653; *The State*, 15 November 1949, pp. 1A, 12A.

WILBURN, Leila Ross (1885-1967) Leila Ross Wilburn was a pioneer female architect in the Southeast. She was educated at Agnes Scott Institute, and worked for Benjamin R. Padgett, architect and builder, before establishing her own architectural office in Atlanta, Georgia, in 1908. She specialized in residential design, and worked in several southeastern states. A large number of residences and apartment houses in Atlanta were designed by Wilburn be-

206

tween 1909 and 1928. The $18,000 Gordon Street Baptist Church building, designed in 1912, was among her larger commissions in Atlanta.

Wilburn advertised her designs in pattern books which were distributed across the Southeast. These books included *Southern Homes and Bungalows*, *Brick and Colonial Homes*, and *Ideal Homes of Today*. *Southern Homes and Bungalows* has photographs and plans for some ninety modest houses, described by the architect as "moderate cost residences where the influence of the English half-timber cottage, the Swiss Chalet and the Mission Bungalow is felt." The designs show a sense of efficiency and convenience, featuring compact halls, built-in furniture, large closets, and multiple bathrooms. Wilburn noted of these houses that:

> . . . all cozy corners and jig-saw work have been abolished, and in place is found such useful built-in furniture and artistic effects as book-cases, window seats, buffets, plate rails, concealed beds, ironing boards, colonnades and beamed ceilings.

Wilburn's designs included many variants of the bungalow style, as well as Colonial Revival and foursquare house types.

South Carolina projects:

1924-1927: William B. King Residence, 604 Elm Street, Conway (Survey files, S.C. Archives.)

Ca. 1926: Charley Webb Residence, 223 Jennings Avenue, Greenwood (Survey files, S.C. Archives.)

Sources: *MR*, various citations; Susan Hunter Smith, "Women Architects in Atlanta, 1895-1979," *The Atlanta Historical Journal*, Vol. XXIII, Number 4, Winter 1979-1980, pp. 85-108; *The State*, 31 January 1915, p. 3; *Who's Who in the South*, 1927, p. 774; Leila Ross Wilburn, *Southern Homes and Bungalows: A Collection of Choice Designs* (Atlanta, Georgia: Leila Ross Wilburn, 1914); Leila Ross Wilburn architectural drawings, Atlanta Historical Society, Atlanta, Georgia.

WILKINS, William J. (active 1891-1932) William J. Wilkins of Florence began his career as a contractor, builder, and architect by 1891. He served as inspector of buildings in Florence in 1900. In 1902 Wilkins was the contractor for the Romanesque-Revival Murchison School in Bennettsville, designed by Colorado architect John J. Huddart (q.v.)

Wilkins's career was materially advanced in 1906 when he pursuaded the Florence County School Board to give him the architectural commission for a proposed school building (Poynor School), a commission entrusted earlier to architect Charles C. Wilson (q.v.) Wilkins would later design four more school buildings for Florence, and at least ten other school buildings in the Pee Dee region of South Carolina.

Two early skyscraper projects in Florence bore Wilkins's signature. In 1920 the Hotel Development Company proposed an eight-story hotel, to be designed by Wilkins; this project may never have been completed. The seven-story Florence Title, Trust & Investment Company building, also designed by Wilkins, was built in 1921-1927. This building is still among the city's largest structures.

Wilkins was associated with Joseph F. Leitner (q.v.) in Florence and Wilmington, North Carolina, in 1906-1908. Frank Vincent Hopkins (q.v.) was associated with Wilkins from 1924 to 1932. The firm continued after Wilkins's death as Hopkins & Baker.

South Carolina projects:

1892: King & Rhodes Opera House, Florence (*MR*, 29 April 1892, p. 44.)

1893: Rebuilding, Central Hotel, Florence (*MR*, 12 May 1893, p. 280.)

1894: Opera Hose, Florence (*MR*, 2 February 1894, p. 13.)

1900: City Hall and Opera House, Florence; $17,315; Hayden, Wheeler & Schwend (q.v.), architects; W.J. Wilkins, contractor (*MR*, 1 March 1900, p. 102; 10 May 1900, p. 273.)

1900: Bank of Florence Building, Florence; W.J. Wilkins, contractor (*MR*, 25 January 1900, p. 16.)

1900: Sisters of St. Francis Convent, Florence; $5000; Dingle & Barbot (q.v.), architects; W.J. Wilkins, contractor (*MR*, 1 November 1900, p. 252.)

1901: City Hall and Opera House, Darlington; $21,000; Frank Milburn (q.v.), architect; W.J. Wilkins, contractor (*MR*, 21 February 1901, p. 96; 14 March 1901, p. 152; 18 April 1901, p. 245; 16 May 1901, p. 318.)

1902: Murchison School, Bennettsville; $32,000; John J. Huddart (q.v.), architect; W.J. Wilkins, contractor (Cornerstone; *MR*, 1 May 1902, p. 269.)

1904-1906: Poynor School, Florence (*MR*, 26 May 1904, p. 431; 9 June 1904, p. 479; 8 September 1904, p. 189; Minutes, Board of Trustees, Florence City Schools, Florence, 6 April 1906, p. 93; 8 May 1906, p. 94; 31 May 1906, p. 96.)

1905: Masonic Temple, Florence; $19,250; W.J. Wilkins, architect and contractor (*MR*, 18 May 1905, p. 415; 17 August 1905, p. 122; 24 August 1905, p. 148; 21 September 1905, p. 250.)

1906: Farmers' Supply Co. Warehouse, Kingstree (*MR*, 15 May 1906, p. 237.)

1906-1908: See **Leitner, Joseph F.** (Leitner & Wilkins)

1909: J.C. Williamson Business Building, Florence; $50,000 (*MR*, 21 October 1909, p. 65.)

1910: Remodeling, Florence County Courthouse, Florence; $12,000 (*MR*, 7 April 1910, p. 82.)

1910: Remodeling, Commercial & Savings Bank, Florence; $12,000 (*MR*, 9 June 1910, p. 65; 30 June 1910, p. 63; 7 July 1910, p. 81.)

1910: Jail, Florence; $6750 (*MR*, 23 June 1910, p. 70.)

1910: Farmers and Merchants' Bank Building, Hartsville; $6000 (*MR*, 4 August 1910, p. 78; 11 August 1910, p. 66.)

1911: J. Saunders McKenzie Residence, Bannockburn; $10,000 (*MR*, 26 January 1911, p. 59.)

1911: Dr. Benjamin Gregg Residence, Florence; $8000 (*MR*, 23 March 1911, p. 68.)

1911: J.F. Muldrow Residence, Florence; $12,000 (*MR*, 13 July 1911, p. 72.)

1912: Two Dormitories, South Carolina Industrial School, Florence; $28,000 (*MR*, 22 August 1912, p. 68.)

1912: First Methodist Episcopal Church South, Florence; $45,167 (*MR*, 26 December 1912, p. 66.)

1914: School, Cheraw; $7800 (*MR*, 29 October 1914, p. 58.)

1914: Dr. E.M. Matthews Store Building, Florence; $12,000 (*MR*, 12 March 1914, p. 73.)

1914-1919: Palmetto Construction Co. Bank and Office Building, W. Evans and S. Irby streets, Florence; $72,000 (*MR*, 28 May 1914, p. 61; 4 June 1914, p. 79; 26 June 1919, p. 139; 3 July 1919, p. 156.)

1915: Park School, Florence; $25,395 (*MR*, 2 December 1915, p. 74.)

1916: Colored School, Florence; $14,103 (*MR*, 15 June 1915, p. 72.)

1919-1920: High School, Florence; $200,000 (*MR*, 27 November 1919, p. 140; 6 May 1920, p. 201; 27 May 1920, p. 126.)

1920: Prize-House, Florence Storage Warehouse Co., Florence; $35,000 (*MR*, 6 May 1920, p. 201.)

1920: Hotel Development Co. Hotel, Florence; $750,000 (*MR*, 22 July 1920, p. 96.)

1921-1927: Florence Title, Trust & Investment Co. Building, Florence; $150,000 (*MR*, 17 November 1921, p. 68; 24 February 1927, p. 105; 10 March 1927, p. 98; 31 March 1927, p. 109.)

1922: Clubhouse, Myrtle Beach Yacht Club, Myrtle Beach (*MR*, 23 March 1922, p. 79.)

1923: High School, Cheraw; $46,000 (*MR*, 22 March 1923, p. 99.)

1923: High School, Lake City; $49,000 (*MR*, 8 March 1923, p. 100; 15 March 1923, p. 100.)

1923: School, Marion; $100,000 (*MR*, 30 August 1923, p. 107.)

Wilkins & Hopkins

1924: Public Library, Florence; $70,159 (*MR*, 5 June 1924, p. 138.)

1924: Dr. M.R. Mobley Residence, Florence; $20,000 (*MR*, 22 May 1924, p. 112.)

1924: Fred Germany & Co. Warehouse, Florence; $13,331 (*MR*, 28 August 1924, p. 116.)

1924: Marion Building & Loan Association Hotel, Marion; $50,000 (*MR*, 18 September 1924, p. 116; 25 September 1924, p. 116.)

1925: Grammar School, Hartsville; $78,379 (*MR*, 6 August 1925, p. 124.)

1927: Grammar School, Florence; $79,000 (*MR*, 7 April 1927, p. 121.)

1927: High and Grammar School, Myrtle Beach; $55,000 (*MR*, 25 August 1927, p. 100.)

1928: High School, Conway; $82,000 (*MR*, 13 September 1928, p. 96.)

1928: Grammar School, Cheraw; $23,000 (*MR*, 19 July 1928, p. 94.)

1928: Addition, High School, Hartsville; $45,000 (*MR*, 5 July 1928, p. 108.)

1928: Sunday School, First Baptist Church, Hartsville; $75,000 (*MR*, 15 November 1928, p. 100.)

1929: Hospital, Conway; $60,000 (*MR*, 12 September 1929, p. 89.)

1929: Robert White Residence, Myrtle Beach; $20,000 (*MR*, 25 April 1929, p. 93.)

1929: Col. Holmes B. Springs Residence, Myrtle Beach (*MR*, 25 April 1929, p. 93.)

1929: Chapin Co. Residence, Myrtle Beach (*MR*, 25 April 1929, p. 93.)

1929: J.E. James Residence, Myrtle Beach (*MR*, 25 April 1929, p. 93.)

1930: Tuberculosis Sanitorium, Florence (*MR*, 2 October 1930, p. 71.)

1932: Masonic Temple, Florence (*MR*, 12 May 1932, p. 70.)

Sources: *Directory of Historic American Architectural Firms*, p. 32; Florence city directories; *MR*, various citations; National Register files, S.C. Archives; *The State*, 6 October 1900, p. 2; Tony P. Wrenn, Washington, D.C., unpublished research.

WILLIAMS, W. Paul (active 1924-1958) W. Paul Williams was a draftsman for S.P. Tinsley (q.v.) in Spartanburg in 1924. He opened his own practice in Spartanburg that same year.

South Carolina projects:

1924: Dr. N.T. Clark and C.C. McMillen, two buildings, Spartanburg; $15,000 (*MR*, 17 April 1924, p. 121.)

1924: Majority Baptist Church Building, S. Liberty and E. Hampton streets, Spartanburg; $20,000 (*MR*, 23 October 1924, p. 107.)

1925: Monaghan Mills Store Building, Greenville; $15,000 (*MR*, 12 March 1925, p. 120.)

1926: School, Duncan (*MR*, 23 September 1926, p. 10.)

1926: High School, Spartanburg County; $70,000 (*MR*, 12 August 1926, p. 98.)

1927: High School, Inman; $311,475 (*MR*, 17 March 1927, p. 123.)

1929: School, Chesnee; $25,975 (*MR*, 19 September 1929, p. 98.)

1929: Geo. D. Jeffries Residence, E. Frederick Street, Gaffney; $15,000 (*MR*, 11 April 1929, p. 89.)

1929: Grade School, Valley Falls; $24,934 (*MR*, 6 June 1929, p. 108.)

Sources: *MR*, various citations; Petty, p. 146; Spartanburg city directories.

WILSON, Charles Coker (1864-1933) Charles Coker Wilson was one of the most influential and successful of South Carolina's architects in the early 20th century. He was the first twentieth-century South Carolina architect to be named a fellow of the American Institute of Architects. Wilson was instrumental in founding the South Carolina chapter of the A.I.A., and he was charter president of the chapter. Under Wilson's leadership, the chapter drafted the legislation to regulate the practice of architecture in the state, and when the South Carolina Board of Architectural Examiners was created in 1917, Wilson was chosen as the Board's first chairman. He also helped draft the state's first building codes.

Wilson was born 20 November 1864, son of Dr. Furman Edwards Wilson and Jane Lide Coker Wilson of Hartsville, South Carolina. He studied civil engineering at South Carolina College in Columbia, receiving his A.B. degree in 1886 and his C.E. degree two years later. He worked as location and construction engineer for the Columbia, Newberry & Laurens Railroad Company (1886-1889) and for the Carolina Southern Railway (1899-1890.)

The work with the railroads may have led Wilson to Roanoke. Roanoke, in the mountains of Virginia, had been a small community called Big Lick with some 700 inhabitants in 1880. In that year the Norfolk & Western and the Shenandoah Valley railroads chose Big Lick as the site for their western machine shops and terminals. The city was renamed Roanoke, and, benefitting from $75 million in railroad investments, grew to a population of 25,000 by 1892. Boasting of its vigor, rising property values, and building boom, Roanoke advertised for "men of money and men of muscle." Wilson and a number of other ambitious men responded to the call. A city history notes that business licenses were issued to 116 house builders, 71 real estate agents, and seven civil engineers and architects in 1890-1891.

Wilson and Henry Hartwell Huggins (q.v.), a fellow South Carolina College graduate, had established an architectural partnership in Roanoke by January 1891. They advertised as specialists in hotel and public building design. The partnership was dissolved by February 1893, with both men remaining in Roanoke. In that same year another South Carolinian and Darlington County native, William Augustus Edwards (q.v.), joined Wilson's office as draftsman.

In 1895 Wilson associated with the established Lynchburg architect Walter P. Tinsley (q.v.) Tinsley & Wilson won a major South Carolina commission, the Anderson Graded School in Anderson, that year. Wilson left Tinsley and relocated to Columbia, South Carolina, with Edwards as his partner. The new partnership thrived; more than fifty buildings designed by Wilson & Edwards between 1896 and 1900 have been identified in the Carolinas, Georgia, Florida, and Virginia. In addition to his architectural practice, Wilson served as city engineer of Columbia and superintendent of the Water Works from 1896 to 1899.

Wilson spent part of 1899 and 1900 traveling in Europe. He obtained his first professional architectural education where he studied briefly in Paris with the Atelier H. Duray at the Ecole des Beaux-Arts.

The partnership with Edwards was dissolved in 1901. Wilson continued to prosper as an architect. His practice included projects in Alabama, Mississippi, and Florida. By 1904 his office suite at 1302 Main Street, Columbia, spread through six rooms with 3,000 square feet of floor space. Among his eleven assistants were Arthur Hamby (q.v.), Paul H. Youmans (q.v.), and James B. Urquhart (q.v.)

Wilson was summoned in 1904 to complete the South Carolina State House, which had been under construction since 1851. Wilson credited the virtues of the design to John R. Niernsee, the building's first architect; but after Niernsee's death in 1885 the work was carried forth by lesser architects. Wilson had entered a proposal in the 1900 architectural competition for the building's completion, but Frank Milburn (q.v.) won the competition, and he designed and built a clumsy central dome. The dome aroused a storm of controversy on aesthetic and structural grounds. Several professionals (including Wilson) were retained in 1903 to evaluate the dome's stability, and after their recommendations were considered, Milburn was dismissed and Wilson was appointed in his place. By 1907 Wilson had redesigned and rebuilt the steel roof trusses, augmented the dome's substructure, and completed the northern and southern porticos. He was not given the option of removing the dome, but he expressed hope that the State House might, some day, be restored to its intended form.

In 1905-1906 Henry Ten Eyck Wendell (q.v.), an architect formerly of New York and Denver, associated with Wilson in Columbia on several projects. Wendell was one of the numerous architects from northern and western states with whom Wilson allied himself during his career. Among the Wilson & Wendell collaborations was Coppin Hall at Allen University in Columbia. Coppin Hall, described as "one of the most imposing buildings ever erected and controlled by the Negro Race," was built by contractor J.D. Smart in 1906-1907.

Wilson reorganized his office in 1907, forming a partnership with Urquhart and Edwin Douglas Sompayrac (q.v.) This same year Wilson was appointed architect of the University of South Carolina (formerly South Carolina College.) As university architect he supervised the renovation of the existing buildings at the campus and prepared a long-range development plan. Four university buildings were designed by Wilson's firm: Davis Hall (1908), LeConte College (1909-1910), Thornwell Dormitory (1912) and Woodrow Dormitory (1913). Wilson also served as chairman of the Columbia Street Commission from 1907 to 1910. He pioneered development of a sand-and-clay pavement for rural roads during his tenure, and by 1909 Columbia and Richland County boasted 250 miles of sand-clay roads.

Wilson's campaign for election to Columbia City Council in 1910 was marred by Fingal Conway Black (q.v.), a disgruntled former subordinate of Wilson on the Columbia Street Commission. Black and his confederates spread rumors at the polling places, accusing Wilson of incompetence and favoritism on several city projects. Although the charges were refuted by other parties, Wilson lost the election. Columbia's newspaper, *The State*, suggested an "Assassination at Polls."

Wilson's maturing powers of architectural design in this period were evident in the J.L. Coker & Company Department Store Building, designed in 1909. The Coker family, in business in Hartsville since the Civil War, provided all manner of merchandise for the community, and had introduced the first rail line and telephone service to Hartsville. Wilson, a cousin of the family, secured the commission for the Coker College Administration Building in Hartsville in 1908. When the old Coker's Store burned in 1909, Wilson, Sompayrac & Urquhart were promptly chosen to design a new department store building.

The scope of the business and the prominence of the Cokers in Hartsville demanded a landmark building. Wilson resolved the program as a single-story heroic arcade three hundred feet long. Eleven triumphal arches defined glass display windows, accommodating the departmentalized merchandise. The arcade was unified by a massive bronze entablature. The monumental scale, the precise workmanship, the classical and heraldic motifs, and the remarkable unity of the design made Coker's Store one of Wilson's foremost architectural achievements.

John Carroll Johnson (q.v.), a graduate of the Armour Institute of Technology in Chicago and the University of Pennsylvania, was hired as chief draftsman around 1910. Louis C. Darnett also entered the office around 1910; Darnett became head draftsman in 1912 and remained with Wilson through 1920. Urquhart left the firm in 1910 and opened his own architectural practice in Columbia.

Sompayrac left Columbia after the World War and took a position with the United States Shipping Board. Wilson hired three new draftsmen: James M. Green, Jr. (q.v.), Jesse W. Wessinger (q.v.), and George R. Berryman (q.v.) The firm opened branch offices in Gastonia and Wilson, North Carolina. Most of Wilson's work in the early postwar years was in North Carolina.

Berryman was promoted to junior associate in 1923. J. Robie Kennedy (q.v.) entered the firm as a draftsman in 1923, and became an associate in 1924. Wilson, Berryman & Kennedy maintained offices in Columbia, Gastonia, and Wilson. The firm's largest commission was the new campus of Meredith College in Raleigh, North Carolina. This project included a first quadrangle of six buildings to cost $1,000,000, with plans for future development to total $3,500,000. The firm also won commissions for several major hospitals; their Halifax District Hospital in Daytona Beach, Florida, which was contracted in 1926 at $536,000, won considerable acclaim when completed.

The partnership with Berryman and Kennedy was ended in 1927, and Wilson consolidated his operations in Columbia. Wilson designed several hospital buildings in these years, including the Alachua County Hospital in Gainesville, Florida (1927) and the St. Luke's Hospital in Tryon, North Carolina (1928). Harold Tatum (q.v.) joined Wilson's office in 1929, and this partnership was maintained until Wilson's death in 1933. Wilson & Tatum prepared plans for a fourteen-story hotel in Columbia in 1930. The project was contracted at $750,000, but never carried out.

Throughout his career, Wilson pursued commissions for school buildings. He designed over fifty school buildings in North and South Carolina. His university work included many buildings at his alma mater, South Carolina College, and at Meredith College in Raleigh, North Carolina. Rudolph E. Lee (q.v.) of Clemson College, in a history of South Carolina public school architecture written in 1910, identified the 1895 Anderson Graded School (Tinsley & Wilson, architects) as "the first attempt in South Carolina at distinctive school architecture." The Anderson Graded School was a two-story brick building with a cross-axis plan, a central four-story Richardsonian entrance tower, and a slate roof. Stairways were located at either end of the longitudi-

nal hallway, and every classroom had substantial window area.

Wilson's 1902-1904 Darlington Graded School, a classically composed building with a colossal Tuscan portico was, in Lee's words, a "marked contrast to the gloomy Tudor and the factory type." Lee praised the functional and utilitarian aspects of the school. He saw that each classroom had large window areas, never less than one-fifth the room's floor area. He admired the logical cross-axis plan with its broad hallways. He described the fire-retardant construction, the tempered-air heating and ventilating system, and the indoor toilets, noting that many public schools in the state were still being built with outdoor privies. The Darlington School "marked the beginning of the present era of school architecture in South Carolina."

After a fire at the Cleveland School, Kershaw County, killed seventy-seven people in 1923, the state determined to define school building codes. Wilson was one of the authors of this code.

Wilson was also involved in the design of several of the region's early tall office buildings. Columbia had only one skyscraper, the National Loan & Exchange Bank Building, in 1911. In the next year three skyscrapers were planned for the city, with Wilson & Sompayrac taking a key role in the development. The first skyscraper designed by the firm, the Gresham Hotel, was begun early in 1912. The six-story, steel-frame building was one of the first steel skeleton frame skyscrapers designed by a South Carolina architect.

When the fifteen-story Palmetto Building was proposed in 1912, Julius Harder of New York (q.v.) was commissioned as designing architect, with Wilson & Sompayrac as supervising architects. This building, the tallest in the state when completed in 1913, was contracted at $300,000 to John J. Cain. The Palmetto Building was constructed with a steel skeleton frame and a sheathing of limestone, buff brick, and terra-cotta, with palmetto tree motifs incorporated in its Gothic-inspired blind arcades. Wilson's association with Harder on this project provided invaluable practical experience in the composition and construction of tall buildings.

South Carolina projects:

Wilson & Huggins

1892: J.J. Ward Store and Office Building, Darlington (*MR*, 26 March 1892, p. 37.)

1892: A. Nachman Store Building, Darlington (*MR*, 26 March 1892, p. 37.)

Charles C. Wilson

1893: Baptist Church, Florence; $10,000 (*MR*, 12 May 1893, p. 280; 7 July 1893, p. 424; "Wilson and Edwards.")

1894: Presbyterian Church, Rock Hill; $12,000 (*MR*, 16 February 1894, p. 46; 23 February 1894, p. 63; 23 March 1894, p. 124; 1 June 1894, p. 302; 15 June 1894, p. 334; "Wilson and Edwards.")

1895: See **Tinsley, Walter P.** (Tinsley & Wilson)

Wilson & Edwards

1896: J.J. Loucas Residence, Society Hill (*MR*, 6 March 1896, p. 99.)

1896: Lutheran Church, Newberry (*MR*, 27 March 1896, p. 151; "Wilson and Edwards.")

1896: Dr. E.B. Miot Residence, Columbia (*MR*, 3 July 1896, p. 386; "Wilson and Edwards.")

1896: D.D. McColl Bank Building, Bennettsville (*MR*, 3 July 1896, p. 386.)

1896: Building, South Carolina State Industrial College, Orangeburg (*MR*, 3 July 1896, p. 386.)

1896: Remodeling, Sumter County Courthouse, Sumter; $15,000 (*MR*, 27 November 1896, p. 301.)

1896-1897: Thomas Memorial Baptist Church, Bennettsville (J.A.W. Thomas, *A History of Marlboro County, with Traditions and Sketches of Numerous Families* (1887: reprint, Ann Arbor, Michigan: University Microfilms, 1965), p. 236; "Wilson and Edwards.")

1896-1897: Greenwood Baptist Church, Greenwood (*Greenwood Journal*, Greenwood, 12 March 1896, p. 3; 30 April 1896, p. 3; 30 July 1896, p. 3; 11 February 1897, p. 3; *MR*, 20 March 1896, p. 134; "Wilson and Edwards.")

1897: Remodeling, Hotel Columbia, Columbia (*MR*, 2 April 1897, p. 178; 9 April 1897, p. 195; "Wilson and Edwards.")

1897: Dr. E.G. Quattlebaum Residence, Columbia (*MR*, 9 April 1897, p. 195; "Wilson and Edwards.")

1897: Second Baptist Church, Columbia (*MR*, 9 April 1897, p. 195; "Wilson and Edwards.")

1897: T.S. Moorman Residence, Columbia (*MR*, 9 April 1897, p. 195.)

1897: J.S. Verner Residence, Columbia (*MR*, 9 April 1897, p. 195.)

1897: J.R. Smith Residence, Greenville (*MR*, 9 April 1897, p. 195.)

1897: O.B. Cagle Residence, Greenville (*MR*, 9 April 1897, p. 195.)

1897: W.E. Lucas Residence, Laurens (*MR*, 9 April 1897, p. 195.)

1897: Floyd L. Liles Residence, Spartanburg (*MR*, 9 April 1897, p. 195.)

1897: Church, Summerville (*MR*, 9 April 1897, p. 195.)

1897: Church, Blackville (*MR*, 9 April 1897, p. 195.)

1897: Church, Walterboro (*MR*, 9 April 1897, p. 195.)

1897: M.M. Ficlen Residence, Columbia (*MR*, 8 October 1897, p. 167.)

1897: A.S. Gilliard Residence, Columbia (*MR*, 8 October 1897, p. 167.)

1897: J.J. Earle Residence, Columbia (*MR*, 8 October 1897, p. 167.)

1897: W.W. Ball Residence, Greenville (*MR*, 8 October 1897, p. 167.)

1897: J.S. Cothran Residence, Greenville (*MR*, 8 October 1897, p. 167.)

1897: Miss M.W. Woodrow Residence, Rock Hill (*MR*, 8 October 1897, p. 167.)

1897: R.B. Cunningham Residence, Rock Hill (*MR*, 8 October 1897, p. 167.)

1897: O.J. Harris Residence, Batesburg (*MR*, 8 October 1897, p. 167.)

1897: J.P. Gossett Residence, Williamston (*MR*, 8 October 1897, p. 167.)

1897: N.S. Gibson Residence, Winona (*MR*, 8 October 1897, p. 167.)

1897: Baptist Church, Lowrys (*MR*, 8 October 1897, p. 167.)

1897: Dr. L.B. Folk Residence, Columbia (*MR*, 5 November 1897, p. 233.)

1898: T.P. Cothran Residence, Greenville (*MR*, 25 March 1898, p. 159.)

1898: August Kohn Residence, Columbia (*MR*, 25 March 1898, p. 159.)

1898: P.H. Nelson Residence, Columbia (*MR*, 25 March 1898, p. 159.)

1898: W.D. Cogshall Residence, Darlington (*MR*, 25 March 1898, p. 159.)

1898: R.E. James Residence, Darlington (*MR*, 25 March 1898, p. 159.)

1898: J.C. and E.W. Robertson Warehouses, Columbia (*MR*, 25 March 1898, p. 159.)

1898: H.L. Elliott Residence, Winnsboro (*MR*, 25 March 1898, p. 160.)

1898-1900: Masonic Temple, Columbia (*MR*, 1 April 1898, p. 176; 15 April 1898, p. 212; 22 July 1898, p. 428; Kline, pp. 8, 14; *The State*, 24 March 1906, p. 8.)

1899: People's Bank Building, Anderson (*MR*, 14 April 1899, p. 201.)

1899: Remodeling, Baptist Church, Chester (*MR*, 30 June 1899, p. 391.)

1899: J.B. Scott Residence, Columbia (*MR*, 20 October 1899, p. 225.)

1899-1900: J.A. McCullough Residence, Greenville; $5000 (*MR*, 20 October 1899, p. 225; 5 April 1900, p. 187.)

1899-1900: Remodeling, Ebenezer Lutheran Church, 1307 Richland Street, Columbia (Council Minutes, Ebenezer Lutheran Church, Columbia, 26 September 1899, 12 December 1899, 25 January 1900.)

1900: Neill O'Donnell Store Building, Sumter; $10,000 (*MR*, 1 February 1900, p. 32.)

1900: Major C.F. Hard Residence, Greenville (*MR*, 26 April 1900, p. 240.)

1900: Dormitory, Welsh Neck High School, Hartsville; $7000 (*MR*, 26 April 1900, p. 240.)

1900: John F. Grandy Residence, Greenville (*MR*, 1 November 1900, p. 252.)

1900: Mrs. G.H. Beckwith School Building, Bennettsville (*MR*, 12 July 1900, p. 426.)

1900: Office Building, Laurens Manufacturing Company, Laurens (*MR*, 12 July 1900, p. 426.)

1900: Mrs. M.S. Habenicht Store Building, Columbia (*MR*, 26 April 1900, p. 240; Kline, p. 14.)

1900: Improvements, Jervey House Hotel, Sumter (*MR*, 11 October 1900, p. 200; 1 November 1900, p. 252.)

1900: Hotel, Pelzer (*MR*, 12 July 1900, p. 426.)

1900: Mt. Pisgah Methodist Church, Sumter (*MR*, 12 July 1900, p. 426.)

1900-1901: Sumter Baptist Church, Sumter; $12,000 (*MR*, 26 April 1900, p. 240; Cornerstone.)

1901: Mess Hall, University of South Carolina, Columbia; Wilson & Edwards, supervising and constructing architects; Walter & Legare (q.v.), designing architects (*The State*, 16 March 1901, p. 8.)

1901: VanMetre Building, Main Street, Columbia (*MR*, 7 February 1901, p. 53; Kline, p. 14; *The State*, 7 March 1901, p. 8.)

1901: Central Presbyterian Church, Anderson (*MR*, 5 September 1901, p. 114.)

Charles C. Wilson

1902: A.R.P. Church, Columbia (*MR*, 27 February 1902, p. 101.)

1902: Bank of Georgetown, Georgetown (*MR*, 10 July 1902, p. 459.)

1902-1903: Hotel Jerome, Main and Lady streets, Columbia; $50,000 (*MR*, 6 February 1902, p. 49; 4 September 1902, p. 120; 2 October 1902, p. 196; 19 March 1903, p. 182; *The State*, 8 November 1903.)

1902-1904: Graded School, Darlington (*The State*, 20 March 1904, p. 20; Lee, "Rural School Improvements.")

1903: Hotel Park in the Pines, Aiken; $200,000 (*MR*, 25 June 1903, p. 470; 23 July 1903, p. 15; 20 August 1903, p. 89; *The State*, 11 October 1903, p. 7.)

1903: Methodist Female College Building, Columbia; $50,000 (*MR*, 23 July 1903, p. 15; 6 August 1903, p. 52.)

1903: Sol Kohn Store Building, Orangeburg (*MR*, 19 February 1903, p. 104.)

1903-1904: J.B. Garfunkel Flats Building, Columbia (*MR*, 3 September 1903, p. 127; 4 February 1904, p. 58.)

1904: Graded School, Charleston (*Southern Architect and Building News*, 3 June 1904, p. 13.)

1904: Operating Building, Columbia Hospital, Columbia (*MR*, 28 July 1904, p. 37.)

1904: First Presbyterian Church, Florence; $20,000 (*MR*, 11 August 1904, p. 84.)

1904: M.E. Rutland Livery Stable, Batesburg (*MR*, 11 August 1904, p. 84.)

1904: Jail, Marion; $12,000 (*MR*, 10 March 1904, p. 166; 14 April 1904, p. 292.)

1904: Clubhouse, Ridgeway (*MR*, 24 March 1904, p. 217.)

1904: McKissick Memorial Library, Connie Maxwell Orphanage, Greenwood (*MR*, 31 March 1904, p. 238; *Southern Architect and Building News*, 8 April 1904, p. 10.)

1904: Williamsburg County Jail, Kingstree (*MR*, 7 April 1904, p. 267.)

1904-1906: Graded School, Florence; $20,000 (*MR*, 9 June 1904, p. 479; 29 March 1906, p. 287; *The State*, 4 June 1904, p. 1; 22 March 1906, p. 10.)

1904-1907: Completion, South Carolina State House, Columbia (*The State*, 26 January 1904, p. 8; 5 June 1904, p. 16; *MR*, 14 April 1904, p. 291; 9 June 1904, p. 479; 7 March 1907, p. 227.)

Ca. 1904: Sligh & Allen Department Store Building, Columbia (Kline, p. 9.)

1905: John Fitzmaurice Store Building, Columbia (*MR*, 23 March 1905, p. 206.)

1905: Marlboro Improvement Company Building, Bennettsville; $10,000 (*MR*, 30 March 1905, p. 228.)

1905: Hotel, Aiken; $250,000 (*MR*, 11 May 1905, p. 384; 15 June 1905, p. 512; 22 June 1905, p. 535.)

1905: Addition, College for Women, Columbia; $20,000 (*MR*, 15 June 1905, p. 512.)

Wilson & Wendell

1905: Twenty-Nine Standard Warehouse Plans, South Carolina Cotton Growers Association (*MR*, 28 September 1905, p. 274; 5 October 1905, p. 301.)

1905: Farmers Warehouse and Storage Company Cotton Warehouse, Johnston (*MR*, 28 September 1905, p. 274.)

1905: Farmers Storage Warehouse Company Cotton Warehouse, Darlington; $5000 (*MR*, 26 October 1905, p. 381.)

1905: Kaminski Hardware Store Building, Georgetown (*MR*, 14 December 1905, p. 581; 21 December 1905, p. 609.)

1906-1907: Coppin Hall, Allen University, Harden Street, Columbia; $12,780 (Cornerstone; *The State*, 17 February 1906, p. 7; 21 February 1906, p. 6; 21 March 1906, p. 6; *MR*, 1 March 1906, p. 183; *The Quadrennial Catalogue of Allen University, Columbia, S.C. 1907-1908* (Columbia: The R.L. Bryan Co., 1907), p. 3.)

1906-1907: First Baptist Church, Hartsville; $18,000 (*MR*, 15 March 1906, p. 237; J.L. Coker, *Hartsville. Its Early Settlers. The Growth of the Town with Sketches of Its Institutions and Enterprises* (n.p., n.p., 1911), p. 54.)

1906-1907: Neville Hall, Presbyterian College, Clinton (*MR*, 12 April 1906, p. 362; Withey, pp. 662-663.)

Charles C. Wilson

1906-1907: First Baptist Church, Newberry (*MR*, 17 May 1906, p. 507; Cornerstone.)

1906: Southern Oaks Sanatorium, Greenville; $10,000 (*MR*, 12 July 1906, p. 733.)

1906: F.C. Cain Hotel, St. Matthews; $25,000 (*MR*, 26 July 1906, p. 44.)

1906-1907: School, Georgetown; $28,310 (*MR*, 16 August 1906, p. 118; 21 February 1907, p. 167; 27 June 1907, p. 771; 11 July 1907, p. 836.)

1907-1908: Woodrow Memorial Presbyterian Church, Columbia; $7500 (*MR*, 25 April 1907, p. 457; *The State*, 11 May 1908.)

1907: Addition, Magnolia Graded School, Greenwood; $10,000 (*MR*, 4 April 1907, p. 356; 9 May 1907, p. 538; 16 May 1907, p. 573; 18 July 1907, p. 22.)

1907: Summerton Methodist Episcopal Church, Summerton (*MR*, 23 May 1907, p. 606.)

1907: Laurens Hall, Presbyterian College, Clinton (*MR*, 11 July 1907, p. 836; Withey, pp. 662-663.)

Wilson, Sompayrac & Urquhart

1907: School, Denmark; $15,000 (*MR*, 13 June 1907, p. 700; 19 September 1907, p. 260; 26 September 1907, p. 83.)

1907: Methodist Episcopal Church South, Denmark; $8500 (*MR*, 22 August 1907, p. 159; 5 September 1907, p. 205.)

1907: First National Bank, Batesburg; $6000 (*MR*, 26 September 1907, p. 83; 3 October 1907, p. 72.)

1907: Masonic Temple, Greenwood; $18,000 (*MR*, 14 November 1907, p. 65; 21 November 1907, p. 64.)

1908: McCall Hotel, Bennettsville; $35,000 (*MR*, 5 March 1908, p. 68; 4 June 1908, p. 70; 23 July 1908, p. 55; *The State*, 17 July 1908, p. 2.)

1908: Development Plan, University of South Carolina, Columbia (*MR*, 4 June 1908, p. 70; Green, pp. 130, 148-149.)

1908: South Carolina Soldier's Home, Columbia (*MR*, 4 June 1908, p. 70.)

1908: Repairs, Existing Buildings, University of South Carolina, Columbia (*The State*, 19 July 1908, p. 12.)

1908: Davis Hall, University of South Carolina, Columbia; $28,763 (*MR*, 12 March 1908, p. 59; 4 June 1908, p. 70; 2 July 1908, p. 70; 13 August 1908, p. 59; *The State*, 2 July 1908, p. 3; 4 August 1908, p. 12; Green, pp. 148, 170.)

1908: State Agricultural and Mechanical Society Exhibit Building, State Fair, Columbia; $8500 (*MR*, 23 July 1908, p. 55.)

1908: State Building, State Fair, Columbia (*The State*, 2 July 1908, p. 3; 8 July 1908, p. 9.)

1908: J.A. Weinberg Residence, Manning; $6500 (*MR*, 6 August 1908, p. 67; 13 August 1908, p. 58.)

1908-1910: Administration Building, Coker College, Hartsville; $25,000 (Cornerstone; *MR*, 4 June 1908, p. 71; 8 October 1908, p. 61; *Hartsville Messenger*, Hartsville, 24 March 1910, p. 1.)

1909: Renovations, Beaufort College Campus, Beaufort; $13,000 (*MR*, 15 July 1909, p. 66.)

1909-1910: J.L. Coker & Co. Department Store Building, Hartsville; $60,000 (*MR*, 8 April 1909, p. 61; 15 April 1909, p. 65; 15 July 1909, p. 66; 9 September 1909, p. 58; 16 September 1909, p. 63; *Hartsville Messenger*, Hartsville, 11 May 1911, p. 1; J.J. Lawton, "Brief History of the Early Days of J.L. Coker & Co. Store Rebuilt," *News & Press*, August 1928, p. 10.)

1909-1910: LeConte (Barnwell) College, University of South Carolina, Columbia; $45,427 (Cornerstone; *MR*, 1 July 1909, p. 72; 8 July 1909, p. 63; 29 July 1909, p. 61; Green, pp. 148, 170.)

1910: Baptist Church, Eastover; $6000 (*MR*, 10 March 1910, p. 62; 17 March 1910, p. 66.)

1910: West End Methodist Church, Georgetown; $10,000 (*MR*, 30 June 1910, p. 63.)

1910: A.F.A.M. Temple Building, Greenville; $100,000 (*MR*, 13 October 1910, p. 67; 24 November 1910, p. 66.)

Wilson & Sompayrac

1910: Farmers and Merchants Bank Building, Eastover (Cornerstone.)

1910: Young Men's Christian Association Building, Greenville; $35,500 (*MR*, 24 November 1910, p. 66; 1 December 1910, p. 86.)

1910: Improvements and Addition, First Presbyterian Church Building, Columbia; $20,000 (*MR*, 4 August 1910, p. 78.)

1911: Y.M.C.A. Building, Sumter (*MR*, 9 February 1911, p. 66.)

1911: City Hall and Market Building, Beaufort; $19,000 (*MR*, 1 June 1911, p. 91.)

1911: Adden Brothers Store and Office Building, Orangeburg (*MR*, 13 July 1911, p. 71.)

1911: Sunday School Room, Central Presbyterian Church, Anderson; $6000 (*MR*, 20 July 1911, p. 70.)

1912: Gresham Hotel, Main Street, Columbia; $86,837 (*The State*, 11 January 1912, p. 8; 12 January 1912, p. 6; *MR*, 18 January 1912, p. 69; 15 February 1912, p. 71.)

1912: Facade, Consolidated Building, 1326-1330 Main Street, Columbia (*The State*, 22 January 1912, p. 8; 17 February 1912, p. 2; *MR*, 29 February 1912, p. 69.)

1912: Thornwell Dormitory, University of South Carolina, Columbia; $40,000 (*MR*, 4 July 1912, p. 86; Green, p. 149; Cornerstone.)

1912: R.L. Bryan & Co. Warehouse, Columbia; $9800 (*MR*, 15 August 1912, p. 69.)

1912: Peoples Bank, Bishopville (Cornerstone.)

1912-1913: Palmetto Building, Washington and Main streets, Columbia; $300,000; Julius H. Harder (q.v.), architect; Wilson & Sompayrac, supervising architects (*The State*, 6 February 1912, p. 10; *MR*, 15 February 1912, pp. 56, 71; *The Columbia Record*, 21 December 1913, pp. 2, 4.)

1912-1913: Logan School, 815 Elmwood Avenue, Columbia; $58,292 (*MR*, 12 December 1912, p. 67; *The State*, 24 June 1913; *Thirtieth Annual Report of the Public Schools, Columbia, S.C. 1912-1913* (Columbia: The State Co., 1913), pp. 13-16.)

1913: Henry Bouchier Store Building, 1722-1724 N. Main Street, Columbia; $26,000 (*The State*, 19 June 1913, p. 14; 27 June 1913, p. 8; *MR*, 26 June 1913, p. 68; 7 August 1913, p. 86.)

1913: Dormitory, Coker College, Hartsville; $50,000 (*MR*, 16 January 1913, p. 74; 6 March 1913, p. 76.)

1913: Woodrow Dormitory, University of South Carolina, Columbia; $23,384 (*MR*, 10 April 1913, p. 74; Green, p. 149; Cornerstone.)

1913: Carnegie Library, Latta; $5000 (*MR*, 27 November 1913, p. 64; George S. Bobinski, *Carnegie Libraries: Their History and Impact on American Public Library Development* (Chicago: American Library Association, 1969), p. 234.)

1914: Remodeling, M.A. Malone Store Building, Columbia (*MR*, 29 January 1914, p. 69.)

1914: Portico, J.L. Mimnaugh Residence, Columbia; $6000 (*MR*, 7 May 1914, p. 80.)

1914: Administration Building and Ward Building, South Carolina Tuberculosis Hospital, Columbia; $8232 (*MR*, 19 November 1914, p. 64.)

Ca. 1914: WinVa Apartment Building, Columbia (*The State*, 17 January 1915, p. 24; 24 January 1915, p. 12.)

1915: Carnegie Library, Camden; $5000 (*MR*, 27 May 1915, p. 51; 3 June 1915, p. 68; Cornerstone; George S. Bobinski, *Carnegie Libraries: Their History and Impact on American Public*

Library Development (Chicago: American Library Association, 1969), p. 212.)

1915: House of Peace Synagogue, 1318 Park Street, Columbia; $3637 (*The State*, 2 March 1915, p. 10; 20 March 1915, p.2; *MR*, 11 March 1915, p. 52.)

1915: Additions, Logan School, Columbia; $31,830 (*MR*, 17 June 1915, p. 59; 24 June 1915, p. 53; 29 July 1915, p. 59.)

1915: Charlie Barron Residence, Columbia; $20,000 (*MR*, 2 December 1915, p. 74.)

1915: Darlington High School, Darlington; $30,000 (*News and Press*, 8 April 1915, p. 1; 8 July 1915, p. 1; *MR*, 29 April 1915, p. 54.)

1915: Dormitory and Gymnasium Building, Coker College, Hartsville; $100,000 (*The State*, 11 April 1915, p. 2; *MR*, 15 April 1915, p. 58.)

1915: Coker & Company Cotton Office, Hartsville (*MR*, 15 July 1915, p. 59.)

1915: William Egleston Residence, Hartsville; $10,000 (*MR*, 30 September 1915, p. 59; 14 October 1915, p. 57.)

1915: Model Village Home #1 Design, State Federation of Women's Clubs (*The State*, 7 March 1915, p. 24.)

1916: Interior Alterations, South Carolina State House, Columbia; $6994 (*MR*, 3 February 1916, p. 80.)

1916: Women's Ward, South Carolina Tuberculosis Hospital, Columbia; $4500 (*MR*, 6 April 1916, p. 82.)

1916: School, Johnsonville; $8000 (*MR*, 25 May 1916, p. 67.)

1916: Graded School, Rowesville; $9290 (*MR*, 29 June 1916, p. 69; 13 July 1916, p. 66.)

1917: Infirmary, Dining Room, and Kitchen, South Carolina Tuberculosis Hospital, Columbia;

$25,278 (*MR*, 8 March 1917, p. 68; 24 May 1917, p. 68.)

1917: Methodist Church, Saluda; $15,910 (*MR*, 29 March 1917, p. 72.)

Ca. 1917: W.E. McGhee Residence, Columbia (*The State*, 21 October 1917, Part 2, p. 8.)

1918: School, Saluda; $25,000 (*MR*, 16 May 1918, p. 84; 30 May 1918, p. 81.)

Charles C. Wilson

1919: St. George Methodist Church and Sunday School, St. George; $27,500 (*MR*, 16 January 1919, p. 104.)

1921: Parsonage, St. Paul's Methodist Episcopal Church, Orangeburg; $28,000 (*MR*, 22 September 1921, p. 84.)

1921: Paul N. Moore Residence, York; $17,400 (*MR*, 29 September 1921, p. 88.)

1921-1922: Camden High School, Lyttleton Street, Camden; $104,994 (*MR*, 16 June 1921, p. 110; Cornerstone.)

1922: Addition, Burroughs School, Conway; $46,700 (*MR*, 18 May 1922, p. 90.)

Wilson & Berryman

1923: Professor's Residence and Apartment Building, Chicora College, Columbia (*MR*, 18 October 1923, p. 118.)

1923-1924: Annex, Lexington County High School, Lexington; $39,500 (*MR*, 27 December 1923, pp. 99-100; 7 January 1924, p. 108.)

Wilson, Berryman & Kennedy

1924: Negro School, Howard Street, Columbia; $51,594 (*MR*, 6 March 1924, p. 151.)

1924: Hamrick Hall of Science, Carroll School of Fine Arts, and President's House, Limestone College, Gaffney; $115,000 (*MR*, 24 April

1924, p. 113; 8 May 1924, p. 113; 18 September 1924, p. 116.)

1924: Boys' High School, Girls' High School, and Manual Training School, Sumter; $33,953 (*MR*, 3 April 1924, p. 154; 19 June 1924, p. 118; 21 August 1924, p. 120.)

1924: Neill O'Donnell Store Building, Sumter; $28,000 (*MR*, 26 June 1924, p. 115.)

1924: Addition, Grammar School, Camden (*MR*, 3 July 1924, p. 138.)

1924: Infirmary and Residence, State Hospital, Columbia; $36,328 (*MR*, 10 July 1924, p. 105.)

1924: Renovations, South Building, Coker College, Hartsville (*MR*, 7 August 1924, p. 133.)

1924: Repairs, South Carolina State House, Columbia; $15,780 (*MR*, 23 October 1924, p. 108.)

1924: Dr. Lemmon Office Building, Sumter; $10,000 (*MR*, 6 November 1924, p. 127.)

1924: Manse, First Presbyterian Church, Sumter (*MR*, 25 December 1924, p. 104.)

1925: Additions, McMaster School, Columbia; $42,370 (*MR*, 23 April 1925, p. 117; 7 May 1925, p. 140.)

1925: Olympia High School, Columbia (*MR*, 18 June 1925, p. 118.)

1925: Rosewood Grammar School, Columbia (*MR*, 18 June 1925, p. 118.)

1925: High School, Greenwood; $151,310; Wilson, Berryman & Kennedy, and James C. Hemphill (q.v.), architects (*MR*, 2 July 1925, p. 131.)

1925: Omar Temple Crippled Childrens' Hospital, Columbia; $30,000 (*MR*, 29 October 1925, p. 98.)

1925-1926: Andrew Jackson Hotel, Rock Hill; $201,389 (*MR*, 31 December 1925, p. 90;

4 March 1926, p. 140; 11 March 1926, p. 113; *The Record*, Rock Hill, 30 December 1926, p. 1.)

Charles C. Wilson

1927: Gymnasium and Natatorium, Limestone College, Gaffney; $32,000 (*MR*, 9 June 1927, p. 115.)

1927: S.J. Watson Residence, Johnston (*MR*, 22 December 1927, p. 92.)

1927-1928: Dormitory and Administration Building, Browning Home, Camden; $115,675 (*MR*, 4 August 1927, p. 118; Cornerstone.)

1928: H.J. Hardy, Eleven Residences, Sumter; $62,000 (*MR*, 5 April 1928, p. 114.)

1928: Sections One and Three, Converse Heights Grammar School, Spartanburg; $190,600 (*MR*, 23 August 1928, p. 85.)

1928: Addition, Grade School, Denmark; $28,400 (*MR*, 25 October 1928, p. 102.)

1929: Classroom and Gymnasium Addition, Greenwood High School, Greenwood; $95,000; Charles C. Wilson, architect; James C. Hemphill (q.v.), associated architect (*MR*, 7 November 1929, p. 101.)

Wilson & Tatum

1929-1930: Tuomey Hospital, Sumter; $97,660 (*MR*, 12 December 1929, p. 87; 5 June 1930, p. 90.)

1930: Hotel, Columbia; $750,000 (*MR*, 15 May 1930, pp. 80-81.)

1931-1932: Post Office, Cheraw; James A. Wetmore (q.v.) and Wilson & Tatum, architects (Cornerstone.)

Sources: *American Art Annual*, Vol. 21, pp. 481-482; Columbia city directories; Crawford, *Who's Who in South Carolina*, p. 215; Garlington, *Men of the Time*, p. 465; Edwin Luther Green, *A History of the University of South Carolina* (Columbia: The State Company, 1916); W.S. Kline, *Illustrated 1904*

Columbia, South Carolina (1904: reprint edition, Columbia: The R.L. Bryan Company, 1962); Rudolph E. Lee, "Rural School Improvement," *The Clemson Agricultural College Extension Work Bulletins*, Vol. VI, #3, July 1910; Leonard, *Who's Who in Engineering*, p. 1395; *MR*, various citations; Wallace, *History of South Carolina*, Vol. IV, p. 1010; "Wilson and Edwards," *The State*, 23 December 1897, p. 7; "Charles C. Wilson Dies At Hospital," *The State*, 27 January 1933, pp. 1, 11; Charles C. Wilson, "Robert Mills, Architect," *Bulletin of the University of South Carolina*, #77, February 1919; Wilson, Lapham, and Petty, *Architectural Practice in South Carolina*; Withey, pp. 662-663.

WILSON BROTHERS (active 1890-1892) Baltimore architects J. Appleton Wilson and W.T. Wilson prepared plans for a Baptist Church in Chesterfield, South Carolina, in 1890.

Sources: Walter C. Kidney, *The Architecture of Choice: Eclecticism in America 1880-1930* (New York: George Braziller, 1974), pp. 72-73; *MR*, 5 April 1890, p. 40, and various other citations.

WINDRIM, James Hamilton (1840-1919) James H. Windrim was supervising architect of the United States Department of the Treasury from 1889 to 1891. He directed the design and construction of federal buildings, including courthouses and post offices, across the nation in this period. The United States Court House and Post Office in Greenville, South Carolina, a majestic Richardsonian Romanesque building, was built according to Windrim's designs in 1889. The United States Courthouse and Post Office in Charleston, South Carolina, was begun under Windrim's supervision in 1891, although the building was carried to completion by architects Willoughby J. Edbrooke (q.v.), Charles E. Kemper (q.v.), William Martin Aiken (q.v.), and John H. Devereux (q.v.)

Windrim was educated at Girard College in Philadelphia, and he had a thriving private practice in Pennsylvania before his appointment to the supervising architect's position.

Sources: *Macmillan Encyclopedia*, Vol. IV, p. 408; *MR*, 28 March 1891, p. 45; S. Dillon Ripley,

Smithsonian Insitution, to Mr. Henry Bacon McKoy, 17 October 1969 (copy in National Register files, S.C. Archives); Smith, *The Office of the Supervising Architect*, p. 44; Tatman/Moss, pp. 871-873; Withey, p. 664; Wodehouse, pp. 224-225.

WITCOVER, Hyman Wallace (1871-1936) Hyman Witcover, a native of Darlington County, South Carolina, was educated in Atlanta. He began professional work in Savannah in the architectural office of Adolph Eichberg (q.v.) in 1897. Witcover opened his own office in Savannah, Georgia, in 1901. He designed many buildings in Savannah, including the city hall, the public library, and the Scottish Rite Temple.

Witcover was initiated into the Ancient and Accepted Scottish Rite of Freemasonry in 1900. He devoted much attention to Masonic duties, and in 1923 he dropped the general practice of architecture to concentrate on Masonic service. His work in these later years included designs for a $350,000 Masonic temple in Jackson, Mississippi, 1923; and a $300,000 "Egyptian type" Scottish Rite Temple in Jacksonville, Florida, 1924.

From 1919 to 1922 Witcover served on the Georgia State Board of Architectural Examiners. His civic service included memberships on the Savannah Public Library Board, the Savannah Kindergarten Association, and other organizations.

South Carolina project:

1914: Hotel Melrose, Darlington; $65,000 (*MR*, 15 January 1914, p. 70; 29 January 1914, p. 69.)

Sources: *MR*, various citations; *The Supreme Council, Thirty-Third Degree* (Louisville, Kentucky: The Standard Printing Company, 1931), pp. 675-676; *Architects and Builders in Georgia*; Withey, p. 667.

WOOD, John A. (active 1871-1901) John A. Wood practiced architecture in New York City from ca. 1871 through the early twentieth century. He prepared plans for several resort hotels in the south-eastern states, including a Tampa Bay Hotel (1899-1901.)

South Carolina project:

1894: F.W. Wagener Hotel, Summerville; $300,000 (*MR*, 12 January 1894, p. 405.)

Sources: Francis, p. 84; *Architects and Builders in Georgia*.

YEATTS, Harold F. (active 1911-1912) Harold Yeatts advertised in the Darlington *News & Press* as an architect. He had an office in the Nachman Building.

Sources: Darlington *News & Press*, 14 December 1911, p. 4; 21 March 1912, p. 4; 8 November 1912, p. 4.

YE PLANRY, Inc. (active 1908-1931) Ye Planry, Inc., of Dallas, Texas, was a ready-made home company, one of many that flourished in the early twentieth century. The firm advertised its buildings in a catalogue called *"Ye Planry" Bungalows*, published in 1908, 1909, 1910, and 1911. The firm's work included the 1931 M.L. Robertson Residence in Goldville, South Carolina.

Sources: Gowans, *The Comfortable House*, p. 228; *MR*, 31 December 1931, p. 38.

YOUMANS, Paul Hammond (1871-1904) Paul Youmans was educated at South Carolina College in Columbia, but did not graduate. He was employed as a draftsman by Charles C. Wilson (q.v.) of Columbia for several years. Youmans was associated with James H. Sams (q.v.) as Sams & Youmans, Architects, from 1898 to 1901.

South Carolina projects:

See **Sams, James Hagood** (Sams & Youmans)

Sources: Columbia city directories; Moore, Vol. 7; *The State*, 29 May 1904, p. 16; 30 May 1904, p. 8.

YOUNGER, Frederick (active 1887) Frederick Younger was listed as a contractor in the 1887 Charleston city directory. F.W. v Younger (sic) was listed as an architect in the business directory of the same volume; he advertised as an architect and contractor, stating a specialty in millwork.

ZEIGLER, Daniel G. (active 1890-1927) Daniel G. Zeigler was an enterprising and much-traveled architect, contractor, and manufacturer active in several South Carolina and Georgia communities. He was born ca. 1869, and commenced architectural practice in Augusta, Georgia, by 1890 as the junior partner of Albert W. Todd (q.v.). During the next twenty years Zeigler traveled often in the Southeast, promoting his concrete block manufacturing machinery and opening architectural offices in many cities, all with limited success.

Many of Zeigler's designs were commercial buildings in the smaller South Carolina towns, including Newberry, Batesburg, and Sumter. A number of these buildings were constructed of cast concrete block; the 1902 Sumter Hospital was designed by Zeigler and built of Zeigler-manufactured concrete block. His *oeuvre* included several ambitious projects that were never built. An eight-story office building proposed by Zeigler for Charleston in 1893 would have been the state's first skyscraper.

Zeigler worked in Augusta until ca. 1892, when he relocated to Charleston, South Carolina. In 1894 he spent brief periods in Haiglers and Cameron before settling in Columbia. He invented a type of concrete block casting machinery about this time, and he promoted the device in most eastern states. In 1908 Zeigler boasted of ten concrete-block manufacturing plants in South Carolina communities and twenty-one plants in other states. The diminishing popularity of cast concrete block construction ultimately terminated this venture. Zeigler pursued his architectural practice in these years as well. In 1901 he attempted to open a branch office in Jacksonville, Florida, where he sought business by offering half rates to a first client.

Zeigler moved his architectural office to Sumter, South Carolina, around 1904. In 1906 a draftsman named Eugene Hogan shot Zeigler following a dispute over some drafting tools. Zeigler recovered from the wound and returned to Columbia, where his practice briefly flourished. He worked in association with Hyman W. Witcover (q.v.) on the 1907 Screven House Hotel improvements in Savannah, Georgia. In 1908 Zeigler sought greater opportunity in Atlanta.

By 1920 Zeigler had abandoned architectural practice and was working in St. Matthews, South Carolina, with the Atlantic Construction Company. He worked in Columbia as a contractor in 1923, and he remained active in this pursuit through 1927, after which time his name was not listed in the city directories.

South Carolina projects:

1890: See **Todd, Albert Whitner** (Todd & Zeigler)

1890: Opera House, Aiken; $10,000 (*MR*, 1 November 1890, p. 44.)

1892: Baptist Church, Charleston; $60,000 (*MR*, 1 July 1892, p. 44.)

1892: B.W. Wohller Residence, Charleston; $8000 (*MR*, 1 July 1892, p. 44.)

1892: J.L. Sheppard Residence, Charleston; $10,000 (*MR*, 1 July 1892, p. 44.)

1892: I.F. Wener Residence, Charleston; $6000 (*MR*, 23 December 1892, p. 431.)

1892: Sumter Hotel Co. Hotel, Sumter; $20,000 (*MR*, 23 December 1892, p. 431.)

1892: Duker & Baltman Store Buildings, Sumter; $15,000 (*MR*, 23 December 1892, p. 431.)

1892: E.D. Ricke Store Buildings, Sumter; $12,000 (*MR*, 23 December 1892, p. 431.)

1892: B.J. Barrett Store Buildings, Sumter; $15,000 (*MR*, 23 December 1892, p. 431.)

1892: D. James Winn Store Building, Sumter; $8000 (*MR*, 23 December 1892, p. 431.)

1893: Office Building, Charleston (*MR*, 9 June 1893, p. 353.)

1893: Claremont Hotel, Claremont (*MR*, 14 April 1893, p. 209.)

1894: W.P. Waltze Residence, Cameron; $5000 (*MR*, 21 December 1894, p. 322.)

1894: Knights of Pythias Hall and Store Building, Charleston; $80,000 (*MR*, 21 December 1894, p. 322.)

1902: Improvements, Hotel Sumter, Sumter (*MR*, 27 November 1902, pp. 357-358.)

1904: Remodeling, Hotel Central, Florence (*MR*, 25 February 1904, p. 119.)

1904: Sumter Hospital, Sumter (*MR*, 11 August 1904, p. 84; 18 August 1904, p. 114; 9 November 1904, p. 189; *Southern Architect and Building News*, 1 September 1904, p. 8; 30 September 1904, p. 13.)

1905: James T. Harris Opera House, Spartanburg; $75,000 (*MR*, 2 November 1905, p. 413; 9 November 1905, p. 439.)

1906: R.L. Zeigler Residence, Allendale; $5000 (*MR*, 11 October 1905, p. 316.)

1906: W.B. Oswald Residence, Appleton; $5000 (*MR*, 11 October 1905, p. 316.)

1906: Planters' Storage Co. Cotton Warehouse, Batesburg; $15,000 (*MR*, 26 July 1906, p. 43.)

1906: M.E. Rutland Hotel, Batesburg; $12,000 (*MR*, 11 October 1906, p. 317.)

1906: St. Matthews Warehouse Co. Warehouse, St. Matthews (*MR*, 21 June 1906, p. 649; 19 July 1906, p. 17.)

1907: H.K. Covington Residence, Bennettsville; $30,000 (*MR*, 10 Octboer 1907, p. 64.)

1907: E.W. Anderson Store, Brunson; $6000 (*MR*, 17 October 1907, p. 68.)

1907: High School, Cross Hill; $5000 (*MR*, 22 August 1907, p. 159.)

1907: Owens Residence, Fairfax; $5000 (*MR*, 2 May 1907, p. 488.)

1907: Bank of Holly Hill Office Building, Holly Hill; $4000 (*MR*, 17 October 1907, p. 69.)

1907: Copeland Brothers Commercial Building, Newberry (*MR*, 2 May 1907, p. 489.)

1907: W.D. Williams Commercial Building, Newberry (*MR*, 2 May 1907, p. 489.)

1907: Mrs. A.C. Shumper Commercial Building, Newberry (*MR*, 2 May 1907, p. 489.)

1907: Sheller & Summer Commercial Building, Newberry (*MR*, 2 May 1907, p. 489.)

1907: Lominick & Livingston Commercial Building, Newberry (*MR*, 2 May 1907, p. 489.)

1907: E.C. Sommenburg Commercial Building, Newberry (*MR*, 2 May 1907, p. 489.)

1907: O. & E. Sobter Commercial Building, Newberry (*MR*, 2 May 1907, p. 489.)

1907: Rev. H.W. Whitticher Commercial Building, Newberry; $6800 (*MR*, 2 May 1907, p. 489; 17 October 1907, p. 68.)

1907: Mrs. A.C. Shumpard Residence, Newberry; $7000 (*MR*, 17 October 1907, p. 68.)

1907: Wm. C. Wolf Opera House, Town Hall, Store, and Market House Building, Orangeburg; $100,000 (*MR*, 2 May 1907, p. 489.)

1907: Lutheran Church, Prosperity; $10,000 (*MR*, 2 May 1907, p. 489.)

1907: Dr. J.K. Fairey Residence, St. Matthews; $5000 (*MR*, 2 May 1907, p. 489.)

1908: Remodeling, Orangeburg County Courthouse, Orangeburg; $20,000 (*MR*, 26 March 1908, p. 59.)

1907: Dr. J.K. Fairey Residence, St. Matthews; $5000 (*MR*, 2 May 1907, p. 489.)

1908: Remodeling, Orangeburg County Courthouse, Orangeburg; $20,000 (*MR*, 26 March 1908, p. 59.)

1908: Remodeling, Orangeburg County Jail, Orangeburg; $20,000 (*MR*, 26 March 1908, p. 59.)

Sources: Atlanta, Georgia, city directories; Augusta, Georgia, city directories; Columbia city directories; *Florida Times-Union and Citizen*, Jacksonville, Florida, 23 July 1901, p. 5; *MR*, various citations; *Mercantile and Industrial Review of Columbia and Richland County, South Carolina* (Portsmouth, Virginia: Seaboard Air Line Railway, n.d.), p. 48; *The State*, 24 March 1906, p. 1; 25 March 1906, p. 1; 28 March 1906, p. 2; 30 March 1906, p. 4; Sumter city directories.

THEMES FOR FURTHER STUDY

"Detail becomes tedious, yet out of all this information emerges an architecture."[15] This data base provides information on a limited range of the state's buildings, and it is not our (present) goal to prepare a definitive South Carolina architectural history. But there are identified in this work themes and patterns of information for future studies, which can further define that history, and enhance appreciation of building in the Southeast and the nation.

Architectural Education and Training. Clemson College was teaching mechanical drawing by 1894, and awarding degrees in architecture by 1924; the program was granted provisional accreditation in 1953. Prior to the maturity of the Clemson program, South Carolina architects received professional education and experience through various means. Many graduates of the civil engineering programs at Clemson and at South Carolina College (later called the University of South Carolina) entered architectural practice. Some architects began their careers in railroad or military engineering and surveying. Still other architects began as contractors, builders, carpenters, or masons. Out-of-state schools, including the Ecole des Beaux-Arts in Paris, also educated architects who practiced in South Carolina.

Expanded South Carolina Architectural Surveys. Field surveys, identifying and recording the built environment, are the foundations of all preservation and cultural conservation programs. Surveys conducted at the South Carolina State Historic Preservation Office in the early 1980s were essential for this project. The primary data on construction projects documented through this study demonstrate the need for expanded or augmented surveys of the historic buildings in all parts of the state.

Black Architects. Architecture has been, and to a large extent still is, a white man's profession. The pioneer black architects in South Carolina, William Wilson Cooke and Miller Fulton Whittaker, and the nation's leading black architect, John A. Lankford, are discussed at length in this study. Other South Carolina buildings were designed by less well known black professionals, and these men, Columbus White, Page Ellington, John H. Blanche, Thomas M. Pinckney, Juan Molina, William W. Smith, and Wallace A. Rayfield, have a forum in this work.

Women Architects. Architect Henrietta C. Dozier, it is said, always wore trousers at job sites and listed her name as "H.C. Dozier," in deference to the male-dominated profession. Six women have been identified as providing design services for South Carolina projects in this period. Leila Ross Wilburn and Henrietta Dozier are well documented, but little is known about New York architects Katherine Cotheal Budd and Fay Kellogg, while South Carolina designers Nell Roper Hair and Minnie Quinn Gassaway are even more obscure. The data included in this study will be essential in tracing the history of women architects in the nation.

Mail-Order Architects and Ready-Made Houses. The impact of prefabricated housing in South Carolina is difficult to evaluate, owing to limited documentation. Studies of national patterns and the available data on South Carolina indicate that such houses were extremely popular in southern towns and cities. Southern architects such as Leila Ross Wilburn advertised their designs in catalogues and magazines. George F. Barber sold not only designs, but complete building materials for houses. Many companies offered prefabricated houses on a national scale, including the Keith Company of Minneapolis; the Minter Homes Company of Huntington, West Virginia; Montgomery Ward; Sears, Roebuck & Co.; Aladdin Readi-Cut Houses of Bay City, Michigan; Ye Planry, Inc.,

---

[15] Aaron Betsky, review of Robert Twombly, *Louis Sullivan: His Life and Work*, in *Progressive Architecture*, March 1987, p. 120.

of Dallas; and others.[16] A South Carolina firm, A.C. Tuxbury Lumber Company of Charleston, manufactured "Quickbuilt Bungalows" ca. 1920.[17] During the Depression, the Federal Government sponsored the Federal Home Building Service Plan in 1938, providing architectural service for homes priced under $7500.[18]

Architects Associated With Church Denominations. Many architects specialized in works for the major Christian denominations. Patrick C. Keely, John T. Comes, George Ignatius Lovatt, and F. Ferdinand Durang did extensive work for the Roman Catholic Church, as did the monk-architect, Reverend Father Michael Joseph McInerney, O.S.B. Harvey Marinus King worked for the Methodist Episcopal Church, and Harry Beauchamp for the Baptists. Herbert L. Cain restricted his practice to church work, with projects for many protestant denominations. Black architects John Lankford and Wallace A. Rayfield did extensive work for the African Methodist Episcopal Church.

Architects Associated With Merchandising Companies. Among the corporations employing company architects were Montgomery-Ward, Coca-Cola, and S.H. Kress. Kress stores by company architects Seymour Burrell and Edward F. Sibbert have been identified in South Carolina and throughout the South.

Railroad Architects. Many railroad depots and warehouses in the state were designed by railroad-employed draftsmen, engineers, and architects. Among these men were Jules L. Bradford, U.H. Johnson, G.M. Poley, A.H. Porter, Joseph Leitner, and Alpheus M. Griffin. There were also primary architects who designed major buildings for the railroads, including Charles C. Hook and Frank P. Milburn.

Theater Architects. Design of the exuberant movie palaces of the early twentieth century was the specialty of a few regional architects. Claude K. Howell, Charles C. Benton, and John McElfatrick were among the nation's theater architects with projects in South Carolina.[19]

Industrial Design and Worker Housing. The architects and engineers who designed and built the state's hydroelectric plants, textile mills, warehouses, and industrial housing included Whaley, Tompkins, Sirrine, the Ladshaws, Shand, and Lockwood, Greene & Co. These projects, far more so than courthouses, schools, commercial buildings, churches, and fashionable residences, shaped South Carolina in the late nineteenth and early twentieth centuries.

South Carolina Skyscrapers. James Brite's National Loan & Exchange Bank was the first building in the state to break the bounds of bearing-wall construction. Earlier projects (never executed) by Daniel Zeigler and W.B.S. Whaley had assaulted this limit. Following Brite's building, (which, though sadly altered, is still the finest skyscraper composition in the state), a substantial body of high-rise banks, office buildings and hotels were built in South Carolina. The early history of high-rise construction in the state, including buildings by northern architects Julius Harder, Thompson & Frohling, Mowbray & Uffinger, and William Stoddart, and the designs by South

---

[16] The Sears, Roebuck houses are described in Katherine Cole Stevenson and H. Ward Jandl, *Houses By Mail: A Guide to Houses from Sears, Roebuck and Company* (Washington, D.C.: National Trust for Historic Preservation, 1986.) See also Gowans, *The Comfortable House*; James L. Garvin, "Mail-Order House Plans and American Victorian Architecture," *Winterthur Portfolio*, Vol. 16, No. 4, Winter 1981; and Cheryl Decosta Evans, "Ready-Mades: A Unique Form of Vernacular Housing," *The Bracket*, Iowa State Historical Department, Summer 1984.

[17] Gowans, *The Comfortable House*, p. 56.

[18] *Architectural Record*, June 1938, pp. 80-82.

[19] See David Naylor, *Great American Movie Theaters* (Washington, D.C.: The Preservation Press, 1987.)

Carolina architects Shand & Lafaye, Cunningham, Wilson & Sompayrac, Beacham & Legrand, Casey & Fant, Baldwin, and Sayre, is outlined in this work.

Charleston architecture from 1865 to 1935. In response to the previously discussed myopic view of Charleston, an analysis of the city's post-war architecture, buildings from "the tasteless '70's and '80's," and "the 'Queen Anne' successors to these 'General Grant' hideousities" is warranted.[20] Themes worthy of study are the resident Charleston architects, including Newcomer, Todd, Simons & Lapham, and Hyer; the Victorian masterpieces such as the Calhoun mansion, the Circular Congregational Church, the Cathedral of St. John the Baptist, St. Matthew's Lutheran Church, and the Federal Courthouse and Post Office (one of the celebrated "Four Corners of Law"); the reconstructions following the 1886 earthquake; the city's early skyscrapers, including the People's Bank Building, the Francis Marion Hotel, and the Fort Sumter Hotel; the vernacular building traditions, which carried the colonial "single-house" form into the mid-twentieth century; and the industrial buildings, including the Walker, Evans & Cogswell Printing Plant, the Charleston Bagging Manufacturing Company, the C.D. Franke Warehouse, and the Cigar Factory.[21]

New York Architects with Projects in Aiken, South Carolina. Aiken was, and is, a haven for wealthy northerners seeking a sporting retreat for the winter months. The "winter cottages" built in Aiken by northern socialites were among the largest and most sophisticated residences built in South Carolina in the early twentieth century. New York architects employed by northerners to build "winter cottages" in Aiken included Peabody & Stearns, Hoppin & Koen, Delano & Aldrich, Thomas Hastings, George Freeman, Alfred H. Hopkins, and Leslie W. Devereux.

---

[20] Samuel Gaillard Stoney, *This Is Charleston* (Charleston: The Carolina Art Association, 1944; revised 1960, 1976), p. 49.

[21] An important study of these utilitarian buildings is Preservation Consultants, Inc., "An Introduction to the Utilitarian and 20th Century Architectural Resources of Charleston, South Carolina" (unpublished typescript, 1984.)

Select Bibliography

Citations in the text to these major sources are given in abbreviated format: the primary author's last name and a shortened title.

Architects Directories

The Architects' Directory for 1894 Including a List of the Architects in the United States and Canada. New York and Chicago: William T. Comstock, 1894.

> The William T. Comstock *Architects' Directory* series, and the earlier J. Arthurs Murphy *Directory of the Architects* and Clark W. Bryan *Directory of Architects* series, have alphabetical lists of persons practicing as architects in the United States. Specific references to the Comstock and Bryan directories are generally not cited in the text of this work.

The Architects' Directory and Specifications Index (1894-1895). New York: William T. Comstock, circa 1895.

The Architects' Directory and Specifications Index (1905-1906.) New York: William T. Comstock, circa 1905.

The Architects' Directory and Specifications Index (1909.) New York: William T. Comstock, circa 1909.

The Architects' Directory and Specifications Index (1913-1914.) New York: William T. Comstock, circa 1913.

Architects of the Middle Atlantic States. Philadelphia: The F.W. Dodge Company, 1921, 1922.

> The F.W. Dodge Company architects directories include volumes on New England (1921, 1922), New York and northern New Jersey (1921, 1922), the central western states (1921, 1922), the north central states (1915), and the northwestern states (1915, 1921, 1922.)

Bishir, Catherine W., Charlotte V. Brown, Carl R. Lounsbury, and Ernest H. Wood, general editors. *Architects and Builders in North Carolina: A History of the Practice of Building.* Chapel Hill, North Carolina: University of North Carolina Press, 1990.

Confidential Reference Book and Directory of the Architects, Builders, Contractors, Carpenters, and Manufacturers. New York: J. Arthurs Murphy & Co., 1873.

Directory of Architects and Classified Directory of First Hands in the Building Trades (1887.) Springfield, Massachusetts, and New York: Clark W. Bryan & Co., 1887.

Directory of Architects and Classified Directory of First Hands in the Building Trades (1890.) Springfield, Massachusetts: Clark W. Bryan & Co., 1890.

Directory of Historic American Architectural Firms. New York: Committee for the Preservation of Architectural Records, Inc., 1979.

Francis, Dennis Steadman. *Architects in Practice in New York City 1840-1900.* New York: Committee for the Preservation of Architectural Records, 1979.

228

Hendricks' Commercial Register of the United States For Buyers and Sellers (1918.) New York: S.E. Hendricks Co., Inc., 1918.

Herndon, Joseph Lucian. *Architects in Tennessee until 1930: A Dictionary.* Masters Thesis, Columbia University, New York, 1970.

> Herndon's thesis, one of the first efforts at cataloguing all the architects to have worked in a geographical region in the nation, is a landmark study. Despite its flaws, it has been an essential resource and guide for the present work. Herndon's preface is particularly relevant.

Koyl, George S., editor. *American Architects Directory (1956.)* New York: R.R. Bowker Co., 1955.

> The *American Architects Directory* was compiled as a parallel piece to the Witheys' biographical directory of deceased architects. It was based on registration records, A.I.A. records, and questionaires prepared by living architects. A second edition of the work was prepared in 1962, and a third edition in 1970. All citations are from the 1956 edition of Koyl unless otherwise indicated.

Petty, Walter F., Charles C. Wilson, and Samuel Lapham. *Architectural Practice in South Carolina 1913-1963.* Columbia: The State Printing Co., 1963.

> This work includes short pieces by Wilson and Lapham on the history of polite architectural practice in South Carolina, focusing on the South Carolina Chapter of the A.I.A.; and an update by Petty, with a list of all members of the Chapter since its founding in 1913. The narrative, especially Petty's sections, concentrates on the social history of the architects' fraternity.

Placzek, Adolph K., editor. *Avery Obituary Index of Architects.* Second Edition. Boston: G.K. Hall & Co., 1980.

Placzek, Adolph K., editor. *Macmillan Encyclopedia of Architects.* Four Volumes. New York: The Free Press, 1982.

> The Macmillan Encyclopedia includes biographical sketches of more than 2400 prominent architects from all periods and cultures. No South Carolina architects from the years 1880-1935 are represented, but the Encyclopedia is a valuable source for other architects of the period. James F. O'Gorman's review (*Journal of the Society of Architectural Historians*, March 1984, pp. 78-79) is relevant.

Pocket Directory of the Architects of Greater New York and State of New Jersey 1914-1915. New York: Martin Publicity Company, 1915.

Ravenel, Beatrice St. Julien. *Architects of Charleston.* Second Edition. Columbia: The R.L. Bryan Company, 1964.

> One of the best works on the state's architectural history, focusing on the antebellum period, but including important entries on some later nineteenth-century architects.

"Registered Architects of South Carolina." N.p., n.p., n.d., circa 1929.

"Registered Architects of South Carolina, August 1st, 1940." Columbia: State Board of Architectural Examiners, 1940.

Tatman, Sandra L. and Roger W. Moss. *Biographical Dictionary of Philadelphia Architects: 1700-1930.* Boston: G.K. Hall & Co., 1985.

> This is the best biographical dictionary of regional American architects published to date, identifying all architects and all known works by each architect.

"Who's Who in Architecture." *American Art Annual,* The American Federation of Arts, Washington, D.C.; Vol. XXI, pp. 360-485.

Withey, Henry F. and Elsie Rathburn Withey. *Biographical Dictionary of American Architects (Deceased.)* 1956: facsimile edition, Los Angeles: Hennessey & Ingalls, 1970.

> The Witheys' dictionary is notorious for typographical and factual errors, but it is absolutely essential for any study of American architects.

Wodehouse, Lawrence. *American Architects from the Civil War to the First World War: A Guide to Information Sources.* Detroit: Gale Research Company, 1976.

Other sources with important lists and biographies of architects

"Annual Report of the Southern Chapter, A.I.A." *Journal of Proceedings*, American Institute of Architects, 1892-1893.

Architects and Builders in Georgia Research Project. Historic Preservation Section, Georgia Department of Natural Resources, Atlanta, Georgia.

> The Georgia State Historic Preservation Office, under the direction of Kenneth H. Thomas, Historian, has compiled extensive information on the architects who worked in that state prior to 1940. A working list of Georgia architects was published in *Southern Architecture and Urban Design Newsletter*, Vol. II, No. 2, January 1983. The records compiled are accessible to the public for research purposes at the Georgia Department of Natural Resources, 205 Butler Street, S.E., Atlanta, Georgia 30334; (404) 656-2840.

Bishir, Catherine W., and Lawrence S. Earley, editors. *Early Twentieth-Century Suburbs in North Carolina.* Raleigh, North Carolina: North Carolina Department of Cultural Resources, 1985.

Bishir, Catherine W. *North Carolina Architecture.* Chapel Hill, North Carolina: University of North Carolina Press, 1990.

Coleman, Kenneth, and Charles Stephen Gurr, editors. *Dictionary of Georgia Biography.* Athens, Georgia: The University of Georgia Press, 1983.

Gowans, Alan. *The Comfortable House: North American Suburban Architecture 1890-1930.* Cambridge, Massachusetts, and London, England: The M.I.T. Press, 1986.

Hewitt, Mark Alan. *The Architect & The American Country House 1890-1940.* New Haven: Yale University Press, 1990.

Leonard, John William. *Who's Who in Engineering, A Biographical Dictionary of Contemporaries 1922-1923.* New York: John W. Leonard Corp., circa 1922.

Morgan, Thomas H. "The Georgia Chapter of the American Institute of Architects." *The Atlanta Historical Bulletin*, Vol. VII, No. 28, September 1943.

Moore, Charles. *The Life and Times of Charles Follen McKim.* 1929: new edition, Boston and New York: Da Capo Press, 1970.

Noffsinger, James Philip. *The Influence of the Ecole des Beaux-Arts on the Architects of the United States.* Washington, D.C.: The Catholic University of America, 1955.

Smith, Darrell Hevenor. *The Office of the Supervising Architect of the Treasury: Its History, Activities, and Organization.* Baltimore: The Johns Hopkins Press, 1923.

White, Norval and Elliot Willensky. *AIA Guide to New York City.* Revised Edition. New York: Macmillan Publishing Co., Inc., 1978.

Wrenn, Tony P. Washington, D.C. Unpublished research.

> Tony Wrenn, Archivist at the American Institute of Architects, has charge of the A.I.A.'s extensive records. He has devoted extensive study to various areas of American architectural history, and he has written an architectural survey of Wilmington, North Carolina.

South Carolina business and biographical directories

Crawford, Geddings H., editor. *Who's Who in South Carolina, A Dictionary of Contemporaries containing Biographical Notices of Eminent Men in South Carolina.* Columbia: McCaw, 1921.

Garlington, J.C. *Men of the Time: Sketches of Living Notables.* Spartanburg: Garlington Publishing Company, 1902.

Hemphill, J.C. *Men of Mark in South Carolina.* Washington, D.C.: Men of Mark Publishing Company, 1909.

Moore, Andrew Charles. *University of South Carolina Alumni Records.* Volume 6. Columbia: no publisher, no date, circa 1910.

Snowden, Yates, editor. *History of South Carolina.* Five Volumes. Chicago: Lewis Publishing, 1920.

South Carolina State Gazetteer and Business Directory, 1880-1881. Charleston: R.A. Smith, 1880.

> The State Gazetteers (including Young's 1900 Directory) attempted to identify all significant persons, including merchants, professionals, government figures, manufacturers, and farmers, in the state by region. Specific references to these directories are routinely not cited in the text of this work.

South Carolina State Gazetteer and Business Directory, 1883. Charleston: Lucas & Richardson, 1883.

South Carolina State Gazetteer and Business Directory, 1898. Charleston: Lucas & Richardson, 1898.

Utsey, Walker Scott, editor. *Who's Who in South Carolina 1934-1935.* Columbia: Current Historical Association, 1935.

Wallace, David Duncan. *History of South Carolina.* Four Volumes. New York: American Historical Society, 1934.

Who's Who in the South 1927. Washington, D.C.: The Mayflower Publishing Company, Inc., 1927.

Young & Co.'s Business and Professional Directory of the Cities and Towns throughout the State of South Carolina. Charleston: Young & Co., 1900.

South Carolina city directories

City directories were widely published in South Carolina in the late nineteenth and early twentieth centuries. These directories are valuable for identifying architects and tracing their careers. The directories are available at the University of South Carolina's South Caroliniana Library, or at the public libraries of the given cities. Specific references to the directories are not cited in the text of this work. The following directories were consulted for this project:

Anderson: 1911-1912, 1913-1914, 1915-1916, 1917-1918, 1920-1921, 1922-1923, 1925, 1927, 1929-1930, 1931, 1934, 1936, 1947-48.

Bennettsville: 1925-1926.

Camden: 1913-1914-1915, 1925-1926.

Charleston: 1867, 1869, 1872, 1874, 1875, 1877, 1878, 1881, 1882, 1883, 1885, 1886, 1887, 1888, 1889, 1890, 1891, 1892, 1895, 1898, 1899, 1901, 1902, 1903, 1904, 1905, 1908, 1909, 1910, 1912, 1913, 1915, 1916, 1917, 1918, 1919, 1920, 1921, 1922, 1923, 1924, 1925, 1927, 1928, 1929, 1930, 1931, 1932, 1934, 1936, 1938, 1940, 1942, 1950, 1958.

Chester: 1909.

Columbia: 1859, 1879-1880, 1888, 1891, 1893, 1895, 1899, 1904-1905, 1906, 1907-1908, 1909, 1910, 1911, 1912, 1913, 1914, 1915, 1916, 1917, 1918, 1920, 1921, 1922, 1923, 1925, 1926, 1927, 1928, 1929, 1930, 1931, 1932, 1934, 1936, 1939, 1951.

Darlington: 1924-1925.

Florence: 1913-1914, 1915-1916, 1929-1930, 1936, 1938.

Greenville: 1883-1884, 1888, 1896, 1899-1900, 1901-1902, 1903-1904, 1907, 1909, 1910, 1912, 1915, 1917-1918, 1919, 1921-1922, 1924, 1928, 1930, 1931, 1933, 1938, 1940, 1965.

Greenwood: 1909, 1914-1915, 1916-1917, 1923-1924, 1927, 1936.

Newberry: 1921-1922.

Orangeburg: 1920-1921, 1938, 1940, 1956.

Rock Hill: 1913-1914, 1925-1926, 1933-1934, 1936, 1938, 1958.

Spartanburg: 1880-1881, 1896-1897, 1899-1900, 1903-1904, 1905, 1908-1909, 1910, 1911, 1913, 1914-1915, 1916-1917, 1918, 1920, 1922, 1924, 1926, 1927-1928, 1929, 1930, 1934, 1936, 1938, 1942, 1954, 1965.

Sumter: 1905-1906, 1928-1929, 1934.

Union: 1911-1912, 1920-1921, 1925-1926.

Directories of many other southeastern cities have been consulted for corroborating evidence. These cities include Jacksonville, Florida; Atlanta, Augusta, Macon, and Savannah, Georgia; Charlotte, Greensboro, Raleigh, and Wilmington, North Carolina; Chattanooga, Memphis, and Nashville, Tennessee; Charlottesville, Lynchburg, Norfolk, Portsmouth, Richmond, and Roanoke, Virginia; Washington, D.C.; and St. Louis, Missouri.

Major South Carolina newspapers

The News and Courier, Charleston.

The State, Columbia.

> *The State* began publication in the 1890s. It has statewide circulation and attempts to cover news in all parts of South Carolina. There are no indexes for most of the paper's editions. Random surveying of *The State* for many years of its publication has provided extensive documentation for this work, but no attempt has been made at comprehensive cataloguing.

The Columbia Record, Columbia.

Darlington News & Press, Darlington.

Greenwood Index, Greenwood.

Greenville Daily News, Greenville.

The Keowee Courier, Walhalla.

The *Manufacturers' Record*

The *Manufacturers' Record* (abbreviated *MR*) was a weekly industrial and business newsjournal covering the southern states (including Oklahoma, Missouri, Kentucky, West Virginia, and Maryland). The journal originated in Baltimore in 1881, focusing on the iron, steel, and industrial hardware trades. By 1885 the journal included a regular "Construction Department" describing factory, railroad, and similar construction projects. This department was expanded by 1890 to include descriptions of most major construction projects in the Southeast: government buildings, churches, schools, and commercial buildings. Residential projects were covered by the later 1890s. Construction notices would usually include the names of the client, architect, and contractor, as well as the contract price.

Other trade journals of the period, including *American Architect and Building News*, *Southern Architect and Building News*, *The Bricklayer and Mason*, and *The Architectural Record* also documented building projects, but none covered southern and South Carolina projects as completely as the *Manufacturers' Record*.

Comprehensive cataloguing of the South Carolina building notices listed in the *MR* from 1890 to 1932 has provided much of the primary data for this study. Extensive cataloguing of the *MR* notices for adjacent states over this same period supplements the South Carolina data base.

The apostrophe was used in the journal's title through 21 July 1910, after which the name was changed to *Manufacturers Record*. The journal changed from weekly to monthly format in June of 1932 and the Construction Department was abbreviated, reflecting the curtailed building efforts during the Depression. Only selected major construction projects were listed after 1932. The journal was renamed *Industrial Development* in the 1950s.

In the 1930s the *MR* introduced a parallel journal, *Construction*, which carried some of the information formerly available in the *MR*. *Construction* was published through the 1940s.

Architects' Drawings

Architects' drawings and other records from the historic offices are staples of architectural history. Drawings of some of the major South Carolina firms have been preserved; the drawings of George E. Lafaye, Joseph E. Sirrine & Co., Joseph Casey and Charles W. Fant, and Lockwood Greene, among others, are available for research. Unfortunately, the drawings and office records of most South Carolina architects have not been preserved.

Where extant, these drawings are essential sources for further study, and for expansion of this data base. The focus of this study, though, is the identification of the architects, and the information which can be derived from in-depth analysis of the architectural drawings is not deemed critical for this identification.

South Carolina Department of Archives and History

The South Carolina State Historic Preservation Office, part of the Department of Archives and History in Columbia, is a critical bank of information on the state's architectural history. The primary and secondary records on the state's cultural history compiled at this office are essential to any study of South Carolina architecture.

A substantial part of this archive's architectural record was assembled in 1979-1985, during which time one or both authors were with the South Carolina Department of Archives and History. Intensive surveys covering parts or all of Abbeville, Aiken, Anderson, Batesburg, Beaufort, Bishopville, Charleston, Chesterfield, Columbia, Conway, Fairfield County, Florence, Gaffney, Greenwood, Greenville, Hartsville, Johnston, Latta, Leesville, Manning, Newberry and Newberry County, Orangeburg, Richland County, Rock Hill, Spartanburg, Sumter, Union, Walterboro, Winnsboro, and other South Carolina urban and rural communities were undertaken in this period. The data gathered in these surveys, and the corresponding comprehension of the state's architectural resources, have helped shape and inspire this study. Historians with the Department who contributed to this study include Martha Walker Fullington, Deborah Allen, Suzanne Pickens, Mary Watson Edmonds, Thomas Shaw, Andrew Chandler, Julie Turner, Norman McCorkle, Charles Lowe, and Rebecca Starr.

INDEX

Two elements of the data base are indexed: project clients (individuals, companies, and institutions, such as E.W. Robertson, S.H. Kress & Co., University of South Carolina, and Jonesville Knitting Mills) and localities, which are sub-indexed by building types. Recurring institutional names like First Baptist Church are sub-indexed by locality. Thus, the First Baptist Church of York can be found in the index under York (Church) and under First Baptist Church (York.) The E.W. Robertson Residence in Columbia can be found under Columbia (Residence) and under Robertson, E.W. Institutions, especially colleges, that sponsored many building projects have the specific projects sub-indexed under the institution name.

We have retained, where possible, the spelling given in the primary sources in these citations. Some communities and institutions in South Carolina changed their names during the study period; thus, we have entries under both Yorkville and York, and under both South Carolina College and the University of South Carolina.

To keep the index within workable parameters, building types have been condensed to relatively few categories. Thus, a grade school, a junior high school, a high school, and an industrial school will all be identified in the index as Schools. Sunday school buildings, parsonages, and rectories, as well as church buildings, are indexed as Churches. City Halls, Courthouses, and similar public buildings are indexed as Government Buildings.